TRAUMATIC REALISM

TRAUMATIC REALISM

The Demands of Holocaust Representation

Michael Rothberg

University of Minnesota Press
Minneapolis
London

The image that appears on the cover and in the introduction is from *The Complete Maus* by Art Spiegelman. Copyright 1973, 1980, 1981, 1982, 1983, 1984, 1985, 1986 by Art Spiegelman. Reprinted by permission of Pantheon Books, a division of Random House, Inc.

Chapter 1 is a slightly revised version of "After Adorno: Culture in the Wake of Catastrophe," an article that appeared in *New German Critique* 72 (fall 1997): 45–81; reprinted with the permission of *New German Critique.* Parts of chapters 3 and 4 were originally published in "Between the Extreme and the Everyday: Ruth Klüger's Traumatic Realism," *a/b: Auto/Biography Studies* 14, no. 2 (fall 1999); reprinted with permission of *a/b: Auto/Biography Studies.* An earlier version of parts of chapter 5 appeared as "We Were Talking Jewish . . . " in *Contemporary Literature* 35, no. 4 (winter 1994): 661–87; copyright 1994, reprinted by permission of the University of Wisconsin Press.

Published by the University of Minnesota Press
111 Third Avenue South, Suite 290
Minneapolis, MN 55401-2520
http://www.upress.umn.edu

Printed in the United States of America on acid-free paper

The University of Minnesota is an equal-opportunity educator and employer.

Library of Congress Cataloging-in-Publication Data

Rothberg, Michael.
Traumatic realism : the demands of Holocaust representation / Michael Rothberg.
p. cm.
Includes bibliographical references (p.) and index.
ISBN 0-8166-3458-0 (hc) – ISBN 0-8166-3459-9 (pb)
1. Holocaust, Jewish (1939-1945) – Historiography. 2. Holocaust, Jewish (1939-1945) – Influence. I. Title.
D804.348 .R68 2000
940.53′18′072 – dc21 00-008299

10 09 08 07 06 05 04 03 02 01 00 10 9 8 7 6 5 4 3 2 1

for YY

Contents

Acknowledgments

During the writing of this book I was frequently asked two questions: Why have you chosen to write about the Holocaust? How do you manage to work on such a subject? In some ways, the first question was easier. Once I began to read and think about the Nazi genocide it became difficult for me not to write about it. The events of the Holocaust seemed to challenge much of what my training in literary and cultural studies had led me to take for granted. At the same time, all of the important questions with which I was concerned intersected in this one series of events, events to which I, as a Jewish American whose family had come to the United States in the early part of the twentieth century, had little direct connection. Thinking through the Holocaust has made me think differently about literature, history, and theory. But thinking as a literary and cultural theorist has also helped me to think differently about the Nazi genocide.

The second question was more difficult, and it was only in writing these acknowledgments that I was able to formulate an answer for myself. I realize now that I was able to dedicate so many years to this project because of the people with whom it has put me in contact. The many communities to which I have belonged — the sense of being part of a larger intellectual and social project — have enabled the solitary work of writing. I am glad to have an opportunity here to acknowledge my intellectual and personal debts. I owe a great deal to writers and scholars I have never met, and I have tried to mark those debts in the endnotes. More immediately, I have benefited from a number of advisers, colleagues, and friends, without whose support this would certainly be a different work.

Nancy K. Miller has accompanied this book from its inception and has followed it through multiple drafts, right to its conclusion. I can't quite imagine what it would have been without her. I am grateful for her sharp wit, incisive commentary, and ongoing friendship. There is no better mentor. While at the CUNY Graduate Center I was also fortunate to work with Vincent Crapanzano, Gerhard Joseph, and Stuart Liebman, all of whom played important roles in the early stages of this book. At CUNY I was aided in initial writing and research by the generosity of the "J. & O. Winter" Fund, administered by Professor Randolph Braham and The Rosenthal Institute for Holocaust Studies.

In the last four years, I have been lucky to be surrounded by a challenging and generous group of colleagues at the University of Miami. I have been inspired in particular by my friends Anthony Barthelemy, Leslie Bow, Russ Castronovo, David Glimp, Jeffrey Shoulson, and Margie Sokoloff. I am especially grateful to Russ for reading sections of my manuscript and offering much-needed advice and assistance, and to David for a last-minute commentary on the introduction. As chairs of the English department, Zack Bowen and Shari Benstock have made it possible for me to complete this work in timely fashion. I was also fortunate to receive two Max Orovitz Summer Awards and one General Research Award from the University of Miami. Peter Hohendahl and the Institute for German Cultural Studies at Cornell University provided a welcome temporary home during the completion of this book and an opportunity to try out some of its ideas before a tough but enthusiastic audience.

My work on the Holocaust has been very much enriched by my association with the Holocaust Educational Foundation. Without the inspirational commitment of Mr. Zev Weiss I would not have had the chance to take part in the foundation's conferences, seminars, and study trips. I would also like to thank Peter Hayes, who ran the Summer Institute on the Holocaust and Jewish Civilization at Northwestern University, and Geoffrey Giles, who led a study trip to central and eastern Europe. On that trip, I was sustained by the companionship of Omer Bartov, Rebecca Boehling, Greg Caplan, David Murphy, and Jeff Peck.

At the University of Minnesota Press I was fortunate to connect with my editor, William Murphy. His enthusiasm for this project has meant a great deal to me. Marianne Hirsch provided more than just a reader's report for the press—to receive encouragement and advice from a scholar for whom I have so much respect has been of the utmost importance. James Berger and Kali Tal also provided thoughtful and engaged responses to the manuscript. While I have not always followed their advice, I always appreciated it. Andreas

Huyssen and Anson Rabinbach provided crucial readings of the first chapter, which appeared in an earlier version in *New German Critique*. I am grateful to the editors of that journal, as well as to the editors of *Contemporary Literature* and *a/b: Auto/Biography Studies,* for permission to reprint material.

Several close friends read and commented on parts of this book in various earlier versions. I am happily beholden to Beth Drenning, Jeffrey Escoffier, Caren Irr, Neil Levi, Stephanie Oppenheim, Florence Stratton, Kassie Temple, Gary Weissman, and Karen Winkler. Meeting Beth, Neil, and Gary, with whom I share so many interests and obsessions, has been one of the most rewarding aspects of writing this book. For the last several years, Jeffrey has been the model for me of what an intellectual can be. Other friends have enriched this project in less direct ways. Julie Ford and Elliot Weininger kept me honest with their social scientific skepticism. My two oldest friends, Carine Montbertrand and Matthew Lore, continue to inspire me through their creativity and vitality. And Molly McGarry always enlivens any discussion with her humor and intelligence.

My parents, Sondra Rothberg and Joseph Rothberg, made the writing of this book possible through their commitment to education and intellectual life. I hope my sister and brother-in-law, Madeleine Rothberg and Dylan Jones, will find something of interest here.

It will come as no surprise to anyone who knows me when I say that without Yasemin Yildiz this book, indeed my whole life, would be a lesser thing. Dedicating this book to her is only the slightest indication of what she means to me.

This drawing by Art Spiegelman first appeared in *Tikkun* magazine, accompanying the article "Saying Goodbye to *Maus*."

Introduction

The Demands of Holocaust Representation

> *As a constellation, theoretical thought circles the concept it would like to unseal, hoping that it may fly open like the lock of a well-guarded safe-deposit box: in response, not to a single key or a single number, but to a combination of numbers.*
>
> — Theodor Adorno

An illustration by Art Spiegelman poses the question at the heart of this book — how to comprehend the Holocaust and its relationship to contemporary culture. Spiegelman is the author of the best-selling comic-book memoir *Maus*. Using a provocative pictorial vocabulary in which Jews are represented as mice, Germans as cats, and so on, *Maus* tells the story both of Spiegelman's father, Vladek, a Holocaust survivor, and of the artist's relationship to his father's story. In a contribution to the magazine *Tikkun* titled "Saying Goodbye to *Maus*," in which he comments on the success of his memoir, Spiegelman draws his characteristic "Maus" self-portrait standing in front of a smiling Mickey Mouse background and gazing mournfully at a "real" mouse (or is it a rat?) that he cups in his hands.

In this drawing, the events of the Holocaust seem at first absent — there are no Nazi cats or Jewish survivors, no swastikas, and none of the barbed wire and guard tower imagery that powerfully evokes Auschwitz in the *Maus* volumes. But perhaps the very absence of the events signals their overwhelming impact. Through indirect means, Spiegelman evokes the Holocaust as a radical problem for understanding. One quickly notices that the image condenses three levels of representation. In the foreground, the mouse is depicted according to realistic drawing codes. The self-portrait, which occupies the middle of the pictorial field, is done in Spiegelman's signature "Maus" stylization. The Mickey Mouse backdrop simulates a mass-cultural icon and corporate logo. What does this pastiche of styles have to do with the Holocaust? This image provides an allegory of the contradictory position of the post-Holocaust artist — an artist who produces formally experimental works about genocide for the smiling, two-dimensional face of the entertainment industry, but everywhere confronts the detritus of the real. It could be argued that such post-Holocaust self-consciousness may tell us something about the dilemmas of the postwar world, but tells us nothing about the Nazi genocide itself. Just this argument was made by a historian during a summer seminar I attended of Holocaust scholars. During a discussion of Spiegelman's book, this historian claimed that he "wouldn't touch *Maus* with a ten-foot pole" because it provides no historical evidence. For a variety of reasons, I find this point of view misguided. Besides the fact that *Maus* represents a version of oral history, comparable to various recent Holocaust documentation projects, Spiegelman's drawings clearly seek to provoke everyone interested in the Holocaust to reflect on how we approach the events of the genocide and how we represent them to ourselves and to others. Among the tasks of this book is to argue for the absolutely central and unavoidable need for reflection on the means and modes of representation in all scholarly and lay approaches to the Holocaust.

The Holocaust, in turn, focuses our attention on, and provides new avenues of access to, disparate aspects of twentieth-century culture and central questions of contemporary cultural theory. Providing both a focused account of the psychic, intellectual, and cultural aftermath of the Holocaust and a broad theoretical intervention into post–World War II thought, this book works on multiple levels. Although the implications of the Holocaust have not been fully confronted in the mainstream of humanities research in the last half century, insights from that research can lead to productive new ways of thinking about the fundamental problems raised by the Nazi genocide. At the same time, the analysis of literary, philosophical, and artistic responses to the Holocaust sheds new light on many familiar debates of the recent "theory wars" about the status of postmodernism and the political implications of poststructuralist theories. Furthermore, close study of this particular historical catastrophe helps us reflect on the insistent presence of related phenomena in our own culture: exploring the recent fascination with the Holocaust means exploring a more general contemporary fascination with trauma, catastrophe, the fragility of memory, and the persistence of ethnic identity. In opening a dialogue between scholars of the Holocaust and cultural theorists I seek to challenge the assumptions of both groups. On the one hand, cultural theorists will find that my insistence on the real of historical catastrophe interrupts the now commonplace insistence on the omnipresence of discourse and the disinterest in questions of reference. On the other hand, I neither retreat to a pretheoretical understanding of the relationship between language and the world nor condone a mystical approach to the uniqueness of the Nazi genocide. Hence, many Holocaust scholars—like the historian in the anecdote about *Maus*—will find themselves confronted with questions of epistemology and cultural critique that they would rather avoid.

The Nazi genocide aimed at a thoroughgoing destruction of both the physical and cultural presence of Jews in Europe — it was, in other words, an "interdisciplinary" project.[1] The near success of the Nazis' murderous program, commonly known in English-speaking countries since the 1960s as the Holocaust, poses problems both familiar and peculiar to attempts at understanding. As such, the Holocaust is best approached through interdisciplinary means. And yet even interdisciplinary approaches to the Holocaust are riven by a series of seemingly irresolvable contradictions: between the event's "uniqueness" and its "typicality," its "extremity" and its "banality," its "incomprehensibility" and its susceptibility to "normal" understanding.[2] Instead of choosing a side, I seek in this book to preserve the tensions between these conflicting understandings of the significance of the Shoah in order to develop a new way forward in thinking about the relationship of culture and barbarism. It is precisely the simultaneity of mutually exclusive claims made on understanding that constitutes the importance of the Nazi genocide for considerations of the history, culture, and politics of modern societies.[3]

Within Holocaust studies broadly defined, two approaches to the question of genocide have dominated, which I will call realist and antirealist. By realist I mean both an epistemological claim that the Holocaust is knowable and a representational claim that this knowledge can be translated into a familiar mimetic universe. The realist approach has characterized the dominant scholarly methodology, that of historians and others who assert the necessity of considering the Holocaust according to "scientific" procedures and inscribing the events within continuous historical narratives. By antirealist I mean both a claim that the Holocaust is not knowable or would be knowable only under radically new regimes of knowledge and that it cannot be captured in traditional representational schemata. The antirealist approach has flourished in more popular discourses, in some survivor testimony and pronouncements, and in many literary, aesthetic, and philosophical considerations of the "uniqueness" of the Shoah. This tendency removes the Holocaust from standard historical, cultural, or autobiographical narratives and situates it as a sublime, unapproachable object beyond discourse and knowledge. In addition to constituting an implicit theory of epistemology and representation, each of these approaches also implies a particular conception of the relationship between the everyday and the extreme, with the realists tending to collapse the two poles or, more often, to situate them on a continuum and the antirealists installing an unbridgeable rupture between the ordinary and the extraordinary.

Emblematic of what I am calling here the realist tendency would be Hannah Arendt's notion of the "banality of evil" — which sought to capture the essence of Nazi genocide in the ordinary figure of the bureaucrat — and her suggestion that "evil is never 'radical,' that it is only extreme, and that it possesses neither depth nor any demonic dimension."[4] Extremity here is not something that breaks with the ordinary dimensions of the modern world but exists on a continuum with it. As scholars committed to empirical historical and social scientific methodologies, both Christopher Browning, with his notion of "ordinary men," *and* Daniel Goldhagen, with his provocative indictment of "ordinary Germans," answer to Michael Marrus's plea for a "normalization" of historical scholarship in the treatment of the Holocaust. Even in Goldhagen's case, seemingly radical evil is situated within an explainable tradition and everyday life-world.[5] Similarly, Zygmunt Bauman's thesis on the "modernity" of the genocide, which is framed as an indictment of the blind spots of a hegemonic sociology, ultimately argues that genocide is indeed explainable with reference to the intersection of very ordinary sociological structures of the modern world. These positions are all realist in that in calling on concepts such as "banality," "ordinariness," "detached, professional" science, and "modernity," they also suggest that the phenomena they describe (whose horror is in no way minimized by them) may be apprehended and comprehended according to already established techniques of representation and analysis.

Proponents of the antirealist tendency are probably more well known among nonspecialists of the Holocaust and, to a certain extent, shape the dominant popular understanding of the events through their access to the resources of the public sphere. They include such significant figures as Elie Wiesel, who has assiduously defended the uniqueness of the destruction of European Jewry and claimed that "Auschwitz cannot be explained nor can it be visualized.... [T]he Holocaust transcends history"; Claude Lanzmann, who asserts that his film *Shoah* forgoes any attempt to represent the Holocaust and declares any attempt to understand the events "obscene"; Arthur Cohen, who gives a theological cast to the discourse with his concept of the "tremendum," a "holocaustal caesura" that renders "[t]hinking and the death camps... incommensurable"; and Jean-François Lyotard, who replaces realism with notions of sublimity and the incommensurability of the "differend."[6] This discourse of "transcendence," "obscenity," "tremendum," and irresolvable "differend" detaches the extreme from the everyday and seeks to disable established modes of representation and understanding.

There are, then, two dramatically different interdisciplinary approaches within Holocaust studies. While all fields of knowledge surely encompass a range of assumptions and arguments, there is something particularly striking about a situation in which two almost entirely incommensurable visions can coexist. Part of the explanation for this fissure lies in the particular "multidisciplinary" structure of Holocaust studies. Multidisciplinarity, as I use it, supposes an institutional umbrella structure that unites scholars from different disciplines, but under which those scholars continue to work according to the procedures and values of their particular fields. Thus, in Holocaust studies, researchers work in history, literature, sociology, psychology, and theology, among other fields. They may read each other's work and sometimes cite it in their own. However, the work that each produces remains for the most part squarely within the disciplinary boundaries of the traditional "home" discipline. Within the dominant realms of Holocaust studies, there have been few attempts to grasp the Holocaust as an event that fundamentally challenges traditional disciplinary divisions and knowledge. While multidisciplinary Holocaust studies has produced vast amounts of essential knowledge about the events and their effects, the lack of a transdisciplinary space of dialogue has contributed to the strange double vision with which the Nazi genocide is today viewed: trapped between Jewish particularity and universalism; between "normal" and "extraordinary" understandings of methodology and representation; and between emphasizing the extreme and everyday elements of the events. Although not aligned uniquely with any one discipline, each side of the realist/antirealist divide tends to fall into a broad coalition: historians and social scientists representing the realist side, while the more speculative and theoretical practitioners of philosophy, religion, literary theory, and some versions of psychoanalysis line up on the other.[7] Perhaps the frequently intoned "impossibility" of comprehending the Holocaust arises in part from the preservation of traditional disciplinary boundaries and structures of knowledge. Questioning those structures will not produce some mythical "full" understanding, but it may open up alternative avenues for exploring the intersection of the psychic and the social, the discursive and the material, and the extreme and the everyday.

The coexistence of such contrasting approaches testifies to an instructive problem of interdisciplinary methodology, but it also indicates something about the nature of the events at issue. As I argue in the two central chapters of this book on Holocaust testimonies, the split between the ordinary and the extraordinary found in scholarship reflects essential characteristics of the Nazi genocide itself and corresponds particularly to the structure of what has been called "the concentrationary universe" of the death camps. I would term *traumatic* the peculiar combination of ordinary and extreme elements that seems to characterize the Nazi genocide in these accounts. When used judiciously trauma is a category that can help illuminate the complexity of both events and methodology. While the traumatic combination of the extreme and the everyday blocks traditional claims to synthetic knowledge, attentiveness to its structure can also lead to new forms of knowledge beyond the realist and antirealist positions and outside of traditional disciplines.[8]

Although seemingly distant from scholarly dispute, Spiegelman's drawing focuses our attention on a set of overlapping and conflicting demands that apply not only to Holocaust art, but to all attempts to confront, understand, and represent the events of the Nazi genocide. The mouse in the artist's hands suggests that some confrontation with the reality of the events is unavoidable no matter how far removed one might seem to be from the past. Meanwhile the idiosyncrasy of the Maus figure highlights the difficult search for a visual, narrative form adequate to that reality, and the Disney logo comically calls for acknowledgment of the "economics" or worldly dimension of Holocaust representation. When it comes to understanding an extreme historical event, the dilemmas of artists, depicted so succinctly here by Spiegelman, are not fundamentally different from those of historians, literary critics, or the interested public. In confronting such a history, we all share the need to find an adequate form for narrating and understanding an extraordinary series of events. Furthermore, in an era of evident fascination with trauma, we need to be aware of how such stories and images circulate in the media, in educational institutions, and in popular culture.

In order to provide an overarching framework for thinking through the perplexities of understanding and representing the Holocaust, I have identified three fundamental demands that confronting the Holocaust makes on attempts at comprehension and representation: a demand for documentation, a demand for reflection on the formal limits of representation, and a demand for the risky public circulation of discourses on the events. These demands do not have a mystical or transcendental source but are of a social nature—they arise from efforts of victims, bystanders, and those born after the Holocaust to engage with the legacy of specific historical events. Yet these demands on representation are relevant not only to the study of the Holocaust, but to all confrontations between culture and history. In order to move Holocaust studies into a broader theoretical conversation, I suggest a connection between those demands and the crucial socio-aesthetic categories of realism, modernism, and postmodernism—categories whose status has been so often contested in recent years in the context of interdisciplinary cultural studies.

This correlation between the demands and modalities of representation arises from extensive engagement with all kinds of Holocaust-related texts, including historical works, literary testimonies, philosophical speculations, films, novels, museums, and television broadcasts. I did not come to the texts with a preformed framework for investigation; the tripartite structure of this book emerged over the course of several years and many drafts. To be sure, in approaching such a diverse corpus of materials one risks incurring the wrath of a panoply of specialists justly eager to defend their disciplinary terrain. Yet by crossing boundaries usually left unquestioned fresh insights and new spaces of dialogue can emerge. Because of inclination, training, and a sense that something valuable is to be gained on all sides, I have sought to open a dialogue between Holocaust studies and cultural studies.

Situating debates about the Holocaust in relation to the terms of discussion in cultural studies allows for a productively mutual estrangement between two fields that have rarely been in contact. Drawing on the socio-aesthetic categories of realism, modernism, and postmodernism helps to pinpoint the significance of the Holocaust in terms of contemporary intellectual debates and practices. At the same time, confrontation with an extreme historical event also forces a reconsideration of the terms of cultural studies. In particular, I seek to supplement the fascination of the everyday in cultural studies with a reminder of the need to confront extremity, and I question the privileging of discourse and representation at the expense of the real. Tracking the theoretical effects of the Holocaust on contemporary thought has, for understandable reasons, not been the first priority of scholars of the genocide or of poststructuralist theorists. Both cultural theorists and Holocaust scholars may be surprised to find the Holocaust situated in the context of debates on theory and cultural studies. But this mutual resistance to thinking differently about history and theory indicates that scholars from both groups will benefit from the unexpected illumination provided by such an unfamiliar conjunction.

In this book, I single out in particular the persistence of the question of realism — starkly emblematized by Spiegelman's foregrounding of the "real" mouse — as one of the central problematics that the Holocaust forces back into view. Since the poststructuralist attack on mimesis in the work of Roland Barthes and the *Tel Quel* group, realism has all but disappeared from theoretical discussion, and, in the 1980s and 1990s, it has been replaced by skirmishes over the distinction between modernism and postmodernism. But the need for a rethinking of realism is signaled by the emergence in the last decades of various new forms of testimonial and documentary art and cultural production. Within cultural studies, this need for further thinking about realism is indicated by the recent obsession with trauma, the body, and extreme historical events and by the impasses of the postmodernism debates. At the center of this book stands the concept of traumatic realism, a concept I derive from Holocaust testimonial writing, but that also has implications for postwar cultural theory.[9] By focusing attention on the intersection of the everyday and the extreme in the experience and writing of Holocaust survivors, traumatic realism provides an aesthetic and cognitive solution to the conflicting demands inherent in representing and understanding genocide. Traumatic realism mediates between the realist and antirealist positions in Holocaust studies and marks the necessity of considering how the ordinary and extraordinary aspects of genocide intersect and coexist.

Reintroducing the problem of realism — for it is not an answer, but a question — has led me to the realization that the categories of realism, modernism, and postmodernism are best thought of not only as styles and periods, as the dominant paradigms would have it. Rather, realism, modernism, and postmodernism can also be understood as persistent responses to the demands of history. Like the demands themselves, these responses are also social; they provide frameworks for the representation and interpretation of history. In the representation of a historical event, in other words, a text's "realist" component seeks strategies for referring to and documenting the world; its "modernist" side questions its ability to document history transparently; and its "postmodern" moment responds to the economic and political conditions of its emergence and public circulation.

There can be no assumption, of course, of a direct access to history. The critique of representation, which has been a hallmark of postwar literary and cultural theory, has aroused an unavoidable suspicion about naive claims of realism. Such suspicion highlights, for example, the fact that the mouse in Spiegelman's drawing only seems "real" in relation to the modern and postmodern playfulness with which it is contrasted within the frame of the image. This overlapping of representational modes points to a second insight that emerges from my bringing together Holocaust studies and cultural studies: the importance of understanding realism, modernism, and postmodernism as relational terms that—at least in a contemporary context—constitute a complex system of understanding.[10] Thinking in terms of relationality and overlap may seem to risk producing an ahistorical account of culture, but in fact it is precisely in the specific modes of interaction between realist, modernist, and postmodernist strategies that historical particularity can be grasped.

The tensions between mouse, Maus, and Mickey Mouse—that is, the relationships between documentation, self-reflexive aesthetic form, and public circulation, or between realism, modernism, and postmodernism—comprise what I call, following Walter Benjamin, a constellation. Benjamin's notion of the constellation—a sort of montage in which diverse elements are brought together through the act of writing—is meant to emphasize the importance of *representation* in the interpretation of history. In his "Theses on the Philosophy of History," Benjamin uses the concept of the constellation in a way that has direct bearing on this project: as the name for the in-between space that ties together the present and past.[11] Written on the eve of the "Final Solution" and Benjamin's ill-fated and fatal attempt to escape the grip of National Socialism, the "Theses" seek to expose and replace the concept of history and time underlying the ideology of progress, an ideology that had failed to predict or combat the forces of Nazism. Benjamin traces this failure to modernity's consciousness of time and argues that the culpable Enlightenment belief in the "irresistible" course of the "infinite perfectibility of mankind . . . cannot be sundered from the concept of [mankind's] progression through a homogenous, empty time" (*Illuminations,* 260–61). The harnessing together of different moments of time in a constellation challenges not just the "progressive" narrative form of modern history, but also its originating gesture. As Michel de Certeau has argued, "modern western history begins with the difference between the *present* and the *past*" (9). This "gesture of division" that historiography repeats everywhere is also the foundation of the concept of historical periods (10). Against the "discourse of separation" (Certeau) that lies behind the concept of "homogenous, empty time," Benjamin proposes that history be viewed as "the object of a construction [*Gegenstand einer Konstruktion*] whose site is... time filled by the presence of the now [*Jetztzeit*]" (*Illuminations,* 261; translation modified). Through this act of construction, Benjamin's historian "grasps the constellation which his own era has formed with a definite earlier one" (263) and is able "to blast open the continuum of history" (262). The present study is premised on the belief that the constellation of elements that makes up modern culture is profitably grasped through the exploration of its extreme moments, the Holocaust prime among them.[12]

The concept of the constellation filled with "the presence of the now," or *Jetztzeit,* also offers an alternative to the periodizing discourse of modern history and opens up the possibility of thinking through the overlapping of historical moments that so many works of Holocaust representation share with Spiegelman's *Maus.* Benjamin's theory of history as constellation also raises the stakes of scholarship because it makes historians and critics accountable for the present as well as the past. In a historical moment — our own — in which genocide seems less a unique event isolatable in the past than an omnipresent possibility, thinking through the constellations that have bound the postwar world to the Holocaust becomes an urgent ethical, political, and, indeed, intellectual task. But, as Spiegelman's drawing also suggests, the "weak Messianic power" posited by Benjamin seems less available after the catastrophe that he only proleptically glimpsed. The past certainly reverberates with the artist's present throughout *Maus* and forms visual constellations of disparate moments in time. Yet these constellations are representative more of history's tendency to weigh on the present than of the historian's revolutionary overcoming of "homogenous, empty time." In this post-Holocaust and post-Marxist period, Benjamin's messianic historian has become an encoder and decoder of constellations that bear witness to the traumatic legacies of modern historical extremity. For better or worse, the expectation of revolution has given way to the more modest, if still elusive, goal of working through — instead of repetitively acting out — the traumas of the past.[13]

With its emphasis on the necessary detour of knowledge through representation and the consequent embeddedness of facts in linguistic, political, and economic structures, cultural studies work inspired by Benjamin helps not only to draw attention to the context in which scholars of the Holocaust write, but also to provide a more integrated approach to an event that was never easily delimitable in time and space.[14] Such a methodology is crucial because, as much recent work has demonstrated, the Holocaust itself has persisted in very real ways beyond the Nazis' own demise, thus throwing into question the easy distinction between events and their aftermaths. This book is thus situated within an emerging interdisciplinary consensus about the importance of taking account of the psychic and social aftermath of genocide, as well as the problem of the transmission of knowledge, in considerations of the Holocaust's significance. While preserving the importance of the events themselves, the shift in focus from events to their transmission and aftermath unsettles the "pastness" of the past. Psychoanalytic research has demonstrated that for the surviving victims of the Nazis the Holocaust has proven to be a traumatic event — that is, according to recent clinical and theoretical perspectives, an event that was not fully experienced at the time of its occurrence and that thus repeatedly returns to haunt the psyches of its victims.[15] Lawrence Langer, in his consideration of the oral testimonies of victims of the Shoah, has radically thrown into question all affirmative accounts of the survival and remembrance of trauma and replaced them with a typology of anguished, humiliated, and unheroic memories that keep the wound of genocide open.[16] In his important study of the history of the United States Holocaust Memorial Museum, Edward Linenthal has provided an analogous typology of forms of public, collective memory and has identified burdensome, treacherous, murderous, and hopeful memories. Others, including James Young and Tom Segev, have looked at the Holocaust's public persistence in postwar societies through a consideration of the memorial, legal, and political processes that not only keep the events present in collective memory, but testify to the active influence of those events in many spheres of contemporary culture.[17]

To this growing body of sophisticated interdisciplinary work in Holocaust studies, this book adds a systematic consideration of the constraints, demands, and possibilities of representations of the extreme — a consideration, that is, of some of the key constellations between the genocide and the postwar world, up to and including the present. Because of my conviction that the extreme is always intertwined with normality and the everyday, an argument I make in the third chapter, these considerations on representation will also have implications for theories of realism, modernism, and postmodernism not directly concerned with the Holocaust or historical extremity. Reading culture through the dim light of the Holocaust provides a new perspective on the fundamental projects, problems, and subjects of realism, modernism, and postmodernism—all of which persist and overlap in a complex constellation. The realist aims at the mimesis of a certain spatial world, but in confronting the structural problem of the relationship between the extreme and the everyday finds herself caught in a traumatic temporality. The modernist, on the other hand, confronts a particular form of progressive time consciousness, but finds his attempt to establish a before and after frustrated as he is pulled back again and again toward the site of a genocidal crime. Finally, the postmodernist interrogates the reign of the pure image or simulacrum and attempts to negotiate between the demands of memory and the omnipresence of mediation and commodification. The constellation of the three categories corresponds to some of the emblematic figures of an era of extreme violence: the survivor, who attempts to document an undocumentable experience; the bystander, who feels impelled to bear an impossible witness to the extreme from a place of relative safety; and the latecomer or representative of the "postmemory" generation, who, like Spiegelman, inherits the detritus of the twentieth century.[18]

The tripartite field that is my subject is not presented as starkly in all of the texts I consider as it is Spiegelman's drawing, although it would be fair to say that some version of this constellation is at work in all Holocaust representations (if often in subtextual or even negative form). While it is important to keep this larger system in mind throughout the various chapters of this book, I have found it useful to address the realist, modernist, and postmodernist responses to the demands of history separately, as constellations in their own right. In three sections, each consisting of two chapters, I interrogate the demands that history makes on representation by way of constellations specific to the Nazi genocide. If these constellations lack the power "to blast open the continuum of history," they may at least provide starting points for a more concrete and complex account of what Maurice Blanchot calls "the writing of the disaster."[19]

Traumatic Realism opens on a philosophical note and considers the dominant modernist discourse in which thinking about the Holocaust as a problem of representation first emerged: Theodor Adorno's often cited and often misunderstood pronouncement that "[t]o write poetry after Auschwitz is barbaric." The first part of the book, "Modernism 'After Auschwitz,' " thus explores the temporal dilemmas of writing in the wake of catastrophe through a close reading and historical contextualization of the very different oeuvres of Adorno and Blanchot, one of the many thinkers who has responded to Adorno. Through a reading of Holocaust memoirs and critical perspectives on them, the second part, "Realism in 'The Concentrationary Universe,' " considers the negotiation between the extreme and the everyday in which accounts of the concentration and extermination camps inevitably engage. In analyzing testimonials by Ruth Klüger and Charlotte Delbo, I develop the concept of traumatic realism, a form of documentation and historical cognition attuned to the demands of extremity. Finally, the chapters comprising the part titled "Postmodernism, or 'The Year of the Holocaust' " explore the dilemmas of the postmodern and highlight the difficult aesthetic, ethical, and political issues involved in the dissemination of knowledge about genocide through mass-cultural forms such as comic books, feature films, and museum exhibits. Works by Philip Roth, Art Spiegelman, Claude Lanzmann, and Steven Spielberg, as well as the exhibit of the United States Holocaust Memorial Museum, reach a much broader audience than any of the texts discussed in the first two parts and thus necessarily raise issues of publicity and the marketplace often overlooked in discussions of Holocaust representations.

The larger trajectory of the book might then profitably be seen as the tracing of a constellation of constellations — a diagnosis, that is, of the cultural scene "after the 'Final Solution.' " In choosing the latter phrase as the title of my conclusion (and in so doing risking the repetition of a Nazi euphemism), I would like to emphasize the paradoxical nature of our actuality — the sense that after the entry of genocide onto the world stage nothing is the same and yet that history nevertheless continues to follow a deadly course, if now with other victims and perpetrators and a whole globe of CNN-watching bystanders. This double consciousness of the simultaneous novelty and deadly sameness of the postwar world leads me to what I hope is a productively critical stance vis-à-vis some of the defining concepts of recent cultural theory. The greater part of the postwar period has been characterized in intellectual life by a suspicion of questions of reference and a flight from the links between discourse and the materiality of history — procedures of avoidance that, as productive of insight as they have been, seem also to be symptomatic of submerged traumatic histories, of which the Holocaust is one. Such a post-Holocaust perspective on history and theory is certainly partial, but in its very partiality it provides a focus through which the resources of contemporary culture can be reassessed.

Part I

MODERNISM "AFTER AUSCHWITZ"

Modernism "After Auschwitz"

Theodor Adorno inaugurated the modernist interrogation of genocide when he proposed in an essay composed in the late 1940s that "to write poetry after Auschwitz is barbaric." During the course of the next twenty years, Adorno continued to repeat and revise that formulation, and it was soon picked up by scholars working across disciplines. The shifting meanings and various interpretations given to the concept of "poetry after Auschwitz" constitute the subject of chapters 1 and 2. Adorno immediately grasped that the problem of representations of the extreme would be in part a temporal one.[1] While it is inevitable that the significance of an event can only be known in retrospect, paying attention to the various articulations of "Auschwitz" in the postwar world reveals that the process of coming to terms with the past is not simply belated but radically uneven. There is no gradual, developmental progress in the "working through" of the implications of genocide — at least on a societal level — that would correspond to the accumulation of knowledge about the Holocaust. What both Adorno and Maurice Blanchot (the subjects of chapters 1 and 2, respectively) demonstrate in their meditations on the "after Auschwitz" epoch is that post-Holocaust history has a traumatic structure — it is repetitive, discontinuous, and characterized by obsessive returns to the past and the troubling of simple chronology.

This traumatic version of modernism differs from realism in that it is primarily concerned not with the practice of representation, but rather with the metanarrative that the modern age tells about itself and its representational practices. Modernism has traditionally been understood as constituting the critical self-understanding of modernity. The aesthetic practices that make up modernism comprise a variety of responses to the self-understanding of modernity as progress; some are skeptical, while others are celebratory — and this is true on both the left and right sides of the political spectrum. Given this multiplicity of responses, many of which predate the Holocaust, how does Auschwitz make a difference in our understanding of modernism? As with realism, the question of modernism and the Holocaust seems belated. World War II is generally thought to mark a border after which begins the institutionalization and decline of modernist art and the gradual emergence of postmodern practices. In some arguments, the Holocaust stands as a sign of this transition, insofar as it brings the master narratives of modernism to crisis and leaves only fragmentary language games in its wake (I refer, of course, to Lyotard's *The Postmodern Condition* and *The Differend*). Thus, even a sympathetic critic, Fredric Jameson, criticizes Adorno's postwar defense of high modernism as reactionary (see his "Reflections in Conclusion" and my discussion in chapter 1). The influence of Adorno's modernist-inflected thinking in discussions of the Holocaust suggests that the event may introduce a certain nonsynchronicity into considerations of theories of the modern. Specifically, the persistence of the question of modernism and the need for self-reflexivity about culture in the wake of catastrophe demonstrate that Lyotard's story of the shift from the modern to the postmodern as a decline in master narratives was always itself a master narrative—that is, a story that glossed over its own contradictions and discontinuities.

There is no single break between the modern and the postmodern — such a concept is itself part of the modern logic of *Neuzeit* that Reinhart Koselleck has mapped out. In *Futures Past,* Koselleck characterizes modernity (which he calls *Neuzeit,* or "new times") in terms of a particular spatiotemporal relationship. Koselleck proposes "that during *Neuzeit* the difference between experience and expectation has increasingly expanded; more precisely, that *Neuzeit* is first understood as a *neue Zeit* from the time that expectations have distanced themselves evermore from all previous experience" (276). In this progressive vision, modernity installs a widening gap between the space of experience and the horizon of expectation, as history becomes "a totality opening toward a progressive future" (281). After Auschwitz, that self-understanding has been radically shaken.[2] The destruction of the European Jews not only was made possible by the technical and bureaucratic expertise of modern society but was, as Zygmunt Bauman has amply demonstrated, *conceived* as a modern project: "It was the combination of growing potency of means and the unconstrained determination to use it in the service of an artificial, designed order, that gave human cruelty its distinctively modern touch and made the Gulag, Auschwitz and Hiroshima possible, perhaps even unavoidable" (219). The project of genocide, in its novelty, drew necessarily on a structure of thought in which the horizon of expectation had radically distanced itself from the space of experience — all was now conceivable. Responses to that genocidal project consequently need to develop a different logic for thinking about history and time.[3]

While modernism participates in this project by immediately raising the question of the relationship of representation to time, in the context of the Holocaust modernism ends by returning again and again to the space of the concentration camp. Modernism "after Auschwitz" thus constitutes a very particular kind of constellation. In revealing the inseparability of space and time in its melding of temporality and place, the phrase "after Auschwitz" becomes what Mikhail Bakhtin terms a "chronotope" — a form of literary expression in which the spatial and temporal axes are intertwined. The articulation of this chronotope by Adorno and Blanchot marks the invasion of modernism by trauma and illustrates how progressive history's fundamental chronological articulation of "before and after" runs aground at the site of murder.

Both Adorno and Blanchot provide tools for a more complex understanding of periodization and discontinuity. The conceptualization of the Holocaust as a clean break between the modern and the postmodern has been facilitated by decontextualized understandings of the phrase "after Auschwitz." While the phrase seems to install a divide between the world leading up to the Nazi genocide and the time of the aftermath, a close reading of Adorno's texts and of Blanchot's reformulation of them reveals a rather different scenario. The late modernism of Adorno and Blanchot involves a turning back against the progressive time consciousness of modernity in order to assert that there is, properly speaking, no era "after Auschwitz." This is true for two reasons. First, as Adorno was at pains to reiterate, the material conditions that made the Nazi genocide possible live on after the "Final Solution" has run its course — a fact confirmed by the globalization of mass slaughter. Second, as Adorno came to realize in his late writings and as Blanchot has implicitly and explicitly testified for the last half-century, the very possibility of a break with the modern conditions of genocide must be premised on a ceaseless witness that returns the subject again and again to the scene of the crime—even when that witnessing subject was not, strictly speaking, present in the first place.

The modernism of Adorno and Blanchot, I argue, is a self-reflexivity of the *bystander* of the extreme. The trauma that modernism undergoes lies in the rupturing of its progressive temporality and of its "modernizing dynamic of innovation or of the 'make it new' " (Jameson, *Signatures,* 160). Adorno and Blanchot retain other elements that, according to Jameson's definition, constitute modernism—such as self-reflexivity and an interest in the breaking of forms—but these are now subordinated to a lifeless temporality of survival (which is explicitly differentiated from living). One of the surprising results of an analysis of the modernisms of Adorno and Blanchot is how much can be learned from two notoriously impersonal writers about the ethics of subject-position "after Auschwitz." If, as Lacan proposes in *The Four Fundamental Concepts of Psycho-analysis,* trauma is part of the structure of the subject's "missed encounter" with the real, the cases of Adorno and Blanchot demonstrate how different the forms of that missed encounter can be.

Adorno, as Jewish refugee from Nazi Germany and as returnee to the Federal Republic, lived an extreme form of the contradiction between being an insider and outsider in the German culture that had formed him. As Miriam Hansen has perceptively remarked in a discussion of the influence of Adorno's concept of experience: "Adorno's return from exile was of more than just symbolic significance: he had come to represent a traumatic absence—that of German-Jewish culture—even though that sense of 'nonidentity' remained largely unacknowledged, encoded in the project of negative dialectics, aesthetic theory, and dissenting sociology" (foreword, xix). This constellation, or, in Hansen's terminology, *Zusammenhang* [context, relation], in which the past maintains itself in the present, is much closer to the meaning of "after Auschwitz" than any notion of pure discontinuity. But the very overlap of cultural moments demonstrates that we are far from a vision of continuity as well. Rather, continuity and discontinuity coexist. In contrast to Hansen, however, I see Adorno's late remarks on Auschwitz, particularly in *Negative Dialectics,* as not simply encoding traumatic absence but raising it into a necessary principle of philosophies of modernity.

In my reading, *Negative Dialectics* marks an important shift in emphasis from the account of modernity two decades earlier in *Dialectic of Enlightenment* as a negative teleology that provides the mirror image of modernity's progressive self-understanding. In the later work, Adorno realizes that the catastrophe of modernity has attained the philosopher's very understanding of it: philosophy itself experiences a "shock" and is traumatized.[4] In place of both the progressive and regressive readings of modernity—which share a belief in the thinker's ability to stand outside historical processes and chart their continuities or discontinuities—modernity is now revealed as the uneven and unpredictable coexistence of continuity and discontinuity. No longer standing outside these processes, the philosopher finds himself personally implicated in the public confrontation with the traumatic legacy of the extreme—hence the emergence in Adorno's postwar work of a commitment to democratic pedagogy.

Blanchot translates Adorno's reflections on Auschwitz into another context and another intellectual register. In constructing a version of "after Auschwitz" that, like Adorno's, seeks to displace the modernist rhetoric of discontinuity, Blanchot rewrites his own revolutionary rhetoric of the 1930s—which he employed as a journalist for right-wing, anti-Semitic journals. The traumatic shock suffered by Blanchot in realizing his proximity to genocide (although he himself was neither pro-Nazi nor a collaborator) does not simply transform him, across the political spectrum, into a left-wing, philo-Semitic mirror image of his earlier self, as is sometimes argued (even if there are moments of such a tendency). Instead, the very terms of his right-wing engagement are reworked and disabled. In their place emerges a vision of eternal vigilance—an endless wake in which the critic commits himself to watching out for the disaster but also recognizes that it has already taken place and that the corpse lies before him.

Until recent contributions by Jeffrey Mehlman, Steven Ungar, Michael Holland, and Leslie Hill little had been said about Blanchot's prewar writings, and the dominant view of the postwar Blanchot was of an apolitical thinker. Even Mehlman, Ungar, Holland, and Hill barely begin the process of reading the prewar writings together with the postwar ones. While certainly much can be gained from intensive readings of either the "political" or "literary" works alone, I propose that by reading them together the vision of an apolitical Blanchot drops out and in its place an important contribution to the project of working through the most serious political complicities emerges. The key category for such a rereading is the psychoanalytic one of *Nachträglichkeit* [deferred action or aftereffect]. Blanchot reads "*après* Auschwitz" as a form of *après coup,* Lacan's translation of *Nachträglichkeit.* Blanchot's understanding of *après coup* is that it is both a form of return of the repressed and a reordering of the past; his innovation is the implicit suggestion that such repetition and reordering can be crucial to a working through of traumatic loss.[5] As in the case of traumatic realism, Blanchot's traumatized modernism can neither let go of nor comfortably grasp the event that lies behind it. Unlike proponents of the realist project, however, Blanchot is primarily interested not in the question of reference and knowledge of the event, but rather in the question of the proper ethical stance to take in relation to the past. It is this sense of the bystander's ambiguous distance from and proximity to the event that mobilizes the otherwise very different modernist projects of both Blanchot and Adorno.

The Spiegelman drawing with which I introduced this book portrays the complexities of the modernist's position as it is theorized by Adorno and Blanchot. That position is characterized by the modernist *auteur*'s very perplexity when faced with a token of the real event that he confronts — the image literalizes the ethical question of how to *hold on* to the real, but also how to begin to *let it go.* The drawing also alerts us to the limits of modernist confrontations with the Holocaust, such as those by Adorno and Blanchot: a reluctance to think through the problem of reference and documentation and an inability to think other than negatively about the fact that representation today is always haunted by the commodity form. Rather than reassert art's autonomy, as Adorno's high modernist position seeks to, Spiegelman both stages an encounter with the real and draws within the environment of the postmodern image. He inscribes both what he calls "MAUS droppings" and the simulacrum of the corporate logo within the frame of his art ("Saying Goodbye," 45). The realist and postmodern moments of representation thus suggest that even the most thoroughly negative and self-reflexive versions of modernism need to acknowledge the violence of history and the marketplace as their conditions of possibility.

Chapter 1

After Adorno

Culture in the Wake of Catastrophe

In an essay written in 1949, the same year that he returned to Germany from exile in the United States, Theodor Adorno inaugurated the modernist reflection on representation in the wake of the Nazi genocide. While much was already known about the Holocaust through such sources as journalism, memoirs, and the Nuremberg trials, Adorno's comments were the first to suggest the impact of the events on literature, philosophy, and art. Drawing on Walter Benjamin's insight that "[t]here is no document of civilization which is not at the same time a document of barbarism" (*Illuminations,* 256), Adorno provocatively proposed that "[t]o write poetry after Auschwitz is barbaric" (*Prisms,* 34). Adorno's phrase (not even a full sentence in the original German) has been quoted, and just as often misquoted, by writers working in a variety of contexts and disciplines, including philosophy, theology, aesthetics, and literary criticism.[1] Rarely has the phrase been read closely, however. Besides the conscious rewritings of Adorno's thought that extend it to fields never mentioned by Adorno; and besides the unconscious distortions of his words — "No poetry after Auschwitz," "After Auschwitz, it is no longer possible to write poems"[2] — the phrase has also circulated with even greater ease in the reduced, ever-malleable form: "after Auschwitz."[3] As a two-word sound bite, "after Auschwitz" has become the intellectual equivalent of the political poster slogan "Never Again!"

Without a doubt, Adorno would be horrified to see his own words on the Nazi genocide turned into an academic truism. He would probably also be unsurprised, finding in the commodification of Holocaust discourse one more proof of the power of the late capitalist totality to reproduce itself and to colonize even the most resistant areas of social life. Yet Adorno's self-citations and his use of the sound-bite version "nach Auschwitz"—which, translated into the English "after Auschwitz," has an ironically poetic effect—have facilitated the frequency with which the concept has circulated.[4] In this case, it is the repetitions, and not the original, that have attracted the most attention. The most frequent allusions to the "after Auschwitz" proposition that actually cite Adorno refer to works in which Adorno was commenting on his earlier statement. Given this pattern, as well as the infamous difficulty of Adorno's thought, it is not surprising that most commentary on this theme has de- and recontextualized the words, often taking them far from whatever meaning Adorno might have intended. Although it is also unlikely that Adorno would have welcomed his inclusion in the field of Holocaust studies, the problems of reception that his writings on Auschwitz have met parallel the problems of multidisciplinarity in work on the Nazi genocide. The interdisciplinary nature of Adorno's writing has, somewhat paradoxically, left a fragmentary intellectual legacy, reaching diverse groups of readers, both hostile and friendly, in isolated institutional locations. Few of Adorno's commentators who have picked up on his Auschwitz hypothesis have been interested in his system of thinking as a whole; rather, they have been concerned with the implications of the proposition for the study of some aspect of culture in the light of the Nazi genocide. Inversely, those who have been concerned with Adorno's philosophical system have tended not to assign a central position to "Auschwitz," relating it, at most, to the "larger" issues of his sociological theory, his relation to other members of the Frankfurt School, his unorthodox Marxism, or his particular version of dialectics. This split in critical approaches makes a more bifocal reading of the significance of the Holocaust in Adorno's thought all the more attractive, if no less daunting.

Because his writings have been so influential in this field, close attention to Adorno's Auschwitz can help to reframe the public and scholarly debates about representing the Holocaust that have grown increasingly heated in recent years. After briefly tracking the way Adorno's proposition has entered the writings of two very different critics (George Steiner and Eric Santner), I will offer a close reading of Adorno's Auschwitz texts and of related works. I want to demonstrate, through an analysis based on Bakhtin's category of the chronotope, how critical and philosophical approaches to the Shoah, even ones that declare its uniqueness, always project theories of history and representation. According to Bakhtin, the chronotope captures the simultaneity of spatial and temporal articulations in cultural practices: in the production of chronotopes, "[t]ime, as it were, thickens, takes on flesh, becomes artistically visible; likewise, space becomes charged and responsive to the movements of time, plot and history" (Bakhtin, 84). As Hayden White remarks, the "socially structured domain" of the chronotope "defines the horizon of possible events, actions, agents, agencies, social roles, and so forth of all imaginative fictions—and all real stories too" ("Historical Emplotment," 341n). While Adorno himself does not use the term "chronotope," his account of culture "after Auschwitz" both constructs a complex philosophical chronotope and provides an original analysis of the effects of genocide on the space and time of representation. The account of history and representation that Adorno develops in his writings on Auschwitz has indeed defined the horizon of many more contemporary considerations of genocide: it sets the stage both for the theory and practice of traumatic realism and for the entry of Holocaust representations into the circuits of the public sphere and commodity culture.

Adorno's Auschwitz chronotope is, in fact, a constellation of concepts that reconfigures itself over the course of two decades. It combines elements of aesthetics ("To write poetry"), temporality ("after"), and place ("Auschwitz") with a morally or politically evaluative predicate ("is barbaric"). My reading of Adorno will mobilize all of those categories in an attempt to reconstruct and examine his successive conceptual constellations. Despite the simplistic symmetry implied by the copula ("is"), neither the phrase as a whole nor its individual particles are transparent, and they all demand interpretation.

A brief consideration of the status of "Auschwitz" serves to unsettle whatever literalist suspicions underlie one's reading of the phrase. As architectural historian Robert-Jan Van Pelt has demonstrated, Auschwitz was initially to be the site of a National Socialist "design for utopia": "Himmler insisted that all Poles and Jews would be removed from the area, and that Auschwitz itself would become a 'paradigm of the settlement in the East.'" Only over the course of time, and relatively late in the camp's existence, did Auschwitz become the "dystopia" that we know it as today—although certainly, I would argue, this second moment was already contained in the "utopian" vision of the first (Van Pelt, 94, 106). As a Germanization by the occupying power of the Polish town of Oswiecim, the name "Auschwitz" already reveals colonial violence. But it is almost immediately clear that "Auschwitz," a place name, is intended to refer not so much to a place as to an event or events. How else could something come "after" it? We know today that the event to which it refers is the slaughter by Nazi Germany of more than one million people (of whom 90 percent were Jewish) during the course of four years (1940–44). The extermination that led to Auschwitz's infamy was, for the most part, carried out at Auschwitz II, known as Birkenau, itself the sight of a razed Polish village, Brzezinka (Young, *Texture of Memory,* 128). At the time that Adorno wrote, however, an accurate account of events at Auschwitz was not yet available, nor was Auschwitz the camp best known to the European and American publics, which were more familiar with the camps liberated by Britain and the United States, such as Belsen, Dachau, and Buchenwald. In disseminating such a formula, it seems unlikely, then, that Adorno meant to refer only to the effects of the events at Auschwitz, since that particular camp was part of a much larger system created and run by the Nazis. Auschwitz takes on both metonymic and synecdochic significance in Adorno's phrase: the place-name refers both to events "proximate" to it and to a totality of events of which it is one part.[5]

Pierre Nora's work on "sites of memory" and James Young's crucial consideration of Holocaust memorials as such sites in *The Texture of Memory* remind us that memory is not indigenous to a (rhetorical or literal) place, but must be created through the ongoing intervention of human agents. In the case of Auschwitz, the process of memorialization had already begun by the time of Adorno's first mention of it: "In 1947, the Polish parliament declared that the [remains] of the camp would be 'forever preserved as a memorial to the martyrdom of the Polish nation and other peoples.'" This incipient nationalization of memory contrasted with another tendency, that of the International Committee of Auschwitz, founded in 1952 in order to put a socialist spin on the memory preserved there (Young, *Texture of Memory,* 130). Unlike the efforts of the Polish and Soviet states, the International Committee, and other groups of survivors, Adorno does not seek to alter the physical topography of Auschwitz. Nevertheless, through his mobilization of the proper name "Auschwitz," he intervenes in Holocaust memory-work and powerfully contributes to the negotiated significance of the death camp as a literal and rhetorical site of remembrance.

"After Auschwitz," Adorno implies, philosophical categories must themselves become chronotopes — "time-places" that serve as imperfect embodiments of historical events and tendencies. Adorno's meditations on Auschwitz ultimately transform his own thinking from within and lead him to reformulate the philosophy of history that had buttressed his writings of the 1940s. One of the later Adorno's most important insights is that the Holocaust forces a confrontation between thought and the event from which neither philosophy nor history can emerge unscathed. In place of the negative teleology of modernity that can be found in the earlier works, *Negative Dialectics* represents modern history as a traumatic shock, a shock that leads to a critical reformulation of enlightenment. The displaced confrontation of Adorno, as refugee and bystander, with historical trauma does not lead to a new practice of documentation and reference, as it will for camp survivors Klüger and Delbo. Instead, it engenders a self-reflexive reconfiguration of the critical faculty and of political practice that pushes his modernist philosophy and aesthetics to their outer limits. Adorno's traumatized modernism provides a theory of Holocaust representation that spurs a rethinking of realism and postmodernism as social categories inseparable from questions of politics and history. Because of his interest in the possibilities of critique, Adorno's focus on Auschwitz is not just turned toward the past. Rather, it creates a constellation between the past and a series of postwar developments in Germany and to a lesser extent in the United States and the Soviet Union. These developments include the persistence of the very modes of thinking and social organization that made the Holocaust possible. Through constant reference to the site of murder, Adorno forces a reevaluation of the time of the modern world — now no longer conceived as a progressive passage from before to after but as threatened from within by potentially deadly repetition. The becoming-historical of thought in Adorno thus corresponds to an ethical and political imperative to prevent the recurrence of Auschwitz, an imperative that entails a critical program of public pedagogy and an ongoing engagement with modernity and democracy.[6]

Rewriting Adorno

Among the rewritings of Adorno, two strategies of interpretation have emerged, one that reads him *à la lettre* and one that takes his words as a jumping off point for even grander claims. Both strategies have produced conflicting evaluations of Adorno, although the great majority of the literalist critics have rejected Adorno's claim. After all, the production of poetry continues apace with no immediately obvious barbaric side effects. Adorno has found more sympathetic readers in those who choose to stretch his insights beyond the restricted realm of poetry, as he himself ultimately did. Many, of course, have read Adorno in both ways, combining a particular attention to poetry or language with considerations of other areas of culture that come readily to mind as vulnerable to the catastrophe of genocide. I have chosen to discuss two particular adaptations here, not because they are necessarily typical of either tendency, but because, even in misreading Adorno, they produce significant variants of his Auschwitz chronotope.

Careful attention to the literal realm of Adorno's proposal (i.e., poetry) does not necessarily result in an Adornian analysis, as the case of George Steiner demonstrates. Adorno's claim has produced sustained reflection by Steiner on the status of poetry and language "after Auschwitz." Steiner, who is probably responsible for the initial impact of the phrase on an English-speaking audience, is one of the few who have taken seriously the effect of Nazi brutality on the writing of poetry. In 1959, and without mentioning Adorno, he diagnosed the German language as not yet free of the contamination produced by years of service to the Third Reich. Steiner impugns not just the human agents of Nazism, but their instruments as well: "[T]he German language was not innocent of the horrors of Nazism.... Nazism found in the language precisely what it needed to give voice to its savagery." What it needed, Steiner implies, was precisely the opposite of the language's rich poetic tradition: Hitler "sensed in German another music than that of Goethe, Heine, and Mann; a rasping cadence, half nebulous jargon, half obscenity" (*Language,* 99).[7] Even fifteen years after the fall of the Reich, Germany's reconstruction was, as the essay's title maintains, a "hollow miracle," because the nation's "language is no longer lived" but propagates "a profound deadness of spirit" (*Language,* 96).

Despite some reconsiderations about the status of contemporary German literature, Steiner reprinted the already controversial essay in his 1967 collection, *Language and Silence.* Although possessing an extremely wide range of reference, this work on "language, literature, and the inhuman" is premised on the Adornian proposition and seems to reflect a reading especially of Adorno's *Noten zur Literatur,* which contains his second, better-known pronouncement on Auschwitz. In the preface, Steiner declares, "We come after. We know now that a man can read Goethe or Rilke in the evening, that he can play Bach and Schubert, and go to his day's work at Auschwitz in the morning" (*Language,* ix). This paradox — that precisely of the relation of poetry and culture to barbarism — stimulates some of the book's fine insights into the spatial and temporal frameworks in which genocide takes place and in which we who come after approach it. In an essay aptly titled "Postscript," Steiner defines his project as an attempt "to discover the relations between those done to death and those alive then, and the relations of both to us; to locate, as exactly as record and imagination are able, the measure of unknowing, indifference, complicity, commission which relates the contemporary or survivor to the slain" (*Language,* 157). Steiner draws (imprecisely) on Adorno's chronotope in a macabre illustration of such a relationship between past and present: " 'No poetry after Auschwitz,' said Adorno, and Sylvia Plath enacted the underlying meaning of his statement in a manner both histrionic and profoundly sincere" (*Language,* 53).

As these formulations indicate, Steiner considers language not just a transparent, instrumental medium — although "The Hollow Miracle" demonstrates how it can be *instrumentalized* — but part of the historical metabolism of the social. Yet Steiner's view of history is profoundly different from Adorno's. Steiner's conception of "after" imports an ideology foreign to Adorno, for, unlike Adorno, Steiner presupposes the existence of what he calls "humane literacy": "We come *after,* and that is the nerve of our condition. After the unprecedented ruin of humane values and hopes by the political bestiality of our age" (*Language,* 4). Such a story of decline is far from Adorno's dialectical evaluation of the legacy of the Enlightenment, as I will argue in the next section. Instead of marking the intimate connection between bourgeois culture and modern terror — explicit in Benjamin and in Adorno's appropriation of him — Steiner laments the terror's emergence at the expense of culture: "The possibility that the political inhumanity of the twentieth century and certain elements of the technological mass-society which has followed on the erosion of European bourgeois values have done injury to language is the underlying theme of this book" (*Language,* 49). Such an idealist understanding of historical change, which places values before material and political determinants, inverts Adorno's thinking. Since at least *Dialectic of Enlightenment*'s reading of *The Odyssey,* Adorno has demonstrated the brutality inherent in the tendential hegemony of "bourgeois values." The message of "after Auschwitz" is not one of nostalgia for a glorious culture where language approximated light or music (*Language,* 41–46), but of the necessity of a new relationship to the future.[8]

If Steiner's account stands or falls on its conception of what comes *before* Auschwitz (which one could contrast, for example, to Adorno's discussion of lyric poetry), other approaches have attempted to move Adorno into a new era "after Auschwitz." In a fascinating study of postwar German film and culture, Eric Santner provides a strong and expansive misreading of the poetry proposition. Santner frames his study, which deals primarily with the mourning and working through of the recent German past, by proposing to investigate the symmetries and asymmetries of the "postwar," "post-Holocaust," and "postmodern" periods. He critically aligns himself with postmodern theory, arguing that it "represent[s] a kind of translation into more global terms of Adorno's famous dictum that there could be no poetry after Auschwitz. After Auschwitz — after this trauma to European modernity — critical theory becomes in large part an ongoing elaboration of a seemingly endless series of 'no longer possibles.' " Santner considers aesthetic, political, cognitive, and social practices as part of that iterative chain of what has becomes impossible: "an inability to tolerate difference, heterogeneity, nonmastery" (*Stranded Objects,* 8–9). He thus understands the phrase "after Auschwitz" as signifying a fundamental transformation in culture that *displaces* the conditions of, and leading up to, Auschwitz.

Santner follows Alice Jardine in giving an affirmative reading of the "no longer possibles." Jardine writes, "I have preferred to speak of our epoch as one of impossibility, and to call for an *ethics* of impossibility: im-possi-bility, the antithesis of *posse / potis / pàtis,* the antithesis of that which relies on power, potency, possessors, despots, husbands, masters."[9] Santner's (and Jardine's) vision of the post-Holocaust future appears as a kind of mirror of Steiner's nostalgic humanism. If the postmodernists emphasize "difference" as opposed to some mythical common culture, they nevertheless both posit a positive vision of an alternative that has existed or does exist. In this they are equally far from Adorno, who, despite the ambiguous formulations of his texts, allows no direct formulation of culture "after Auschwitz" and proposes no such absolute break in modernity (whether or not it has in fact taken place).

While Santner distances himself from some postmodern tendencies to erase historical specificity, his appropriation of Adorno leaves it unclear whether the "no longer possibles" that he and Jardine enumerate are sketches of an ethical imperative or the actually existing condition of our "epoch." Santner's translation of Adorno's "poetry after Auschwitz" dictum into the postmodern ethical demand "to tolerate difference, heterogeneity, nonmastery" elides the materialist and radically negative dimensions of Adorno's thought and replaces them with a liberal pluralist discourse. Adorno's comments are not so much a call for opposition to power, as are Jardine's, but a questioning of the possibility of such resistance. In bringing these two very different discourses together, Santner risks reversing the significance of Adorno's thought without remarking on it. At the least, such a translation would need to specify the relationship between ideological / theoretical formulations of "difference" and the material conditions in which they take place. If this problem remains unresolved in Santner's text, Santner nevertheless poses the important question of how to "[undo] a certain repetition compulsion of modern European history" that "found its ultimate staging in Auschwitz" (*Stranded Objects,* 9). In turning to Adorno's oeuvre the question becomes: In what ways does Adorno's philosophical "restaging" of Auschwitz entail (or not entail) a break with the condition of modernity that constitutes the matrix of the Nazi genocide?

Adorno on Auschwitz

Adorno's philosophizing takes place in a complicated tension with the modernist chronotope of progress — the belief in a constant movement forward through a homogenous space / time that continuously breaks with the past.[10] From his *Dialectic of Enlightenment*, written with Max Horkheimer, to his *Negative Dialectics*, Adorno simultaneously reveals the lacunae in the progressive vision of history and holds out for more enlightenment, as opposed to an impossible return to the premodern.[11] Much of Adorno's writing during his exile from Nazi Germany in the 1940s, in particular, concerns the links between modernity, fascism, capitalism, and culture. This is true for the grand theorizing of *Dialectic of Enlightenment* (written 1944; published 1947), as for the fragmentary, more personal insights of *Minima Moralia* (written 1944–47; published 1951). These works set the stage for the Auschwitz comments, which appear first in the essay "Cultural Criticism and Society" (written 1949; published 1951).

"Cultural Criticism and Society" does not primarily concern the effects of World War II or the implications of genocide. Adorno dedicates the majority of the essay to a kind of *Aufhebung* of cultural criticism. In good Hegelian Marxist fashion, he first demonstrates the implication of such criticism in "sinister, integrated society" (*Prisms*, 34) and in the culture that "shares the guilt of society" (26). He then argues that cultural criticism can be surpassed by the dialectical critic:

> To accept culture as a whole is to deprive it of the ferment which is its very truth — negation. The joyous appropriation of culture harmonizes with a climate of military music and paintings of battle-scenes. What distinguishes dialectical from cultural criticism is that it heightens cultural criticism until the notion of culture is itself negated, fulfilled and surmounted in one. (28)

The dialectical method, for Adorno, entails a double movement back and forth between "the knowledge of society as a totality" and "the specific content of the object" (33). Cultural criticism, in contrast, either reduces the object to a simplified notion of the social or exalts culture as a source of humane values. Against these tendencies, Adorno respectively castigates vulgar class analysis and insists that "only insofar as it withdraws from Man, can culture be faithful to man" (30, 23).

Adorno's stated goal as dialectical critic is "to shed light on an object in itself hermetic by casting a glance at society [and] to present society with the bill which the object does not redeem" (33). What, then, can we make of the intrusion of Auschwitz in the essay's final paragraph? This last passage exemplifies Adorno's characteristic absolutism and puts the Auschwitz phrase in a context not usually considered in citations of Adorno:

> The more total society becomes, the greater the reification of the mind and the more paradoxical its effort to escape reification on its own. Even the most extreme consciousness of doom threatens to degenerate into idle chatter. Cultural criticism finds itself faced with the final stage of the dialectic of culture and barbarism. To write poetry after Auschwitz is barbaric. And this corrodes even the knowledge of why it has become impossible to write poetry today. Absolute reification, which presupposed intellectual progress as one of its elements, is now preparing to absorb the mind entirely. Critical intelligence cannot be equal to this challenge as long as it confines itself to self-satisfied contemplation. (34)[12]

As the movement of this passage (and the essay from which it is taken) demonstrates, "Auschwitz" does not stand alone but is part of a historical process. Adorno assigns Auschwitz a critical position in this history, but less as an autonomous entity than as a *moment:* Auschwitz is "the final stage of the dialectic of culture and barbarism." This does not necessarily entail a position on the "uniqueness" of the event, but it does demonstrate what is missing from critics of Adorno who ignore the place of genocide in "society as a totality."

The complicated and ambiguous structure of Adorno's German (as well as the tendency to decontextualize the Auschwitz phrase — a tendency facilitated by its English translation into a separate sentence) reveals the source of the mistaken interpretation that Adorno is declaring Auschwitz the source of poetry's "impossibility." The context reveals that the agent of the impossibility is "absolute reification," the process that "absorb[s] the mind entirely." In this essay at least, Adorno places Auschwitz within his larger critique of capitalist modernity and the Enlightenment, forces that stand behind the movement of reification. Adorno assigns Auschwitz a particular position as the apotheosis of barbarism, but the significance of barbarism emerges from its place in what he sees as its Enlightenment dialectic with culture. The specificity of Nazi barbarism does not rupture, but continues, the dangerous blend of instrumentally rational means and irrational ends that the Frankfurt School understands as the primary legacy of modernity.

The barbarism or irrationality of "poetry after Auschwitz" is that, against its implicit intentions, it cannot produce knowledge of its own impossible social status. This impossibility is neither technical nor even moral, for Adorno clearly does not see barbarism as the result of individual abilities, actions, or attitudes; it results instead from an objective and objectifying social process that tends toward the liquidation of the individual. As a form of ostensibly free individual expression, the writing of poetry contributes to that mystifying "semblance of freedom [that] makes reflection upon one's own unfreedom incomparably more difficult" (*Prisms,* 21). That semblance is false since the tendential expansion of capitalist society "integrates" the individual as well as relatively autonomous spheres such as culture and unifies them according to the identificatory logic of exchange. In Adorno's reading even Marxist theory must change to keep up with the logic of capital since the latter "no longer tolerates even those relatively independent, distinct moments to which the theory of causal dependence of superstructure on base once referred. In the open-air prison which the world is becoming, it is no longer so important to know what depends on what, such is the extent to which everything is one" (34). The dark vision of this passage is self-evident, but it also leaves open possibilities for a less absolutist position. First, the emphasis on "becoming" is a crucial qualifier to Adorno's totalizing critique, implying that domination has not yet eliminated all possible resistance. Second, the change in relation between base and superstructure signals an increased role for cultural politics since the cultural realm appears no longer derivative of economics. Yet, however other critics or a later Adorno might exploit these openings, in "Cultural Criticism" no such optimism is to be found.

In this essay, experience and expectation collapse into each other, as the mind is "absorbed," creating a surface on which domination plays itself out with deadeningly repetitive blows. Time is reduced to a series of stages whose difference is one of degree but not kind. Meanwhile space suffers a similar iterative demise as the concentration camp replicates itself in the places of public life: the world becomes an "open-air prison." If the citizens of the world do not recognize Auschwitz as the reflection of their lives, that is only, according to Adorno, because terror functions more abstractly outside of the camps through the very logic of identity that laid the groundwork for genocide and has not yet disappeared. The triumph of exchange value, another name for identity in Adorno, prepared the way for mass murder by rendering human life indifferent and therefore expendable. The two words of the phrase "after Auschwitz" are thus equivocal: they mark the limits of an era, but one that was already on its way and that remains today; and they locate a crisis, but only in order to extend its effects well beyond its original space of experience.

The form that Adorno's reflections take here seems as much a product of Adorno's exile in the United States during the 1930s and 1940s as it does of the situation in Europe. Adorno's experience of what he called "late capitalism" in the United States did not initially leave him with much belief in the existence of alternatives to the logic of fascism.[13] To the contrary, Horkheimer and Adorno's analysis in *Dialectic of Enlightenment* — with its adjacent chapters on the culture industry and anti-Semitism — suggests a parallel between American-style monopoly capitalism and Hitlerian National Socialism. Passages in the culture industry chapter make those similarities explicit:

> "No one must go hungry or thirsty; if anyone does, he's for the concentration camp!" This joke from Hitler's Germany might shine forth as a maxim from above all the portals of the culture industry.... Under liberalism the poor were thought to be lazy; now they are automatically objects of suspicion. Anybody who is not provided for outside should be in a concentration camp, or at any rate in the hell of the most degrading work and the slums. (Horkheimer and Adorno, 149–50)

Whatever its truth-value (and who can deny its grain of truth in an era of homeless "shelters" and welfare "reform"), Adorno's argument demonstrates the spatiotemporal situatedness of the production of chronotopes, which always takes place from within other chronotopes. First, Adorno's writing bears obvious traces of his American location, as his later writings will intervene in a more strictly German context. Second, I think it is arguable that such a "comic" comparison could only take place at a moment *before* the camps had been sacralized as sites of ultimate and unspeakable terror — before Auschwitz was "Auschwitz." This is not to say that there was not already consciousness of the camps that Adorno "cites" in creating this phrase, for indeed there were already memoirs, films, and other accounts. But it is to suggest that the temporal break that we retroactively infer in the phrase "after Auschwitz" had not yet taken place in 1940s' public consciousness. The response to, and the form of, some of the texts of the late 1940s (including Adorno's) confirm that the afterlife of an event needs to be periodized as carefully as the event itself. An event alone does not always rupture history; rather, the constellation that that event forms with later events creates the conditions in which epochal discontinuity can be thought.

The tenuous, if not imaginary, quality of the individual and of nonreified production in "administered society" is certainly one of Adorno's great themes, one that he expressed most emphatically in the culture industry chapter of *Dialectic of Enlightenment.* But poetry, to which Adorno refers in this context, presents a particular aesthetic case that should not be immediately subsumed under Adorno's general view of culture under late capitalism. In reflecting on the specificity of poetry in Adorno's system we observe the emergence of inconsistencies. In his 1957 essay "On Lyric Poetry and Society" Adorno shows the limits of lyric poetry — "the most fragile thing that exists" — in the attempt "to attain universality through unrestrained individuation" (*Notes,* 1:37–38). The process of individuation fails, and the lyric cannot remain aloof from the "bustle and commotion" of society, because "the demand that the lyric world be virginal, is itself social in nature. It implies a protest against a social situation that every individual experiences as hostile, alien, cold, oppressive" (*Notes,* 1:37, 39). Poetry cannot actualize its own ideal and stand outside the forces of the rationalized social totality. However, the essay on lyric poetry does not entirely endorse the pessimism about culture evident in the cultural criticism essay because it shows poetry as registering an element of protest. Poetry is not simply an ideological attempt "to falsely present some particular values as general ones," Adorno warns in 1957. The essence of poems, and other works of art, "consists in giving form to the crucial contradictions in real existence": in direct contradiction to the ideas of ideology critique, "the greatness of works of art... consists solely in the fact that they give voice to what ideology hides" (*Notes,* 1:39). For Adorno in the late 1950s, poetry has an important mimetic function, one that consists not in reproducing the harmonious narrative of traditional realist forms, but rather in expressing the rifts that realist mimesis represses. The distinction between this revelatory notion of art as expression and the earlier idea that "poetry after Auschwitz" mystifies knowledge of the social points to the existence of a dual theory of poetry in Adorno. When, in a later discussion, Adorno switches from "poetry after Auschwitz" to "lyric poetry after Auschwitz," he also shifts his conception of the aesthetic from that in "Cultural Criticism and Society" to that in "On Lyric Poetry in Society."

Thirteen years after first measuring the possibility of post-Auschwitz culture, and after much intervening public debate, Adorno returned to the theme in his essay "Commitment." This work, which seems to be better known than "Cultural Criticism and Society," criticizes Sartre's then fashionable notion of engaged literature. The Auschwitz section, titled "The Problem of Suffering" (in one of its English translations), serves as a hinge between a critique of Sartre's and, especially, Brecht's politicized aesthetic and a defense of the "autonomous" art of Kafka and Beckett. Adorno devastatingly reveals the contradictions of Sartre's conception of art, demonstrating that his plays are "bad models of his own existentialism": "they display in their respect for truth the whole administered universe which his philosophy ignores; the lesson we learn from them is one of unfreedom" ("Commitment," 304). Adorno similarly exposes the lack of fit between form and content in Brecht's satire of fascism. Brecht trivializes fascism, making it appear "mere hazard, like an accident or crime," so that its "true horror... is conjured away." Adorno is not immune to Brecht's political claims, but he remains unimpressed by the political level of the work: "If we take Brecht at his word and make politics the criterion by which to judge his committed theatre, by the same token it proves untrue" ("Commitment," 308–9). Thus far, then, Adorno seems to confirm the aesthetic pessimism we saw in the earlier essay, now extending it beyond bourgeois individualist production into the engaged art of "the people."

The example of Auschwitz reveals a third possibility beyond the antinomy of political/apolitical art. Adorno begins by self-consciously reiterating his earlier claim, now specified as a citational "saying" about *lyric* poetry, and then goes on to complicate (if not contradict) it:

> I have no wish to soften the saying that to write lyric poetry after Auschwitz is barbaric; it expresses in negative form the impulse which inspires committed literature.... But [Hans Magnus] Enzensberger's retort also remains true, that literature must resist this verdict, in other words, be such that its mere existence after Auschwitz is not a surrender to cynicism.[14]

The paradoxical situation of art is that this cynicism can be avoided only when kept at bay by a full recognition and remembrance of the horrors of the age. The purpose of art is neither to represent the interests of the proletariat or the individual, nor to grant meaning to abstract humanity, but to remain true to suffering: "The abundance of real suffering tolerates no forgetting.... Yet this suffering, what Hegel called consciousness of adversity, also demands the continued existence of art while it prohibits it; it is now virtually in art alone that suffering can still find its own voice, consolation, without immediately being betrayed by it" ("Commitment," 312). The impossible demand put on art more closely resembles the status of lyric poetry in the 1957 essay — the anguished individual expression of social contradictions — than it does the notion of poetry as that which prevents the comprehension of its own impossibility. But, although lyric poetry is mentioned by Adorno, it does not serve as the primary example of post-Auschwitz aesthetics.

"Commitment" mobilizes a different aesthetic in the wake of the catastrophe from that dismissed in "Cultural Criticism and Society" or partially rescued in "Lyric Poetry and Society" — its name is Beckett. For Adorno, Beckett's writings (as well as Kafka's) enact what others only proclaim: "Kafka and Beckett arouse the fear which existentialism merely talks about. By dismantling appearance, they explode from within the art which committed proclamation subjugates from without, and hence only in appearance" ("Commitment," 314–15). In these writers — one who proleptically internalized the disaster, the other who retrospectively maintains its absent "presence" — the notion of art's barbarity is not refuted but enacted in order to present the barbarity of the age. This allows them to avoid the more chilling paradox present in "the so-called artistic representation" of historical terror: "When genocide becomes part of the cultural heritage in the themes of committed literature, it becomes easier to continue to play along with the culture which gave birth to murder" ("Commitment," 312–13). Representational art creates the possibility for sadistic identification in members of the audience because it contains a surplus of pleasure: "The so-called artistic representation of the sheer physical pain of people beaten to the ground by rifle butts contains, however remotely, the power to elicit enjoyment out of it" ("Commitment," 312). The problem of pleasure is intrinsic to the nonsynchronicity of representation — in retrospect, it seems, any historical situation can be mobilized for the enjoyment of the spectator who consumes history at a spatial and temporal distance. Beckett's art, Adorno claims, evades this problem through its refusal of realist figuration, but one is justified in asking why it too cannot be appropriated by the culture industry. This is precisely what happens, according to Jameson, during the transition to postmodernism. Calling Adorno's essay an "antipolitical revival of the ideology of modernism," Jameson draws attention to the way that "what was once an oppositional and anti-social phenomenon in the early years of the century, has today become the dominant style of commodity production" (Jameson, "Reflections," 209). Adorno's defense of high modernism need not be understood uniquely, however, as a transcendental defense of a particular ideology of style. Reading Adorno in context demonstrates the specificity of his intervention in a post-Auschwitz culture, even as it inevitably illustrates the contextual limitations of his political and aesthetic vision.

Adorno makes clear that "autonomous" art's apparent avoidance of social realism should not be confused with ahistoricism. In "Trying to Understand *Endgame,*" written contemporaneously with "Commitment," he gives a more complete analysis of Beckett and uses this play to add to the "after Auschwitz" chronotope already under construction in his other essays. Adorno once again contrasts Beckett to existentialism, claiming that "French existentialism had tackled the problem of history. In Beckett, history swallows up existentialism." In its refusal to find any figment of humanity within the postcatastrophic landscape, *Endgame* figures forth "the historical horror of anonymity" (*Notes,* 1:244–45). The subject, and the subject's historical sense, may have atrophied, but, for Adorno, this is itself a historical process for which Beckett's play serves as a registration of the real. If existentialism "negat[es] precisely the particularity, individuation in time and space, that makes existence existence and not the mere concept of existence," "Beckett poses the decisive antithesis. . . . Instead of omitting what is temporal in existence — which can be existence only in time — he subtracts from existence what time, the historical tendency, is in reality preparing to get rid of." Beckett's chronotope is thus one of space and time's tendential erasure — not an abstract negation of particularity, but a concrete process affecting "consciousness' power to conceive [history], the power to remember" (*Notes,* 1:246–47).

This chronotope, while certainly incorporating the temporality of the atomic age, among other factors, has intimate ties with the post-Holocaust era. Hiroshima and Auschwitz combine to transform living into half-life, or better, *after*life: "After the Second World War, everything, including a resurrected culture, has been destroyed without realizing it; humankind continues to vegetate, creeping along after events that even the survivors cannot really survive, on a rubbish heap that has made even reflection on one's damaged state useless" (*Notes,* 1:244). The emphasis in "Cultural Criticism and Society" was on the extermination camp as the "final stage" of reification owing its existence to the triumph of an instrumental reason unleashed by the Enlightenment and capitalism. This tendential reading of history — itself a kind of inverted reflection of the concept of progress — is certainly still present, but Adorno's reflections on Beckett put more emphasis on what comes after the "Final Solution," on the survival of the ultimate barbarism into an era premised on reparation or *Wiedergutmachung.*

Adorno was writing in the wake of a period of postwar reconstruction during which there was an ongoing attempt to normalize and legitimate West German democracy and its "economic miracle"; this could only work through a selective forgetting of the recent past and an instrumentalization of the state's financial reparations to individual Jews and to Israel. According to Johannes von Moltke, West Germany's official "politics of memory" vis-à-vis the Holocaust and Jews served (and, to a certain extent, continue to serve) as "the Federal Republic's entry-ticket into the Western alliance" ("Exhibiting," 15).[15] Adorno was dubious about the break with the past that this instrumentalization of memory implied. He went so far as to suggest in 1959 that he "consider[ed] the continued existence of National Socialism *within* democracy potentially more threatening than the continued existence of fascist tendencies *against* democracy" ("What Does Coming to Terms with the Past Mean?" 115). Bearing the message that all cannot be made good again, Beckett's plays and Adorno's essays intervene in the affirmative postwar cultural politics of Western, and particularly German, society. Adorno finds evidence of the underside of the postwar European "rebirth" in the fate of the characters Nagg and Nell, which represents the hypocrisy of the "welfare system": "*Endgame* prepares us for a state of affairs in which everyone who lifts the lid of the nearest trashcan can expect to find his own parents in it. . . . The Nazis have irrevocably overthrown the taboo on old age. Beckett's trashcans are emblems of the culture rebuilt after Auschwitz" (*Notes,* 1:266–67). The "state of affairs" uncovered by Adorno recalls George Steiner's controversial denunciation, which I discussed above, of what he termed Germany's "hollow miracle." Steiner, who would a few years later bring Adorno's ideas about Auschwitz to an English-language readership, argued in 1959 that the German language itself was tainted by the afterlife of the Shoah (*Language,* 95–109). Adorno attempts to expose that hollowness from a strategic position within the Federal Republic, but his account of the cultural devastation extends beyond national boundaries, as ultimately does Steiner's.

Both of the essays that privilege Beckett's autonomous art — finding in them that to which "has fallen the burden of wordlessly expressing what is barred to politics" — end, unsurprisingly, with a paradox. "Commitment" evokes Paul Klee's painting *Angelus Novus* (the model for Benjamin's Angel of History) in order to capture the ambiguity of the chronotope of "after Auschwitz": "The machine angel's enigmatic eyes force the onlooker to try to decide whether he is announcing the culmination of disaster or salvation hidden within it" ("Commitment," 318). In the *Endgame* essay, Adorno claims that in Beckett's "imageless image of death . . . the distinction between absolute domination — the hell in which time is completely confined within space, in which absolutely nothing changes any more — and the messianic state in which everything would be in its right place, disappears" (*Notes,* 1:274). Although Adorno's writing often seems to find in this "last absurdity" confirmation for what he calls in *Minima Moralia* his "melancholy science," we might also find in these later essays that science's "standpoint of redemption" (*Minima,* 15, 247).

Perhaps because of the melancholic's refusal to break with a traumatic event, some historical sense is preserved, even if only in the form of the "imageless image" or the "wordless expression." "Trying to Understand *Endgame*" is dedicated, after all, "To S.B., *in memory* of Paris, Fall 1958" (*Notes,* 1:241; emphasis added). The patently Benjaminian language and themes of these passages raise interesting questions about the relationship between Adorno and the author of "Theses on the Philosophy of History."[16] Most significant for this project would be the impetus that Adorno takes from the theses for the construction of a chronotopic constellation between the *Hitlerzeit* and the postwar era that Benjamin never knew. Differentiating historical materialism from historicism, Benjamin claims that the materialist understands historicity as a retrospective quality of events: facts "[become] historical posthumously." The historical materialist "grasps the constellation which his own era has formed with a definite earlier one. Thus he establishes a conception of the present as the 'time of the now' [*Jetztzeit*] which is shot through with chips of Messianic time" (*Illuminations,* 263). The kind of memory Adorno produces in Beckett's texts is the effect of a constellation connecting Europe and the Federal Republic with its recent past. But while Benjamin is primarily concerned with "blast[ing] open the continuum of history" (262), Adorno's rather different concern here is to exhibit the continuity that underlies a superficially discontinuous German history.

In a famous study from the late 1960s, Alexander and Margarete Mitscherlich argued that the vast majority of German people had never come to terms with their relationship to the crimes of the Nazi era, but had, instead, repetitively and unconsciously attempted to break entirely with the past: "That so few signs of melancholia or even of mourning are to be seen among the great masses of the population can be attributed only to a collective denial of the past" (cited in Santner, *Stranded Objects,* 4). Adorno anticipated this diagnosis of Germany's "inability to mourn" in his 1959 discussion of working through the past [*Aufarbeitung der Vergangenheit*]. He reads what the Mitscherlichs term "rupture" with the past as a surface phenomenon that indicates a deeper continuity: "This collective narcissism [whereby powerless individuals were gratified through identification with the whole] was grievously damaged by the collapse of the Hitler regime; a damage which, however, occurred in the realm of simple fact, without each individual becoming conscious of it and thereby getting over it" ("What Does Coming to Terms with the Past Mean?" 122; cited in Santner, *Stranded Objects,* 5).

In his writings from the late 1950s and early 1960s, we see Adorno refining and reshaping the conception of Auschwitz first mentioned in "Cultural Criticism." Here he is concerned with the production and reception of culture in a context where rupture and continuity coexist—where, in other words, different layers of space and time can cluster around a single name, Auschwitz. He writes from *within* a situation in which the historicity of Auschwitz has not yet settled into a "fact." Rather, it floats within certain institutionally determined parameters, as a fact in the making and thus as one of the means and the stakes of various political negotiations. His concern is obviously not with the individual psychology of Germans but with objective "conditions over which [the majority of people] have no control, thereby keeping this majority in a condition of political immaturity [*Unmündigkeit*]" ("What Does Coming to Terms with the Past Mean?" 124). To combat such immaturity he recognizes the need to wage a battle over the construction of chronotopes, hence his championing of forms of cultural production, such as that of Beckett, that represent contemporary history as the persistence of dark forces from the recent past. Adorno considers such a historical vision necessary to the opening of alternative futures and not a retreat into defeatism. In his late writings, Adorno will continue this discussion in the realm of metaphilosophical discourse, emphasizing the austere pedagogical and theoretical praxis necessary for activating what Benjamin called the messianic potential of the present.

While I have pointed to a break or shift in Adorno's thinking between the first two moments of his continuing "after Auschwitz" discourse, the historical period that encompasses those two moments does not so much witness a break as mark the development of Germany's postwar reconstruction. Adorno's second reiteration of "poetry after Auschwitz," however, not only shifts the tenor of his thinking, but was also published in a cultural context where the meaning of the events of World War II was in the process of transforming itself significantly. Because of the different emotional and historical forces unleashed by the Eichmann trial in Israel in 1961, the Auschwitz trials in Germany in the mid-1960s, the 1967 Arab-Israeli war, and the 1968 international student revolts, the 1960s saw a rapid and uneven development of "Holocaust consciousness."[17] The belated emergence of this historical consciousness varied according to national context, as well as more local and psychological factors, but it remains a social fact that, somewhere in that decade, "Auschwitz" took on a new significance. The repetition of "after Auschwitz" by Adorno and his followers such as George Steiner both reflects this emergence and helped to shape it.

Adorno's testimony to the persistence of historical memory in unlikely cultural locations (i.e., the writings of Beckett) makes clear that the near-silence and imagelessness of art after Auschwitz should not be confused with actual silence or with a ban on representation *tout court*. "Not even silence gets us out of the circle" of culture and barbarism after Auschwitz, Adorno writes in *Negative Dialectics*. "In silence we simply use the state of objective truth to rationalize our subjective incapacity, once more degrading truth into a lie" (*Negative Dialectics,* 367). Here, Adorno preempts the reading of his proposition that implies that because the horror of the annihilation of the Jews cannot be perfectly imitated or reproduced according to the ideals of a naive realism (as if anything could be), all artistic representation should cease. Adorno disallows evidence of the subject's incapacity to represent total horror as grounds for the abdication of art. Such a negative aesthetic of silence, he argues, would only be motivated by the desire "to rationalize" its own predestined failure. But this would be no refusal of the administered society that made Auschwitz possible since "to instrumentalize art is to undercut the opposition art mounts against instrumentalism" (*Aesthetic Theory,* 442). Art's role is its "afunctionality," and thus its success lies in its very failure (although not *any* failure). Hence the *proximity* to silence of the art Adorno values. This proximity is not an abdication but an articulation of suffering. Adorno finds this quality in the poetry of Paul Celan, whom he compares to Beckett on the basis of a common "anorganic" writing practice: "[Celan's] poetry is permeated by a sense of shame stemming from the fact that art is unable either to experience or to sublimate suffering. Celan's poems articulate unspeakable horror by being silent, thus turning their truth content into a negative quality" (*Aesthetic Theory,* 311, 444). Such an assessment of Celan in Adorno's final work takes on added significance given that the original statement about poetry after Auschwitz is considered in popular mythology a pointed rejoinder to the former's "Todesfuge."[18]

After the disavowal in postmodernism of the "great divide," as Andreas Huyssen calls it ("Mapping," 249), between high and mass culture, Adorno has frequently been criticized for his conception of an aesthetic realm autonomous from the social. Yet Adorno's comments about art after Auschwitz demonstrate his understanding of the social content of the "silent" aesthetic. In *Negative Dialectics,* Adorno echoes his comments in "Commitment" and goes on to suggest links between art and historical understanding: "Perennial suffering has as much right to expression as a tortured man has to scream; hence it may have been wrong to say that after Auschwitz you could no longer write poems." He then immediately renders this recantation ambiguous: "But it is not wrong to raise the less cultural question whether after Auschwitz you can go on living."[19] This last thought brings Adorno's philosophy to the edge of the abyss, but it is only in this position that he finds the resources for a thoroughgoing negation of *what is.*

The guilt of surviving the "Final Solution," Adorno suggests in this emotionally charged passage, "is irreconcilable with living": "And the guilt does not cease to reproduce itself, because not for an instant can it be made fully present to consciousness [*weil sie dem Bewußtsein in keinem Augenblick ganz gegenwärtig sein kann*]. This, nothing else, is what compels us to philosophize. And in philosophy we experience a shock: the deeper, the more vigorous its penetration, the greater our suspicion that philosophy removes us from things as they are" (*Negative Dialectics,* 364; translation modified). This passage anticipates psychological insights about what has come to be known as "survivor's guilt," but, more importantly, recognizes the implications of those insights for culture at large and points us toward the social framework in which this condition's symptoms should be read. The surprising *personal* quality that Adorno's writing exhibits testifies to a *social* context in which, during and after the Eichmann trial, survivors were beginning to be recognized as a group that had been silently haunted by a particular set of experiences and expectations about life "after Auschwitz."[20]

In this light, it is interesting to compare the reflections in *Negative Dialectics* with the famous Eichmann testimony of Holocaust novelist Yehiel De-Nur (whose pen name, Ka-Tzetnik, is derived from the German acronym for concentration camp). Before collapsing on the stand, in "one of the most dramatic moments in the country's history," according to an Israeli journalist (Segev, 4), De-Nur described his experience of the camps in words that Adorno's formulation echoes: "Time there was different from what is here on earth. . . . And the inhabitants of that planet had no names. . . . They were not born there nor did anyone give birth. Even their breathing was regulated by the laws of another nature. They did not live, nor did they die, in accordance with the laws of this world" (cited in Segev, 3). These words could come from Adorno's description of the universe of a Beckett play. This public evocation of the "Auschwitz" death-world, from someone who, unlike Adorno, had been at its center, contributed to the climate in which an "after Auschwitz" chronotope could also be spoken. Only beginning in the 1960s could survivors and others who come after begin to bring their respective experiences and expectations to bear on each other in the public sphere. Such a delayed "event" (or the doubling of the event in its acting out or working through) also necessitates reflection on the preexisting modes of reflection. Adorno's late work attempts to bring theory into line with the cultural confrontation with trauma and the attempts at the work of mourning happening all around him.

The passage from *Negative Dialectics* in which Adorno assesses the "guilt" of the post-Holocaust world also, as Sigrid Weigel has recently argued, marks the limits of philosophy itself. What compels philosophy is not only guilt but the nonsynchronicity of guilt and consciousness, those moments that consciousness cannot fully grasp and that therefore return ceaselessly. But if consciousness of "the other of consciousness," that is, genocide and its aftermath, grounds philosophy after Auschwitz, it also strips away its ground, since it produces the traumatic "shock" that these nonintegratable moments of guilt cannot be reconciled with any already existing philosophy of history (Weigel, " 'Kein philosophisches Staunen,' "

129–30). Thinking modern history under the sign of trauma does not, however, lead Adorno to abandon his engagement with modernity, but rather to reformulate it.

The "after Auschwitz" context forces a recognition that philosophy itself has been transformed by the material forces of history that led to the Shoah; in fact, it forces that very materialism of history "upon metaphysics." Such a process makes for some ironic philosophical actors: "a new categorical imperative has been imposed by Hitler upon unfree mankind: to arrange their thoughts and actions so that Auschwitz will not repeat itself" (*Negative Dialectics,* 365). This mutation of philosophy, however, should not be seen simplistically as the symptom of a complete historical break that would install a radically new stage in Western culture, although much of the rhetoric of "after Auschwitz" would seem to imply this. As Adorno makes clear in a radio broadcast from the same year as *Negative Dialectics,* the categorical imperative not to repeat Auschwitz — here considered as the primary goal of education — is necessary precisely because such a break has *not* taken place. In "Erziehung nach Auschwitz" [Education after Auschwitz], Adorno encourages the attempt to build consciousness of the links between civilization and barbarism for the very reason that "the fundamental structure of society and its members, which brought it on, are today the same." Adorno locates the roots of genocide in the development of modern nationalism and inscribes its potential in a "societal tendency" that cannot be separated from the "great tendencies of progress, of Enlightenment" (*Gesammelte Schriften,* 10.2:675; my translation).

While in "Cultural Criticism and Society" Adorno seemed to subscribe to a notion of history as the inverse of progress — a theoretical position that appeared to leave no room for the possible redirection of social tendencies — in his later work he mobilizes a more complex view of history, but one that at first glance seems even gloomier. In *Negative Dialectics* he at once negates and affirms different notions of the kind of universal history implicit in the notion of Auschwitz as a "stage" in a process of reification: "No universal history leads from savagery to humanitarianism, but there is one leading from the slingshot to the megaton bomb." The domination of nature and humanity — epitomized in the Nazi genocide and the threat of nuclear annihilation — "is the unity that cements the discontinuous, chaotically splintered moments and phases of history. . . . History is the unity of continuity and discontinuity" (*Negative Dialectics,* 320). In order to provoke a liberating discontinuity that would not be irrational chaos, it will not do to locate a parallel or parasitic progress alongside or within the universal history of barbarism. For Adorno, thought's resistance to universality comes not from a celebration of difference (what he would call the nonidentical), as in much poststructuralism, but rather from a refusal to rationalize or grant meaning to that which already exists. Thus, while the desirability of universality is denied, its stranglehold on history is not. Adorno replaces the affirmation of difference in the present with an appeal to a version of "the theological ban on images" that defers the emergence of difference to a post-totalitarian world that has not yet arrived.[21] Echoing his assessment of Celan and Beckett, Adorno holds that "[m]aterialism brought that ban into secular form by not permitting utopia to be positively pictured; this is the substance of its negativity" (*Negative Dialectics,* 207). Here the aesthetic and the political are shown to possess a similar critical engagement with the present. There are clear links between the ban on articulating utopia and on Celan's imageless image and Beckett's wordless expression. The latter are the artistic and discursive correlates of utopia in a theory that doubles historical time, asserting the coexistence of a "linear" regression and a discontinuous hope that can only be voiced through determined and determinate negation.

Adorno proposes this theory not *as* "universal history" but as the product, once again, *of* history. Philosophy becomes materialist because "after Auschwitz there is no word tinged from on high, not even a theological one, that has any right to exist unless it underwent a transformation" (*Negative Dialectics,* 367). Not only history as such but also the philosophy of history responds to material forces. If Adorno ascribes the overarching lines of force to the progressive history of capitalism, he does so in order to complicate the question of causality, and he reserves a particular place in this history for Auschwitz:

> [T]he capitalist system's increasingly integrative trend, the fact that its elements entwine into a more and more total context of functions, is precisely what makes the old question about the cause — as opposed to the constellation — more and more precarious. We need no epistemological critique to make us pursue

> constellations; the search for them is forced upon us by the real course of history. (*Negative Dialectics,* 166)

Drawing attention to the spatiotemporal dimensions of the Benjaminian constellation in this passage, Fredric Jameson observes "the way in which Adorno here uses the spatiality of the figure of the constellation to argue explicitly against 'linear causality,' but in the name of history itself" (Jameson, *Late Marxism,* 59). The paradox is that this spatialization of historical understanding is, in some way, the product of the movements of a more "progressive," "linear" history: the "increasingly integrative trend" of capitalism and Enlightenment. The Nazis were, Adorno sometimes implies, the agents of the qualitative transformation whereby history reached a new spatialized stage. The exemplary space of this stage is the concentration, or more accurately, extermination camp: "Genocide is the absolute integration. It is on its way wherever men are leveled off — 'polished off,' as the German military called it — until one exterminates them literally, as deviations from the concept of their total nullity. Auschwitz confirmed the philosopheme of pure identity as death" (*Negative Dialectics,* 362). In Adorno, the language of "identity," of "leveling," is directly connected with the domination of exchange value that capitalism sets in place. Thus Auschwitz is at once an "effect" of reification and the ultimate fulfillment of its tendency to eliminate particularity, in this case the particularity of those human beings not integrated into the Aryan "race."

The name that Adorno gives in *Negative Dialectics* for this relationship that Auschwitz has with the social totality is the "model." The third part of that work is divided into three sections, which Adorno names "models of negative dialectics," and the last, "Meditations on Metaphysics," includes his most extensive reflections on Auschwitz. Adorno's explanation of what he means by "models" is crucial to understanding how the Holocaust intersects with his thought:

> They are not examples; they do not simply elucidate general reflections. Guiding into the substantive realm, they seek simultaneously to do justice to the topical intention of what has initially, of necessity, been generally treated — as opposed to the use of examples which Plato introduced and philosophy repeated ever since: as matters of indifference in themselves. The

> models are to make plain what negative dialectics is and to bring it into the realm of reality, in line with its own concept. (*Negative Dialectics,* xx)

The prominence given to Auschwitz in Adorno's critique of metaphysics makes it almost a model among models. In *The Differend,* Jean-François Lyotard chooses the "after Auschwitz" model as his designation for "an 'experience' of language that brings speculative discourse to a halt." Such a view of the stakes of Adorno's text derives from an understanding of the model as "the name for a kind of experience where dialectics would encounter a non-negatable negative [*un négatif non niable*], and would abide in the impossibility of redoubling that negative into a 'result' " (*Differend,* 88). Lyotard quite correctly reads Adorno's meditations as a critique of Hegelian dialectics in which the negation of the negation produces an affirmative result. When this experience or encounter with that which cannot be raised up into a positive term takes the form of the Auschwitz event, it results in a shift in the horizon of human expectation. The Holocaust leaves a permanent wound in the self-conception of humanity that cannot be overcome, but can at best be prevented from reoccurring.[22] Hence Lyotard insists that what results from this event is a lack of result, and Adorno emphasizes the meaninglessness of the event and thus seeks to shelter it from "committed" or sentimental works of art.

Despite its lack of affirmative result or meaning, the form of the "model" event must henceforth be factored into philosophical discourse as the becoming-temporal of thought. In opening his "Meditations on Metaphysics," Adorno declared, "We cannot say any more that the immutable is truth, and that the mobile, transitory is appearance. The mutual indifference of temporality and eternal ideas is no longer tenable" (*Negative Dialectics,* 361). After Auschwitz, culture — the avowed realm of "eternal ideas" — is folded back into barbarism and the corrosive passage of time. The production of the model is an attempt to think from a place no longer determined by antimaterialist idealism. As the ultimate instance of modern culture's definitive subordination to barbarism, as the rationalized production of death, Auschwitz not only models the model but casts a retroactive judgment on the ideology of Enlightenment with its trust in reason and the sanctity of culture. This rejection of an optimistic account of progressive reason does not entail that Adorno abandon reason for the delirium of the irrational since he does not place his hopes in the progressive narrative. Here, Adorno diverges from Lyotard, whose "postmodern" disavowal of the "grand narratives" of Enlightenment reason is much more thoroughgoing.[23] Lyotard rejects enlightened modernity even as he remains, like Adorno, faithful to aesthetic modernism.[24] Adorno, on the other hand, attempts — through a reworking of philosophical form in the light of the catastrophe — to wrench reason free from its instrumental determinations.

Thus, the concept of the model necessitates a new form of philosophical representation. Adorno borrows the concept of the model, Jameson suggests, from music, and specifically from Schönberg's serialism. In twelve-tone composition the model is "the raw material of a specific composition, . . . the particular order and configuration of the twelve notes of the scale which, chosen and arranged in advance, *becomes* the composition, in so far as this last is 'nothing more' than an elaborate series of variations and permutations . . . of that starting point" (Jameson, *Late Marxism,* 61). The significance of Jameson's understanding of the model, and that which opposes it to the tenor of Lyotard's post-Marxist argument, is that in this musical reading the model is revealed as that fragment that already contains the totality within it. Jameson's wording, however, is somewhat ambiguous and seems to imply that the relationship between the model and the totality (the composition) is one of what Althusser termed "expressive causality."[25] In other words, the relationship between part and whole in Jameson's musical metaphor seems too simple, a combinatorial logic where the part immediately generates the whole.

Jameson's Hegelian reading does not properly account for the process of "structural causality" that Adorno's account of the model seems to suggest. In this case, we do not simply derive Auschwitz from a history that moves externally to it (as we would in a mechanistic deduction); we grasp that history through the necessary mediation of Auschwitz. But the process is not mere induction either, since Auschwitz does not "generate" or "reflect" the totality of the history of modernity. Yet had it not "taken place," the history to be grasped would clearly not be the same. After Auschwitz, modernity and Shoah need to be read in light of each other; our understanding of each is mediated by the other.[26] The model is not a matter of indifference, as is the example in speculative thought, nor is it simply an element in a permutational series. The manner in which thought can arrive at some understanding of that which the model models is less direct. As Adorno wrote about "the essay as form," "the essay has to cause the totality to be illuminated in a *partial* feature, whether the feature be chosen or merely happened upon, without asserting the presence of the totality" (emphasis added). From his account of the essay, we can presume that Adorno's use of the model is not an attempt to be "systematic," as Jameson's metaphor suggests, but rather has the "characteristic of an intention groping its way" (Adorno, *Notes,* 1:16). The nonassertive, almost blind illumination of essayistic thought is once again the "imageless image," and *its* model is autonomous art. With the selection of "poetry after Auschwitz" as the partial feature through which to illuminate the Holocaust and its relation to modernity, Adorno preserves a tension between part and whole that maintains both the power of the modern totality and the truth content of its various local expressions.

We can now grasp something of the temporality and location of "after Auschwitz" as Adorno employs it in his late works. In fact, the famous opening line of *Negative Dialectics* — "Philosophy, which once seemed obsolete, lives on because the moment to realize it was missed" (3) — expresses the defunct temporality of lifeless survival that the "experience" of Auschwitz inaugurates, according to the text's final "meditations on metaphysics." And the place of this thought is revealed as that constricted zone of nearly annihilated expectation, the death camp: "Beckett has given us the only fitting reaction to the situation of the concentration camps — a situation he never calls by name, as if it were subject to an image ban. What is, he says, is like a concentration camp. At one time he speaks of a lifelong death penalty" (*Negative Dialectics,* 380–81). If, in Beckett, the concentration camp is the "unnamable," in Adorno the camp (Auschwitz) is the repetitively invoked name for something else that must be grasped in a situation of indirect illumination.

That something else is, strangely enough, the yearning for utopia, that which has no-place. Faced with the "lifelong death penalty," Beckett's writing

> seems stoical but is full of inaudible cries that things should be different. Such nihilism implies the contrary of identification

> with nothingness. To Beckett, as to the Gnostics, the created world is radically evil, and its negation is the chance of another world that is not yet. As long as the world is as it is, all pictures of reconciliation, peace, and quiet resemble the picture of death. (*Negative Dialectics,* 381)

The significance of positing "another world that is not yet" derives not from any positive qualities of that world (which fall under the image ban), but from the coexistence of an alternative chronotope — the *concept* of another space and time — in a field where the replacement of experience with integrated, administered consciousness obliterates expectation and hope. Elsewhere, Adorno formulates this concept in terms of the indexicality of thought: "utopia is essentially in the determined negation . . . of that which merely is, and by concretizing itself as something false, it always points at the same time to what should be."[27] In Bakhtin's formulation the indexical function of the chronotope points backward toward the event — thus underlining representation's belatedness in relation to that event. In Adorno the necessity of coming after the catastrophe coexists with an anticipatory temporality. The construction of the chronotope blocks the event itself but in so doing casts a shadow whose outline registers utopia. If we always come *after* the event in Adorno's thought (both historically and epistemologically), we are also always *too early* to grasp it. We live in a world where reconciliation has not yet taken place and thus has not yet provided the standpoint from which to view the event from outside the flow of "damaged life." The repeated citation of Auschwitz is an attempt to make one's way through that flux, to provide a temporary map of the historical present as the means to a future that would install a break with the conditions that nurtured fascism.

In a sense we return to Adorno's initial phrasing of "after Auschwitz" where he castigated poetry for blocking knowledge of the "radically evil" social totality. Now, however, we see that some poetic practices (e.g., Celan's, Beckett's) and Adorno's writings on poetry seek, through their direct or indirect invocation of Auschwitz, to block a positive comprehension of what, after Auschwitz, can only be known negatively. Only by avoiding "faded positivities" can writing avoid "conspiring with all extant malice, and eventually with the destructive principle itself" (*Negative Dialec-*

tics, 381). The repeated performance of the terrifying chronotope, "after Auschwitz," holds a place for a time not yet emergent.

Conclusion: After Adorno

If the space-time "after Auschwitz" occupies some middle zone between past and future events that defy representation, its own substance remains conceptual, which is not to say imaginary. After Adorno one cannot conceive of genocide or its effects in quite the same fashion. But when or what is "after Adorno"? Irving Howe remarked, quite correctly, that it is difficult "to think of another area of literary discourse in which a single writer has exerted so strong, if diffused, an influence as Theodor Adorno has on discussions of literature and the Holocaust" (Howe, 178). Yet Howe also realized, as did Adorno, that the "speculation that human consciousness could no longer be what it had previously been" after Auschwitz was unfortunately not true (Howe, 198). We can certainly explain this latter fact in Marxist terms, arguing that a change of consciousness could only follow a change in the material organization of society—this is precisely Adorno's critique of postwar European culture. But Howe's remark on Adorno's influence reasserts the question of consciousness and intellectual intervention, while it suggests that that intervention should lie elsewhere than in "speculations" on consciousness.

If Adorno is correct in *Negative Dialectics,* speculation must give way to a new form of dialectical materialist analysis in the wake of Auschwitz. One consequence of this proposition would be the need to take into account the material effects of philosophizing. Instead of seeking in Adorno the reflection of a historical break called "Auschwitz," we might understand him as producing a series of concepts (in the form of chronotopes) that retroactively pose the possibility of a break, at the same time that they illuminate the eternal return of the same in those places that have not yet worked through the Auschwitz model. Thought "alone" cannot alter history, but, in citing and resignifying a discursive chain (such as that connecting Auschwitz to "Auschwitz"), it can keep the past present and the future open. The production of concepts also helps structure the field out of which the agency to alter the parameters of the present must emerge.

As Howe implies, the major influence of Adorno's Auschwitz

writings has taken place in aesthetic realms. This must be taken for its negative as well as its positive implications. Adorno provides complex, contradictory, and frequently misunderstood concepts for evaluating "Holocaust art." Despite those discouraging adjectives, various interpretations of Adorno continue to structure critical response to such art in the present (even when Adorno's name is not mentioned). One potentially positive effect of my reading of Adorno would be to shift this terrain from what remains a primarily *moralizing* discourse to a *materialist* and *ethical* critique. In other words, instead of evaluating a work's "decorum" according to principles assumed to adhere in the event itself, we can recognize our ambiguous distance from the event and inquire into the relationship a work establishes between the past it mobilizes and its contemporary context. Reading Adorno's works as interventions in concrete situations meant to produce effects deprives them of their oracular quality, but also increases their relevance and their usefulness in the present.

It is equally true, however, that the particular way in which Adorno's thought structures the field of possibilities limits the kinds of interventions that he would promote. Adorno's aesthetics remain, as Jameson points out, strictly modernist.[28] Since modernism no longer represents a challenge to quiescent ideologies, a more properly postmodernist critique would offer a crucial reconsideration of mass culture.[29] In particular, a full-blown consumer society demands an acknowledgment of the status of the Holocaust commodity. In the midst of postmodernism's proliferation of aesthetic techniques new kinds of historical art are taking shape.[30] Some postmodern works, such as Art Spiegelman's *Maus,* challenge the assumptions about the necessary "autonomy" of art after Auschwitz that have emerged from Adorno's (albeit critical) reception, even as those same works recognize the risks of commodification.

Equally limiting to the project of confronting the historical legacy of genocide is the way in which Adorno focuses primarily on aesthetic objects, even as he refers them back to the conditions of their production. This is of course ironic since his initial statement of the problematic seems deliberately antiaesthetic. Adorno's subsequent reformulations, and most of his writings, refine the status of the aesthetic, granting authentic or autonomous art a role of absolute importance in articulating a critique of capitalist society.

But the wholesale substitution of reflective and aesthetic practice for other forms of praxis hardly seems justifiable on political or theoretical grounds.

This is not all there is, however, in late Adorno. If the ethico-political call to arms after Auschwitz derives from the necessity of preventing its recurrence, then the pedagogical moment that sometimes surfaces in Adorno's writings and, especially, speeches and radio talks ought to be kept in mind. In those more obviously conjunctural interventions, Adorno stresses the concept of education to maturity, *Erziehung zur Mündigkeit*. In sketching this notion of "democratic" or "mature political pedagogy," Adorno not only leaves the autonomy of the aesthetic realm but suggests a project of "public enlightenment" whose formulation and actualization remain today as critical as they do unfinished.[31] Ultimately, this relocation of the confrontation with Auschwitz in the public sphere of democratic education may be as great a contribution to the process of coming to terms with the past as the more famous reflections on representation. In fact, the realms of representation and the public sphere are not so easily separable. The lively debates surrounding many recent films, literary and historical texts, memorials, and museums seem to indicate a renewed interest in historical understanding that has been spurred precisely by controversies about representation. Viewed retrospectively from the vantage point of such debates, Adorno's contribution is all the more impressive; he brought together the questions of Holocaust representation and education at a moment when they had not yet been fully articulated.

Through the articulation of the "after Auschwitz" chronotope, Adorno thus provides the theoretical impetus for what will later emerge as new realist and postmodernist forms of representation and cognition. In beginning the process of working through the implications of extremity for literature, philosophy, and politics, Adorno's writings also suggest the need for new forms of representation capable of registering the traumatic shock of modern genocide and for new forms of publicity that will translate knowledge of extremity for a mass audience. Although his modernist sensibilities would probably prevent him from recognizing the cognitive and pedagogical values of what I call traumatic realism and the postmodern Holocaust commodity, Adorno's reflections have helped to make these forms both conceivable and desirable.

Chapter 2

Before Auschwitz

Maurice Blanchot, From Now On

Comme un guetteur qui n'est pas là que pour veiller, se maintenir en éveil, attendre par une attention active où s'exprime moins le souci de soi-même que le souci des autres.

— MAURICE BLANCHOT, "Les intellectuels en question"

Writing the Disaster

Adorno's critical engagement with the possibilities of Enlightenment reason in the wake of the man-made modern catastrophe of the Nazi genocide transforms his philosophy of history from within. The recognition in *Negative Dialectics* that "[w]e cannot say anymore that the immutable is truth, and that the mobile, transitory is appearance" (361) shifts the philosophy of history from a discourse *about* time into one marked and marred *by* temporality. Such a recognition helps Adorno to disentangle his thinking from the progressive legacy of modernity, which had previously lived on in his work in negative form. The more complicated — but no more affirmative — conception of history that results actually encourages a reengagement with certain aspects of modernity, including experimental modes of representation and the democratic public sphere. It is precisely Adorno's grasp of the disastrous and discontinuous temporalities of history that provides a small space for agency and for the preservation of a kind of utopian thinking. In citing and modifying Adorno's "poetry after Auschwitz" dictum, Maurice Blanchot also provides a self-reflexive rethinking of history and representation, but from a radically different historical, political, and ethical situation. Blanchot's explicit grappling with Auschwitz emerges decades after Adorno's "Cultural Criticism" essay — thus indicating again the discontinuity of the waves of Holocaust memory. However, reflecting specifically on the issues of traumatic temporality in these two "modernist" writers encourages a return to Blanchot's earlier work — both immediately before and immediately after the war — in order to reread their significance in the dim light of the Shoah. Through a rethinking of literary representation under the sign of trauma Blanchot implicitly returns us to his own traumatic site and provokes further consideration of the limits of representation and of the ethical situation of the witness-bystander.

The works of Blanchot indeed provide a fascinating lens through which to establish both the epistemological and political importance of the Holocaust in a contemporary context. Yet as much as Blanchot's writings on Auschwitz and on the "writing of the disaster" help us to grasp the limits of representation and the simultaneous estrangement and implication of language, terror, and trauma, his bio-bibliography also presents its own challenges to that understanding. One of the most important and influential, although least understood, writers and thinkers of the amorphous movement known in the United States as "French poststructuralism," Blanchot was also a prolific intellectual contributor to the quasi-fascist French "Jeune Droite" during the 1930s. In political and literary writings for such journals as *Réaction, Combat,* and *L'Insurgé,* Blanchot shared the pages with extreme nationalist figures, including Robert Brasillach, Thierry Maulnier, Maurice Bardèche, and Pierre Andreu. These articles, which number in the hundreds, represent a significant right-wing political engagement, one made all the more mysterious by Blanchot's sudden ideological reversal after the Nazi occupation of France. If Blanchot's own political line was never pro-Nazi, as that of some of his colleagues was, it nevertheless clearly illustrates the 1930s mix of anti-Semitism, extreme nationalism, and opposition to democracy, capitalism, and communism that historian Jean-Louis Loubet del Bayle has termed "non-conformism." On the other hand, Blanchot's social and political commitments since the war have been inverted and include opposition to the Algerian War, a role in the May 1968 uprising, a vigilant critique of anti-Semitism, and intellectual friendships with the most prominent contemporary French Jewish thinkers.

The complexity of the Blanchot case is redoubled by another biographical factor, his well-known withdrawal from public after the war (given up briefly during May 1968), as well as by the deliberate, but productive, obscurity of many of his writings since then. Blanchot's withdrawal and his radically impersonal public persona include an almost total silence about his own past, even as his work has come, over the years, to engage more and more directly with the significance and status of the Nazi genocide. In *L'écriture du désastre* [*The Writing of the Disaster*] (1980) and *Après coup* [*Vicious Circles*] (1983), Blanchot's meditations on the Shoah take on increased gravity, although explicit discussion of the implications of the genocide occurs as early as *L'entretien infini* [*The Infinite Conversation*] (1969), *Le pas au-delà* [*The Step Not Beyond*] (1973), and *L'amitié* [Friendship] (1973).[1] Blanchot's case is thus significantly different from the more well known one of Paul de Man. While their early writings bear some resemblance, de Man's later work does not integrate the disaster the way that Blanchot's writings do. Not only do Blanchot's late texts constitute one of the major efforts to "think" the Holocaust, they also suggest the need for a rereading of his entire oeuvre. In this reconsideration, the silently passed-over right-wing journalism suddenly assumes a central position and even the so-called apolitical texts of the 1940s and 1950s appear as determinate political responses to a troubling history. The knowledge that arises from a consideration of the late texts alongside those from the 1930s and 1940s concerns the ethical and political stakes of writing, reading, and remembrance. In this process of rereading, however, the early texts cannot be allowed to disappear behind the more palatable, post-1968 philosophical reflections, as they do in much Blanchot criticism. The constellation of texts and ethico-political positions that emerges extends the modernist reflection on representation and its limits — and also begins to indicate the very limits of that modernist project.

Where Jeffrey Mehlman, one of the few critics until late to pursue the "missing" texts, finds in Blanchot's pre- and post-Occupation work a continuity in the guise of a break with the past ("Blanchot"), I see a critical political and theoretical rupture premised on an inability to overcome the past. Like Adorno, Blanchot transforms a recognition of the traumatic impact of his relationship to the Nazi genocide into a critical philosophical strategy. Blanchot's melancholic refusal to overcome the past is no doubt psychologically and ethically ambivalent.[2] Yet in rewriting history as trauma Blanchot takes limitless responsibility for his position as an implicated bystander. In addition, however, the impossibility of making history and politics disappear also displaces part of the ethical bind back onto Blanchot's critics, creating an imperative to reexamine that about which Blanchot himself remains silent. In doing so, sympathetic critics cannot hesitate to suggest certain unsavory aftereffects that shadow Blanchot's texts: in order to speak with Blanchot in the *entretien infini* [infinite conversation] we must sometimes speak against him. Preserving the memory of Blanchot's engagement with the Jeune Droite within any consideration of the more valuable later writings prevents ahistorical and antipolitical misreadings of Blanchot's significance to postwar thought — a significance central to the critique of representation after the "Final Solution." That significance concerns, above all, the temporality and the ethics of the "post," that is, the relationship in a posttraumatic culture between past and present (and future), between before and after. Blanchot hints enigmatically at that relationship when he paraphrases Adorno in *Après coup:* "A quelque date qu'il puisse être écrit, tout récit désormais sera d'avant Auschwitz" (99) [No matter when it is written, every narrative (*récit*) from now on will be from before Auschwitz (*Vicious Circles,* 69; translation modified)]. The discontinuous temporality that this peculiar phrase figures forth reasserts the question of representation, tacking writing to history at three points: the paradigmatic event of the past (Auschwitz), the now (the *date*) of the text, and some open-ended conception of the future (*désormais*). If, as Shoshana Felman has asserted, language and occurrence are essentially foreign to each other (Felman and Laub, *Testimony,* 212), they nevertheless encounter each other everywhere, establishing a constellation of the utmost ethical and political importance.

Critical Challenges

Until recently, most critics have maintained a respectful silence with regard to Blanchot's right-wing political journalism of the 1930s, and only a few have taken seriously his texts of those years. Writing in the mid-1980s, Steven Ungar challenged Blanchot critics to read this multidimensional oeuvre "within history" and posed a series of questions for future research: "Is the political venture a master key on which the later fiction and criticism are somewhat dependent? Do the early writings explain or account for inconsistencies and gaps? Or should they instead be added to the existing body of his writings without special consideration? . . . How much does the political supplement enrich our understanding of Blanchot's place in literary modernity? ("Paulhan," 79, 78). It has taken ten years before most of these questions have begun to be addressed. Only in the late 1990s has a thoroughgoing reevaluation of Blanchot's career along those lines begun among the growing number of Blanchot scholars. The first major work was done by Ungar himself in his 1995 book *Scandal and Aftereffect,* and several works appearing in 1997 continued the discussion.[3] Yet even some recent criticism continues the tactful but mystifying silence. Indeed, the first full-length study of Blanchot in English, published in 1994, manages to survey at length both the fictional and nonfictional postwar writings but makes no mention at all of the political or literary critical writings of the 1930s.[4] Many of those critics who do allude to Blanchot's prewar political positions tend to assert their irrelevance to contemporary investigation, thus unwittingly contributing to processes of historical forgetting that, at the limit, take far uglier forms.[5]

To be sure, Blanchot's political positions of the 1930s were already known to those who were interested before Ungar's call to action. There are occasional references to Blanchot's role in the French right in such historical studies as Zeev Sternhell's *Ni droite ni gauche* and Jean-Louis Loubet del Bayle's *Les non-conformistes des années 30,*[6] but the most exhaustive theoretical account of his early political positions (before Ungar's book) can be found in a long essay by Mike Holland and Patrick Rousseau, "Topographie-parcours d'une (contre-) révolution." Holland and Rousseau trace the context and itinerary of Blanchot's ideology, placing him in line with a Maurrasian heritage of anti-Semitic nationalism. They demonstrate the logical contradictions that resulted from the German threat, thus explaining at a formal level, which is not entirely satisfactory, the reason for his abrupt abandonment of his 1930s positions. By not considering these early works in the light of later writings, Holland and Rousseau reproduce the notion of a "clean break" that cannot address the persistence of motifs and elements from the 1930s into the post-Occupation era.

The most significant early study that attempts to connect

Blanchot's political writings with his postwar literary influence is Jeffrey Mehlman's "Blanchot at *Combat:* Of Literature and Terror" in *Legacies of Anti-Semitism in France.* Instead of foregrounding Maurras, Mehlman stresses the connection, through Bernanos, to Drumont, the late-nineteenth-century author of the massive, best-selling diatribe *La France juive.* In considering Blanchot's approving reflections on Montherlant's collaboration-marked *Solstice du Juin* in *Faux Pas* (1943), Mehlman suggests disturbing continuities between the pre- and post-Occupation writings.[7] While Holland and Rousseau emphasize the internal contradictions, and ultimate logical impossibility, of the revolutionary thought of the Jeune Droite, Mehlman places the emphasis on external contingencies; he argues that the Occupation and Nazi genocide radically transformed the French intellectual landscape, creating a break after which the currency of prewar anti-Semitism became untenable. However, instead of finding Blanchot working through his right-wing engagements in his wartime writings (i.e., after his political break), Mehlman sees a mirrored reversal where the embarrassing past is "liquidated" and anti-Semitism becomes philo-Semitism without transforming the structure of the theoretical apparatus. Mehlman wrote his essay on Blanchot before the appearance of *The Writing of the Disaster* and *Après coup,* both of which serve to alter retrospectively the relationship between Blanchot's pre- and postwar writings. These two texts of the 1980s do not disprove Mehlman's assertions, which are convincing as long as they remain historically situated in the early postwar period, but they complicate the relationship between Blanchot's antagonistic personae, and they allow for a less pessimistic appraisal of French literary and philosophical modernity than the one underwritten by Mehlman's account.

Steven Ungar's *Scandal and Aftereffect: Blanchot and France since 1930* significantly alters the critical landscape and has already begun to effect a major displacement in the ways that Blanchot is read. Ungar both extends the Blanchot corpus, so that the dozens of articles from the 1930s can no longer be ignored, and inquires into the logic of *Nachträglichkeit* (which he translates as "aftereffect") in order to explain the scandalous return of interwar and wartime texts that has disrupted previous understandings of literary modernity. At the same time that he acknowledges the significance of Blanchot's postwar political transformation, Ungar (not unlike Mehlman) argues that "the post-1958 writings contained enough traces of abject dissidence to question the common belief that Blanchot emerged from the war as though converted" (135). Ungar's project is to reveal how Blanchot's various "disclosures" of the fascist past are in fact double-edged and serve both to "reveal and hide" his own involvement in that history (136).

Although absolutely convinced of the importance of Ungar's work for the reevaluation of Blanchot and modernity, I nevertheless have several interrelated problems with his approach: (*a*) Ungar puts too much stress on the formal pattern of "dissidence," a kind of structural stylistics that allows him to compare, for example, a 1986 critique of apartheid with 1930s anti-Semitic rhetoric without taking into account the radically different contexts and objects of the two polemics. (*b*) While he demonstrates the ambivalence of Blanchot's postwar reassessments of fascism and anti-Semitism, Ungar seems at times to desire a "full disclosure" (136) or confession on Blanchot's part (although at other times he writes that one should not "project accountability directly onto the figure of the individual" [164]). But the point should be not to put the Vichy and pre-Vichy periods on trial in order to denounce them summarily, but rather to increase understanding of the periods. Given that the offending texts are already known, it is not entirely clear to me what a personal avowal of responsibility on Blanchot's part would add to these processes.[8] (*c*) The stress on disclosure is in part based on Ungar's reading of *Nachträglichkeit* as aftereffect or return of the repressed (2); hence, according to this logic, what is not avowed returns in displaced form. Because this return is especially pertinent to the processing of traumatic experiences, *Nachträglichkeit* plays an important role in Blanchot's consideration of Auschwitz. But Blanchot himself (following Lacan) also transforms Freud's term, using the French *après coup* specifically in relation to the interwar period in order to connote not just a carrying forward of a repressed past into the future, but a retrospective and reevaluative return from the present to the past. Thus, despite the lack of full disclosure, a process of working through is significantly at play in Blanchot's later texts, especially those that address (in personal and nonpersonal ways) the underlying events and ideologies at issue. (*d*) Because of this double movement of *Nachträglichkeit,* a reading of Blanchot that moves back and forth across the war is necessary to capture the full position of his work in French literary and philosophical modernity. Ungar makes some of these moves, but, because of the groundbreaking nature of his archival work, he chooses to focus on the 1930s at the expense of texts such as *Après coup* and *The Writing of the Disaster.* When read in dialogue with the early journalism, however, these latter, speculative texts provide more access to the past than the genre of confession would, and thus already enrich the understanding of the interwar and immediate postwar periods and of Blanchot's place in them. (*e*) The dialogic approach, which I attempt here, contradicts the received opposition in virtually all Blanchot criticism that Ungar reproduces between "the binding of literature and politics in Blanchot's articles in *Le Rempart, Combat,* and *L'Insurgé* [and] the postwar conception of literary space from which history and politics were more or less elided" (169). The reading of Blanchot that follows from these methodological principles, which I have developed in relation to Ungar because he provides the most complete consideration of the 1930s texts, serves as neither condemnation of nor apology for Blanchot. I share Ungar's desire to rehistoricize the work of a writer who has too frequently been removed from history and politics. Because Blanchot's writing already contains meditation on the intersections between representation, politics, and history with respect to the Holocaust, it serves as a better model than, say, Heidegger and de Man for coming to terms with the past. Specifically, Blanchot provides an intensive reflection on the position of the bystander or contemporary of deadly events, and he renders a critique of the limits of representation that should be read as arising out of that vexed subject-position.

First and Last Words

The structure of the brief collection *Après coup*[9] suggests the difficulty of establishing the time of Blanchot's writings, but also points toward the importance of history, and particularly the history of Nazi genocide, in the postwar Blanchot. The book consists of three pieces—two short stories and one philosophical reflection musing on the stories. The stories were both written in the mid-1930s, but only published together well after the war in 1951 as *Le ressassement éternel.* One of the texts, "Le dernier mot" [The last word], was, according to Blanchot, not "destined for publication." Nevertheless, he sought to publish it in 1947 in a literary series that, he claims ironically, no sooner reached its last word and stopped appearing. In the 1983 edition, the two stories from before (and after?) the war are joined by the short retrospective essay, "Après coup" [After the fact]. United in one book despite and perhaps because of their radically discontinuous provenance, these texts have much to say about the continuity and discontinuity of history. They also suggest, albeit allegorically, modes of reading and reconsidering the specificity of Blanchot's political journalism of the 1930s. The strategies of rereading that emerge from Blanchot's later work stand in opposition to the lack of tools for historically specific reading provided by the later Paul de Man.

Written in 1935–36, but abortively published a dozen years later, the disappearing story, "Le dernier mot," is also concerned primarily with disappearance. Well before his own exit from public life, Blanchot uses the short story to stage the evacuation of the speaking / writing "I." Since this "last word" proved ironically to be a work of initiation for what would become a career of disappearances (because of both Blanchot's withdrawal and the ceaseless negations of his writing), it helps to consider Blanchot's life / work in terms of different genres of disappearance. I will propose here that two significant versions exist, just as Kristin Ross has found in Blanchot two versions of the everyday. While Ross's schema turns around the break initiated by May 1968, my own pivots around the centrality of Auschwitz (although this is not unrelated to the *changement d'époque* postulated by Blanchot in the late 1960s). The turning in Blanchot is not simply from activism to *écriture,* as Mehlman implies — "a dream of *action française* gives way to the infinite passivity... of *l'espace littéraire*" (*Legacies,* 13). At stake, rather, is the ethical status of the subject and its relationship to history.

Illustrative of the first version of disappearance, the first-person narration of "Le dernier mot" briefly recounts the wanderings of an "I" through a landscape in which language has lost its links with authority: " 'Since the watchword was done away with,' I said, 'reading is free. If you think I talk without knowing what I'm saying, you are within your rights. I'm only one voice among many' " (*Vicious Circles,* 47). In keeping with the reactionary rhetoric of the era, "Le dernier mot" demonstrates how, when the hierarchy of voices is leveled, discourse floats free of "proper" names and the legitimacy of law enters into crisis. After being assigned and resisting the positions of teacher and judge, the narrator of this early story comes at last to a tower—the Tower of Babel, Blanchot will tell us. There he meets a man who claims to be its owner [*propriétaire*]; although an apocalyptic storm rages outside, the owner claims his tower will never crumble. Of course it does, but before even this can happen Blanchot "disappears" his narrator, seeming to imply by this move the impossibility of narration in a postdeluvian world where the signifier has become unstuck from the signified. These are the crucial sentences, in which we witness the destruction of the witness and the owner:

> [B]ecause I treated him as master, I chained him to his sovereignty. And we were bound together in such a way that for him to become who he was again, he had to say to me: "I'm laughing at you because I'm no more than a beast," but with that confession my adoration became twice as great, and in the end there was nothing left but a sad animal, watched over by a servant who swatted away the flies. A ray of sunlight, erect like a stone, enclosed both of them in an illusion of eternity. They blissfully sank into repose. (54)[10]

The narrator's "I," first metamorphosing into the apparent metaphor of the animal and servant, disappears for good in the next line, which syntactically and semantically objectifies both male characters and renders them speechless. Moments later, we approach the fatal silence that resides in the last word. In the story's final, truncated exchange, one of Blanchot's ubiquitous female characters asks the transformed *propriétaire* whether the ground beneath them was missing, and he responds silently: "But he reassured her with his calmness, and when the tower collapsed and threw them outside, all three of them fell without saying a word" (55).

Such a narrative leads me to ask, as Blanchot did of the writings of Bataille in the eponymous last essay of *L'amitié,* "Who was the subject of that experience?" But, as Blanchot remarks, the form of that question already delimits the answer: "In substituting the opening of a who? without answer for the closed and unique 'I,'" we participate in the becoming-impersonal of language, a process "without end" in which we grasp our own subjectivity as "the unknown and slippery being of an indefinite 'who?' " (328).[11] However, as nicely as Blanchot's theorization of the subject *sous rature* would at first glance seem to fit "Le dernier mot," written thirty-five years earlier, the short story fails in at least one crucial place to fulfill the guidelines Blanchot set for impersonalization: it ends. This motif of impersonalization and disappearance is marked retrospectively in "Après coup" as politically ambivalent. The texts that Blanchot will go on to write, *Thomas l'Obscur* [*Thomas the Obscure*] crucial among them, emerge out of this realization that the disappearance initiated by his early story requires a movement "without end," an avoidance of foreclosure—of actually arriving at "the last word"—that in Blanchot becomes linked with the most serious ethical and political errors. This also explains why, in fact, the "I" does not disappear from Blanchot's writing and instead remains under constant interrogation in his essays as well as his *récits,* which, in Geoffrey Hartman's words, attack "the notion of the sincere and even of the authorial 'I' " (*Beyond Formalism,* 101). Blanchot's writings from after what he called the "absolute" personal and historical divide of World War II (*L'amitié,* 128–29) repeat this movement from the initial temptation of disappearance to a second version: the disappearance of the possibility of total disappearance.

The situatedness of this transformation in proximity to the war is precisely what makes the mode of disappearance more than an abstract linguistic game, as it looks from the decontextualized vantage point common to most Blanchot criticism. The moment at which Blanchot was writing "Le dernier mot" (1935–36) was also, we recall, the moment at which he was writing regularly for journals of the Jeune Droite like *L'Insurgé* and *Combat.* While his published political commitments go back to the beginning of the 1930s, the writings for these latter journals took place after the 1933 break in right-wing ideology. According to Holland and Rousseau, the coming to power of Hitler, and the belated experience of the world financial crisis in France, made 1933 the year when the calls for conservative spiritual renewal became demands for revolutionary nationalist insurrection (23–29). Upon the rise of Léon Blum's Popular Front, Blanchot turned to the pages of *Combat* and *L'Insurgé* with a vengeance. These anticommunist and anti-Semitic articles also presented "increasingly strident calls to acts of violence against the regime" of Léon Blum (Mehlman, *Legacies,* 10): "Léon Blum, You Were Warned" was the threatening title of one jointly authored statement in *L'Insurgé* (11 [24 March 1937]: 3), while another of Blanchot's articles saw some small hope in a group of workers carrying signs that read "Death to Blum" ("Préparons la vengeance," *L'Insurgé* 11 [24 March 1937]).[12]

In order to read essays such as these and such as those, in some ways analogous, of Paul de Man in *Le Soir,* it helps to meditate on what separates us — the *déchirement,* in Blanchot's words — as contemporary North American readers from the cultures out of which these writings emerged. Jeffrey Mehlman suggests that the "pivot" of any study of French anti-Semitism must be "Hitler's liquidation of antisemitism as a tenable option for a French intellectual" (*Legacies,* 3). Before World War II, anti-Semitism was not the sole province of reactionaries, but, as Zeev Sternhell's work shows, served as one of the relays through which some socialist and communist writers passed over to the radical right (*Neither Right,* 40). Against this historical background of the engaged intellectual, whether left or right, we must differentiate our own institutional locations. In an important essay on the de Man "scandal," Alice Kaplan reminds us that North American critics have traditionally tended to "view any political involvement with art as exotic and aberrant" while "European critics . . . have traditionally had a declared political identity linked to their intellectual one." In other words, for Blanchot as for de Man, "it is entirely misleading to think that because he was to become a unique and original critic, his wartime activities were themselves a unique phenomenon" ("Paul de Man," 279, 267). And, thus, our readings of prewar and occupation writings should be "ultimately less dependent on any category of intentionality than on the sustaining effects of a cultural *milieu* that at times seems — or seemed — anti-Jewish in its essence" (Mehlman, *Legacies,* 3).

Yet, given Blanchot's and de Man's very different postwar relationship to the writings of their youth (Blanchot was in fact several years older than de Man at the time of their respective right-wing engagements), the notion of milieu cannot fully explain either writer. In the case of Blanchot, the offending articles are more offensive than those of de Man (although they are not, strictly speaking, collaborationist or pro-Nazi) and bespeak a more serious ideological engagement, but the writing of Blanchot in the wake of the disaster more explicitly comes to terms with the intellectual and political challenge of the genocide than anything in de Man. The interest of comparing de Man and Blanchot probably derives more from their related postwar influence in French and American literary circles than their somewhat different positions in the 1930s and during the war. Nonetheless, they superficially share a certain aesthetic theory in their early criticism. Considering the relationship of the early thought of each critic to their later work illuminates the divergent itineraries that were possible in traversing the void of the war. As such, this brief comparison also suggests the need to reassess the contemporary moment in terms of its inherited version of modernity. As with the question of Blanchot's relationship to pre- and postwar politics, the contrast turns on the question of whether a rupture is established or continuity preserved.

Consistent with his postwar positions, de Man's *Le Soir* essays attempt to extricate literature and culture from politics, even as his own cultural production was at its most *engagé*. De Man's review of Robert Brasillach's *Notre avant-guerre* illustrates this, as he praises Brasillach's evocation of prewar culture and gently castigates his political commentaries (such as the infamous description of the 1934 Nuremberg rallies): "[O]ne feels he is losing his way in a domain which is not his own." In order to understand the prewar period, writes de Man, "it is necessary clearly to separate its political aspects from its artistic or cultural aspects" (12 August 1941: 2).[13] Such a position allows him to minimize the significance of the war as a potential rupture when he comes to write the article titled "La littérature française devant les événements" [French literature in the face of the events] (20 January 1942: 2). In that article, he praises the quiescence of Montherlant, Drieu la Rochelle, and other collaborationists because of its salutary aesthetic correlates:

> From a purely artistic point of view, that attitude proves itself fruitful and productive, since it quarters [*cantonne*] literature in a clearly limited domain in which it enjoys complete liberty. That attitude thus brings about no change in questions of style since it does not impede normal developments. In fact, there is thus no gap between the French literature from before and from after the campaign of 1940, and the reader will not at any moment be disoriented by an unusual manner of writing.[14]

Certainly, de Man's language could be seen as working against itself in this passage, with the verb *cantonner* signifying both the act of division separating the war from literature and the return of the war into literature (insofar as *cantonner* applies to the quartering of soldiers). The war metaphor ironically points to the vanity of de Man's project: an attempt to cut himself off from the political context — to which he owes his position in the first place — through a fetishistic denial of the rupture of the Occupation. In fact, de Man's rhetorical move here might, with reference to Eric Santner, be termed "critical fetishism."[15] In other words, his essay seeks to disavow the rupture that called it into being in the first place. It will be precisely by working through trauma that critics like Blanchot and memoirists like Klüger and Delbo will arrive at a nonfetishistic account of representation in times of war and crisis. In the case of the two memoirists, such a nonfetishistic project, which I call traumatic realism, builds on a recognition of the intertwining of everyday and extreme conditions in genocidal situations. The ambivalence of de Man's position reveals itself, on the other hand, in the notion that complete liberty would be available in an admittedly limited domain, an attitude all too salutary to the repression of the *everyday, journalistic collaboration* to which (regardless of his "true" ideological beliefs) he had succumbed. Although de Man could have known nothing of the specifics of the "Final Solution," his infamous *Le Soir* essay, "Les Juifs dans la littérature actuelle" [Jews in contemporary literature] (4 March 1941: 10, written before the Wannsee Conference or the ordering of the genocide), makes it clear that, in his thinking at the time, even the disappearance of the Jews from Europe would not have ruptured the happy continuity and "normal development" of Western culture.

While de Man's post-Holocaust attitudes toward Jews and toward Nazism are not at stake — for the simple, but troublesome, reason that no explicit published analysis exists — we can demonstrate the persistence of certain of his ideas about the relationship of culture to history and politics during and after the war. Unlike Blanchot, de Man develops no significant account of "being-toward-the-past," but, rather, everywhere puts into question the possibility of witness and testimony. In the present context, the following passage from his well-known essay on Blanchot illustrates the continuity in de Man's thought and the limits of his brilliant contribution to postwar literary culture. In general, the surgical separation of culture from the complexities of history and, in particular, the avoidance of World War II in an account of Blanchot's place in modernity do justice neither to the contemporary cultural scene nor to Blanchot's own role in it. According to the later de Man, writing in 1966, Blanchot is

> an intensely private figure, who has kept his personal affairs strictly to himself and whose pronouncements on public issues, literary or political, have been very scarce. . . . A sizeable group of readers have followed his essays, often appearing in the form of topical bookreviews in various journals none of which is particularly esoteric or avant-garde: *Journal des débats, Critique,* and more recently in *La Nouvelle revue française.* (*Blindness and Insight,* 61)

This passage resonates only too obviously with its author's own career.[16] The blatant contradictoriness of these sentences — the implicit idea, for example, that topical book reviews do not constitute pronouncements on public literary issues — seeks to displace the evacuation of those public *political* issues that Blanchot did address, both from the right and from the left, both before and after the war. (De Man also leaves out any mention of *L'Insurgé, Combat,* or other extremist political journals.) In his effort to purge the aesthetic of the political and the public, de Man sounds what Kaplan calls the one consistent note of his career as journalist and critic ("Paul de Man") and misreads the significance of the silences in Blanchot's writing.

The forgetting of Blanchot's prewar writings by later critics such as de Man detracts even from the purely literary analysis (whatever that would mean) of his works, since it was in *L'Insurgé* that Blanchot began writing regular literary columns.[17] Furthermore, a common logic operates across genres in Blanchot's fiction, criticism, and polemic during the 1930s. In "De la révolution à la littérature" [From revolution to literature] (*L'Insurgé* 1 [13 January 1937]: 3), a short essay that may be his first programmatic statement on the relationship of literature to politics, Blanchot at first glance seems to describe an aesthetic not dissimilar to that of de Man. Blanchot carefully separates his conception of literature from anything resembling a *littérature engagée* of whatever political hue, but then he suggests the necessity to explore the links that de Man simply banishes from consideration: "Criticism which escapes on principle from the indelicate infiltrations of the party spirit, which is the opposite of the critical spirit, cannot escape from a question which is essential and which leads it to wonder whether, at a moment when the revolution is desirable, there are not some affinities to be recognized between the idea of revolution and literary values."[18] This essential question of the desired revolution puts some distance between the young Blanchot and the young de Man, although, to be sure, Blanchot's answer is far from straightforward. Blanchot distances himself from those political aesthetics that would put literature at the service of a revolution, "*même véritable*" [even a true one], or of a style politics valuing only the shock of the new. De Man would make similar arguments in *Le Soir*, even as his collaborationist articles were at the service of a very particular revolution. But, unlike de Man, Blanchot formulates an explicit (although not necessarily less contradictory) answer to the question of literature and revolution, one that turns (in well-nigh Bloomian terms) on the notion of the great work's intrinsic will-to-power:

> What is more important is the oppositional force which is expressed in the work itself. This force is measured by the power which a work has to suppress other works or to abolish a part of ordinary reality, as well as by the power to call into existence new works which are as strong, or stronger than it, or to determine a superior reality. What also counts is the force of resistance that the author opposed to his work through the ease and license which he has refused to it, the instincts which he has mastered, and the rigor by which he submits it to himself.[19]

In the majority of the following issues of *L'Insurgé*, Blanchot's literary column, "Les lectures de *L'Insurgé*" [The readings of *L'Insurgé*], in which he explored the autonomous "force" and "power" of various works, ran parallel to his strictly political columns. Despite his theoretical attempt to separate aesthetics from "vulgar" political positions, the rhetoric of "De la révolution à la littérature" does not depart from his nonconformist analysis of France's political situation under the Popular Front.

Just as Blanchot's literary program turns on the opposition between strong and weak works, his view of the contemporary status of French politics opposes an ideal, forceful nation with the actual, decadent state.[20] Blanchot (like his colleagues) tends to figure the weakness of the state through the "foreign" body of its Jewish leader, Léon Blum — hence, the mobilizing role of anti-Semitic insinuation in these texts. The "decomposition" of the country's "rotten system" is frequently linked to the "anti-French ends" supposedly supported by Blum. Because the state's leader represents the interests of "a foreign race," one must "distinguish the Blum government from the politics of France, the regime from the nation" [distinguer le gouvernement Blum de la politique de la France, le régime de la nation] ("Nous, les complices de Blum...," *L'Insurgé* 2 [20 January 1937]: 4). What Blum lacks is that from which literature also derives its "perfection" — force and the heritage of civilization, with the latter being conceived in quasi-biological terms: "He is the interlocutor whom no one fears because he never speaks of force, but only of disarmament;...the adversary whom no one respects because he has not even inherited the civilization he is supposed to defend" ("Blum, notre chance de salut..." 3 [27 January 1937]).[21] Just as "De la révolution" proposes that great works of literature must contain an "oppositional force" able to "suppress other works," the political columns suggest that "at the moment, the only way to save our country is by demolishing it in that which best represents its abjection" ("M. Delbos a raison," *L'Insurgé* 15 [14 April 1937]: 4).[22] Holland and Rousseau argue that this contradiction between nation and state accounts for Blanchot's ultimate break with the right since it "is revealed as impossible to maintain in the face of Hitler's unsupportable nationalism and because the nationalist state is incapable of installing itself."[23] However, I do not see this logical impossibility as a sign of "*la perte de la révolution*" [the loss of the revolution] (Holland and Rousseau, 34–35), but precisely as an ideological strategy in the waging of the right-wing nationalist revolution. Desperate and often hysterical as the rhetoric seems, we should not minimize the possible role such ideas played in setting the stage both for direct collaboration and for the racist politics of Vichy. Blanchot saw France's crisis as authorization for an abandonment of faith in democracy. The "fundamental passivity" of the state can only be righted by a violent, antidemocratic coup (see "La France condamnée à avoir tort," *L'Insurgé* 18 [12 May 1937]: 4). It would not be long before an even greater crisis would reveal the depths of France's weakness and a regime would rise up to answer Blanchot's call in *L'Insurgé* and reunite the state and nation.[24]

Après (le) Coup

My analyses of "Le dernier mot" and the *Insurgé* writings, as well as Blanchot's comments on his early stories, suggest that Blanchot's political and literary/critical texts from the 1930s took the form of two parallel tracks with a common deep structure. Premised on the decadence of the present—the loss of authority staged in "Le dernier mot," the "passivity" and "weakness" of the French state and its corrupted culture—these writings propose a forceful and definitive solution to the civilizational crisis: some literary works will need to be abolished by the power of the new culture; some politicians will have to disappear ("Death to Blum"). In what ways can Blanchot be said to break with the form, as well as the content, of that thought? It helps to witness again the terms of the political writings, so as to grasp more clearly their determinate negation (as Adorno might say) elsewhere in Blanchot's oeuvre. That negation also demonstrates the implicit politics of Blanchot's later writings. He does not, as most critics suggest, "correct" or "liquidate" (according to one's degree of sympathy) his political errors by separating literature once and for all from politics, but rather, he works through those errors by combining the aesthetic and the political in a new syncretism. Starting perhaps with *Thomas the Obscure,* Blanchot's writing of the last half-century questions not only the terror but also the very terms of writing such as the following, from April 1936:

> The shameful Sarraut government, which seems to have received the mission of humiliating France as it had not been humiliated in twenty-five years, has driven this disorder to a pitch. . . . It began by hearing the appeals of unfettered revolutionaries and Jews, whose theological furor demanded against Hitler all possible sanctions immediately. . . . Nothing could be as perfidious as that propaganda for national honor, executed by foreigners suspected by the offices of the Quai d'Orsay, to precipitate young Frenchmen, in the name of Moscow or Israel, into an immediate conflict. (Cited and translated in Mehlman, 11)[25]

Other writings by Blanchot in *Combat* propose a solution to this "shameful state": "It is necessary that [the] revolution be violent because one does not tap a people as enervated as our own for the strength and passions appropriate to a regeneration through measures of decency, but through a series of bloody shocks, a storm that will overwhelm — and thus awaken — it" (cited and translated in Mehlman, 11).[26] Unlike the storm that Thomas experiences at the beginning of the 1950 *récit* (*Thomas the Obscure,* 7), there is no sense, in these journalistic texts, of a "calm" at the heart of the tempest — the space of contemplation and reading, the "pure interval" of friendship (*L'Amitié,* 328) — that would always contradict the apocalyptic finality of Blanchot's political rhetoric in *Combat.* His postwar writing practice, in which the author is considered as a "path" between the "not yet" and the "no longer" (*Après coup,* 86), suggests a temporality utterly foreign to the "bloody shocks" [*secousses sanglantes*] that punctuate the depiction of fascist revolution.

It is no accident that the article from which I took the long anti-Semitic quotation above was titled "Après le coup de force germanique" [After the Germanic bid for power] and that Blanchot titled his reflections on his early stories and on Auschwitz "Après coup." Although Blanchot does not mention his political writings there, his comments on the "silent decision" in the stories, and his assessment that "every narrative from now on will be from before Auschwitz" (*Vicious Circles,* 99), ask to be read as a displaced critique of the apocalyptic political narrative of a nationalistic new order to which he temporarily decided to subscribe.[27] What the *Combat* and *Insurgé* articles share with the two formative stories is a belief that the last word can arrive — in the form of revolution, apocalypse, or disappearance. The project that *Thomas the Obscure* inaugurates works to forestall that end, even in recognizing that it has also always already arrived and that the calm at the eye of the storm is also the silence of a past destruction: "[T]here reigned a silence and a calm which gave the impression that everything was already destroyed" (*Thomas the Obscure,* 7). I would not know how to measure the extent to which the irreality of Blanchot's texts derives from this historical rupture that produces a new writing subject out of the ruins of the old. What is sure, however, is the extent to which Blanchot's own writing works against attempts to separate his historical experience as a writing subject at the heart of a political storm from his later, more "aesthetic" work. In its contrast to the violent teleology of the early writings, with their continual movement toward the disaster, the "always already" of the destruction in later Blanchot presupposes that a rupture has occurred in civilization as in his own work. However, as a further consideration of "Après coup" illustrates, that divide is not one that would permit a break with the already broken past. Any attempt to flee from or toward the disaster ignores its claim on the present.

In that 1983 afterword to the republication of "Le dernier mot" and "L'Idylle," Blanchot explicitly contrasts the failure of "these innocent stories that resound with murderous echoes of the future" to *Thomas the Obscure:*

> (it would be dishonest to forget that, at the same time or in the meantime, I was writing *Thomas the Obscure,* which was perhaps about the same thing, but precisely did not have done with it and, on the contrary, encountered in the search for annihilation (absence) the impossibility of escaping being (presence)—which was not even a contradiction in fact, but the demand of an endlessness that is unhappy even in dying). In this sense, the story was an attempt to short circuit the other book that was being written, in order to overcome that endlessness and reach a silent decision, reach it through a more linear narrative that was nevertheless painfully complex. (*Vicious Circles,* 63)

Blanchot is of course discussing the original 1941 version of *Thomas,* which itself has, in some sense, disappeared in turn behind the second, 1950 version. In the words of Jean Starobinski, the images of the first version "were offered only in order to disappear" (502). The fact that Blanchot felt the need to write a second version, and to speculate in its prefatory note on the "infinity of possible variants" for all texts, indicates how closely *Thomas the Obscure* is linked with his aesthetic of (non)disappearance.

"Après coup," as the previous citation illustrates, connects this aesthetic explicitly with ethics and politics. If the stories take place in a murderous future tense (*les présages meurtriers des temps futurs*), the essay attempts to establish an ethical means of writing in the past tense. In its title, and in its methodology, "Après coup" makes reference to the Freudian notion of *Nachträglichkeit* (translated in French as *après coup*), in which events of the past repeat themselves but are simultaneously restructured from the perspective of the present. *Nachträglichkeit,* especially as used by Blanchot, bears a double, condensed temporal structure in which repetition and retrospection combine. Although such a temporality could be understood as pertinent to an understanding of consciousness generally, the *après coup* applies particularly, as Anne Tomiche demonstrates, to events or scenes of a traumatic nature ("Rephrasing," 51). According to Lacan's restructuring of Freud, in this act of "recollection [*remémoration*], that is, of history," "it is not a question of reality, but of truth, because the effect of full speech is to reorder past contingencies by conferring on them the sense of necessities to come, such as they are constituted by the little freedom through which the subject makes them present" (*Ecrits: A Selection,* 48). Lacan defines this act of reordering—"this assumption of his history by the subject, in so far as it is constituted by the speech addressed to the other" (*Ecrits: A Selection,* 48)—as an ethical act that founds the psychoanalytic method.

Two possible divergences emerge between Lacan's definition and Blanchot's practice of the *après coup*. First of all, in his reordering, Blanchot does not fully and explicitly "assume his history"; rather, he maintains a reserve about his political writings, alluding to them only through the displaced reference to the two short stories. This leaves open the possibility that, insofar as it appears to repress certain *histoires,* the return of the past in discourse also might constitute an acting out or return of the repressed.[28] The second divergence complicates the first. It is not at all clear that Blanchot seeks to give past contingencies "the sense of necessities to come"; or, if he does, he attempts to mark out two separate necessary histories, one that would imply some kind of partial responsibility for genocide, the other that would suggest the genealogy of his later resistance. On the one hand, he remarks on the way the stories do disturbingly foreshadow the "concentrationary universe," but, on the other hand, he also attempts to bring to light an alternate history, symbolized by *Thomas the Obscure,* that was on the point of emergence. It is the peculiarity of Blanchot's career that both of these constructions of history are necessary in that both describe with some accuracy his political trajectory.

Blanchot's disavowal of the possibility of total disappearance, but also of pure presence, accounts for the traumatic nature of his discourse. The trauma is neither in the original scene (his right-wing commitments, Auschwitz), nor in the scene of recollection (the refusal of the past to disappear), but rather "the trauma is in the sequence of the two scenes and in their linkage." The very act of memory "functions as a source of traumatic energy," even as it provides the only means of working through the trauma and interrupting its repetition. Yet according to certain contemporary rereadings of Freud's concept of *Nachträglichkeit,* there is something that eludes memory: the initial traumatic scene that produces affect but no representation of the event itself (Tomiche, "Rephrasing," 51, 53). Blanchot's reworking of Freud has precisely to do with this traumatic void and its effects on time and narrative. Blanchot hollows out the event, not in order to minimize its importance but indeed to heighten its effects. Blanchot's discourse, in other words, not only acts out a traumatic past (as critics imply) but actively constructs the past as traumatic. This constructive side of the *après coup* represents a strategy meant to provoke working through, even if it might be of an endless, melancholic sort—it is, in any case, a strategy at the furthest remove from de Man's critical fetishism vis-à-vis history. Rewriting Adorno, Blanchot gives the name of Auschwitz to that occurrence that, on the one hand, eludes representation and, on the other, marks all subsequent acts of representation and, indeed, alters the historicity of representation. In reconsidering his two early stories in *Après coup,* Blanchot comes to the following conclusion:

> That is why, in my opinion—and in a way different from the one that led Adorno to decide with absolute correctness—I will say there can be no fiction-narrative [*récit-fiction*] about Auschwitz (I am alluding to *Sophie's Choice*). The need to bear witness is the obligation of a testimony that can only be given—and given only in the singularity of each individual—by the impossible witnesses—the witnesses of the impossible—; . . . No matter when it is written, every narrative [*récit*] from now on will be from before Auschwitz. (*Vicious Circles,* 68–69; translation modified)

In this passage, Blanchot provides two different readings of Adorno's famous proposition that "[t]o write poetry after Auschwitz is barbaric" (itself repeated in different contexts and with different nuances). First, Blanchot asserts Auschwitz's resistance to fictional mimesis and the very different impossibility of survivor testimony: "[A]ll narration, even all poetry, has lost the foundation on which another language could be raised" (68). This assertion, however extreme, does not go beyond the many paraphrases of Adorno that have proliferated since the 1960s, particularly after its popularization by George Steiner.

But Blanchot goes further. In linking Auschwitz to the logic of trauma, he rethinks the limits of representation in a way that not only confirms but also extends Adorno's thoughts in *Negative Dialectics.* Recognizing that narrative will proceed even without foundation — "Forgetfulness no doubt does its work and allows for works to be made again" (68) — Blanchot goes on to evoke an other temporality to account for this untimely survival. In this reading, Auschwitz affects not just postwar culture but history in a far broader sense ("No matter when it is written"). Auschwitz does indeed rupture history's continuity, but not simply in order to divide it into two symmetrical pieces, before and after. The world "after Auschwitz" becomes a kind of palimpsest in which pre-Holocaust traces continue to exist in the postnarrative world as so many reminders of what has been destroyed. This anachronous remainder recalls the impossibility of disappearance [*l'impossibilité d'échapper à l'être*] that defines the key concept of sur-vival in Blanchot: "[S]ome have survived, but there sur-vival [*sur-vie*] is no longer life, it is the break from living affirmation, the attestation that the good that is life (not narcissistic life, but life for others) has undergone the decisive blow that leaves nothing intact" (*Vicious Circles,* 68; translation modified).[29] The fact that nothing has been left intact does not mean that nothing has been left. The comfort of oblivion is not an option, even if the traumatic kernel of the catastrophe cannot be represented. As one critic has written, "We are marked by events, bound to them and compelled to acknowledge them, precisely to the extent that we cannot recover them, cannot preserve them, cannot remedy them. Irremediability, or loss, is what implicates us" (Shaviro, "Complicity," 829).

Blanchot's revision of the *après coup* reverses the temporal vectors of trauma. Instead of a condensed, centripetal relationship between the present and the past moment of the trauma, Blanchot's version is centrifugal: time recedes on either side of the present, running backward toward and beyond Auschwitz and floundering in repetition and rupture "from now on." In addition, the relationship to the other [*autrui*], which Lacan notes as the foundation of the psychoanalytic approach to trauma, is shattered: "Perhaps life continues," but not "life for others" [*la vie pour autrui*] (*Vicious Circles,* 69, 68). For Blanchot, it is a question not of psychoanalytic method but of the conditions in which narrative and speech can take place. Thus, the logic of Blanchot's claim implies, working through the past is ultimately impossible because the trauma is forever being displaced into the future and the narrative means for coming to terms with the event merely testify to a failure to come to terms ("every narrative will be from before Auschwitz"). Yet working through the past is also required, since the "non-presence of the past, its irrecuperability, is equally its failure to be altogether absent" (Shaviro, "Complicity," 829). This necessity of the return of the repressed, which the *après coup* marks, reveals, even as it hides, the fact that what is at stake is not only Auschwitz but indeed something from before it: Blanchot's anti-Semitic engagement and whatever indirect and almost incalculably minor role it had in setting the stage for genocide. However small this role was, it cannot, dictates Blanchot's theory, disappear. In exposing this truth, even as it hides it, Blanchot's text demonstrates what Dominick LaCapra has repeatedly argued: that acting out may be a necessary element of attempts at working through (see *Representing* and *History and Memory*).

From Now On

There is an odd, supplemental word in Blanchot's phrasing of the relationship between narrative and Auschwitz, one that further complicates the notion of the present in Blanchot: *désormais* [from now on]. What function does this word play in the proposition? Referring to the moment of enunciation of "Après coup" (1983), it would seem to bear no connection to the question of Auschwitz. Indeed, the question of why, at this particular moment, Blanchot would begin again to speak of Auschwitz is somewhat obscure, although the mention of *Sophie's Choice* and the proximity to the broadcast of the *Holocaust* television series suggest that Blanchot may be responding to a new level of commodification of Shoah narratives. At a more general level, however, the *désormais* self-reflexively signals the importance of the noncontemporaneity of all events, of their tendency to be understood only retrospectively (*après coup*). This is indeed the theme of Blanchot's dialogical essay from *The Infinite Conversation,* "On a Change of Epoch: The Exigency of Return." In that essay, Blanchot theorizes why, if an event is to come to represent an epochal change, it can only do so retroactively when, at a later moment, someone says, "from now on, things will not be the same." As one of Blanchot's fictional interlocutors suggests, "The fact of our belonging to this moment at which a change of epoch, if there is one, is being accomplished also takes hold of the certain knowledge that would want to determine it." The other participant in the fictional dialogue develops the point, quoting Nietzsche: "The greatest events and thoughts are comprehended last; the generations that are contemporaneous with them do not experience such events — they live right past them" (*Infinite Conversation,* 264). As with trauma, it is neither the event itself nor the moment of its remembrance that is sufficient to break the continuity of time, but the connection established between those moments, the yoking of the present to a time that, nevertheless, cannot be found anew (as in Proust's *temps retrouvé*). The "from now on" of Blanchot's "Après coup" signifies that at some point (or series of points) we have become contemporaries of the Holocaust.[30]

Theorizing Auschwitz in terms of the noncontemporaneous *désormais* provides a map for rereading Blanchot's postwar work, where the past remains but in radically different form. The notion of the "from now on" means not that time is divided in two, with a void (Auschwitz) at the center, but that successive moments establish different relationships to that past as the void propagates itself in a series of uncomprehending presents. The change of era is still figured as a storm (as in the 1930s), but now it has "a discrete force" [*une force discrète*], and the words that carry it to us, *pace* Nietzsche, are "the most silent" (*Infinite Conversation,* 264; translation modified). Blanchot constantly, although silently, recalls his faux pas as a member of the Jeune Droite by repeating concepts from those writings, but shifting their significance 180 degrees. Thus in Blanchot's postwar metaphorics, force becomes discrete, the tempest falls silent, disappearance fails to disappear, and passivity metamorphoses from a sign of decadence to a valued resistance to terror. A rupture has occurred (unlike in de Man), but the past is not therefore liquidated. Tracking the significance of silence and death, and their relation to each other, in Blanchot's postwar writings allows us to trace the fault lines of his survival.

Not surprisingly, silence and its links with genocide have been a major preoccupation of Holocaust discourse. In an influential discussion of historical revisionism and the Nazi concentration camps in *The Differend,* for example, Lyotard notes at least four possible meanings of the silences of camp survivors in the face of questioning about their experiences:

> The survivors remain silent, and it can be understood (1) that the situation in question (the case) is not the addressee's business ... or (2) that it never took place (this is what Faurisson [the revisionist] understands); or (3) that there is nothing to say about it (the situation is senseless, inexpressible); or (4) that it is not the survivors' business to be talking about it.... Or, several of these negations together. (No. 26)

Putting aside the question of how we might evaluate Lyotard's distinctions in the case of survivors, how do we analyze the silences of Blanchot and de Man, not survivors of the camps but bystanders and agents of a certain self-imposed, other-directed written violence?

Commenting upon the relationship between de Man's wartime writings and his later criticism, Shoshana Felman argues that his silence about the *Le Soir* writings falls roughly into Lyotard's third category, the silence of the inexpressible:

> Incorporating the silence of the witness who has returned mute into his very writing, de Man's entire work and his later theories bear implicit witness to the Holocaust, not as its (impossible and failed) narrator (a narrator-journalist whom the war had dispossessed of his own voice) but as a witness to the very blindness of his own, and others', witness, a firsthand witness to the Holocaust's historical disintegration of the witness. (Felman and Laub, 139)

Felman later suggests (201n) that such an analysis of the "radical — and inescapable — *complicity*" of all acts of witness could equally well apply to Blanchot's work. I find a danger, however, in eliding the differences, not only between the different types of silence (as in de Man's reading of Blanchot as a nonpolitical thinker) but between the different subjects of those silences. And, in fact, Felman's larger project in *Testimony* contradicts her apologetic stance toward de Man and Blanchot, insofar as it is concerned with the witness's "utterly unique and irreplaceable topographical *position* with respect to an occurrence" (206). To group collaborators of whatever degree of commitment with concentration camp survivors under the abstraction of "the Holocaust's historical disintegration of the witness" reifies this disintegration, stripping it of the collective agency that lies behind it. "Complicity" and "implicit witness" are terms too vague to capture the significant wartime and postwar divergences in Blanchot's and de Man's actions and in their attitudes toward the relationship of language to history.

I would locate the important difference that emerges between de Man and Blanchot — despite the similarity in their use of the trope of chiasmus, which *does* bear witness to a certain crisis in witnessing — in Blanchot's refusal of de Man's generative opposition between the historical and the literary. The work around the question of World War II that culminates in *The Writing of the Disaster* provokes a rereading of early works such as *Thomas the Obscure* and *Death Sentence* in a way that nothing in de Man's oeuvre can. The weight of absent bodies haunts Blanchot's postwar writings and registers itself long before "Auschwitz" became the rhetorical place in which a historical rupture was located. At a moment in the 1940s when Adorno was speaking of the "Final Solution" as a "stage" in the dialectic of Enlightenment, and when even French-Jewish survivors were reluctant to express the particularity of their experience as Jews (Wieviorka, "Jewish Identity"), certain texts by Blanchot already anticipate the singularity with which the Holocaust would come to be described. At the same time, those texts rigorously refuse to name the event, preserving a sometimes troubling vagueness toward historical specificity — what Ungar calls a lack of "full disclosure" (*Scandal,* 136) — whose ambivalent effects need to be kept in mind.

Reading retrospectively by the dim light of the disaster helps to explain the aura of irreality, of deathlessness, in Blanchot's *récits,* as it explains the importance he ascribes to the failure of his early stories, to the terrible fact that they end, somehow, too smoothly. Death by extermination rewrites death and demands that writing itself be re-formed. Lyotard theorizes what we also experience in *Thomas the Obscure,* that "sacrifice is not available to the deportee, nor for that reason accession to an immortal, collective name. . . . The individual name must be killed (whence the use of serial numbers), and the collective name (Jew) must also be killed in such a way that no we bearing this name might remain which could take the deportee's death into itself and eternalize it. This death must therefore be killed, and that is what is worse than death" (*Differend,* no. 157). Killing death. This paradox plays itself out in Blanchot's writing. In *Thomas the Obscure,* we read of Anne's dying, during which

> [t]he doctor bent over her and thought that she was dying according to the laws of death, not perceiving that she had already reached that instant when, in her, the laws were dying. She made an imperceptible motion; no one understood that she was floundering in the instant when death, destroying everything, might also destroy the possibility of annihilation. (*Thomas the Obscure,* 84–85)

After the *déchirement* of genocide, the possibility not only of the philosopher's "beautiful death" disappears, but of any death as resolution. Mass death destroys not just the individual but individual death, death according to the laws. The death of death, of course, does not leave life in its wake, but rather lifeless survival.

A passage from the 1950 version of *Thomas* (present in almost identical form in the 1941 version) will illustrate the way history and literature are implicated in what I have called the second version of disappearance, a mode described by Ann Smock as the moment when "everything has disappeared [and] disappearance, the disappearance of everything, appears" (9). Late in the *récit,* when Anne has performed the impossible and died, Thomas speaks for the only time in an extended monologue using first-person narration. Thomas remembers writing on a wall "I think, therefore I am not," a slogan that causes a strange vision to rise before him:

> In the midst of an immense countryside, a flaming lens received the dispersed rays of the sun and, by those fires, became conscious of itself as a monstrous I, not at the points at which it received them, but at the point at which it projected and united them in a single beam [*un faisceau unique*]. . . . [T]he entire universe became a flame at the point at which the lens touched it; and the lens did not leave it until it was destroyed. Nevertheless,

> I perceived that this mirror was like a living animal consumed by its own fire. (99)

This imaginary machine — at once human and animal, subject and object of destruction, life force and death blow — subsequently begins to speak and thus displaces, but does not eradicate, the "I" of Thomas in the remainder of his monologue. Such a passage, and I could have chosen many others even in this same short text, enacts the appearance of disappearance, presenting a figure for the subject unable to disappear because the forces of total destruction have gone so far as to destroy their own ability to destroy totally. It does not seem accidental to me that this subject-machine is described at one point as a *faisceau,* a word connected etymologically to "fascism," for it is precisely the fascist as subject of a total violence that is radically put into question here — even as it is recognized that that subject is so close to the narrative voice that the voice of the "monstrous I" "seemed to come from the bottom of my heart" (99). By exposing, in *Thomas,* the proximity of the narrative to the fascist voice, but simultaneously warding off the possibility of total destruction, Blanchot could be seen as developing a counterlogic for working through the right-wing rhetoric of destruction to which he had subscribed in the very years when he had begun to write this *récit.*

At first glance, the scene described also seems to be a kind of holocaust — literally a total consumption by fire or a burnt offering — or, in Blanchot's words in *The Writing of the Disaster,* "*the* absolute *event of history . . . that utter-burn where all history took fire*" (47). But this latter definition of the Holocaust as absolute event contradicts the auspicious de-absolutizing of destruction characteristic of the passage from *Thomas* and of the second version of disappearance in general. The absolutizing of "the Holocaust" represents a troublesome philo-Semitic temptation in Blanchot's postwar thinking because it places Jewish experience before that of others and because it momentarily forgets that there is no "last word" in destruction and that even Jews may be its agents. Even in *The Writing of the Disaster,* however, the notion of the "absolute" is more often in question than affirmed; the hints of philo-Semitism, for which Mehlman and others take Blanchot to task, are limited and eclipsed by the ethics and politics developed in the wake of May 1968.

The Persistence of the Death-World and the Ethics of Waking

Aspects of Blanchot's postwar writing, in which he considers the paradoxes of total destruction, are illuminated by philosopher Edith Wyschogrod's critique of the phenomenological concept of the life-world, which she evaluates according to the example of the death-world of the Nazi genocide. Under ordinary circumstances, the human life-world has three components: an inanimate base; a vital world of movement, temporal flux, and inner experience; and an "ethical dimension in which other persons are apprehended as centers of value" ("Concentration Camps," 328). Wyschogrod argues that

> [a]t the vital level of the life-world . . . the concentration camp succeeded in suppressing the primordial modes of man's being in the world. . . . For the life-world now and in the future includes in collective experience and shared history the death-world of the camp. *Once the death-world has existed it continues to exist, in the mode of eternity, as it were, for it becomes part of the sediment that is the irrevocable past.* (335; emphasis in original)

This destruction of the vital life-world is part of what constitutes "survival" in passages like the previous one from *Thomas the Obscure:* the mutual contamination of life and death. In Wyschogrod's words, "Life perdures but the life-world ceases to exist" (328). However, in neither Blanchot's works nor Wyschogrod's speculations does the persistence of death within life mark the complete eradication of the life-world. The Nazi's totalizing desires were foiled: "[W]hile the modes of significance were destroyed by the camp system at the vital level of existence, this collapse of meaning did not come about at the ethical level in the manner intended by the camp's executioners. . . . [S]o long as and wherever the other is recognized as a node of value the ethical level of the life-world is continued" (337–38). The recognition of the other, which in Wyschogrod's thinking owes much to the work of Lévinas—himself a lifelong friend and intellectual companion of Blanchot—is an important element of many post-Holocaust writings. In such writings, the question of the other inevitably raises the problem of mourning and memorialization, two processes that seek to establish a relationship to an absent other.

The many confrontations with the opacity of the other staged in Blanchot's *récits* indicate a similar ethical obsession. *L'arrêt de mort* [*Death Sentence*] (1948) is, for example, a remarkable literary enactment of the situation described by Wyschogrod, the overlap of the post-Holocaust persistence of the death-world with the survival of the ethical dimension. For the purposes of this essay, the section of that work that interests me most is the opening half of the book in which the narrator describes the strange (non-)events surrounding the fatal sickness of his friend "J." The impossibility of death — itself a symptom of the permanent incursion of death into the life-world — is an experience that unites the narrator and his subject: "Her doctor had told me that from 1936 on he had considered her dead. Of course the same doctor, who treated me several times, once told me, too: 'Since you should have been dead two years ago, everything that remains of your life is a reprieve.' He had just given me six more months to live and that was seven years ago" (*Death Sentence*, 5). This common problem of survival that the narrator and J. share — "something much worse" than death — confirms what the scriptural similarity between "Je" and "J." already suggests: J. is one of the many uncanny doubles who haunt Blanchot's texts. If, as Freud argues, the double is often an uncanny figure marking a site of repression, to what return of the repressed does this double, J., testify?

It is frequently remarked in the extensive critical literature on *Death Sentence* that Blanchot parallels the descriptions of J.'s endless dying with historical references to the events of Munich in 1938. In Kristin Ross's words, for example, "The rhythm of her struggle is the rhythm of political crisis: episodic, punctuated by frequent dramatic turning points, triumphs and reversals. The rhetoric of war and combat dominates the description of her relationship to her illness" (32). Ross reads the historical allusions as signs of a struggle between private and public horror in which "[t]he narrator . . . borrows the gravity of the historical only to use it as a weapon against the historical; he uses it to triumph over it by alluding to a far worse eventuality" (34). This reading of the text is convincing, as is the suggestion that this *récit* foreshadows the politicization of the everyday that emerges in *The Infinite Conversation.* I would suggest, however, once again the value of rereading *Death Sentence* in the light of Blanchot's actual activities during the period that the text concerns. Barely occluded by the doubling and displacement between the narrator and J., and between public and private suffering, are the same events hidden and revealed by Blanchot's *après coup* consideration of his early stories. For indeed, to paraphrase Ross, the rhetoric of *Combat* is at stake in this text. And 1936, the date mentioned in the passage when J. was supposed to have died, is a year in which Blanchot wrote some of his most vociferous and violent journalistic texts in *Combat.* Up until just a few months before the late 1938 capitulation to Hitler that the Munich events signify, Blanchot's own writing in *Combat* and *L'Insurgé,* although never pro-Nazi, took a decidedly ambivalent stance. In a short article titled "Le chantage à l'antihitlerisme" [The anti-Hitler blackmail], Blanchot admits that Germany represents *le péril le plus grand* [the greatest peril] for France, but, at the same time, he declares: "It is truly shameful to see so many Frenchmen lose their composure when Hitler is mentioned, and fear appearing less patriotic than the communists if they don't condemn Germany severely enough" (*L'Insurgé* 22 [9 June 1937]).[31] Throughout Blanchot's 1930s journalism, the German "peril" is consistently downplayed in the interests of a fanatical anticommunism meant to set the stage for a toppling of France's democratic government. In *Death Sentence,* the references to Munich and the text's incessant dating of events serve as screens that both distract from and ultimately point toward an unspoken historical engagement.

If, then, the sickness of J. in *Death Sentence* is metonymically associated with the fatal diplomacy of Munich, and if that connection points back toward Blanchot's own discourse of those "darkest" days (*Death Sentence,* 11), what is the position of the *récit*'s narrator in relation to that network of associations? The narrator literally brings J. back from the dead — "this young woman was dead, and returned to life at my bidding" (30) — ensuring the survival of her living death and completing a story of failed disappearance. Between those events of 1938 and their recounting in this narrative nine years later, the narrator tells us, he had attempted other times to write the story and to do away with it once and for all. These multiple writings represent so many attempts *après coup* to come to terms with events of which the narrator seems only partially to grasp the significance:

> If I have written books, it has been in the hope that they would put an end to it all. If I have written novels, they have come into being just as the words began to shrink back from the truth. I am not frightened of the truth. I am not afraid to tell a secret. But until now, words have been frailer and more cunning than I would have liked. I know this guile is a warning. It would be in the best interests of the truth to keep it hidden. But, now, I hope to be done with it soon. (*Death Sentence,* 1)

Given Blanchot's many postwar critical and theoretical texts, not to mention the very enigmatic structure of this *récit,* the narrator's desire for closure can only be understood ironically. A great deal of the text treats the narrator's absence from the events that ostensibly concern him and the absence of meaning in the encounters at which he is, in some sense, present. It is precisely "this non-presence, this absence of relation [that] weighs so heavily upon" the narrator (Shaviro, "Complicity," 829). And it is in the oscillation that the previous passage charts between a sense that the truth is lacking from language and a need to testify despite this inevitable failure that a new model of witnessing emerges.

The narrator's relationship to J. (and thus to the Munich events that led to the war that intervenes between the story and the narrator's discourse) represents a variation on the Orphic theme dear to Blanchot. According to Blanchot's reading of that myth in *The Space of Literature,* Orpheus's gaze inscribes the double movement of the creation of the work of art: "[I]t links inspiration to *desire.* It introduces into concern for the work the movement of *unconcern* in which the work is sacrificed: the work's ultimate law is broken; the work is betrayed in favor of Eurydice, in favor of the shade" (175). In the breaking of the work's law, in Orpheus's gaze, "the work can surpass itself, be united with its origin and consecrated in impossibility" (174). In *Death Sentence,* however, the narrator's gaze does not kill J., but, to the contrary, brings her back to life. Upon entering the room of the dead J. in order to observe her body, the narrator is struck by the withered look of her hands, "so much too weak for the immense battle [*combat*] which that great soul had fought, all alone." Moved by the marks of combat, the narrator recounts, in a passage that resembles *Thomas*'s doctor at Anne's bedside: "I leaned over her, I called to her by her first name; and immediately . . . a sort of breath came out of her compressed mouth" (20). This resurrection, stimulated by voice and gaze, would seem to reverse the Orpheus story, except that the life / light to which J./Eurydice is brought back is one of "nocturnal obscurity" in which "living in her [is] the plenitude of her death" (*Space,* 172). In the *récit,* the result of the gaze and voice of the work is not death, but that "*quelque chose de plus grave*" that the refusal of the events to disappear represents. If the typical Orpheus / Eurydice story exiles the feminine in order to create a masculine work founded on feminine absence, this retelling asserts the impossibility of making the feminine disappear and links this preservation of an asymmetrical sexual difference to the ethics of historical understanding.[32]

While in *Death Sentence,* and in Blanchot's other *récits* and early novels, this ethics of the gaze remains historically abstract, Blanchot's later, more explicitly philosophical work prompts the type of rereading I have proposed. *Death Sentence* certainly foreshadows, as Kristin Ross argues, the *changement d'époque* that Blanchot concretized and theorized in *The Infinite Conversation.* Because of that foreshadowing, it is necessary to keep in mind Blanchot's reflections in that latter text on the deferred action and belated contemporaneity of events; 1968 was not simply a turning point because of the social upheavals for which the month of May serves as shorthand. It was also the moment when a constellation emerged — including a variety of only partially understood sociological, psychological, and political reasons — that retroactively changed the meaning of the Holocaust. At that late date, Blanchot, and many others in France and throughout European and North American cultures, began to experience the full effects of a genocide that had occurred twenty-five years earlier. Even if references to the Holocaust remain relatively few in Blanchot's writing of the late 1960s, he had already grasped an important general dynamic of historical periodization: its basis in the belated coming together of seemingly unlike times and places in a constellation. Another decade would pass before the effects registered at the end of the 1960s would reach their culmination in Blanchot's thought with the publication of *Après coup* and *The Writing of the Disaster.* If *Après coup* illuminates the break in time produced by the unrepresentable Shoah, *The Writing of the Disaster* outlines a difficult strategy for confronting that catastrophe that goes beyond regression into the certainties of total disappearance and beyond the potentially apologetic recognition of inevitable complicity.

Throughout Blanchot's meditations on Auschwitz, Robert Antelme's memoir of the camps, *L'espèce humaine,* occupies a privileged place. I find it significant that Blanchot chooses Antelme, a political prisoner of the Nazis, and not a Jewish memoirist of the camps, such as Primo Levi. This choice demonstrates again the extent of Blanchot's witness to his own past actions and inactions since, although he could never have been a Jewish victim, he could have been in the position of Antelme, deported as an active member of the resistance. Blanchot's writings on Antelme are, then, another *après coup,* another way of keeping watch over past mistakes that continue to reawaken the critic from an uneasy sleep. Hence, the strange resonance of the passage in his 1984 essay, "Les intellectuels en question" [Intellectuals in question], where he finds the cause of intellectuals exemplified in the wartime "defense of an innocent Jew: that which justified their writing, knowledge, and thought. The strangeness of their intervention is that it was collective yet it exalted the singular" (8; my translation).[33] Like so many of his compatriots Blanchot's own wartime activities are mired in obscurity, with indications both of temporary collaboration with Vichy and of life-saving actions on behalf of the family of his friend Emmanuel Lévinas. The complexity, which the previous citation suggests, of coexisting imperatives toward collectivity and singularity — toward politics and ethics, in other words — is expressed in the juxtaposition (in the section titled "The Indestructible" in *The Infinite Conversation*) between the chapters on *être juif* [being Jewish] and on *l'espèce humaine.*[34] These adjacent essays testify to the need for an ethics of the singular — for Lévinas's *l'exigence de l'étrangeté* [demand of the foreign] (Blanchot, *Entretien,* 189) — but also (and less often glimpsed in Blanchot) for a collective response of the type in which Antelme was involved.[35] Antelme, Blanchot writes, helps us to see "[t]hat man can be destroyed . . . but that because of and despite this, and in this very movement, man remains [*reste*] indestructible" (*Infinite Conversation,* 130; translation modified). This indestructibility of "man" is not a form of naive humanism on Blanchot's part, but a statement of the witness's ceaseless responsibility to confront movements of destruction.

In a passage on Antelme in *The Writing of the Disaster,* Blanchot brings to fruition the theory of witnessing first suggested in early writings such as *Thomas the Obscure* and *Death Sentence. L'espèce humaine* inspires there a meditation on hunger in the death camps in which Blanchot locates the critic "after Auschwitz" in a state of terminal waking (both awake and at the wake of history). Speculating on the gaze that accompanies the ultimate starvation, Blanchot initially suggests, would allow the critic momentarily to glimpse some absolute knowledge: "[W]ith this gaze which is a last gaze, bread is given us as bread.... In this ultimate moment when dying is exchanged for the life of bread, ... need—in need—also dies as simple need. And it exalts, it glorifies—by making it into something inhuman (withdrawn from all satisfaction)—the need of bread which has become an empty absolute where henceforth we can all only ever lose ourselves." Stopping at this point would leave a troubling exaltation of suffering. But Blanchot immediately contradicts this tendency; the "last gaze," like the "last word," proves to be an ethical mirage. The critic's desire for *consommation*—for transcendence of the human in the nothingness of the "empty absolute"—runs up against the silencing voices of the survivors. Blanchot defines the responsibility that arises from the encounter with those voices in a passage that rhetorically resembles that of the almost-all-consuming fire in *Thomas:*

> [T]he danger (here) of words in their theoretical insignificance is perhaps that they claim to evoke the annihilation where all sinks always, without hearing the "be silent" addressed to those who have known only partially, or from a distance the interruption of history. And yet to watch and to wake, to keep the ceaseless vigil over the immeasurable absence is necessary, for what took up again from this end (Israel, all of us) is marked by this end, from which we cannot come to the end of waking again. (*Writing,* 84)

This passage moves two steps beyond the search for self-annihilation in the empty absolute. When confronted with their implication in the disaster, and after receiving the commandment of silence, most people, including some of the most important thinkers of the twentieth century, would seem to stop. Blanchot, on the other hand, proposes a necessary second step (a *pas,* and thus also a negation) that contradicts the silence of the first step and therefore must be introduced with "and yet" (*cependant:* a word whose second syllable echoes the *pas*). Blanchot adds the vigil, the watching over [*veiller*], to the tasks confronting the critic in the wake of the disaster; as in the epigraph to this chapter, the intellectual becomes a lookout in the care, not of the self, but of others. The ceaselessness of this watch radically reimagines the Orphic gaze and suggests an inability to break definitively from the past: the "end" of the interruption of history also serves as a negative origin for the survival of everyone. All living is living on—the impossibility of death, of disappearance; the persistence of presence, of the "last word" that ceaselessly repeats itself even when its author would prefer not to recognize his own guilty authorship. Republication of the early stories ("Le dernier mot" and "L'Idylle") becomes a political act that de Man, committed only to silence and to the inevitability of complicity, could never perform. The ceaselessness of the wake in Blanchot takes place in a double temporal frame, that of the enigmatic pronouncement that "all narratives from now on will be from before Auschwitz." The insomniac witness is at once yoked to the disaster that has already occurred and watchful over its contemporary and future reappearances.

Yet the question of Blanchot's passive withdrawal, like that of Adorno's modernist aestheticism and primarily reflective politics, also survives "from now on." Are these modernist engagements with the limits of representation enough? Surely they are both necessary and at the same time insufficient. Indeed, while I have read Blanchot primarily in terms of the demand for reflection on the limits of representation, there are, as one of his best critics has suggested, always two demands at work in his thought: "[F]or every demand addressed to the act of writing by virtue of its own absence of worldly foundation or justification, there is always another demand requiring that justice be done without delay in the world. These two demands . . . function according to different rhythms, different temporalities, and different logics of possibility and impossibility" (Hill, 210). Nevertheless, it could be argued that the second, worldly demand never achieves in Blanchot the importance of the ethics of writing—never, that is, except perhaps in his early journalism! In his later writings on the Nazi genocide and that which "is intolerable in the world," Blanchot marks the place of the second demand, but as an impossible site: "That the fact of the concentration camps, the extermination of the Jews and the death camps where death continued its work, are for history an absolute which interrupted history, this one *must* say, without, however, being able to say anything else. Discourse cannot be developed from this point" (*Step,* 114; Blanchot's emphasis). In underlining the demand for the remarking of a "fact," Blanchot suggests the need for documentation and reference. Yet, in assuming that discourse must halt with this remark, he remains unable to think other new forms of representation that have emerged out of this confrontation with trauma and the limits of writing. The writing that I call traumatic realism in the next two chapters does not ignore the demand to confront the unfounded nature of writing, but it nevertheless attempts to develop new forms of "documentary" and "referential" discourse out of that very traumatic void.

Both Blanchot and Adorno might also be read as opening a path toward the postmodern engagement with the Holocaust as a highly mediated public discourse, which I discuss in part 3. Their writings provide some of the most profound and sophisticated reflections on the position of the bystander—a position that, in the age of instantaneous telecommunications, has been generalized to include most of the globe. The problems of knowledge and responsibility that arise from such a situation demand solutions that are attuned both to the ethical issues addressed by the two modernist thinkers and to the questions of technology, commodification, and spectacle that are inevitable in a postmodern context. While both Adorno and Blanchot do occupy the public sphere with their critical discourses of pedagogy and witness, they also tend to shun the market and the society of the spectacle where contemporary meanings are made. The postmodern engagement with the demands of Holocaust representation builds on the claims of realism and modernism for reference and reflection but focuses on a recognition of the power of the image and the commodity.

Part II

REALISM IN "THE CONCENTRATIONARY UNIVERSE"

Realism in "The Concentrationary Universe"

As anyone who has been occupied with the Nazi genocide can attest, the desire for realism and referentiality is one of the defining features of study of the Holocaust. Perhaps because it is so difficult to construct a recognizable narrative out of extremity or because so much of the narrative must turn on absence, a commitment to documentation and realistic discourse has come to hold an almost sacred position in confrontations with genocide. At the same time, realism's "strange power of making absent objects not only present but credible" (Furst, viii) also raises suspicion in many who live in the aftermath of the Holocaust. Realism's very character seems to affirm "what is" and to suggest the possibility of a resurrection of the dead — an affirmation and a resurrection that traduce the unsurpassable negativity of genocide. The ambivalence that surrounds the question of realism and the Holocaust arises from the contradictory nature of the demands for documentation and self-reflexivity made on the literary genre by the historical event.

In formulating the concept of *traumatic realism* I seek to preserve these contradictions, while attempting to show that they do not simply undermine the realist project, but can also produce a rejuvenation of realism. The problematics of representing and coming to terms with an extreme historical event push the realist project — based, as it tends to be, on the depiction of modern, everyday life — to its limits. But traumatic realism, as the examples of Klüger and Delbo suggest, often entails a survival of the claims of realism into a discourse that would otherwise be identified in terms of literary history or style as modernist or even postmodernist. It is the very persistence of the problem of reference and documentation that makes these memoirs realist in my vocabulary. My discussion of realism begins with the question of how to represent the *space* of the concentrationary universe and moves to a recognition that this space can only be represented traumatically as the registration of a repetitive structure of *time*.

In postwar literary studies, realism has been one of the most maligned concepts. For a critic such as Georg Lukács in the 1930s, realist depiction had represented a revolutionary force that was a natural correlative of proletarian struggle. For Erich Auerbach, writing in exile during the war, a defense of realism amounted to a much-needed affirmation of civilization in the face of barbarism. In the following years, however, the successive waves of structuralism and poststructuralism reversed this positive evaluation and tended to equate realism with a noxious bourgeois ideology, or even with ideology as such. While the vanguard moment of theory is over, and multiple theoretical positions now interact in the intellectual marketplace, it would be safe to say that the concept of realism has not yet recovered its previous status. As an intervention into the contemporary theoretical scene, my use of the concept of traumatic realism is not meant as a return either to a naive pretheoretical belief in transparent mimesis or to a relatively orthodox Marxist position, with its belief in the ultimately determining instance of the economic infrastructure. Rather, I seek to open up a new space for reading narratives of extremity by drawing attention to how certain works exceed the frameworks of both classical realism and the poststructuralist critique of representation.[1] Such a project is all the more necessary given the recent obsession with the real in contemporary art, accounted for powerfully by Hal Foster, and in other realms of literature, such as the family memoir or photograph (see N. K. Miller, *Bequest;* and Hirsch, *Family Frames*).

Traumatic realism develops out of and in response to the demand for documentation that an extreme historical event poses to those who would seek to understand it. "Documentation" consists of two elements — reference and narrative — that correspond to its nominal and verbal meanings. On the one hand, the demand for documentation calls for an archive of facts or details referring to the event. On the other hand, the active sense of documentation indicates the need for the construction of a realistic narrative that would shape those details into a coherent story. Poststructuralist critics have called both elements of documentation into question and have substituted for them the "play" or "drift" of writing detached from reference or meaning. Traumatic realist texts, however, search for a form of documentation beyond direct reference and coherent narrative but do not fully abandon the possibility for some kind of reference and some kind of narrative.

Roland Barthes's famous essay "The Reality Effect" is paradigmatic of poststructuralism's skeptical characterization of reference. Barthes defines realism as "any discourse which accepts statements whose only justification is their referent" (16). In "The Reality Effect," such statements include in particular descriptions of objects or details detached from the narrative. His essay is significant in that, unlike most discussions of realism, which are limited to questions of fiction, it considers literature and history as equally exemplary of the will to realism. It is not only Flaubert's famous barometer from *Un coeur simple* but also a "little door" mentioned by Michelet in his *Histoire de France* that constitute Barthes's examples of details that say *"we are the real"* (16). Barthes himself is dubious about the possibilities for such a "*direct* collusion of a referent and a signifier," preferring to understand realism as the ideological production of a "reality effect" and not the summoning of reality. The factual details that realist discourse seems to amass in acts of documentation are mere ruses that simulate and do not refer to reality.

Parallel to the critique of the "concrete detail" as simulation instead of reference runs the critique of the narrative through which discourse is given order and meaning. Here, Hayden White's considerations of historiography have been definitive. White argues that historians "have transformed narrativity from a manner of speaking into a paradigm of the form which reality itself displays to a 'realistic' consciousness. [They] have made narrativity into a value, the presence of which in a discourse having to do with real events signals at once its objectivity, its seriousness, and its realism." In fitting reality into a narrative paradigm, however, the writing of history (or realist literature) imposes a layer of contingent meaning between the understanding and its object. White suggests that the desire of narrative in fact turns out to be quite different from, and ultimately contradictory to, that of reference: "[T]his value attached to narrativity in the representation of real events arises out of a desire to have real events display the coherence, integrity, fullness, and closure of an image of life that is and can only be imaginary" ("Value of Narrativity," 23). As does Barthes, White ultimately removes the discourse of realism from "real events" and the demand for documentation and stresses instead that it is an "imaginary" genre (in the sense that it responds to desires other than those of approaching the real). Just as Barthes's realist detail turns out not to be concrete at all but rather a simulation of concreteness, White's "narrativity" covers over the very events it claims to present through an unwarranted gesture of closure.

The force of the two-pronged critique of realism levied by Barthes and White is indisputable, and it is significant for an interdisciplinary study of Holocaust representation because of the rigorous standard it sets for the continuing use of the concept of realism. Yet the stakes are high, since unlike other literary genres, realism makes what Fredric Jameson calls "simultaneous, yet incompatible, aesthetic and epistemological claims." The "possibility of *knowledge*"—the epistemological claim—that inhabits realist texts and desires makes it difficult merely to dismiss realism as ideology, even when the constructionist, aesthetic side of the realist project is foregrounded. Or rather, ideology itself needs to be rethought as "not a form of *error*" but "a form of social or cognitive mapping, which . . . it would be perverse to imagine doing away with" (Jameson, *Signatures,* 158, 165). But what kind of knowledge does awareness of the aesthetic construction of realism still permit? Jameson is more sanguine than either Barthes or White about the epistemological possibilities of realism. He argues that, regardless of the seeming incoherence of its conflicting claims, realism should still be understood as producing knowledge *of* and effects *in* the real:

> [R]ealism and its specific narrative forms construct their new world by *programming* their readers; by training them in new habits and practices, which amount to whole new subject-positions in a new kind of space; producing new kinds of action, but by way of the production of new categories of the event and of experience, of temporality and of causality, which also preside over what will now come to be thought of as reality. Indeed, such narratives must ultimately produce the very category of Reality itself, of reference and of the referent, of the real, of the "objective" or "external" world. (*Signatures,* 166)

In Jameson's more historicist understanding, realism is not mere illusion, but a social fact or force that has consequences for material practice as well as the understanding of events.[2] The "new world" to which Jameson refers here is that of nineteenth-century bourgeois society, but the productive and programming functions of realism he identifies can be usefully brought to bear on representations of the Holocaust — representations, that is, of another new world, one at once very far from and very close to the everyday life of modern Europe.

Much of Holocaust discourse shares the realist desires for both reference and the coherence that only narrative can provide, and it similarly attempts to "program" its readers. But it also demands another kind of reference and another kind of narrative than those provided by traditional realist discourses, because the category of reality that it seeks to register and produce demands an alternative account of the relationship between writers, readers, and the event. Jameson's formulation of realism as a form of *production* helps to clarify as well the stakes of traumatic realism. Instead of understanding the traumatic realist project as an attempt to reflect the traumatic event in an act of passive mimesis, I would suggest that traumatic realism is an attempt to produce the traumatic event as an object of knowledge and to program and thus transform its readers so that they are forced to acknowledge their relationship to posttraumatic culture. Because it seeks both to construct access to a previously unknowable object and to instruct an audience in how to approach that object, the stakes of traumatic realism are both epistemological and pedagogical.

Reading Spiegelman's drawing as a Benjaminian constellation is once again helpful in clarifying the limits and claims of realism, as well as the Holocaust's particular "traumatic" relationship to them. The contrast between mouse, Maus, and Mickey Mouse constitutes a reality effect that simultaneously marks the place of the real through its differentiation from other levels of aesthetic stylization and locates the limits of the aesthetic by framing it on either side with signifiers of economic and corporeal materiality. In Spiegelman's work there is clearly no desire for what Barthes calls a "*direct* collusion of a referent and a signifier" — that is, after all, one of the points of the animal motif. Instead there emerges the possibility of *indirect* reference through the self-conscious staging of the conundrum of representing historical extremity.[3] The mouse that the artist holds in his hands is not the real itself, but it is an object of knowledge and an effect of the real that points toward the real's foundational absence from representation. The abject and unsightly body of the mouse *moves us* toward the site of trauma.

Reading the detail as *pointing to* the real instead of claiming *to be* the real (as in Barthes's reading) suggests that the detail in traumatic realist texts may be akin to the type of sign that Charles Sanders Peirce called an "index."[4] An index is a sign that relates to a referent as an effect relates to a cause — the classic example is the weathervane that points in the direction that the wind is blowing. However, the index in traumatic circumstances functions differently than the traditional version. Instead of indicating an object or phenomenon that caused it, and in that sense making the referent present, the traumatic index points to a necessary absence. As with other traumatic details that I will discuss in the course of this book, such as Klüger's socks and Delbo's teddy bear or broken clock, the mouse in Art's hand does not embody the real but evokes it as a felt lack, as the startling impact of that which cannot be known immediately. This potential indexical quality of realism is missing from Barthes's and White's notions of realism as ideological error or imaginary construct and suggests that even a reality effect contains the possibility of knowledge of the real. Traumatic realism is counterideological precisely because it does not produce an imaginary resolution, but rather programs readers to recognize the absence of the real.

Traumatic realist texts, moreover, challenge the narrative form of realism as well as its conventional indexical function. Although an image obviously appears static, there is a narrative dimension to Spiegelman's illustration that emerges when we situate it in the context of his larger oeuvre. This image comes from Spiegelman's "goodbye to *Maus*" and is presented as a visual reflection on his completed memoir. Knowing that this image reacts to the post-*Maus* context suggests that it may be an emblem of the failure of the comic book. There is a sense in which the abject real of the mouse does not simply lie outside of or before the act of representation, but has been produced by the book's very inability to fulfill the claims of realism. The narrative logic of the drawing highlights how Spiegelman's culture industry success has led not to a working through of a traumatic history, but to that history's displaced return. As a literalization of the artist's metaphorical formal vocabulary, the mouse is a real object both in that it is an embodiment of the memoir's inability to touch directly the real of the Holocaust and in that it signifies Spiegelman's inability to control the material effects of his own representational universe. The "narrativity" of this image, then, produces a very different effect than the realist narrative described by White, yet it does so by acknowledging the unavoidable illusory coherence that narrative tends to grant to the fragments of the real. Spiegelman's ability to turn a real historical event into narrative has produced his material success, illustrated in the drawing by the "backing" of the culture industry. That success has not eliminated, however, the artist's failure to capture the real — signaled by the reappearance of the real under a displaced form (the mouse — and the possibility that it may in fact be a rat!). Yet, in a final twist, that very displaced return inaugurates a new realist project. In its engagement with the reality effect and the narrative account of realism, Spiegelman's work demonstrates a dual commitment: it seeks to present the real by representing the fictionality of the realist contract; and it recognizes realist discourse's production of the real as an accidental effect of representation. As such, this drawing is an example of what I call traumatic realism.

In chapter 3, I continue my reflections on realism through a critique of the ways that theories of realism connect texts to history. Working from the important contributions of Georg Lukács and Erich Auerbach I reveal the logic of everyday historical realism as one that connects the microcosm of the text to the macrocosm of a historical totality — be it conceived in Marxist or humanist terms. David Rousset's concentration camp memoir, *L'univers concentrationnaire,* provides the terms for a discussion of realism in the context of the Holocaust. Rousset names the "new world," in Jameson's terms, that this realism will have to grapple with and seek to produce in the minds of its readers — *the concentrationary universe.* Furthermore, he identifies a structural problem, the relationship of the extreme to the everyday, that lies at the basis of attempts to think Holocaust representation in relation to the realist demand for reference and documentation. Recent works by Lawrence Langer and Tzvetan Todorov on camp memoirs provide an opportunity to observe how two opposed, but structurally similar, critical works come to terms with the relationship (or nonrelationship) between extremity and normality. A deconstruction of their approaches leads me to reconceive the camp world as a hybrid of contradictory elements — a conception I find exemplified in Ruth Klüger's memoir *weiter leben* (chapter 3) and Charlotte Delbo's trilogy *Auschwitz and After* (chapter 4).

But once the relationship between the catastrophe and the everyday has been unsettled, what are the possibilities for realist representation? I argue that Klüger and Delbo, like Spiegelman, offer versions of *traumatic* realism—a realism in which the scars that mark the relationship of discourse to the real are not fetishistically denied, but exposed; a realism in which the claims of reference live on, but so does the traumatic extremity that disables realist representation as usual. Both Klüger and Delbo additionally invent new narrative forms in response to the claims of the traumatically real. Klüger interrupts her autobiographical account with critical commentary on Holocaust representation and the reception of the genocide in Europe and the United States. She thus provides a literary response to Saul Friedlander's call for a self-conscious writing of Holocaust history that simultaneously brings us closer to the events and, through the use of commentary, discourages the facile embrace of closure and coherence found in the typical realist narrative.[5] While Delbo also combines the documentary impulse of history or autobiography with the self-reflexivity of commentary, she adds a further collective dimension to her testimony. Her later texts anticipate the archival innovations of video documentary collections, as they provide space for a multiplicity of testimonial voices without hiding the contradictions and rifts of the real behind a totalizing organizational principle.

Chapter 3

"The Barbed Wire of the Postwar World"

Ruth Klüger's Traumatic Realism

Everyday problems do not interest us.
— Heinrich Himmler

The program that followed from Himmler's dismissal of daily life rapidly left the realm of the everyday to become a defining moment in what Eric Hobsbawm has called the "age of extremes." But the traffic between the everyday and the extreme is never simple. Hobsbawm's naming is meant to capture the coexistence of the wars, revolutions, mass killings, and ideological battles that haunt this century alongside unprecedented technological progress. Because his task is the monumental reconstruction and comprehension of what he terms "a coherent historical period" (5), Hobsbawm does not pose the question of the nature of extremity or of the theoretical and methodological tools necessary to its comprehension. He does not let the violent extremity of his subject matter interfere with his nimble traversal of disparate realms of knowledge and culture or with the "coherence" of his approach. Coherence, however, is not always so easily obtained. When violence takes extreme forms, forms of knowledge are also implicated. Characterizing an age as extreme necessitates reflection on the character and epistemology of extremity.

Within accounts of twentieth-century extremity, the Nazi genocide has occupied a privileged and paradigmatic position because of its singular mobilization of new techniques of destruction. Works of interdisciplinary Holocaust studies have attempted through various means to account for that extremity, although, as I have argued, they have often done so at cross purposes. The deadlock I have identified between realist and antirealist approaches to the Holocaust arises from the difficulty of thinking through the relationship between the everyday and the extreme, a relationship that was of concern to the Nazis themselves (as the quotation from Himmler demonstrates), as well as to scholars of the Holocaust and the twentieth century. While the multifaceted character of Holocaust studies has meant that it has produced a fascinating and pluralist corpus of insights, it has also led to a situation in which Holocaust representations, whether literary or historical, tend to be evaluated according to two apparently contradictory sets of criteria. On the one hand, a demand that representations of the genocide be realistic registers the desire for an undistorted documentation of history and the fear that flights of the imagination or of philosophical speculation will trivialize the events, mock the "literalness" of the victims' suffering, and lend ammunition to Holocaust negationists.[1] An antirealist tendency within Holocaust studies, on the other hand, argues that the reluctance to attempt epistemologically challenging analyses of the Nazi genocide has blocked from view the very aspects of the Holocaust that constitute its specificity. Indeed, just as frequent as the calls for realism and "the facts" are assertions of the Holocaust's uniqueness and exteriority to understanding and normalizing writing practices. Here, instead of calls for realism, are found attacks on realism and calls for silence.[2]

The fact that this deadlock persists despite the impressive advances of the field indicates that the questions at issue may derive from a traumatic situation—a situation that, I argue, is relevant to both the methodology and the object of Holocaust studies, as well as the relationship between the two. Instead of abandoning the need either for documentation or for recognition of the Holocaust's specific challenge to representation, I propose that a rereading of realism under the sign of trauma may be the most productive way out of the current dilemma. To challenge realist epistemology is not to deny either the need for or possibility of knowledge of historical events. Conversely, to reassert the importance of representation for historical cognition need not be a step backward into an epistemologically naive past that screens out the rupture of genocide and the critique of mimesis. Rather, pursuing the question of realism under traumatic conditions demonstrates the extent to which theories of history and theories of representation depend upon each other — and the extent to which the specificity of extreme historical events poses challenges to both.

In this chapter, I first lay bare the mechanisms of realism in general. Drawing on the work of Georg Lukács, Erich Auerbach, and Christopher Prendergast, I demonstrate that realism has been understood as a movement from textual surface to historical depth. This hierarchical movement relies on a logic linking microcosm to macrocosm and presupposes either a totalizing notion of history or of socially shared conventions that underwrite such a logic. A concentration camp testimony by David Rousset both exposes the weakness of those theories of realism in accounting for the Holocaust and proposes an alternative articulation between extreme violence and the everyday bases of society. The constellation of the extreme and the everyday — which Rousset names "the concentrationary universe" — serves as the grounds for a critique of Lawrence Langer's and Tzvetan Todorov's influential accounts of Holocaust testimonies. Through a deconstruction of their seemingly opposed projects I arrive at a new understanding of the concentrationary universe of the Nazi camps as a borderland of extreme and everyday elements. In my reading, Ruth Klüger's memoir *weiter leben: Eine Jugend* [living on: A Youth] provides a concrete instance of the articulation of the extreme and the everyday that leads me to formulate a new mode of representation and historical cognition under the name of traumatic realism. Drawing on Fredric Jameson's notion of the "programming" and "productive" qualities of realist discourse, I use the concept of traumatic realism as both an epistemological and a social category in order to resolve one of the dominant antinomies of Holocaust studies: the seemingly irresolvable opposition between realist and antirealist tendencies. While Adorno and Blanchot also situate thought, writing, and history after Auschwitz under the sign of trauma, traumatic realists like Klüger do not only interrogate the limits of representation but contribute to a revitalization of the documentary function. By representing a site of extreme violence as a borderland of extremity and everydayness, traumatic realism attempts to produce the traumatic event as an object of knowledge and to program and transform its readers so that they are forced to acknowledge their relationship to posttraumatic culture.

Realism in the Balance

What does it mean to demand realistic representations of the Holocaust? Before this question can be answered, it is important to consider the meaning of realism in literary history and criticism. It is precisely in the field of fiction that the concept of realism has been most fully described and indeed questioned, but the impact of such work has implications for representation more generally, including testimonial and historical works. The two most common analogies for realist writing come from the field of the visual. The text is described as either a mirror of or a window onto the world, with the emphasis in either case on the "picture-perfect" clarity of the text. Such figures are obviously inadequate, not least because their metaphorical basis in images does not answer the question of what constitutes a realistic depiction. Rather, the "mirror" or "window" metaphor displaces the problem into another medium without making explicit the connection between realistic literary *narrative* and realistic visual *depiction,* and without in any way considering the problems specific to the visual medium.

Georg Lukács, one of this century's most important theorists and defenders of realism, attempts to overcome the weaknesses of such "reflection" theories by insisting on the necessary "mediations" between the text and the world it purports to depict:

> If literature is a particular form by means of which objective reality is reflected, then it becomes of crucial importance for it to grasp that reality as it truly is, and not merely to confine itself to reproducing whatever manifests itself immediately and on the surface. If a writer strives to represent reality as it truly is, i.e. if he is an authentic realist, then the question of totality plays a decisive role, no matter how the writer actually conceives the problem intellectually.... So the crux of the matter is to understand the correct dialectical unity of appearance and essence. ("Realism in the Balance," 33)

Lukács insists on the difference between a photographic conception of realism, which merely "mirrors the original," and his dialectical notion, which "express[es] the wealth and diversity of reality, reflecting forces as yet submerged beneath the surface" (48). The question remains, however, as to what authorizes the grasping of "reality as it truly is" in a "dialectical unity of appearance and essence." Lukács, famously and problematically, solves this problem with reference to the Marxist notion of the relationship between base and superstructure. Representing reality "as it truly is" means understanding the surface image as an aspect of the superstructure and thus as a distorted reflection of the real material conditions of society: "Every Marxist knows that the basic economic categories of capitalism are always reflected in the minds of men, directly, but always back to front" (32). Lukács's connection between the question of literary realism and material historical processes marks a crucial theoretical insight in moving beyond the purely and superficially "visual" understanding of realism.

When realism is revealed as not simply a "picture" of reality but a *mediated cognition of history,* its importance for literary and historical Holocaust representations correspondingly increases. But Lukács's reference to the base-superstructure problematic immediately creates further problems insofar as it displaces the problem of representation one step back onto the assumption of an already known historical totality — capitalism — that grounds, or ought to ground, both realist texts and their interpretations. Reality is knowable by virtue of the correspondence between superstructural appearance and economic base, and realism earns its name by exposing these connections between what is immediately experienceable and what lies below the surface. The base-superstructure model presents an opportunity for complex historical understanding through the focus on mediations that link culture and economics in inseparable heterogeneity. But if this model is used rigidly and deterministically, it ends up eliding the importance of mediation and thus collapses back into a form of reflection theory. In this case, historical understanding is only rendered as an abstraction, and the specificity of events disappears. This problem is particularly crucial for the case of genocide, which takes place outside of, and even in contradiction to, economic logic; no abstract notion of historical determination will be able to comprehend its particularity. Lukács's connection of the problem of realism to the base-superstructure problematic is an important theoretical advance — because it locates the intersection of history and representation in mediation — but confronting the question of Holocaust realism means reworking the Marxist model in a more thoroughgoing fashion than Lukács would have accepted.

In *Mimesis,* an extended and influential consideration of "the representation of reality in European literature," Erich Auerbach presents a version of realism that preserves the connection between the surface of the text and history, but without the same reliance on economic determinism. In contrast to Lukács, whose theory led him to a normative model of realist representation, Auerbach emphasizes the multiplicity of possible realisms — addressing a series of texts from *The Odyssey* to Virginia Woolf's modernist experimentation. Yet this very inclusiveness also testifies to a fundamental and grounding totality in Auerbach's thought: that of an unquestioned Western tradition. Auerbach provides a two-sided definition of realism: "The serious treatment of everyday reality, the rise of more extensive and socially inferior human groups to the position of subject matter for problematic-existential representation, on the one hand; on the other, the embedding of random persons and events in the general course of contemporary history" (491).[3] Auerbach specifies the realist project by connecting it to a depiction of everyday life in which "the people" at once come to voice and are situated in a larger historical process. Lukács also takes part in this optimism because of his evolutionary Hegelian Marxist framework. Even in his justly famous discussion of the historical novels of Walter Scott, in which he brings the categories of historical catastrophe and crisis onto center stage, Lukács ultimately seeks to demonstrate how such crises provide an opportunity in which "human greatness . . . is liberated" (*Historical Novel,* 51). No less than Lukács, Auerbach sees a political dimension in realism, which he allies with modern processes of democratization. The realist commitments both to depicting "socially inferior human groups" and situating those groups within modern history are among the conditions of possibility for the project of Holocaust realism, and yet problems in the applicability of Auerbach's theory clearly persist.

While not reliant on the ready-made conceptual framework of the base and superstructure, Auerbach, like Lukács, nonetheless also grounds his understanding of realism in a vision of history that events such as the Holocaust belie. To be sure, Auerbach's work on realism was immediately and directly set against Nazi terror and disdain for truth, both in its composition in exile from Nazi Germany and in its democratic claims for literature. Nevertheless, the confidence his text expresses in the critic's ability to grasp "the general course of contemporary history" seems as out of touch with the actual course of history at the time of the book's writing as the orthodox Marxist's belief that fascism and the Holocaust could be explained by the ultimately determining instance of the economy. While Auerbach was writing a book that he hoped would "contribute to bringing together again those whose love for our western history has serenely preserved" (557), the Nazis and their allies were serenely shredding the fabric of universality upon which that history saw itself founded. As the full impact of the Nazi genocide emerged in the postwar years, Auerbach's imagined community of the faithful would be much depleted. With its profound investment in the transmissible tradition of Western culture, Auerbach's text registers and reproduces the Enlightenment belief in a progressive, continuous movement of Western history that the events of the two world wars and the Holocaust have thrown radically into question.

As Christopher Prendergast has argued, both Auerbach and Lukács, despite their many differences, rely on an equally problematic notion of history as totality: they take for granted "the principle which allows for the unproblematic passage from microcosm to macrocosm, the criteria by which the writer decides, and which enable the reader to accept, that one set of selections and combinations is representative, where another is random or arbitrary" (26). These accounts of realism are haunted, in other words, by the fact that there will always be a degree of randomness or arbitrariness in all decisions that distinguish between the necessary and the random or arbitrary. By making explicit the implicit grounding of realism in the relationship between the realist text, its author, and its reading public, however, Prendergast also reveals the way that, despite theoretical problems, texts are still read as realistic: "For the text to be accredited with mimetic values, the narrator's assertions must command the assent of the reader. There must be a certain 'concord' between narrator and reader, a necessary condition of which is the existence of a socially shared universe of meaning" (30). If a "socially shared" consensus were to exist about what constitutes appropriate material and appropriate treatment of material in a realist text, then realism would become thinkable again. But instead of transcending its superficial historical conditions in the revelation of historical essence, literature would then be condemned to reproducing stereotypes or ideologies of history and not "the real thing" (cf. Prendergast, 31).

The stakes for Holocaust literature are high, since most works of testimony and history are created with the assumption that the particular microcosm of the events they recount has implications for the macrocosmic understanding of history. In "realist" accounts of testimonial works, the movement from particular to general is grounded by the category of eyewitness experience, which bears the authority of legal evidence. Historical works, of course, have an even more elaborately legitimated methodology for turning documents into evidence and evidence into truth. But the realist movement from the microcosm to the macrocosm that grounds testimonial literature and dominant historiography runs into multiple problems when the events to be considered are those of the Nazi genocide. As I have already remarked, attempts to ground realism in the notion of the historical totality as an expression either of the economic base or of a continually progressing Western culture run aground at the fact of genocide. The attempt to exterminate totally a people and a culture cannot be reduced to economic laws of capitalism, nor can such a breach of continuity be reintegrated into an affirmative version of European history. If most works of Holocaust testimony or history do not share these particular totalizing moves, the authority they are often granted as evidence still implicitly partakes of a concept of historical totality. The legal or historical conceptions of evidence tend to fall within the more pragmatic concept of realism as the expression of a "concord" within a "socially shared universe of meaning"—a concept that ultimately does not avoid the pitfalls of the teleologies of Lukács or Auerbach. It is precisely the confrontation with the lack of shared meaning between narrator and reader that characterizes both the genre of Holocaust testimony and works of historiography that do not seek simply to reinsert the Holocaust in the continuous flow of German, European, or world history. If there is a specificity to the Holocaust, it must reside in the difficulties it poses to the concepts of history, culture, and communication that underlie most theories of realism. Nevertheless, in explaining these difficulties, aspects of the classic theories of realism—such as Lukács's concept of mediation and Auerbach's focus on the everyday life of marginal groups—will prove crucial. In the following pages, I explore the specificity of the Holocaust's challenge to realism by focusing on testimonial and critical works that attempt to chart the Nazi genocide's place in history.

In the Concentrationary Universe

Back from sixteen months in the death-worlds of Buchenwald, Neuengamme, and other Nazi concentration camps, which he inhabited because of his political engagement as a communist member of the French resistance, David Rousset continued his opposition to fascism by engaging immediately in a prolific literary production. Within months he had written an influential testimonial account of the camps, and by the end of 1946 he had also written a 760-page nonfictional novelistic version, *Les jours de nôtre mort.* Although less frequently read today than many of the testimonies either published or rediscovered later (as in the case of Elie Wiesel's *Night* or Primo Levi's *Survival in Auschwitz,* respectively), Rousset's work has nevertheless contributed one of the most important concepts for thinking about the Holocaust: *l'univers concentrationnaire,* the concentrationary universe.[4] How does this "universe" compare to the "socially shared universe of meaning" that realism presupposes and posits?

In drawing attention to the Nazi's creation of an unprecedented parallel world of genocidal murder, Rousset's formulation has provided a useful way of conceptualizing the singularity of the Shoah, even if—as a prisoner of concentration and not extermination camps—he was never a direct witness to genocide. And yet as valuable as the notion of a concentrationary universe may be for understanding the psychological, social, and literary implications of the death camps and for providing a conceptual space through which to think about Holocaust realism, it also raises difficult questions about what constitutes the Holocaust and about the frameworks through which it should be understood. On the one hand, as a historical process, the Holocaust was clearly much more than the creation of concentration camps. On the other hand, the camps had industrial and punitive functions other than those associated with the murder of European Jews. In considering the concentrationary universe as a concept through which the specificity of the Nazi genocide has been produced and expressed, certain questions immediately arise: Does the concept include the ghettos where Jews were concentrated before being sent to their death? Does it include both "normal" concentration camps and extermination camps? How does one conceptualize a camp such as Auschwitz that had prison, industrial, and annihilatory features?

How does one account for the different "categories" of prisoners within the concentrationary world? There is no one correct answer to these questions, but neither is the problem a trivial one of semantics. Rather, the necessity of defining the contours of the concentrationary universe — and thus deciding what is a "realistic" account of it — has significant implications for how one situates the Holocaust in history. Acts of definition and representation determine the kinds of lessons one can draw from the study of the history of genocide: the problems of history and representation are inseparable, if nonetheless irreducible to each other.

In Rousset's account, the concentrationary universe emerges as a contradictory phenomenon. On the one hand, it is a place beyond the bounds of normality where "everything is possible" and where concentrationees "are set apart from the rest of the world by an experience impossible to communicate" (*Other Kingdom,* 168–69). On the other hand, those very extreme qualities of the camps reveal "the sheer fact of living, in itself, brutal, entirely stripped of all superstructures." In other words, that which is impossible to communicate proves to be the essence of historical reality: "the dependence of man's condition on economic and social structures, the true material relations that determine behavior" (*Other Kingdom,* 171). In order to communicate the incommunicable, Rousset draws on the Marxist conceptualization of society as consisting of two hierarchically interrelated levels, the economic base ("the true material relations that determine behavior") and the cultural and political superstructure ("man's condition") that needs to be stripped away in order to unveil the essence of history ("the sheer fact of living"). This account also draws on a logic that links and ultimately reduces the microcosm to the macrocosm, the specific fact of the camps to the question of human history in general. In this way, the concentrationary universe is rendered amenable to a simplified version of Lukács's notion of realism that has had key mediating links taken out. Rousset's Marxist vocabulary seems, especially from today's vantage point, fatally flawed as a means of conceptualizing the Nazi system. Few historians (and fewer camp survivors) would propose that the Nazi camp system served primarily rational goals or could be derived from laws of economic necessity (however rationally the Nazis may themselves have conceived their actions and however partially integrated the camps were into industrial and military production).

Yet despite these obvious flaws, Rousset's formulation also proves a fruitful starting point for a reconsideration of realist documentation of the Nazi genocide. If the base-superstructure model employed by Rousset seems inadequate, the intimacy that his account implies between the extreme and the normal bases of social life is in fact central to many accounts of the Holocaust. Focusing on the possible mediations between these poles may produce a more adequate framework from which to pursue the possibilities of a concentrationary realism in literary or historical narration. There are two dominant ways of thinking about the relationship between the extreme and the everyday in relation to the Nazi genocide, which I have termed realist and antirealist. Zygmunt Bauman provides a representative example of the realist tendency when he describes the "uniqueness" of the Holocaust in terms not unlike Rousset's: "*[I]t stands unique against the quotidianity of modern society because it brings together some ordinary factors of modernity which normally are kept apart. . . .* [O]nly the combination of factors is unusual and rare, not the factors that are combined" (94; emphasis in original). This argument, which bears a family resemblance to Hannah Arendt's notion of the "banality of evil," proposes that catastrophic events are generated from within a matrix of the everyday, and thus that extremity is just a particularly volatile mixture of quotidian elements.[5] In a post-Marxist era, the concept of "modernity" has come to substitute for the economic base as the grounding totality of historical explanation. Claude Lanzmann articulates a paradigmatic version of the antirealist position when he claims that "between all these conditions" of the Holocaust's possibility "and the gassing of three thousand persons, men, women, children, in a gas chamber, all together, there is an unbreachable discrepancy. It is simply not possible to engender one out of the other. There is no solution of continuity between the two; there is rather a gap, an *abyss*, and this abyss will never be bridged" ("Obscenity," 206). Lanzmann opposes this "abyss" that separates the everyday from the extreme to what he calls "the obscenity of the project of understanding" (207). Bauman, on the one hand, substitutes one historical totality for another outmoded one, without questioning the subsumption of the particularity of the event under the universalizing explanatory model. Lanzmann, on the other hand, risks taking the Holocaust completely outside of history by disconnecting the extreme event from any account of social processes. Beyond this deadlock between the "abyss" and the banality of evil, it is in the nonreductive articulation of the extreme and the everyday that I find the possibility for a reworking of realism under the sign of trauma.

At the Limits of the Concentrationary Universe

Lawrence Langer's *Holocaust Testimonies: The Ruins of Memory* and Tzvetan Todorov's *Facing the Extreme: Moral Life in the Concentration Camps* are two critical works that, in their flawed attempts to work through the relationship between the extreme and the everyday, point the way toward a more complex version of Holocaust realism. Langer takes the notion of a concentrationary universe seriously and proposes that the experiences of Jews (and sometimes other prisoners) in the ghettos and camps of Nazi-occupied Europe lie wholly and uniquely outside the confines of everyday imagination. Todorov's work consists of a close examination of texts concerning both Nazi and Soviet camps, which he considers essentially related. Although his work is based on camp testimonies, and thus relies methodologically on the notion of an autonomous concentrationary universe, his book aims to collapse that world back into the everyday in order to draw moral lessons for ordinary circumstances.

These two books represent important contributions to the conceptualization of the concentrationary universe both in the tasks they set for themselves and in those they refuse to consider. Langer forcefully demonstrates the specificity of the experience of the Holocaust and its unsettling of traditional historical and moral accounts. He also contributes to an appreciation of the particularities of the genre of oral testimony, although he refuses to treat it as a representational medium that is mediated and governed by conventions just as is written work — even if by *other,* not yet fully understood conventions (see especially chapter 1 of *Holocaust Testimonies*). Todorov rightly refuses to give up in advance on attempts to understand, evaluate, and judge extreme phenomena. His consideration of a full range of experiential subject-positions — from death camp commandant to ghetto leader to rescuer and beyond — adds a comprehensive quality to his discourse that suggests the ways that extreme events and situations are articulated to a range of institutions and communities, not all of which are themselves situated in the concentrationary universe. By tracing the contradictions and limits of these two important critical works and by sharpening the distinctions between and relationships among the history, experience, and representation of the Nazi genocide, I seek to formulate an alternative conception of the concentrationary universe and an account of realism commensurate with it.

The goal of Langer's account of Holocaust testimonies and memoirs is to remove victims' experiences from pathologization, sentimentalization, and other inadequate responses rendered by a world anxious to avoid coming to terms with the extreme conditions produced during the twentieth century in the heart of the modern world. Langer thus aims to remove the camps and ghettos from everyday moral frameworks that rely on notions of choice and individual agency. For Langer, and certainly for many victims, the concentrationary universe can be understood as providing only "choiceless choices" between equally problematic options. Ordinary notions of agency and humanity disappear, as do possibilities of heroism and resistance (*Holocaust Testimonies,* 26). Langer radically separates the truth of the concentrationary universe from the ordinariness of human social relations. He thereby also implicitly suggests the need for a new version of realism, one premised on his understanding of oral as opposed to written testimony. In a critique of the artifice of one particular memoir, Langer observes that the author "seeks to transform individual doom in Auschwitz into a model of universal history and man's fate in time, thereby affirming a continuity that the deathcamp was determined to divide" (*Holocaust Testimonies,* 58). Both the movement from the particular to the general and the assertion of historical continuity are familiar leitmotifs of realism against which Langer seeks to develop an alternative model more adequate to the fact of extremity.

Langer is concerned primarily with what he calls, in one form or another, "the experience of the Holocaust," primarily that of its "former victims."[6] Focusing on the "experience" of the ghettos and concentration and extermination camps allows Langer to develop a notion of absolute discontinuity between the everyday world and the concentrationary universe.[7] This absolute discontinuity draws on what Langer has called Rousset's "definitive" formula of the singularity of the concentrationary world (*Holo-*

caust and Literary Imagination, 15–16). But, while admitting that the concentrationary universe "wasn't the antiworld, but the world as Nazi Germany decided it should be" (*Admitting,* 6), Langer — because of his focus on the *experience* of extremity — does not usually grant conceptual importance to the worldliness of Nazi Germany and its embeddedness in economic and social structures and material relations. He thus not only rejects the hierarchical and deterministic subsumption of the Holocaust in material relations that underlies Rousset's realism, but risks rejecting any attempt to make sense of the Holocaust in historical context.

In *Holocaust Testimonies,* he characterizes the experience of the Holocaust as arriving from the past through oral testimony without mediation by representation or historical contingency: "Writing about Holocaust *literature,* or even written memoirs, . . . challenges the imagination through the mediation of a *text.* . . . Nothing, however, distracts us from the immediacy and the intimacy of conducting interviews with former victims (which I have done) or watching them on a screen" (*Holocaust Testimonies,* xii–xiii). Langer's stress on immediacy is problematic first because of the indefensible position that oral testimony is not inflected by rhetoric, the social context of the interview's production, and intervening historical factors. Equally odd, however, for a literary critic, is Langer's situating of the immediacy of the experience on the side of the interviewer and viewers. This double displacement of experience's mediation by text and history has a series of consequences: it allows Langer to "admit" the social production of the history of the Holocaust while ignoring its consequences, and it legitimates the nonvictim's role in the production of knowledge of the extreme that ought to be beyond the nonvictim's reach. Thus, while Langer's critique of literary accounts of genocide denaturalizes the conventions of realism, it does so in the interests of a renaturalization of the realism of orally rendered experience.

The exclusionary gesture of focusing on experience at the expense of history and representation ultimately leads Langer to exclude as well all experiential evidence that does not fit his thesis about the radical rupture of extremity. Any testimony that might support the idea of a continuity between the experience of the concentrationary universe and the values of the outside world is dismissed, as are any accounts that deny the ultimate contamination of the survivor's post-Holocaust world by the death-world of mass murder. While Langer frequently recognizes that even experience of the extreme might be heterogeneous, his interpretation again and again seeks to "cancel" all traces of normality. In discussing Nathan A.'s testimony, for example, Langer notes that the survivor had "reclaimed some of his lost dignity" in his postwar life in Israel:

> This allows him today to establish a precarious balance between the atrocities he witnessed and endured in the camps and the integrated self that yearns to leave them behind. But the content of his testimony, which cannot and indeed refuses to form a hierarchy of values, preferring to juxtapose affirmation with negation, leaves us with an intricate legacy in which infinite death trespasses on natural death, canceling the balance that Nathan A. seeks valiantly to sustain. (*Holocaust Testimonies,* 136–37)

In passages such as these, Langer overwrites the experience of his subjects through a process of cancellation whose agency is ambiguous. Ultimately, the subject of the canceling can only be Langer, in whose judgment the dignity, balance, and juxtaposition of experience that he himself admits make up Nathan A.'s testimony must be replaced with the trespassing of the negative on the affirmative. Similarly, Langer reports Edith P.'s claim that the Nazis "wanted us to become animals and I haven't seen one, not one"; after commenting that "for *her* this assertion of humanity is certainly valid," he concludes that "[a]bsence here cancels presence" (107; emphasis added). To be sure, Edith P.'s story is a horrific one (as are all of those that Langer recounts), but the rhetoric of cancellation ends up asserting the interpreter's authority over the witness in deciding how to weigh the balance of experience.

In a typical passage from the introduction to his collection *Admitting the Holocaust,* Langer employs a contradictory spatial metaphor that illustrates his methodology: "When we speak of the survivor instead of the victim and of martyrdom instead of murder, regard being gassed as a pattern for dying with dignity, or evoke the redemptive rather than the grievous power of memory, we draw on an arsenal of words that urges us to build *verbal fences* between the atrocities of the camps and ghettos and what we are mentally willing—or able—to face" (*Admitting,* 6; emphasis added). Excluding the fact that Langer's argument here evokes a mixture of reasonable and absurd oppositions (much like Daniel Goldhagen's use of false oppositions in *Hitler's Willing Executioners*), what is most striking in this passage is the way that Langer projects his own "verbal fences" onto his unnamed opponents. Despite the warning that directly precedes this passage that one should not conceive of Auschwitz as "another universe," Langer's purification of the vocabulary appropriate for discussing the Holocaust is in fact premised on just such an absolute dichotomy between normal and extreme worlds. The "verbal fence" is his own, and it runs throughout his work. As he writes in *Holocaust Testimonies,* "normal circumstances" are "the opposite of the Holocaust universe," and to think otherwise is to enter the realm of "myths" (*Holocaust Testimonies,* 212n, 166). There is thus an obvious circularity in Langer's account of the concentrationary universe: its existence is first assumed and then confirmed by evidence either selectively chosen to fit its hypothesization or produced by its initial conceptualization as an experience and not the representation of a historical site. Because of this circularity, the possibility of an alternative conception of realism consonant with the Holocaust is reduced to a mere mirror image of the "canceled" and disavowed "literary" version—in place of the mimesis of the everyday Langer substitutes the confrontation with extremity, and in place of the continuity between the world of the text and general historical processes Langer finds only discontinuity.

Although Todorov does not cite Langer, his project in *Facing the Extreme* aims to contradict directly the arguments of *Holocaust Testimonies,* as well as the explicit pronouncements of various survivors from both Nazi and Soviet camps.[8] While recognizing the extremity of experiences in death camps and the various reasons why survivors might portray the concentrationary universe as a place of absolute moral degradation — including the desire to capture their limit-experience in its uniqueness—Todorov asks whether the camps can nevertheless be understood as "a place for moral life" (as he titles the second half of his prologue). Todorov answers in the affirmative and cites numerous examples that demonstrate moral choice and ethical behavior toward others. In order to demonstrate that the possibilities for morality were not, as Langer suggests, rendered irrelevant by the camp experience, Todorov does not attempt to ameliorate intellectually the actually existing conditions of the camps. Rather, he argues, again based on survivor testimony, that degrees of moral choice were present and recognized as such: "Matters of conscience are not at all rare in extreme situations, and their very existence attests to the possibility of choice, and thus of moral life.... It is not true that life in the camps obeyed the law of the jungle. The rules of camp society may have been different but they still existed" (*Facing,* 36). By relating incidents that reveal the continued presence of social life in the camps, Todorov's purpose is to avoid reproducing the kinds of deterministic theories that made the Nazi and Soviet camps possible in the first place (although one could certainly argue that he fails to differentiate adequately between those two very different ideological systems).

Todorov's humanism leads him to the opposite conclusion from Langer — he "affirm[s] the continuity between everyday experience and that of the camps" (translation modified). At the same time, however, he must qualify his affirmation, and thus the previous sentence continues, "except where the latter [camp experience] crosses beyond the threshold of the bearable" (*Facing,* 40). This "threshold of suffering" refers to the extreme conditions of hunger and deprivation beyond which moral questions do indeed become irrelevant in Todorov's account (*Facing,* 38–39). Yet he has already assured us that "I will not dwell at length on situations where that threshold has been crossed" (*Facing,* 39), since beyond the threshold "an individual's actions teach us nothing more about the individual but only about the mechanical reactions that unbearable suffering elicits" (*Facing,* 38–39; translation modified). As Todorov's formulations imply, beyond the threshold lies the "uniqueness of the Judeocide" [*unicité du judéocide*] that he does not deny but that must be "put to the side" [*mis à part*] by his analysis (*Face,* 313; my translation). The exclusion of the specific aspects of the Nazi genocide from the consideration of the world of the camps suggests that Todorov's project is undertaken less by "facing the extreme" than by turning away from its most extreme manifestations. This turning away from the threshold nevertheless constitutes the heart of his analysis in that it brings the concentrationary universe closer to the everyday world, facilitates the conceptual collapse of the Nazi and Soviet regimes, and preserves the hope that moral lessons can be drawn from the camps and applied unproblematically to the present.[9]

Although coming to opposed conclusions about the experience

of the camps, both Todorov and Langer are forced to perform similarly excluding acts of border patrol. Interestingly, the line that they draw between what is worthy of comment and what is not runs not between the concentrationary universe and the outside world but, paradoxically, through the center of the death-world itself. Langer excludes the impingement of normal social relations (or of social relations as such) on the Nazi's construct, while Todorov chooses to ignore the very extreme phenomena that for Langer and many others define the novelty of the Nazi camps. In their studies, Todorov and Langer remain on either side of this threshold that they have themselves established without more than acknowledging that the two sides of the concentrationary universe might coexist in a heterogeneous amalgam. Todorov aims to erase the line between the concentrationary and the everyday, but in order to do so he needs to draw another line through the concentrationary that differentiates extreme from ordinary experiences within it, and then ignores the former experiences. Langer aims to sharpen the line between the concentrationary and the everyday, but in order to do so he also needs to draw a line through the concentrationary. His line performs the same differentiation, yet expels, instead, reports of ordinary aspects of the concentrationary as ideological holdovers or myths that have not come to terms with Auschwitz. In both cases, the concept of the concentrationary universe — whether it be formulated in order to be erased as an autonomous region or held up as a "hermetic ordeal" (*Holocaust Testimonies,* 49) — turns out to rely on a logically prior threshold that the critics use to classify the very accounts of that universe that serve as their evidence. The internal division within the concentrationary universe precedes and in fact produces the inside / outside division that makes that universe thinkable in the first place.

Todorov and Langer lack a coherent historical account of the universe whose moral life they evaluate, and they sidestep questions of representation in the accounts they interpret and in the very constitution of the camp world. The lack of a theory of history also limits the possibilities for a theory of realism. Such a restricted methodology produces results purified of the contingency and complexity of historical processes and representational practices. Although both critics accept a certain diversity within the realm of experience they choose as their terrain, the original division of the concentrationary universe between the extreme and the ordinary limits in advance the kinds of experiences that will count. Around the question of the historicity of the Holocaust, their methodologies again converge from opposing intellectual positions.

Langer excludes questions of history by asserting that victims' experiences and their articulations of their experiences violate the tenets of historical thinking. Drawing on Nietzsche, Langer defines history as a "life-promoting" project meant to "[mirror] insights from the past that enable us to confront the future with a more informed sense of ourselves as human beings in time" (*Holocaust Testimonies,* 78–79). He later quotes Hayden White's critique of historical emplotment that holds that "[i]nsofar as historical stories can be completed, can be given narrative closure, can be shown to have had a plot all along, they give to reality the odor of the ideal" (*Holocaust Testimonies,* 120). Langer understandably finds in the Nazi genocide no grounds for future-oriented projects capable of transforming the putrid reality of Auschwitz into the odor of human ideals. He thus claims that the "humiliated memory" of many survivors "negates the impulse to historical inquiry" (*Holocaust Testimonies,* 79). But if Langer's critique of modern history with reference to the Holocaust appears accurate in its dismissal of Nietzsche's "historical men," for whom "looking into the past urges them toward the future" filled with hope (Langer, *Holocaust Testimonies,* 78 [citing Nietzsche]), he refuses to take the next step and articulate a properly post-Holocaust historical project.

And yet Langer's own discussion of oral testimonies implies the need for a rethinking of history and its relationship to experience, memory, and realist representation. In analyzing a segment of the oral testimony of survivor Alex H., Langer shows how the narration of "chronological sequence" gives way to "another voice": "He shifts from the mode of *in medias res* — which views the Holocaust as an event sandwiched between prewar and postwar periods — to what might be called the mode of *in principio,* where, according to most testimony of surviving victims, the Holocaust has a different beginning for each witness and provides closure for none." According to Langer, this narrative shift "introduces a *discontinuity* into his account that detaches it from his previous efforts at chronology" (*Holocaust Testimonies,* 66). In this passage, Langer provides a characteristically insightful reading of oral testimony, one that opens a path toward a discussion of history and representation that, however, is not fully realized. Langer's project aims at confronting the post-Holocaust world with the testimony of the concentrationary universe in order to provoke a rethinking of identity, modernity, and the image of the human.[10] Yet without taking account of the mediation of surviving victims' experiences through representation or of their social circulation in historical discourses (be they literary, testimonial, or "scientific"), those experiences are doomed precisely to the isolation and impotence that Langer movingly charts.

Todorov, on the other hand, explicitly attempts to move his discussion of victims', perpetrators', and bystanders' historical experiences and actions into the center of a consideration of everyday human morality premised on a notion of realist mimesis. But his tendency to separate moral questions from historical questions—"all phases of history are not equally propitious for moral action" (*Face,* 259; my translation)—leads him to discount the specificity of the Nazi genocide, a move that subsequently allows him to avoid a reconsideration of either history or morality "after Auschwitz." This establishment of a threshold between the moral and the historical—which is not unrelated to the line Todorov draws between the extreme and the ordinary in the camps—simplifies the conception in *Facing the Extreme* of both sides of the divide. Todorov aligns history only with questions of force and power and reduces morality to the choice "to imitate or to reject" (one of the chapters of the section titled "Facing Evil"). Todorov concerns himself in his evaluation of the responses of survivors and bystanders with whether those responses imitate or refuse to imitate the terrible means of the Nazi or Soviet perpetrators. But this notion of imitation, as he demonstrates particularly in his analysis of Claude Lanzmann's film *Shoah,* has less to do with actions than with states of mind. The argument relies on a simplistic notion of mimesis as mirroring that fails to address the kinds of historical questions Lukács and Auerbach moved to the center of theories of realism (in however flawed a way).

Todorov applies his critique to Lanzmann's controversial pronouncements on his refusal to attempt to "comprehend" the Holocaust, but rather to provoke a "reenactment" in the present. Recognizing that explanations of the genocide will always come up against "something unintelligible," Todorov suggests that, nonetheless, "there is still much to understand, and understanding makes it possible to prevent the return of horror, certainly better than does the repetition of those same practices" (*Facing,* 277; translation modified). What is extraordinary here is the way that both Lanzmann and Todorov slip between questions of history and questions of representation. Lanzmann's refusal to comprehend derives from a belief that to conceive of the genocide, to represent it in thought, text, or film, would amount to a reproduction of the genocide's historical logic by making it acceptable. Yet Lanzmann paradoxically believes that his particular form of mise en scène of the genocide in artificial, but nonfictional, stagings (e.g., his renting of trains, the scene in the barbershop) brings the event back without the detour of mediation; the event cannot be explained or represented, but it can be reexperienced!

Todorov believes the genocide can be understood and represented as well as any other event because he, unlike Lanzmann, conceives of the concentrationary universe as continuous with the everyday world. But in accusing Lanzmann of a "repetition of the same practices" used by the Nazis in his technique of reenactment, Todorov forgets the rather significant gap between representational practices and the enactment of genocide. Both Lanzmann and Todorov elide the difference between discourses (be they cognitive or aesthetic) and events, an elision that permits them to leave representation unthought, either because it can be by-passed in experience (as Lanzmann and Langer believe) or because in the field of morality such a difference has no place (Todorov). Condemning Lanzmann for having made his film the expression of hate toward the Nazis, Todorov suggests that "one of the worst effects of that occupation, of that war, was that the victims of the Nazis began to become like them" (*Face,* 257; my translation). The theme of victims becoming victimizers is not foreign to Holocaust literature dealing with the aftermath of genocide, but in collapsing the production of images and texts with the perpetration of crimes against humanity Todorov obscures the uneven relationship between experience, representation, and history. Todorov's concept of "imitation" excludes history and, ironically (given the proximity of imitation to mimesis), representation from playing necessary but autonomous roles in his discussion. He thus reduces the potential of his inquiry into morality under extreme circumstances as surely as he does by excluding the extremes of extremity—that is, the specificity of the Nazi genocide of Jews—from discussion.

Reading Langer and Todorov together for their very different contributions suggests the heterogeneity of the significance of the concentrationary universe. Revealing the problems common to their books opens the way for further research into literary and historical representations of the Holocaust. Langer and Todorov share a purifying gesture that serves to characterize the death-world as either discontinuous or continuous with the world that produced it. In fact, this purifying gesture is self-subversive in that it rather reveals a discontinuity (which remains to be specified) within the experience of the camps. In neither book does a new account emerge of how concentrationary experience would lead to a reconceptualization of history—in Langer's case because he suggests that the deconstruction of modern history represents the deconstruction of history as such; in Todorov's because his exclusion of the genocide from his discussion leaves him untroubled in his account of the separation of morality from history. Both books rely on a belief in an unmediated access to experience and thus leave questions of representation by the wayside. Todorov occasionally bases his arguments on a conception of representations as equivalents to historical events. The nonsensical moral judgments that result from such a collapse of specificity and lack of mediation inadvertently demonstrate the necessity of preserving the distinction between the various levels of the concentrationary universe, even as analysis must hold them together in a conceptual constellation.

Taken together, the different analytic operations performed by Langer and Todorov reflect the methodological scenario of multidisciplinarity in which Holocaust studies breaks down into realist and antirealist schools. The degree to which the methodological a priori determines the outcome of the analysis suggests that the problem with multidisciplinarity is not only the absence of transdisciplinary dialogue and "fellowship" but an impoverished understanding of history itself. Yet out of the very inadequacies of such discourses emerges an alternative conception of the concentrationary universe as a complex object—at once extreme and everyday, historically produced and reproduced, experienced from a multitude of subject-positions, and accessible only through discursive practices. The purpose of the preceding analysis was not to suggest that the drawing of lines and the marking of thresholds are avoidable practices; rather, instead of proceeding from one binary cut, I assume that there are multiple and crisscrossing lines that divide the world of the concentrationary, both within and without. The concentrationary universe is a specific version of the "borderland," as Gloria Anzaldúa has conceived it — a space not merely divided between inside and outside, but consisting precisely of the coexistence of that which the border seeks to keep separate.[11] In Primo Levi's words, "the Lagers constituted an extensive and complex system which profoundly compenetrated the daily life of the country; one has with good reason spoken of the *univers concentrationnaire,* but it was not a closed universe" (*Drowned and Saved,* 15). Preserving the conceptual openness of that universe means revealing the constant redrawing of boundaries that takes place as that world is produced, experienced, represented, and maintained as an object of memory, discourse, and political struggle. Formulating a version of interdisciplinarity attuned to the complexity of extreme events necessitates not just reconceptualizing the camp world but reconceptualizing the very tools through which it is thought. Following the lead of Jameson's rethinking of realism, I turn to a text that combines aesthetics, historical cognition, and a transformative social project in order to begin establishing how traumatic realism can productively alter our understanding of the Holocaust.

Ruth Klüger's Traumatic Realism

Through its combination of autobiographical narration and essayistic commentary, Ruth Klüger's memoir *weiter leben: Eine Jugend* [living on: A Youth] constitutes an interdisciplinary text that takes part in both the redrawing of boundaries and the interrogation of the stakes and significance of representing the Holocaust.[12] *Weiter leben* tells the story of Klüger's coming of age as a Jewish child under National Socialism in Vienna and recounts her early teenage years spent in concentration camps. After the war, Klüger and her mother spent a few years in Germany before emigrating to the United States, where she later became a professor of German. Klüger's memoir provides a map of the concentrationary universe as a borderland in which extremity and everydayness coexist and abut each other, but without resolving into a new unity. In her text, the extreme and the everyday are neither opposed, collapsed, nor transcended through a dialectical synthesis — instead, they are at once held together and kept forever apart in a mode of representation I call traumatic realism.

Klüger's mapping of the concentrationary universe can be glimpsed through attention to the primary and often-repeated image through which she figures boundaries: barbed wire. A frequently reproduced and cited "piece" of the camp world, barbed wire serves in much Holocaust literature (and visual art) not only as a metaphor that immediately calls up certain well-worn associations of evil but as a metonymy that stands in for a particular topography. As Sidra Ezrahi has shown, such internally chosen, metonymic figures generally function to emphasize the "closedness" of the camp world, since through them language itself is revealed as trapped within the limited options of the concentrationary (49–66; see especially 55). Through a critique and refunctioning of the image, Klüger transforms barbed wire — which might be *the* stereotypical trope for indexing the Holocaust — into a tool for prying open the multiplicity of relations within the camps and between victims and their nonvictimized contemporaries (both during and after the war).

In an epilogue to her memoir, Klüger describes the "primal scene" that generates the literary narration of her life story. Back in Germany after forty years as a visiting professor of German literature, Klüger is run down by a bicyclist on Göttingen's Jüdenstraße [Jew Street!]. It is during her recovery from this accident that she begins to write her memoirs. In her reconstruction of her thoughts as the bicyclist bore down on her, the bicycle and headlight are transformed into barbed wire and a spotlight:

> I believe he is pursuing [*verfolgt*] me, wants to run me down, bright desperation, light in the dark, his headlight, metal, like a spotlight over barbed wire, I want to defend myself, push him back, both arms outstretched, impact, Germany, a moment like a hand-to-hand fight, *that* struggle I lose, metal, Germany again, what am I doing here, what did I come back for, was I ever gone? (272)

In her description of this occurrence, Klüger creates a constellation consisting of the constricting threat of barbed wire, the accidental impact of extreme events, and the restlessness of the memory of the camps that reverberates back through the entire memoir. By merging divergent locations in time and space, she suggests the essentially traumatic origin of her story. This "origin" is at once located at the moment of the memoir's enunciation and in the open wounds of the memories that it probes. Because it suggests a simultaneously porous but painful marking of boundaries, barbed wire in *weiter leben* comes to play a significant role in figuring the complex relationship between past and present, and here and there. While all memoirists must negotiate this charged borderland of experience and memory, survivors of trauma have the added burden of having to grapple continuously with the interplay of the extreme and the everyday.

Barbed wire imagery begins in the section of *weiter leben* titled "The Camps" and continues throughout the rest of the book. Significantly, however, the image first appears not in a description of the author's experience but rather in the lengthy essayistic discourse which opens "The Camps." This reversal of the expected order of memoiristic presentation — experience followed by reflection — highlights the impossibility of direct access to events and the necessity of working through the preexisting discourses that mediate and circumscribe experience. Introducing her time in Theresienstadt, Auschwitz-Birkenau, and Christianstadt, Klüger reflects on the multiplicity of types of camps and ghettos in the concentrationary universe and on the disinclination of the general public to recognize it:

> The disinclination of most people . . . to note the names of smaller camps perhaps is attributable to the fact that one would like to keep the camps as unified as possible and under the large labels of the concentration camps that have become famous. That is less tiring for the mind and emotions than coming to terms with differentiations. I insist on these distinctions . . . in order to break through the curtain of barbed wire that the postwar world has hung before the camps. There is a separation between then and now, us and them, which doesn't serve truth, but rather laziness. (82)

In its insistence on differentiation, Klüger's conceptualization of the concentrationary universe implicitly sets itself against both Langer and Todorov. According to Klüger, neither the experience nor the history of the camps was "unified," as Langer would have it, but nor was it continuous with everyday life, as Todorov argues. Coming to terms with differentiation, however, proves also to necessitate coming to terms with connectedness. The "barbed wire curtain" not only screens out distinctions between camps but also installs a "lazy" "separation" between the camps and the postwar world. Differentiation does not mean distancing the events from the present; this passage implies that — for "outsiders" and perhaps for former inmates as well — overcoming that distancing is in fact a prerequisite for understanding and "coming to terms with" the specificities of the concentrationary universe. Breaking through the barbed wire means learning to differentiate between differentiation and separation. Separation recalls the line-drawing that both Langer and Todorov unself-consciously perform. Differentiation, on the other hand, can be seen as a nontotalizing process of distinction whereby differences are held together, while simultaneously a "displacement of the clear borderlines of thought" also takes place (86). The proximity in Klüger's text of "borderlines of thought" to the material borders of the camps makes clear that undermining the "disciplinary" function of barbed wire means challenging not only *what* we think about the camps but the *way* we think about them.

Displacement of borderlines is not equivalent to their erasure; indeed, it throws into question all attempts at equation.[13] Pondering the communicability of extreme experiences, Klüger criticizes Gisela, her foil throughout the book, out of whose comparisons equations continually emerge — "nur wurden aus ihrer Vergleichen gleich Gleichungen" — and yet she notes that "one cannot get by without comparisons" (111). Distinction, comparison, and displacement constitute the conceptual tools through which Klüger both experiences and represents the events of the Holocaust. But if "in reality this reality was also different for everyone" (83), what is the fate of attempts to represent that reality? How can realism come to terms with such multiplicity, such displacement?

The "truth" of the concentrationary universe is that it is not one: "Behind the barbed-wire curtain everyone is not the same; concentration camp does not equal concentration camp" (83). Barbed wire is, nonetheless, not only the name for a negative rhetorical tool that must be dispensed with since it produces only equation or separation. It remains simultaneously a metonymy tied to the material conditions of the camps, a border behind which "literal" death indeed took place. And yet "literal" death cannot be represented, not only because language always has a figural side but because, as Klüger notes, "she who writes, lives" (140). The "living" medium itself gives the lie to its message of death. How does the self-reflexive memoirist—committed both to narrative and to commentary—represent "realistically" this abyss, this exteriority of death, this space behind the barbed wire curtain? How can a language that must remain ordinary portray the extreme without banalizing it?

Klüger uses at least two techniques to address this impossibility. On the one hand, she undermines the authority of experience by refusing to present her story as if it could serve as an all-encompassing origin or synecdoche for a complete narrative of the Holocaust. Describing the fate of the people with whom she had been deported to Auschwitz, but whom she left behind for another, "safer" camp, she writes: "On July 7, 1944, the remaining prisoners of the Theresienstadt family camp in Birkenau were gassed. That can be found in books. I looked it up" (139). "Looking up" the fate of her fellow victims does not mean abandoning all authority to history (what can be "found in books"), but revealing the necessary heterogeneity of both experiences and the modes or sources through which they come to be represented. Autobiography and history supplement each other without bringing forth the totality of the event. They reveal, instead, what is almost perceivable and yet which always lacks—mass death behind the barbed wire.

Extremity is not, however, only that which falls out of language, it is also what remains caught in its net—the impossibility of discourse to free itself from the demand for a reckoning with trauma. Drawing on the physical topography of Birkenau, in which various subcamps were situated adjacent to each other and separated only by barbed wire, Klüger represents a situation in which proximity and distance coexist. A brief paragraph describes the narrator and her mother's encounter with two Hungarian prisoners, victims of one of the last and most massive phases of the Nazi genocide:

> One day, the camp next to ours was full of Hungarian women. They had come directly from home, and they knew nothing yet. Through the barbed wire we talked with them, quickly, hectically, without being able to say much. I realized how far ahead of them I was with my experience from Theresienstadt. There was a woman, who spoke good German, and her daughter, ap-

> proximately my age. . . . My mother remembered that we had an extra pair of wool socks, went to fetch them, and set about throwing them over the wire. I interfered, I could throw better, give them to me. My mother refused, threw, threw badly, and the socks remained hanging overhead in the barbed wire. Words of regret on both sides. Futile gestures. The next day the Hungarian women were gone, the camp stood ghostly empty, in the barbed wire our socks still hung. (123)

In this passage, Klüger mixes identification and dis-identification, familiarity and estrangement. The Hungarian mother-and-daughter pair mirror the narrator and her mother. They speak the same language, the daughter is the narrator's age, and they seem to be accessible across the barbed wire. At the same time, the throwing of the socks is an everyday gesture of care for the body's extremities. And yet the "homeliness" and familiarity of the women, and the everyday gesture of the mother, are rendered uncanny by the context — an uncanniness that helps the narrator to see her own self-estrangement through the experience of the camps. The same barbed wire whose porousness allows communication between camps also establishes a limit beyond which gestures are futile, words tinged with regret. When the Hungarian women disappear, their end can be conceived, but not represented, through a mimetic gesture. Nevertheless, their absence is marked by the socks that hang in the barbed wire. Not quite across the line into the ghostly emptiness, but no longer in the possession of the living on the near side, the socks mediate between the everyday and the extreme. The dead possess the living insofar as they dispossess them — of words, gestures, and other everyday objects.

In this scene, Klüger's text carries on an implicit dialogue with theories of realism. Auerbach's major discussion of modern realism comes in a chapter of *Mimesis* titled "The Brown Stocking." Auerbach focuses on Virginia Woolf's *To the Lighthouse* and draws attention in particular to the figure of Mrs. Ramsay, depicted in the act of knitting a stocking. What interests Auerbach about Woolf is the way that "[s]he holds to minor, unimpressive, random events: measuring the stocking, a fragment of conversation with the maid, a telephone call. Great changes, exterior turning points, let alone catastrophes, do not occur" (483). If Auerbach's account of Woolf is accurate, Klüger could be seen as taking a step beyond modern realism in bringing together — through the figure of the socks — the minor and the catastrophic. This is indeed one place that traumatic realism draws on and deviates from the traditionally understood realist project.[14]

As victims of extremity, the dead cannot be the objects of an everyday realism, because they embody "something more real than the reality we ordinarily inhabit" (Hartman, "Traumatic Knowledge," 542). They are, instead, traumatically real. Indeed, the extreme, as Klüger has narrated it and I have described it thus far, bears a strong resemblance to the Lacanian notion of the real, as characterized by Slavoj Zizek: "[I]t is impossible to *occupy* its position. But, Lacan adds, it is even more difficult simply to *avoid* it. One cannot *attain* it, but one also cannot *escape* it" (156; emphasis in original). In a subsection of *The Return of the Real,* Hal Foster has drawn on this understanding of Lacan to describe an aesthetic of "traumatic realism." Foster uses this concept of the real to supplement readings of contemporary neo-avant-garde art, especially those of the work of Andy Warhol, as either purely simulacral or purely referential (130). In Foster's fine reading, Warhol's repetitive images of accidents both "*screen* the real understood as traumatic" and *point* to the real that "*ruptures* the screen of repetition" (132). The repetition produces a paradoxical situation much like that described by Zizek: "[W]e seem almost to touch the real, which the repetition of images at once distances and rushes toward us" (136). The notion of traumatic realism I develop by way of Klüger has a similar double relationship to the real. The barbed wire serves as a version of the Lacanian screen, which seems both to offer access to the real and to frustrate attempts to "touch" it; the socks provide a condensation of this doubleness. Yet if the extreme bears a strong resemblance to the real in *weiter leben,* it does not equal it, and neither can it be equated with trauma — the relationship is more complex and demands further differentiation.

Unlike the barbed wire curtain of the postwar world — which attempts to avoid the traumatically real by separating now and then, us and them, the extraordinary and the banal — Klüger's barbed wire occupies an intermediary space and reveals a tangled legacy of differentiation from which it is impossible to extricate oneself. This is the space of the camp as borderland. The story of the Hungarian women illustrates how, even in Birkenau, in the middle of the concentrationary universe, the relation between extremity and normality is constantly being displaced according to position and perspective: while situated within the shadow of the crematorium, the narrator and her mother find themselves, incredibly, on this side of extremity and returned to a caretaking, everyday role. Although it is produced from within the ordinary, the extreme remains an outside limit, always situated on the other side of the fence. When we try to grab hold of the extreme with language, as in testimony, history, or other genres committed to some notion of realism and reference, it slips away, leaving the grounds "ghostly empty." When we try to avoid it, however, it returns, or rather, reveals that it was there all along, like socks caught in barbed wire.

This contradictory quality of the extreme, the fact that it always exceeds language but always inhabits it, also constitutes its implication in the everyday. This implication represents in turn the traumatic potential of extremity. Trauma resides not in the extreme event itself but in the barbed wire that holds together and separates life and death, the inside and the outside, the familiar and the radically foreign. This understanding of trauma is slightly, but significantly, at an angle to dominant contemporary understandings, such as Foster's. Foster suggests that "a confusion of subject and world, inside and outside, . . . is an aspect of trauma; indeed it may be this confusion that *is* trauma" (134).[15] At least in Klüger's representation, however, the traumatic nature of the experience results not so much from a confusion of inside and outside, but rather from the narrator's location in the face of an unsurpassable coexistence of inside and outside, subject and world. This shared/divided place—where, for instance, Klüger encounters the Hungarians—is a place of trauma because its coincidence of opposites overwhelms the everyday structures of understanding, which nevertheless remain present.[16] As Cathy Caruth writes, trauma is not an event but "the *structure of its experience*" ("Trauma and Experience," 4; emphasis in original). This structure is one in which the event remains unintegrated into "narrative memory." This lack of integration recalls the socks that mark the crossroad of inside and outside, but also the maintenance of the boundary. It is the insistence of this seemingly banal object that poses a challenge to understanding: "For the survivor of trauma, then, the truth of the event may reside not only in its brutal facts, but also in the way that their occurrence defies simple comprehension" (Caruth, "Recapturing," 153). What is crucial here, but easily unremarked, is that the "defi[ance of] *simple* comprehension" does not simply annihilate comprehension, but rather *displaces* it. This displacement, as Caruth makes clear, derives from the fact that trauma involves both "the encounter with death" and "the ongoing experience of having survived it." Thus traumatic texts, such as Klüger's, represent "the inextricability of the story of one's life from the story of a death" (Caruth, *Unclaimed Experience,* 7, 8). She who writes lives — but she lives an other life.

Trauma theory, as it has been developed recently by Caruth, Hartman, Zizek, and Foster, among others, helps to overcome the fetishistic "separation" [*Trennung*] identified by Klüger as the denial of trauma's impact. To claim that the extreme is implicated in the everyday as a nonintegrated presence, and that this implication constitutes the traumatic, is not necessarily to claim, however, that the reverse is also true. That is, the extreme is not always a part of the everyday and the everyday is not only a place of trauma. Without this distinction, a trap different from separation emerges: equation threatens to replace comparison and differentiation. A potential risk of trauma theory based on Lacan's rereading of Freud is the collapse of distinction between the real and the traumatic — the notion, in Foster's reading for instance, of "the real understood as traumatic" (132). In my rereading of Lacan through Klüger, I depart from Foster and seek to install a rift between the two categories in order to specify the differentiated relationship between the real, the everyday, the extreme, and the traumatic.[17]

As Klüger suggests when she describes how she came to write her memoir after being run down by a bicyclist on a German street, trauma and its witnessing emerge in the context of accidents. In *The Four Fundamental Concepts of Psycho-analysis,* one of contemporary trauma theory's foundational texts, Lacan comes close to defining the essence of the real as trauma, but he also highlights the importance of the accident in the constitution of trauma: "The function of the *tuché,* of the real as encounter — the encounter in so far as it may be missed, in so far as it is essentially the missed encounter — first presented itself in the history of psycho-analysis in a form that was in itself already enough to arouse our attention, that of the trauma" (55). While it is possible to read these lines as asserting the identity of the real and the trauma, I would rather hold that Lacan presents the "missed encounter" of trauma as a particular modality of the real. It is crucial to preserve the space between the specific example of trauma and the general category of the real, as the next line makes clear: "Is it not remarkable that, at the origin of the analytic experience, the real should have presented itself in the form of that which is *unassimilable* in it—in the form of the trauma, determining all that follows, and imposing on it an apparently accidental origin?" (55). The real is always a "missed encounter," but within that category only trauma is radically "unassimilable" and "accidental."[18] To equate the real with the traumatic would be to generalize the unassimilable and thus deprive it of its accidental nature.[19] Under nontraumatic, everyday circumstances, the missed encounter that characterizes confrontation with the real does not have the status of the "shocking and unexpected occurrence of an accident" (Caruth, *Unclaimed Experience,* 6). Rather, the *méconnaissance* of the real under everyday circumstances is precisely that which is expected, and thus its potentially traumatic nature is mediated by social structures of community, communication, and empathy.[20] As that which nevertheless resists symbolization and escapes what Hartman calls "the 'pointing' or 'bullseye' pretension of language — our wish to achieve a perfect marker" ("Traumatic Knowledge," 541), the missed encounter of the real in everyday life can be a site of play and aesthetic experimentation. Under extreme circumstances, in contrast, the unexpected and overwhelming breakdown of communicative structures results in what Shoshana Felman calls an "accidenting" of knowledge (Felman and Laub, 17–25).[21]

Klüger's text makes clear that the trauma's conditions of possibility lie in surviving the accident of the extreme. In the narrator's missed encounter with the disappearance of the Hungarian women, it is not the latter who are traumatized by the extreme; they are its victims. The narrator is traumatized insofar as she lives on beyond extremity into a new world of everydayness — hence the book's title, *weiter leben* [living on]. Without the distinction between the traumatic and the extreme, the difference so crucial to Klüger between the dead and the living, both surviving victims and nonvictims, disappears. The extreme's implication in the everyday is spatial, but trauma's relationship to that place is temporal. Trauma always entails a coming after: "[T]he impact of the traumatic event lies precisely in its belatedness, in its refusal to be simply located" (Caruth, "Trauma and Experience," 9). In fact, the scene I have been describing in Birkenau is constituted by the layering of at least three temporally different moments: one in which the narrator encounters the Hungarians, one in which the narrator observes their absence, and one in which the narrator retells the story. Again, the socks snared in the barbed wire provide the link. They do not only testify to the spatial inextricability of the extreme and the everyday — they *hang* there, they persist beyond the murder of the women, and this persistence invokes the "ghostly" belatedness of trauma.

Even under everyday circumstances, the missed encounter of the real — its resistance to full and transparent symbolization — certainly troubles dominant theories of realism. It is indeed not easy to penetrate beyond the surface reality of the world to the real of the historical totality, as Lukács proposes in the Marxist tradition. Nor is the "serious treatment of everyday reality" — a phrase with which Auerbach famously characterizes the realist project — as straightforward as it may sometimes appear (Auerbach, 491). The problems with these assumptions from theories of realism become especially glaring under what I have characterized as traumatic circumstances. On the one hand, something always slips away — in this case, the Hungarian women — leaving a gap that undermines the movement from the microcosm of the text to the macrocosm of the social world. On the other hand, something always inexplicably persists as a remainder / reminder — like the socks — that links surface to depth without allowing passage from one into the other. In a sense, then, to carry on the classical project of realism in relation to an extreme event such as the Holocaust is to risk falling into what Eric Santner has called "narrative fetishism": "the construction and deployment of a narrative consciously or unconsciously designed to expunge the traces of the trauma or loss that called that narrative into being in the first place" ("History," 144). Like the fetishist, the realist attempts to use a piece of reality to convert a hole in the real into a real whole.

The writing I call traumatic realism, in contrast, seeks to bring forth "traces of trauma," to preserve and even expose the abyss between everyday reality and real extremity. That abyss frustrates the mechanisms that make up realism's conditions of possibility: the movement from surface to depth and from part to whole, the positing of a "socially shared universe of meaning" (Prendergast,

30). But traumatic realism differs from other forms of writing and art that also recognize the nonsymbolizable remainder of the real and move in the direction of nonrepresentational or nonreferential aesthetic practices. Under traumatic conditions, there is a socially shared universe of meaning, but it is defamiliarized by its inextricability from an other world: in this case, the concentrationary universe. If traumatic realism shares a distrust of representation with modernist formal experimentation and postmodern pastiche, it nevertheless cannot free itself from the claims of mimesis, and it remains committed to a project of historical cognition through the mediation of culture. The abyss at the heart of trauma entails not only the exile of the real but also its insistence. Traumatic realism is marked by the survival of extremity into the everyday world and is dedicated to mapping the complex temporal and spatial patterns by which the absence of the real, a real absence, makes itself felt in the familiar plenitude of reality. In the wake of modern and postmodern skepticism, traumatic realism revives the project of realism — but only because it knows it cannot revive the dead.

As an aesthetic bound to survival, traumatic realism meets its limits not so much in the impossibility of direct reference or transparent mimesis as in the dilemma of belated temporality — the impossibility of reviving the dead. But traumatic realism is not turned only toward the past and its tendency to reappear in haunting repetition. By virtue of its performative address to a posttraumatic context, this kind of writing possesses a future orientation.[22] The traumatic realist project is an attempt not to reflect the traumatic event mimetically but to *produce* it as an object of knowledge and to *transform* its readers so that they are forced to acknowledge their relationship to posttraumatic culture. Hence, barbed wire functions in *weiter leben* both as a metaphor for the postwar generation's refusal to acknowledge extremity and as a textual screen across which that generation is given a controlled access to the past. Klüger's self-reflexive use of the concentration camp stereotype does not allow a naturalized, mimetic consumption of the extreme, but it also refuses to accept the postmodern version of the bystander's lament whereby "we didn't know" is transformed into "we can't know." Because it seeks both to construct access to a previously unknowable object and to instruct an audience in how to approach that object, the stakes of traumatic realism are at once epistemological and pedagogical, or, in other words, political.

Chapter 4

Unbearable Witness

Charlotte Delbo's Traumatic Timescapes

Arrivals, Departures

Auschwitz and After, Charlotte Delbo's ambitious and original trilogy, which attempts to create a literary representation of the concentrationary universe, opens by engaging with the problem of the conceptual dissonance of the ordinary and the extreme. Under the heading "Arrivals, Departures," Delbo begins the first volume, *None of Us Will Return,* with the poetic prose that marks much of her trilogy:

> People arrive. They look through the crowd of those who are waiting, those who await them. They kiss them and say the trip exhausted them.
>
> People leave. They say good-bye to those who are not leaving and hug the children.
>
> There is a street for people who arrive and a street for people who leave.
>
> There is a café called "Arrivals" and a café called "Departures."
>
> There are people who arrive and people who leave. (3)

In the first lines of the volume, Delbo constructs a vision of the ordinary. Through a foregrounding of the symmetry of arrival and departure and through the repetition in the French original of that most reassuring of phrases, *il y a,* Delbo sketches the contours of everyday life. Everything is expected, everything is in its proper place, everything is normalized. And then, in the very next lines, the first hints of trouble:

> But there is a station where those who arrive are those who are leaving
> a station where those who arrive have never arrived, where those who have left never came back.
> It is the largest station in the world. (3)

The repetitive rhythm of the opening is interrupted, if not completely dispensed with, and the reassuring symmetry breaks down. The categories of arrival and departure, while initially self-contained, now flow into each other. As a result, their meanings are thrown into question: arrival is not arrival, departure is now of another order. In the next pages, the contrast becomes clear even without being explicitly named, as Delbo evokes well-known details of arrival at Auschwitz — separation of men and women, selection, the presence of barbed wire.

Because Delbo's work is cited with admiration by both Todorov and Langer — and her conception of memory in *Days and Memory* is, in fact, one of the bases of *Holocaust Testimonies* — it makes an interesting test case for the conception of the concentrationary universe. How is it that her testimony has served to buttress two such different theories? In these first two stanzas, Delbo takes on precisely the question of the relationship between the ordinary and the extreme under traumatic circumstances, which was the subject of the previous chapter. What is the relationship between those two poles in Delbo's opening? On the one hand, there is an attempt to illustrate the absolute gap between the normality of travel and the horror of arrival in the concentrationary universe. She does not attempt to represent this contrast through a radical break in diction, but through subtle modulations of style and, especially, through a revelation of the inadequacy of received vocabulary to encompass entry into Auschwitz. "Arrival" is no longer arrival, but nor has it become something else that can be given a name of its own. This is a paradoxical attempt to represent radical otherness, since its success can only be attained by a recognition of its failure. It also, however, mimes the experience of those whom it describes, who do not themselves have a vocabulary or framework for what is happening to them: "They expect the worst — not the unthinkable" (4). In not attempting to find words for the "unthinkable," Delbo succeeds in representing an aspect of the *experience* of the victims.

But there is another way to read this opening contrast that places the emphasis rather on the "ordinary" aspects of the Nazi genocide. For indeed, from a historical perspective, the train station in the first stanza could easily be *the very same station* as in the second (in other death camps, if not in the particular case of Auschwitz). One of the particularities of the Holocaust is the extent to which the Nazis drew on already existing structures — of bureaucracy, manpower, and means of communication — in order to perpetrate an extreme crime. In this sense, the relationship between the unthinkable and the everyday is parasitical: the former is built on the site of the latter, just as Delbo's evocation of the extreme passes through the language of the everyday. Far from banalizing the singularity of the Nazi genocide, this recognition of the mutual implication of daily life and mass murder heightens the question of how to think Auschwitz. The tension between inconceivable experience and explainable historical phenomenon constitutes the very material out of which Delbo's traumatic realist project emerges. Through an exploitation of that tension, Delbo produces a representation of the concentrationary universe as borderland — a zone that not only borders on the everyday world of the past but impinges on the postwar world as well. Like Klüger, Delbo helps us to move beyond the realist/antirealist deadlock in Holocaust studies.

In charting what Primo Levi called the "compenetration" of death-world and daily life, survivors, critics, and historians can mark the singularity of the Holocaust without removing it from human history and social relations. In *Auschwitz and After,* Charlotte Delbo's project is not simply empirical in nature, whatever the significance of her contribution to history or to the sociology of camp life perfected by Levi in *Survival in Auschwitz.* Her texts also possess a testimonial function that exceeds the "facts" and bears witness to what Shoshana Felman and Dori Laub have called a "crisis in truth": "[O]ur cultural frames of reference and our preexisting categories which delimit and determine our perception of reality have failed, essentially, both to contain, and to account for, the scale of what has happened in contemporary history." Against this background of traumatic crisis, of which the Holocaust is a prime instance, "testimony cannot be subsumed by its familiar notion. . . . [T]exts that testify do not simply *report facts* but, in different ways, encounter — and make us encounter — *strangeness*" (xv, 7). Delbo does indeed lead us to an encounter with strangeness, but she also suggests the need for a modification in Felman's account of testimony.

Without disparaging the reporting of facts, Delbo's testimony manages to perform a double function: it maps the way that the radical strangeness of the concentrationary universe opens onto the familiarity of the known world; and at the same time, it forces a recognition that the familiar categories and frameworks available for the accomplishment of such a task need themselves to be estranged through a confrontation with the impossibility of a full witnessing of the experiences of the Holocaust. These two functions correspond respectively to the desire to capture the everydayness of an event historically and to index its experiential extremity. Delbo's accomplishment of such a double task is in turn made possible by another realm: that of the literary, the site of the representation of the chronotope *Auschwitz and After.*

A reading of Delbo attentive to this doubleness is necessary because most literary critical responses have stressed experiential extremity at the expense of a full engagement with Delbo's attention to the everyday. In *The Age of Atrocity,* for instance, Langer offers an important and detailed reading of Delbo's trilogy. As in his later *Holocaust Testimonies,* he is concerned primarily with the hermetic "experience of atrocity," which "is sealed in the moment of its occurrence, resisting efforts to establish it as part of continuous time" (*Age,* 206). There is significant evidence for such a view, especially in the first volume, which I will discuss below. In my reading, however, this "hermetic" notion of experience cannot describe all experience of atrocity in Delbo's book (unless it is defined with the same "purifying" acts I criticized in the previous chapter). The major difference in my interpretation is that I am interested in mapping the testimonial representation of the *contradictions* between the experience and history of atrocity instead of concentrating on the experience of atrocity alone. Such a shift in emphasis reveals that Delbo's text works across and through the multiple boundaries between the everyday and the extreme that define the concentrationary universe once it is reconceptualized as a borderland.

Like Klüger, Delbo offers an example of traumatic realism in which the unsymbolizable real persists within and disrupts the mimetic narrative of everyday reality. The traumatic disruption of the real is marked in Delbo's testimony by unintegrated objects like stuffed bears and stopped clocks, comparable to Klüger's socks. Even more dramatically than Klüger, Delbo invents a new form of narration to capture the trauma of genocide. While Klüger employs a conjunction of narrative and commentary in order to bring together experience and history, Delbo's multiperspectival, fragmented narratives provide a formal correlative to the unintegrated details that haunt her testimony. In these different manners, both writers can be said to move beyond the critique of the limits of representation diagnosed by Adorno and to reinvent post-Auschwitz aesthetics. The fragmentary narratives and unintegrated details of Delbo's texts should be read as *petits récits* that fill the void left after the postmodern, postgenocidal decline of master narratives diagnosed by Jean-François Lyotard. Delbo, however, does not simply reproduce a splintered, traumatic world. Especially in her later work, Delbo's version of traumatic realism seeks to produce a new understanding of history and a new vision of community by transforming testimony into a collective project: literature becomes an archive of trauma in which the ruins of the real are collected in order to disrupt the fetishized separation of the everyday and the extreme, the individual and history, then and now.

Boundaries, Differences, Chains, and the Space of Witness

Charlotte Delbo's writing is at once intensely autobiographical and at the limits of the conventions of life-writing. Although her work generally refuses to give an orderly (i.e., chronological) account of her experiences, for reasons that will become clear, a short summary of her itinerary through the concentrationary universe is helpful in establishing initial points of reference. Delbo was arrested with her husband, Georges Dudach, in Paris on 2 March 1942; they had both been members of the anti-Nazi resistance. Delbo had returned to France several months earlier from safety in Argentina, where she had been working with the theater group of Louis Jouvet. Knowing full well the risks she ran in returning to a Nazi-occupied zone, Delbo nonetheless acted out of a sense of responsibility and solidarity toward her communist and resistant comrades. Upon their arrest Charlotte and Georges were taken to the Santé prison. In May, Georges was executed at the Mont-Valérien prison, along with other captured men from the resistance. In August of that year, Delbo was sent to the fort at Romainville, and from there was deported to Auschwitz with a convoy of 230 French women on 24 January 1943. After six months in the women's camp at Birkenau, Delbo, along with some of the survivors of her convoy, was sent to work in a nearby agricultural laboratory, Raisko, where the conditions were significantly better than in the main camp. Six months after that, in January 1944, the Nazis moved several of the French women, including Delbo, within Germany to the Ravensbrück camp. She was liberated from Ravensbrück by the Red Cross on 23 April 1945 and taken to Sweden before her return to France a few months later.[1] In the forty years between her return and her death in 1985, Delbo wrote the three-volume memoir *Auschwitz and After,* as well as plays and other works addressing both the camp experience and a variety of contemporary historical events, including the Algerian War (*Les belles lettres,* 1961) and the May 1968 uprising (*La théorie et la pratique,* 1969).

The earliest chronological moment of Delbo's experience narrated in her memoir comes at the beginning of the second volume, *Useless Knowledge,* on the eve of deportation. Returning to a moment before Auschwitz allows Delbo to mark the threshold of the concentrationary universe, while at the same time drawing attention to the difficulties inherent in performing such a definitional act. This volume opens with two short narratives, separated by a poem, set in the French prison where Delbo and her arrested comrades await deportation. In the opening chapter, "The Men," Delbo evokes the assassinations of a group of male prisoners through the reactions of the women in the prison. The period of waiting before the deaths is characterized by different kinds of performances. The women perceive that the men are suffering not just from imprisonment but from "the sting of the decline of strength and manly duty since they could do nothing for the women" (117). In an attempt to lessen the men's suffering, the women perform as if their situation was not so grave and as if their everyday virtues [*vertus . . . de tous les jours*] were still intact. This allows the men to attempt to return to their *naturel quotidien* (*Aucun,* 11). These exaggerated everyday gender roles are then literally staged in theatrical productions that the women create:

> Every Sunday, they staged an entertainment in the prison yard, which the men could watch standing behind the barbed-wire fence erected between the two quarters. All week the women were hard at work sewing and rehearsing for the coming Sunday. . . . For the men, they sang and danced, putting on a merry, carefree air. (118)

As in Klüger's encounter with the Hungarian women, the barbed wire of the concentrationary universe serves as both a mark of division and a permeable boundary through which some form of communication takes place. While the narrator recognizes these performances as "preposterous," she also notes that they succeed at times in arousing a theatrical suspension of disbelief and a "liveliness [that] occasionally seem[s] real" (118). But theater ultimately fails to forestall the inevitable. The eve of the men's executions is marked by the end of performances: "This particular Sunday was sadder than any other. The fort's commanding officer had forbidden the entertainment [*interdit la représentation*]. The men were confined to their rooms, the women to theirs" (118). The "ban on representation" [*interdi(ction de) la représentation*] — akin, perhaps, to Adorno's discussion of "poetry after Auschwitz" — is revealed here as put into effect by a Nazi prison commandant and thus becomes one of the markers that divide Auschwitz and Nazi mass murder from their prehistory.

This lack of fit between language and death is literalized in Delbo's next narrative, which describes yet another execution — this time, of four resisters "who spoke up [*pris la parole*] right in the Buci market" (131) in order to denounce the German occupation. As they take their last steps up to the guillotine scaffold on the way to death, the men begin to sing the Marseillaise:

> But after the first two words of the refrain, there are only three voices, still as even, articulating clearly all the words, then two, then one lone voice which swells and rises to the highest pitch, in order to be heard alone by all the prisoners, one lone voice in turn cut short. The head fell in the middle of a word. A word left hanging, severed, intolerably silenced. (132)

Although the victims' song is after a moment taken up by the other prisoners in their cells, that act of resistance can only be read through the knowledge that those prisoners are soon to experience death of a whole other order in Auschwitz. Executions are after all still individual affairs, and particularly in this case, there is a semblance of "logic" linking the men's actions with their punishments — from the "taking of the word" [*pris la parole*] to its mutilation. Those deported will find a much more tenuous and cruel link between everyday behavior and the degradation of the concentrationary universe. Their own speech acts, like those of the women in the previous scenario, will soon also be cut off as they move further into a world whose core tolerates no resistance and more radically removes the possibility of a full linguistic response. The "word left hanging," like Klüger's socks, promises only death.

In this outpost of the concentrationary universe, life and death still proceed according to recognizable patterns—of gender roles, resistance, patriotism, revenge, and punishment — even if such everyday concepts are pushed to the limits of their usefulness. If the Nazis and their collaborators demonstrate here at the threshold of the concentrationary world the power to forbid, suspend, or even cut language, what hope can there be for the narrator's own testimony? Delbo demonstrates her awareness of this problem by quoting immediately after the performance of the Marseillaise a newspaper article from 1960 reporting the execution by the French of an Algerian, who was also accompanied to the scaffold by singing (32). The point of this addition is not only to compare Nazi terror with colonial violence—although in this pre-Auschwitz world such a comparison still holds validity. Rather, the more important point has to do with the possibilities for bearing witness when language itself is susceptible to political violence. As Delbo writes elsewhere, pursuing this analogy: "Torture in Algeria / Men have made of my tongue [*langue*] the language of torturers" (*Mémoire,* 133; my translation). The play on *langue* as tongue and language suggests the fluidity of the movement from bodily torture to a crisis of witnessing and recalls Jean Améry's autobiographical reflections on torture as "instruction in etymology" (Améry, 33). Even for the victim, there is no pure language of testimony with which to respond to injustice.[2]

Once within the core of the concentrationary world, the question of the survival of language and testimony is heightened by the narrator's proximity to the Nazi genocide. Thus, one aspect of Delbo's work that must be taken into account if we are to use it in an exploration of that universe is the fact that she entered it as a political prisoner and not as a Jew. From the point of view of the Nazis this was obviously a radical difference, and it also had radical implications for the kinds of suffering their victims underwent. In fact, the survival rate of Delbo's non-Jewish convoy, even at less than 25 percent, was still significantly greater than that for deported French Jews. At the same time, from the point of view of individual experience, suffering and death resist such easy categorization. Whatever their diverse reasons for being sent to Auschwitz, Delbo's dead comrades and the Jews murdered in the Nazi genocide all died at the hands of the same system, and both groups make demands on our memory and conscience. Rather than disqualifying Delbo's testimony from consideration in elucidating the Holocaust, her non-Jewishness and proximity to genocide point to the importance of positionality in reconstructing a notion of the concentrationary universe as borderland.

Indeed, her work can be read in part as an elaborate account of how differences in position within that world influenced survival. The extremity of cruelty found in the concentrationary universe should not distract from the more subtle shadings of "life" there—what Levi called, in another context, "the gray zone." In her formulation of the differences between Jewish and non-Jewish prisoners in Auschwitz, Delbo encompasses both their proximity and their distance from each other, just as in her narratives of camp life Jewish and gypsy prisoners are present in various capacities but suffer a singular fate:

> Jews and non-Jews both found themselves at Auschwitz; where was the difference? The difference was great, and from the moment of arrival. Upon getting out of the train, there was the selection for Jewish convoys.... Often there was no selection: the entire convoy went to the gas chamber.
>
> Certainly in Birkenau the conditions were practically the same. Practically, but at that level the least aggravation led immediately to a greater mortality. (*Convoi,* 16)[3]

When minute differences take on the ultimate significance, the borderline between the ordinary and the extraordinary is also rendered unstable—it is "displaced," in Klüger's vocabulary. Extreme conditions result from relatively ordinary differences, which means that even the apparently ordinary may only be understandable as part of a unique universe, while at the same time that universe is not outside of history but part of a particular conjuncture of recognizable historical elements.

As example of the extraordinary stakes of ordinary phenomena, Delbo frequently highlights the role of language in the camps. Continuing her discussion of differences between prisoner groups in *Le convoi,* Delbo points out that groups of Jewish women, because they had only been brought together on the eve of deportation, "didn't form homogenous, unified groups. Mixed in with Jews of other countries, whose language they didn't understand, they encountered neither friendship nor assistance." On the other hand, for the women of Delbo's group, "Language was defense, comfort, hope. In speaking of what we had been before, of our life, we continued that before, we held on to our reality" (17). In the camps, the presence of the homogeneity or heterogeneity of languages, such as might be lived by any urban-dweller or tourist, came to play a determinant role in the prisoners' experience of the concentrationary universe and was even linked to the temporality of that universe.[4] The politically active, non-Jewish women in Delbo's group were able to preserve some modicum of *continuity* between the everyday and the extreme—which resulted in an "exceptional, unique" survival rate (17)—while the Jewish prisoners suffered a discontinuity that was at once linguistic, temporal, and geographical.

Yet Delbo's dilemma as witness to the concentrationary universe is in many crucial ways not different from that of Jewish survivors. In a famous passage from his last book, *The Drowned and the Saved,* Primo Levi meditated on the problems of testimony about the camp world:

> At a distance of years one can today definitely affirm that the history of the Lagers [camps] has been written almost exclusively by those who, like myself, never fathomed them to the bottom. Those who did so did not return, or their capacity for observation was paralyzed by suffering and incomprehension.
>
> On the other hand, the "privileged" witnesses could avail themselves of a certainly better observatory, if only because it was higher up and hence took in a more extensive horizon; but it was to a greater or lesser degree also falsified by the privilege itself. (17–18)[5]

Levi, one of the most acute chroniclers of the camps, has, of course, been chided for his excessive modesty, since neither his memoir, *Survival in Auschwitz,* nor his essays contain "falsification" of any meaningful sort. And yet Levi points to a significant and necessary gap in testimony — that of those who "did not return." This experiential hole in our knowledge of the camps is the one that works of testimony seek to fill, but it also represents the limit where they fail. Even Delbo's documentary work, *Le convoi du 24 janvier,* which attempts to tell something of the lives and experiences of all the women who accompanied her in deportation, ends with photographs of women who could not be recognized. The significance of the work of Delbo is that she inscribes those gaps identified by Levi into the content and form of her testimony.

This internalization of holes in experience represents a significant way in which Delbo's work differs from that of historians or critics such as Langer and Todorov who attempt to generalize, indeed totalize, their particular perspectives. Hers is an interdisciplinarity that points to that which falls between the totalized examples of disciplinary knowledge. If the particular version of the concentrationary universe depicted by Delbo goes under the name Auschwitz — as it also does in historical and critical accounts — she also points to the potential for "falsification" in the giving of that name. In one of the poems from *Useless Knowledge,* the second volume of her trilogy, Delbo describes Auschwitz as a "black spot at the core of Europe," "the nameless place" [*un lieu sans nom*], and "the un-named" [*l'in-nommé*] (137). This placing, or more accurately dis-placing, of the sites of death is not just a metaphorical attempt to evade the "common places" [*lieux communs*] (25) through which those who were not there attempt to evoke the unimaginable. Rather, for Delbo, Auschwitz is in essence an "un-named," uncommon place, because of the concrete experiences of some of its victims upon their arrival.

Although *None of Us Will Return* opens with a poetic-philosophical meditation on the meaning of arrival in Auschwitz, Delbo only gives an account of her group's particular arrival midway through her trilogy. At the beginning of the trilogy, Delbo had asked how one can arrive in a station where "there is no arriving.... [and] that will remain nameless" (4–5). But why does Auschwitz have no name? In the second volume she provides an answer:

> We arrived on a morning in January 1943.
>
> The doors of the cattle cars were pushed open, revealing the edge of an icy plain. It was a place from before geography. Where were we? We were to find out — later, at least two months hence; we, that is those of us who were still alive two months later —

> that this place was called Auschwitz. We couldn't have given it a name. (167)[6]

The name Auschwitz is insufficient in two senses. On the one hand, the survivors cannot give any conventional name to their experiences: they cannot map "a place from before geography." On the other hand, according to Delbo's testimony, dozens from her convoy died in Auschwitz shortly after arrival without even knowing where they were. Thus, although "Auschwitz" figures prominently in Delbo's vocabulary as the synecdochal name for the concentrationary universe, it must be read as an *im*proper name. As a rhetorical figure, it is a part that stands not for the whole, but for the hole at the center of experience.

In fact, the discrepancy in experiences indicated here by Delbo is even greater because the account of her own group's arrival is immediately preceded by the description of another arrival — of a convoy of Jews — that seems to trigger this story. That chapter begins, innocuously enough, with the description of a Christmas spent in the Raisko laboratory. While certainly melancholy, this episode seems to represent one of those "moments of reprieve," as Levi named them, during which these "privileged" prisoners were almost able to obtain an experience of normality at the heart of extremity. The festivities conclude with the exchange of small gifts, one of which, given to a young girl, is a teddy bear. This most innocent of gifts turns out to have a "terrible" provenance, which, recounted by the narrator, shatters the normality of the entire scene:

> One morning, as we passed near the railway station on our way to the fields, our column was stopped by the arrival of a Jewish convoy. . . . This is how a doll, a teddy bear [*un ours en peluche*], arrives in Auschwitz. In the arms of a little girl who will leave her toy with her clothing, carefully folded, at the entrance to "the showers." A prisoner from the "heaven commando," as they called those who worked in the crematoria, had found it among the objects piled up in the showers' antechamber and exchanged it for a couple of onions. (166)

In this small, but emblematic, anecdote, a chain of contamination connecting the murder of a Jewish girl with the celebration of a Christian holiday stretches across various regions of the camp world — from the crematoria, through the chambers and antechambers of death, into the commerce of concentrationary society. The very same process that produces an extraordinary genocide is revealed as enhancing an ordinary celebration at the "privileged" end of the camp hierarchy. In its circulation from one "little girl" to another, the narrator recognizes the bear as the carrier (bearer?) of an uncanny double heritage. In the face of the extreme, the price of normality is high indeed. And yet it is not clear that the Christmas party has been a failure, . . . except that the narrator has by chance seen the bear's original owner, an accident that ensures that the chain of evidence leading from murder to celebration will survive. From that accidental survival comes the testimony of traumatic realism — the delivery of a terrible message that contaminates the receiver with useless knowledge.

The path of the bear from arrival to circulation within the concentrationary universe embodies the metonymic narrative structure through which Delbo reveals the relationship between the everyday world of play (and, as we will see, work) and the deathworld of the camps. The metaphor of the "chain" connecting related, but different, elements proves to be crucial to *Useless Knowledge*. In the next two examples the chains once again bring together signification and death, but — somewhat differently from the earlier stories of execution — language and murder are in these cases not opposed, but fatally interwoven. The chronologically later example comes from Delbo's time in Ravensbrück and follows immediately after a theatrical anecdote — one in which the narrator exchanges a ration of bread with another prisoner against a copy of *Le misanthrope* and proceeds to memorize the play and keep it at her breast until the moment of her liberation. The next chapter opens with the prisoners in the camp workshop, no longer enjoying the narrator's literary recitations:

> Each at her place, each sitting at her machine, the seamstresses were leaning over their work [*l'ouvrage*]. The pieces [*pièces*] went from the one assembling them, to another who sewed in the sleeves, a third who attached the collar, a fourth who made the buttonholes, and the last who did the lining. A chain . . . [T]he uniforms kept piling up in spite of our slowdown, and all that was left to do was sew the shield with the double S onto the lapels. (189)

Between the literary oeuvre of Molière and the concentration camp *ouvrage* would seem to lie an untraversable chasm, and yet the machine at which the prisoners labor in their production of *pièces* [pieces or plays] is also a kind of Kafkaesque writing machine or a deadly chain of signification. Delbo demonstrates how the masters of the concentrationary universe integrate prisoners, production, and language itself into their oeuvre, forcing them all to stitch the signifier of their power.

Although the SS rules its empire absolutely, with the only survival being accidental, Delbo's conception of the concentrationary universe is nonetheless, like Levi's, open. This openness is no window allowing escape—either physically or through the imagination. It is rather the hole through which prisoners from the outside world arrive and chains of products and information circulate. Testimony can become part of that circulation, but only by virtue of a passage in proximity to death. The chapter "Lily" recounts the story of a young Jewish woman in the Raisko laboratory who became engaged to a Polish prisoner "by exchanging a few words without looking at one another, without seeming to talk, since an SS could appear at any moment and catch them breaking the law" (159). As part of her courtship, Lily daringly adds an illegal white collar to her striped uniform and goes out to walk near her beloved. "[T]o find a piece of cloth for a collar, thread and a needle, was a difficult, complex task. However, there was a human chain between the men's camp sewing workroom — where female prisoners worked for the SS — and the lab with which the garden commando had established a liaison operation" (159–60). Here, the concentrationary chain seems to lead initially back from the SS to the prisoners, as Lily produces, through sewing, a sign very different from that produced by the workshop in Ravensbrück.

Lily and her lover are never described as touching; their relationship passes through the mediation of signs, especially through the letters they leave for each other under the leaves of a pumpkin. Naturally, this was also extremely risky since "[i]t was strictly forbidden to write to the men, forbidden to write in general" (160). The persistence of writing in the concentrationary universe despite its ban can be read as a form of resistance (similar to, but less avowedly "political," than that of the Marseillaise singers), but it also establishes a chain leading to death. One day, Lily's fiancé could not come. One of his comrades delivers his letter and picks up Lily's, but then, "[w]alking through the entrance gate to the camp — the gate with a motto inscribed above it, 'Work Makes You Free' — after coming back from work in the evening, the comrade had lost the note.... An SS picked up the note, and having summoned the comrade, had taken him to the Politische where he was interrogated.... [F]or the Gestapo everything was coded, and love letters must convey political instructions" (160–61). The deadly interpretation of the SS wins out over the fragile language of love, just as the hypocritical sign, "Arbeit macht frei," is allowed to translate with perverse irony the experience of the camps. Lily's letter arrives at a destination that rapidly leads to the execution of the letter's sender, its receiver, and its bearer. And yet the narrator also learns of the letter's content and passes it on to the reader: " 'We are here like plants full of life and sap, like plants wanting to grow and live, and I cannot help thinking that these plants are not meant to live.' A man who worked at the Politische told us this" (161). The testimonial chain is not broken — only the message that it bears.[7]

Delbo's subtle juxtaposition of the two "arrivals" at Auschwitz and her chaining together of different camp "scenes" reveal a whole conception of the concentrationary universe. Delbo reiterates the difference between Jewish and non-Jewish prisoners by situating an elliptical narrative of immediate death by gas next to one of rapid, but partial, death through sickness and starvation. At the same time, she reveals this difference as essentially relational, as layered and connected, not cordoned off by an infrangible line of demarcation. Finally, Delbo situates testimony at the middle of this terrible double heritage of difference and connectedness. Material evidence remains, information circulates, and places can be given names or integrated into normal geography, but the dead cannot be revived and language itself is integrated into the process of killing and torture. How can a witness testify from within such a situation?

Traumatic realism provides a testimonial form adequate to that situation because it refuses both to supply a redemptive ending (in its focus on isolated traumatic details) and to give up on attempts to communicate the extreme (in its mapping of the openness of the concentrationary universe). In the words of Felman, "[t]o bear witness is to *bear the solitude* of a responsibility, and to *bear the responsibility,* precisely, of that solitude." At the same time, "[b]y virtue of the fact that the testimony is *addressed* to others, the witness, from within the solitude of his own stance, is the vehicle of an occurrence, a reality, a stance or a dimension *beyond himself*" (Felman and Laub, 3). Testimony gathers the remains, whether of survivors (the narrator and her comrades) or surviving traces of victims (the Jewish girl's bear, Lily's letter), in order to bear witness to a story that leads at once to death and to communication with others. Although historians (including survivors) can account for the dead, explain everything about the process of their death in the concentrationary universe, and even give that world the proper name "Auschwitz," the *experience* of those who died without knowing where they were, in "a place from before geography," cannot be told. Similarly, the weight of those scraps that do remain as the evidence of experience proves too great to be borne. Since the messenger cannot hold on to it, Lily's letter falls into the wrong hands, which are also those of the narrator, those of the reader: even its testimonial publication is a violation of the intimacy of its message. Traumatic realism produces knowledge, but not consolation.

The Time and Untimeliness of Testimony

Testimony, like the concentrationary universe, has both a spatial and a temporal side. In *Useless Knowledge,* the ruling figure of the chain helps sketch a geography of multiple and interpenetrating thresholds that runs from the black hole of the gas chambers through the various economies of camp trade and industrial production. The branching of this chain between death and the accidental survival of evidence also provides the fragile and contradictory space of witness and the traumatic realist text. As the verb in its title suggests (one of two in her oeuvre), the first volume of Delbo's trilogy, *None of Us Will Return,* concerns itself with the experience of time in the concentrationary universe. This title, like that of the play that serves as a companion to it, *Who Will Carry the Word?* negates or puts into question the future tense in order to interrogate the possibility and meaning of survival and return. In moving to the final work of the trilogy, *The Measure of Our Days,* and Delbo's last book, *Days and Memory* (whose titles also highlight time), the paradox becomes how to represent survival when return has already been deemed impossible.

Time takes on unusual significance in Delbo's description of

Auschwitz precisely because there, at the core of the concentrationary, space turns in on itself. As opposed to the chain, which provides a semblance of openness, at least to prisoners at the privileged end, the guiding metaphor in the first volume of the trilogy is either of an emptiness repeated ad infinitum ("Marshes to infinity [*à l'infini*]. An infinite expanse of icy plain" [44; translation modified]) or of a closed circle. Both metaphors use repetition to figure a universe sufficient unto itself. Toward the end of *None of Us Will Return,* Delbo describes an absurd torture designed by the SS to select out the weak to send to the antechamber of death, Block 25. While male prisoners stand ready with shovels, the women are made to run in circles, collecting dirt from the men and then depositing it elsewhere — all the while being beaten by Kapos and guards. In this situation, even language, that which is possible, is reduced to such a circular form. The narrator's comrades notice one French prisoner among the men and use ruses to talk to him: "We try to exchange a couple of words. . . . Three rounds [*tours*] are required for a full sentence" (92; translation modified). This circuit lasts for hours, during which women collapse and even volunteer to go to Block 25, and ultimately becomes a hallucinatory frenzy:

> Run — schnell — the gate — schnell — the plank — empty out the earth — schnell — barbed wire — schnell — the gate — schnell — run — apron — run — run run run schnell schnell schnell schnell schnell. A maniacal run . . . The round goes on. (94)

While the words in the first sentence appear to figure a hyphenated chain, the repetition of vocabulary and the ultimate passage from French to German, as well as the final syntactical breakdown, concretize the reduction of the narrator's world to a circle of decreasing magnitude.

When the concentrationary world becomes hermetically sealed, repetition can mean only death. The repetitive temporality of that world constitutes a significant challenge to the possibility of testimony. Different locations within the geographical terrain of the camp are necessary for testimony to arrive at the witness, and testimony would be impossible if all potential witnesses shared the fate of the victims. Similarly, a differentiated temporality is necessary to narrate the story of the camps. Traumatic realism, as my reading of Klüger suggested, derives from the paradoxes of the survival of extremity. But Delbo puts into question the possibility both of marking time within the concentrationary universe and of surviving it in order to tell. When she writes that the women "will die the next day or a day close to it" (110), she uses the concepts of "the next day" and "a day" ironically. Most of the section titles in *None of Us Will Return* consist of time markers such as those — "The Same Day," "Daytime," "Morning," "Night" — but because all orientation to the outside world has been stripped away in this isolated universe, such words cannot be attached to a referent and their repetition only emphasizes the absurdity of such attempts. Or, if they can, the gap opened up between word and referent by the conditions of the concentration camp destabilizes the semantics of time. Thus, the chapter narrating the circular dance of death described above ends with the sentences, "The sky was blue, the sun had reappeared [*le soleil retrouvé*]. It was a Sunday in March" (94). Far from representing *le temps retrouvé,* the rediscovery that this was an early spring day, which should have been a "day of rest," only heightens the difficulty of placing the narrative in relation to everyday time.

Much of Delbo's memoir takes place in an in-between time specific to camp conditions in which prisoners are awakened in the middle of the night for absurd and endless *Appells:* "when the whistle blows reveille there are still the straits of eternity to traverse between night and day" (57). Such a transformed relationship to time demands a narrative that resists narrating. In her trilogy, Delbo does not reject narration altogether, for some semblance of storytelling is essential in order to bear witness, but she dispenses with a master narrative that might tie all of the concentrationary universe's scenes together. In place of the singular *grand récit,* she collects a series of *petits récits.* The collection of micronarratives constitutes a narrative form that has strong affinities to the project of traumatic realism — the form signals simultaneously the impossibility of a seamless account of the events that make up Nazi genocide and the necessity for an accounting of its effects and affects. Traumatic realism neither fully endorses nor rejects either of the two most important elements of realism: the significant detail and the narrative transmission of events.

In one scene that illustrates Delbo's tense relationship to narrative, titled "One Day," the narrator recounts the Sisyphean struggles of a near-dead woman to climb a hill as the other women look on from the *Appelplatz.* Sensing the desperate futility of the woman's attempts — which will end in a death more terrible than the punishment suffered by Sisyphus — the narrator turns away and attempts to look elsewhere, but finds only death: "Elsewhere — ahead of us — is the gate of Block 25." There she sees a figure "wrapped in a blanket, a child, a little boy." The figure, "jump[ing] up and down ceaselessly with a frenzy," turns out, however, to be a woman. Or on second thought, she turns out to be a "female skeleton. She is naked.... She pulls the blanket up to her shoulders while continuing to dance. The dance of an automaton. A dancing female skeleton... There are living skeletons that dance." At this point, Delbo senses that the allegorical quality of her narrative is beginning to diverge from the time and space of the concentrationary universe and so breaks off her account: "Presently I am writing this story in a café — it is turning into a story" (26). Delbo's entry into the text, uncharacteristic in this volume, emphasizes that the "elsewhere" sought by the narrator in Auschwitz can only be realized outside of, or after, Auschwitz. It serves as a reminder that survival is a precondition of narration, but that for that very reason narrative traduces the time and space of the narrated events. In breaking off the story Delbo manages to ward off the possibility of its becoming a "master" narrative. Through such strategies of rupture and deliberate incompleteness, she attempts to fix the scene in the reader's memory and transmit its traumatic reality.

It is, finally, both with and against this knowledge of the untimeliness of testimony that Delbo has written *None of Us Will Return.* The text's last two lines, from which the title is taken, are posed (in the original version) on facing pages: "None of us will return. / None of us was meant to return" (113–14) [Aucun de nous ne reviendra. / Aucun de nous n'aurait dû revenir (182–83)]. Between the two lines lies a blank space. How to cross that gap between a future-oriented statement of fact and a past-conditional moral evaluation? The problem of how to understand these sentences will prove to be not so different from coming to terms with the variations and dialectical contradictions of Adorno's "poetry after Auschwitz" dictum.[8] These lines follow a chapter in which Delbo first reaches the depths of the camp experience — with a description of women who rehearse their own death — and then experiences an awakening of memory: "Spring sang in the memory, in my memory. . . . Why among all these beings have I alone kept this memory? In my memory spring was singing. Why this difference? . . . Why this injustice?" (111). In this scene, the intrusion of the everyday on the extreme serves not as a source of comfort, but as a precondition for traumatic memory: as one of the few survivors of her convoy, the narrator will feel compelled to repeat her experiences in painful testimony. No matter how impoverished [*images si pauvres*] or bloodless [*exsangue*] is the memory of normality that intrudes upon the narrator's experience, this experience of nonsynchronicity chooses her as the bearer of a witness that will become a burden of future memory.

Memory is not, however, the thing itself, and its anguish, in Langer's terms, derives also from that knowledge (see *Holocaust Testimonies,* chapter 2). As the narrator already senses with her awakening memory, her ability to narrate the experiences of those who do not return will be contingent on her *inability* to capture the language in which they were experienced. In the last lines of the memoir, immediately preceding the final couplet, the narrator fails to respond to the call of a dying comrade:

> My neighbor. Is she calling? Why does she call? All of a sudden the mask of death covered her face . . . death in her fingers that twist and knot like twigs devoured by the flames, and she speaks in a foreign tongue words I do not understand. . . .
>
> Did she call out to me? She lies motionless now, her head fallen in the dirty dust.
>
> Far beyond the barbed-wire enclosure, spring is singing.
>
> Her eyes grew empty
> And we lost our memory. (113)

If death is a flame that gnaws at the human form, testimony works through the soiled remains of the "dirty dust" [*la poussière souillée*] left behind. The inability to respond to the call of the dying, to comprehend the call, or even to know whether the call took place constitutes for the narrator the content and form of her future memory. At the same time, the unknown language of the dead will remain foreign, their experience will be voided, and they will be lost to recall. This loss is one not just *of* individual memory, but *in* collective memory.

Even when among the remains to be gathered are the last words of the dying, the language remains foreign to the uninitiated:

> So you believed that only solemn words rise to the lips of the dying....
>
> Naked on the charnel house's pallets, almost all our comrades said, "I'm going to kick the bucket.... "
>
> They did not realize that they were making the task of the survivors more difficult when they would have to report their last words to their relatives.... [S]ince they didn't expect that even one would survive they never left any kind of message. (108)

The lack of future-oriented consciousness in the victims proves a further hindrance to the transmissibility of the experience of the concentrationary universe. The only words for the witness to transmit are ones that cannot be heard by the general *vous* to whom she confides her testimony. This absence of testamentary message contrasts to the eager letter-writing of the women in the very trains that carried them from France to Auschwitz: "The train didn't move. We took paper and pencil from our bags and wrote letters.... Viva always finished with: 'I will return," underlined" (*Convoi,* 10).[9] No better testimony to the corrosion of testimony by Auschwitz than the contrast between "I will return" and "None of us will return."

But the contrast between the future tense and its negation in those two lines from either side of the concentrationary universe remains too symmetrical. The difficulty of *None of Us Will Return*'s last lines lies in the tension of the irresolvably paradoxical situation of the witness. Taken literally, "None of us will return" is a sentence that erodes the possibility of its own enunciation as testimonial memoir; in that, it is not unlike the concentrationary universe itself, which sought to curtail the future of its victims, not only physically but spiritually. Understood metaphorically, it suggests that no one can return whole; that humanity itself does not return whole from genocide; that return does not equal survival. Crossing to the other side of the page we are met with a differently modulated claim: "None of us was meant to return" [*Aucun de nous n'aurait dû revenir*]. On the one hand, this mimes the Nazi point of view, identifies the telos of their project. Genocide differs qualitatively from mass murder in that reproduction, the continuation of a "race" in the future, is targeted. Indeed, the first mention of the phrase "none of us will return" follows the description of the humiliating sterilization of male prisoners (95–96). On the other hand, the moral framework implied by the conditional form of *devoir* [should have, was meant to] suggests the unseemliness and arbitrariness of survival. As the narrator remarks, "I know then that all those who pass by [on the stretcher of the dead] are passing for me, that all those who died died for me" (67).

Barely spoken, and lying between the lines, is the fact that there would be no moral or literary dilemma if the narrator had not herself returned. The world that seemed to permit of no future and no past proved fallible, if only accidentally and at the greatest cost. This accidental release from the extreme, which does not constitute a release from the demands of the extreme, recalls the definition of trauma I developed in the previous chapter. The shift in tense from future to past-conditional registers the time lag between testimony and the events to which it bears witness. The coexistence of two temporalities suggests that time itself has become traumatic. Through no choice of her own (or, at least, not solely through the exercise of volition), the narrator finds herself condemned to live a future weighted with memory. There is therefore a performative contradiction in the last lines of the text: what it says is not the same as what it does. What the text does, as opposed to what it says, is not just to register the fact of return but also to attempt some form of communication even when it claims that the experience it relates is incomprehensible. This attempt at communication, at testimony, is above all else ethical — that is, it *should* be undertaken, even if the value of its results is far from obvious, and even if what is communicated is the very failure or limit of communication. The text manages to work on both sides of the border where Langer and Todorov stop. In other words, it constitutes an attempt at an ethical act in the nonconcentrationary world, but one that refuses to compromise that attempt by turning its back on extremity.

Maladies of Time and Space: *The Measure of Our Days* and *Days and Memory*

The first two volumes of *Auschwitz and After* delineate the possibilities and limits of testimony by confronting the potential witness with a spatial and temporal map of the concentrationary universe. In demonstrating that testimony is only possible when the time and space of that world are not utterly enclosed, *None of Us Will Return* and *Useless Knowledge* necessarily end by turning toward the troubling and uncertain question of the future, of return. Even as it asserts that "you should not speak with death / for it is useless knowledge" (225), Delbo's work extends precisely that conversation into the postwar period and unsettles expectations about the boundaries of the concentrationary universe. If history as a discipline often keeps a wary distance from memoir as a source, because of the distortions and limited perspectives of individual memory and its narration, Delbo's later writings question the possibility of understanding the concentrationary universe from a purely historical perspective. The experiences of the aftermath that Delbo collects and shapes reveal not only traumatic histories, but history as trauma, as a malady of time and space. Of course, the traditional memoir or autobiography, with its chronological or teleological frame, is no less subverted by what Delbo discovers. Thus, the problem in those later volumes becomes the invention of representational practices adequate to the aftermath. The questions are not just, "*[W]ho* will carry the word[?]" and "Can we act a play where the characters die before you've had time to know them?" (*Who Will Carry,* 309), but *How* can the word be carried upon returning? and How should people be portrayed who keep on dying as long as you know them?

The Measure of Our Days, written during the late 1960s as the last volume of the trilogy, and *Days and Memory,* published in the mid-1980s, represent a breakthrough in documentary art. They simultaneously draw on earlier oral history projects, anticipate the video archives of Holocaust testimonies that have been established since the 1970s, offer insights into the psychic world of survivors that have since been developed by psychologists, and unsettle the division between literature and history. Both works combine "transcripts" of survivor (and occasionally bystander) interviews done years after the fact with meditations and poetic texts by the author on her own experiences and on postwar history. For the most part, in the interview sections Delbo presents uninterrupted monologues by others, a format that provides access to a multiplicity of contradictory points of view, not all of which seem to mesh with the author's own. At the same time, the unnaturally long, unbroken narratives highlight the artificiality of this form of testimony, and indeed, Delbo gives no guarantee that these are literal transcripts or that they have not, at the least, been edited and recontextualized. The tension between the authenticity and the artifice of these works reproduces the lack of immediate correspondence between history, experience, and representation and bears witness to their mutual interaction.

The rhetoric of "days," which in *None of Us Will Return* testified to the warped temporality of the concentrationary universe, now also constitutes a reflection on the everyday in the wake of the catastrophe. Taken together, Delbo's work demonstrates the interpenetration of everyday time and concentrationary time both during and after the war. *None of Us Will Return* had already revealed that even when belief in survival was small it was nevertheless paradoxically a necessary prerequisite of survival: "To talk meant that we could make plans about going home, because to trust we would return was a way of forcing luck's hand. The women who had stopped believing they would return were as good as dead" (102). The aftermath was thus already a margin of existence at the very heart of the concentrationary universe, even if the women could never actually represent liberation to themselves: " 'How do you envision getting out?' . . . we let the question sink in silence" (102). The "anxiety" provoked among the women by this question implies that, upon the return, the problem of the limits of representation would prove a haunting one for those who survive.

The Measure of Our Days suggests that even in the postwar period an answer to the problem of the aftermath is not forthcoming, and precisely this lack ensures that the concentrationary universe will carry over into the present. Poupette, a survivor of Auschwitz who was deported as a sixteen year old and lost her mother and sister there, expresses the feeling of Delbo and many of her comrades, even if her memory of what exactly was discussed in the camps differs from Delbo's own:

> Returning was hard. We should have expected it. However, least of all did we think of what would follow. . . . Our flights of imagination, which soared up to wondrous, supernatural heights whenever we envisioned crossing the barbed-wire fence, stopped right there. Beyond that barbed wire, freedom lay in wait. That was all. (271)

In Poupette's testimony the barbed wire comes to signify not just physical imprisonment but the limitation on imagination and representation that simultaneously separates the concentrationary universe from the "beyond" and leads to the extension of the concentrationary into the space and time of postwar everyday life: "Once we were free and had resumed our daily lives we mourned as we had not done over there. The empty places were noted more keenly, we missed intensely those we lost" (271). In the testimonies of *The Measure of Our Days,* twenty years have elapsed since the entry into freedom, but the "empty places" of unfinished mourning continue to mark a rediscovered everyday life.

The persistence of the concentrationary universe shows itself in what I call maladies of time and space. The unsettling of spatiotemporal boundaries documented by Delbo's work serves as evidence not only of psychological traumatization but of the failure of ordinary society to respond to the message borne by survivors and of postwar history to alter its course accordingly. In her own voice, Delbo writes of her failed attempts to make nonsurvivors understand "the difference between our time here and time over there, between time over there, which was empty yet heavy with all the dead, ... and the time over here, which is hollow" (343–44). Most troublesome about this difference for many of the survivors is the coexistence of the two temporalities that they experience and the self-splitting that that layering entails.[10] As Ida, a Jewish survivor, reports, "I was double and unable to meld the two parts of me into one. There was a ghost inside me wanting to adhere to its double yet unable to do so" (299). The ghost [here, *spectre,* but also *revenant*] who haunts Ida is a sign of a trauma that is temporal in two senses: it returns without warning, thereby upsetting the continuity of everyday time, and it seems to derive from a rupture of generational continuity.

After struggling to establish herself upon her return, Ida and her husband have a child: "We were wild with joy.... And then I don't know what happened to me. *One day* [*Un jour*], just when everything was going well ... I was seized with an insurmountable anguish. My throat was choking, an iron hoop crushing my chest, my heart was smothering me" (298; emphasis added). This alteration between contentedness and anguish becomes the dominant motif of Ida's life as the crisis repeats itself in uncontrollable fashion: "There are times when I feel fine, very very well.... And all of a sudden, without knowing why and how, why at this moment rather than another, without the least forewarning, I feel the same anxiety rise in me, the one I experienced shortly after Sophie's birth" (299). The randomness of these crises, which fragment time into disconnected moments, and their clear connection to reproduction indicate the extent to which the trauma has emerged out of the fracturing of the family and the continuity of generational change.

Indeed, both of Ida's parents were killed by the Nazis. Yet the traumatic event seems to lie not only in the parents' death but especially in Ida's encounter with her father in Auschwitz. This encounter is linked with Ida's description of the origin of her crisis both psychologically and linguistically. Each narrative begins with the same vague temporal indicator, "one day" [*un jour*], that connects trauma to time, but not only to historical time:

> *One day* [*Un jour*], in a column of men walking in the direction of the factory, I recognized my father. How he had changed! Old, thin, dressed in tatters. He who had always been so well dressed... You can imagine, he was a tailor. I shouted, "Papa! Papa! It's Ida! Ida!"... At the sound of my name, he turned around and threw a frightened look in my direction. The column went on walking. My father did not recognize me among the others. (297–98; emphasis added)

It is precisely the lack of recognition on the part of the father, as well as the radical transformation he has undergone, that constitutes Ida's trauma, distinguishes genocide from murder, and tears this event out of the continuity of everyday time. In contrast to her mother, who was deported and killed without Ida's direct knowledge, her father's fate represents an insurmountable void:

> It seems to me that I've forgotten all of it. I've only kept very tender memories of Mama: her voice, her hair, her skin.... My father... He's disappeared. So then, these feelings of anxiety that assail me when I least expect it, this ghost which detaches itself from me and wants to assume its place... I don't understand. (300)

The specter returns to fill a place that cannot be filled, just as the new generation represented by Ida's child cannot take the place of the old as it should under ordinary circumstances of generational continuity. The surviving victim is left uncomprehending. The gaps that mark Ida's narration belie the possibility of forgetting and bear witness once again to the specificity of genocide as a disruption of time. Ida's story illustrates Dori Laub's insight that trauma and its working through are *multigenerational* events.[11] Genocidal time is not contained by the barbed wire that seems to mark its limit.[12]

If Ida's narrative testifies to the death-world's ability to traumatize through an unfixing of time that outlasts that world's materiality, other examples demonstrate a freezing of time that is no less traumatic. With the fixing of time, the past is at once completely present, because trauma stops time, and completely distant, because such time is not susceptible to transformation. The most radical example of this comes in *Kalavrita of the Thousand Antigones* [*Kalavrita des mille Antigone*], published first in 1979 and then integrated into *Days and Memory.*[13] In this narrative, a Greek woman recounts to a "voyager," Delbo, how, in December 1943, the Germans entered Kalavrita, a Peloponessian village, and massacred all of the men, while the women and children were held in the village school. Much of *Kalavrita* recounts the efforts of the women to bury the thirteen hundred men, hence the reference to Antigone.

The woman's story begins by transporting the reader, along with the author, to the route that the men were forced to take on their way to be massacred: "Here it is. It's here. That's the path that they took." But if the opening lines seem to promise unmediated access to the past, the Greek narrator quickly recants:

> That isn't the earth that they treaded on. Those aren't the stones which rolled under their feet. . . . That, that was their real path. The real path is under the stairs, these gilded stone stairs that we have sealed over the real path so that its trace is not lost, so that the real path is not worn away. The gilded stone stairs lead to the monument. . . . The real path led them to death. (*Mémoire,* 103)

The villager makes an essential distinction between the victim and the outsider by differentiating between the "real path" and the path that has been constructed alongside it. It is the difference not simply between an original and its copy, but rather between two unassimilable experiences: the true path leads to death and thus oblivion, while the gilded path of the visitor leads to a site of memory. The memorial path helps the true path to keep its trace of the events of the past, but only at the cost of being radically separate from it and them.

For the women of the village, including the narrator of this story, who were alive at the time of the massacre, the separation between event and recollection is different from that of the "memory tourist." The memorial they have constructed is not for them, for there is no worry of their forgetting: "The war had long been finished, the soldiers, with their boots and helmets, had long since gone home, when the monument was erected. / So that one remembers" (124). The impersonal "one" that must remember corresponds to the visitor and the future generations, not to the collective "we" of the women whose husbands, fathers, and sons were killed. It is also only for the tourist that the war could be construed as finished, as the narrative makes clear. Nevertheless, the women neither were eyewitnesses of the slaughter nor possess in the wake of the massacre a plenitude of living memory that would make memorialization unnecessary. As in the case of events in the concentrationary universe, the story of the massacre is only made possible by a chain of testimony deriving from a fortuitous survival. Two men managed to escape from the columns of the condemned and were able to bring back the story, even if they were unable to prevent its occurrence: "They slipped, living, between the dead" (110). As with the industrial genocide of the camps, these deaths extend beyond physical annihilation, so that life henceforth is lived "between the dead":

> The memory of the country was lost with the men who fell that day.... There no longer exists anyone who remembers the way the cabinetmaker aged his oak, and there's also an entire language that was lost, the language of men's professions.... Those to whom they showed their dexterity, the companions who would have taken up after them, died at the same time they did. (115)

As in the case of Ida (and in the Nazi genocide of European Jews of which that individual case is a part), the crime against humanity perpetrated in Kalavrita disrupts the continuity of the generations, in this instance because the means of communication for the transmission of aspects of the collective memory are shattered. The willed destruction of the social structure to which this example bears witness demonstrates that the extension of the concentrationary universe into the postwar world is a question not only of the victims' and survivors' experiences but also of the process of history itself.

For the women of Kalavrita, the result of such a genocidal war on civilians is a disruption of the conventions of the mourning process, and this disruption impinges upon the very experience of time. Faced with the masses of the dead, the women found themselves "immobile. Mute. What should they do? What should they really do? For ordinary deaths, one knows. But for those ... That enormous heap of the dead. The enormous heap" (114; ellipses in original). The narrative again makes clear that the difference between genocide and ordinary death is not one of scale, but of social organization. "For the funerary toilet, everyone knows what to do. / For the burial ... The gravedigger was there, dead with the others. ... And the coffins? The carpenter was there, dead with the others" (119; first ellipses in original). The problem of burying thirteen hundred men exceeds the individual faculties, which might accomplish the "toilet," but which are rendered helpless by genocide's utter destruction of the community. "Ordinary" means for burying extraordinary dead prove insufficient when the gravedigger, the carpenter, and even the priest have been murdered together.

In improvising a communal grave for the men, the women of the village also show extraordinary commitment to the task of burying and honoring the dead: "[W]e performed for our dead all of the duties that one owes to the dead" (123). But the tale's uncanny end reveals the extent to which the standards and practices of the everyday have been destroyed, at least for the survivors of the massacre:

> Goodbye, voyager. / When you cross the village to find the road and return home, look at the hour on the clock in the square. / The hour that you will read on the face of the clock is the hour of that day. The spring of the clock broke with the first volley. We didn't repair it. It's the hour of that day. (124)

As material evidence of a crime, the stopping of the Kalavrita clock becomes a monumental index of genocide and a metaphor for its traumatic persistence. The narrator's envoi and Delbo's recording of it also attempt to transmit this trauma to the reader / voyager, who is able to read the signs of violence but is also safely on the tourist's path home — a path not so different from that taken by the perpetrators as they proceeded home unscathed. The narrator's trauma lies in part in the recognition of this tension between the rupture of home and time in the village and the continuity that will finally bury the traces of the dead. That different times and places coexist can itself be traumatic, but it also represents the only possibility for memorialization. In order for the story to be passed on, "so that one remembers," the narrator needs the voyager, even if the voyager's experience can only be the vicarious one of the gilded memorial stairs. The dilemma of the modern Antigone lies in this traumatic dialectic between the eroding passage of time, which threatens the preservation of memory, and the fixing of time, in which memory overwhelms the activities of the present.

The Measure of Our Days offers a similar example of temporal disruption, which, if it at first appears more intimately individual, opens onto questions about the social conditions of trauma. Françoise's monologue consists of a meditation on the phrase "to start life over again" [*refaire sa vie*] and particularly on the impossibility of overcoming the past: "Erase and cover with writing words that were there before. . . . It doesn't seem possible." As for Ida and the women of Kalavrita, the malady of time suffered by Françoise derives from the destruction of the family by the wagers of total war. She recounts how she was called to say goodbye to her husband, who was going to be executed in a French prison on the same day as Delbo's own husband: "When I was called that morning, something in me stopped, and nothing can set it off again, like the watch that stops when the wearer stops living" (*Auschwitz,* 348). The complexity of this image links the couple through the watch, sign of the everyday regulation of time, which when interrupted testifies not only to death but to the arresting of time in life. The "thing" inside her is not dead, but rather stopped, and therefore persists traumatically.

This temporal fixing, which prevents her from remaking or rewriting her life, also disrupts the *space* of the everyday:

> To make one's life over, what an expression . . . I returned. I resumed my professional life. I have a noble profession; I'm a nurse. Those I care for need me. It is not that I live without Paul, but that I live with the sick. Nothing forces me to leave them when my turn of duty is over. All of me belongs to them. The part of me that knows how to care for the sick is wholly

> theirs. I go back to our apartment to sleep. I still say "our place." I've never succeeded in saying "my place." (350–51; ellipses in original)

The extent to which Françoise has returned is marked by her return to her profession. But this represents less a taking up again of life than a continuous confrontation between life and death — between her *malades* [the sick] and her own "maladies." Unable to reconstitute a space of her own after the destruction of "our place" [*chez nous*], Françoise lives a continuation of the betweenness of the concentrationary universe: "I've been living so many years in a state of suspension. . . . I'm a sleepwalker" (350–51).

The traumatization of space, especially of the *chez soi* and the relationship between home and homelessness, recurs frequently in Delbo's stories of the aftermath. At the extremes are the cases of Loulou, on the one hand, and Gaby, on the other. Loulou returned from the camps with six of his comrades, but once back in Paris "each one went his way" (302). Return proves to be an isolating experience for Loulou since none of his family has returned from deportation, the family apartment has been requisitioned by strangers, and even his camp comrades have regained some semblance of postwar life (even if it is often as isolated as his). Deprived at all levels of home, Loulou finds himself first on the streets and then in a mental asylum, although he is not mad so much as shorn of the supporting structures of normalcy. When the hospital prepares to release him, Loulou asks to stay since he has nowhere to go and no money or profession. He spends the next twenty years in the asylum until he is finally tracked down by the comrade who narrates his story. Loulou's homelessness and his reconstitution of home in the benign enclosure of the asylum repeat his experience in the concentrationary universe with a difference: he continues to dwell under "free" conditions in what must be for him both a version and an inversion of Auschwitz. This evidence of Loulou's spatial malaise is connected to a disruption of temporality. As his unnamed comrade who tells the story reports, Loulou "remembers everything. He may even have better recall than you and I — for him the past is closer than it is for us — except that he feels it didn't happen to him. He has a past that is not his" (305).[14] In a manner related to but significantly different from the memorialization of the Kalavrita massacre, Loulou demonstrates that the price of memory is loss — in his case, loss of the possibility of reclaiming living space after the experience of the death-world and loss of *la notion du temps* (*Mesure,* 133), the time sense, which connects experience to identity.

While Loulou voluntarily encloses himself in the institutional universe of the state, Gaby encloses herself in her own home: "I don't go out because I feel cold. . . . Even in summer I feel cold. We heat the house almost all year. Just to go to the door to open it, look, my fingers turn white" (*Auschwitz,* 328). For Gaby, a well-heated home is the only defense against recollection that is not intellectual but tactile, sense-based: "As soon as I feel cold, I imagine myself over there. Frozen roads, frozen mud, wind, snow, snow squalls at roll call. . . . Just talking about it, as I do now, I start shivering, crawl into my armchair all wrapped up in a warm shawl. At home I feel good" (330). As a kind of second skin, the well-warmed house recalls Delbo's metaphor in *Days and Memory* figuring the radical difference between "deep memory" [*la mémoire profonde*] and "external memory" [*la mémoire externe*]: "Auschwitz is so deeply engraved in my memory that I don't forget a single instant of it. . . . Auschwitz is there, unalterable, precise, but enveloped in the skin of memory, an impermeable skin which isolates me from my present self" (*Mémoire,* 13). External memory serves as a skin that keeps the unalterably engraved concentrationary experiences at bay. For Gaby, Delbo, and for some of the others, such memory serves as a kind of prosthesis, an instrument that keeps subjects both in touch with and separate from their past. The Auschwitz self is always present, but "housed" (institutionalized, in Loulou's case) within or alongside [*à côté* (*Mémoire,* 13)] the everyday.

The risk in reading each of these accounts lies in the possibility of only seeing them as psychological testimony of individual illness. In fact trauma, like genocide, has a historical side as well, and the maladies of time and space that Delbo catalogues are social maladies that extend beyond the lives of particular survivors. Rather than pathologizing the victims, but also without minimalizing their pain, the point is to reveal the historical contexts that blocked the construction of a truly post-Auschwitz world and that prevented those who returned from working through their experiences. To reprise Ruth Klüger's phrase, trauma arises for many of these survivors because "the barbed wire of the postwar world" (Klüger, 82) represents a continuation of the concentrationary universe by other means. In the case of Delbo and many of her comrades, this postponed traumatization arises both from the uncomprehending reception of the significance of Auschwitz by "ordinary" people and from the failure of attempts to construct a utopia that would counter the concentrationary dystopia.

In Françoise's narrative, for example, there are hints that her inability to "start life over again" derives not only from a personal loss but from a larger failure of political movements to reinvent life. Part of her bitterness derives from the fact that the struggle in which she and Paul were engaged, and for which he gave his life, has failed to fulfill their hopes. Communist social revolution, on whose promise their antifascism was premised, was revealed as capable of crimes of a comparable magnitude to those of the Nazis: "Why struggle now . . . now that we know, now that the scandal has surfaced, the lie been unveiled" (*Auschwitz*, 348; ellipses in original). The revelation of Stalinist terror leaves her without the "taste for that new dawn" (350) that had inspired her life with Paul, and utopia shades into dystopia. Jacques, another communist survivor, returns from the camps devastated both by his own experiences and by the discovery that his family had been killed by a bombing attack. But the traumatic event he relates is rather the abandonment by his former comrades that he experiences upon his return because they mistakenly think he had betrayed his resistance network. Even after the mistake is admitted and Jacques is rehabilitated, his disillusionment persists: "Although I realize that in their place I'd have done the same thing — because I was also a diehard [*j'étais intransigeant*] — I can't feel the same about the comrades, not the way I felt before" (325; translation modified). For Jacques, as for Françoise and others, the new dawn offered by communism has been tarnished by the war and its aftermath.[15] The knowledge of the gulag weighs especially heavily on Delbo's later writings. Should this new dawn now come, writes Delbo in the lyric that concludes her trilogy, it could no longer mean the same thing: "now / it is called break of day / Beggar / this dawn stained by their blood" (354).

Not only the disappointment of Stalinism in the Soviet Union and French communist circles but the revelation of the *uselessness* of the concentrationary experience haunts the women. In Delbo's texts uselessness often signifies the lack of correspondence between ordinary vocabulary and narrative and the experience of the concentrationary universe. Here, it also indicates the "outside" world's refusal to confront and learn from the extreme, and thus the responsibility an unchanged world bears in abetting the propagation of trauma. For Gaby, enclosure in the protective skin of her home is an attempt to avoid the fact that the "ordinary" world has taken on characteristics of the extreme. Gaby's recognition of that slippage stops at the negative gesture of attempting to expel that world from the safe-zone of the house: "We don't have television. One sees too many horrors. We used to have it, but when it broke down Jean didn't have it fixed. It was during the war in Algeria. Uniforms, soldiers, machine guns . . . " (330; ellipsis in original). Reading the Algerian War in light of World War II may or may not be good history, but, for many survivors, a recognition that the world has not changed comes with the persistence of postwar atrocity: "Everything is the same" (263).

In Mado's words, which resemble at many points Delbo's own:

> I am not time-worn. Far worse than being care-worn is to be empty of life. . . . How can we not be disillusionized when after suffering what we suffered, sacrificed so much and held such high hopes, we see that all of this came to naught, that we continue waging wars, that we are threatened by still more cruel wars, that injustice and fanaticism reign and the world must still be altered? (260)

Mado cannot separate the emptiness of her postwar existence from the repetitive history that has unfolded in the wake of the disaster. If the last words of the passage suggest the survival of a hope that the world still can be changed, Mado quickly retracts it: "When I make these statements, I am using my reason. This reasoning self is distinct and alien from my real self" (260). The estrangement of reason itself represents the ultimate victory of the uselessness and irrationality of the concentrationary universe constructed by the Nazis. It can be argued that the possibility of finding "reason in history" — which grounded the thought of such modern philosophers of history as Hegel and Marx, and the actions of *résistants* and communist activists like Delbo and her comrades — ran aground in the aftermath of Auschwitz.[16] Not only the event itself as experienced by the victims, but also the fact that it *did not* represent a turning point in history for those who triumphed over fascism ensure that the concentrationary universe will not so quickly become a historical curiosity. It is not only for survivors that time has been fixed and space traumatized; taking the "measure of our days" means observing the deadly traces of an immeasurable past under society's path toward the future.

Conclusion: Auschwitz and After – the Nonsynchronicity of the Concentrationary Universe

As untranscendable as Mado's critique of the rationality of history might be, the context of its position in a work of testimony needs to be taken into account. Although it breaks with traditional modes of bearing witness and narrating history, Delbo's traumatic realist writing does not dispense with history or testimony as such. Instead, she fashions an ethical-aesthetic practice that maintains the history-negating "experience" of Auschwitz while insisting on historical specificity and difference, and on the overlap of the everyday and the extreme. *Auschwitz and After* works with at least three different narrative modes that capture different aspects of the concentrationary universe: *None of Us Will Return* assembles micronarratives that in their isolation reveal the spatial closure and repetitive temporality of Auschwitz; *Useless Knowledge* renders narrative as a metonymic chain that both traces and transgresses the various internal and external borders of the concentrationary universe, a universe whose heterogeneity both allows and forbids the testimonial act; and *The Measure of Our Days* (along with *Days and Memory*) presents a contradictory collective of individual voices that upsets the temporality of before / during / after by extending the experience and social significance of genocide beyond the death-world into psychologically and historically grounded maladies of time and space.

Throughout her works, Delbo joins the sense of solidarity that comes with political activism to the writer's openness to the singular in order to draw attention to the simultaneously individual and collective nature of history and experience. The "situatedness" of Delbo's testimony about the camps — as survivor, non-Jew, and thus "privileged" — is in no way a hindrance to knowledge, but rather the very "partial" position from which she constructs her account of the continuities, discontinuities, and internal differences of the concentrationary universe.[17] In drawing attention to the deficits and destructiveness that have followed in the wake of Auschwitz, as well as to the necessary burden of testimony, Delbo challenges readers to take responsibility for a history they have inherited, if not directly experienced. In this sense, she refuses to submit to the separation of then and now, of us and them, that, in Klüger's words, serves only laziness (82). At the same time, in her comparisons Delbo does not in any way relativize the events or experiences she describes: "then and now" and "us and them" are still useful epistemological and existential categories that both divide people and times and provide the rhetorical "places" from which "our" (nonsurvivor) knowledge of extremity begins. Delbo thus sets the stage and the terms for a consideration of bystander and second-generation responses to the "Final Solution."

Reading Delbo's trilogy in order to chart the relationships between the concentrationary universe, testimony, and representations of time and space leads finally to an understanding of the title and rubric under which this project takes place: *Auschwitz and After.* At first glance, the trilogy's title seems to tell a story of progress by means of a most reduced narrative: first came Auschwitz, then came the aftermath. The title also performs certain operations on time and space: on the one hand, it opposes the two orders by differentiating Auschwitz the place from the time that comes after; on the other hand, it asserts the continuity of space and time by temporalizing Auschwitz, making it into what Ruth Klüger calls a "timescape" [*Zeitschaft* (78)], so that a place becomes something that can come *before* something else. The title also obviously refers to the phrase "after Auschwitz," which was already in circulation by the time of the publication of the trilogy, if not at the time of the writing of the first two volumes soon after the war (see chapter 1, above, on Adorno). These resonances constitute the texts' diachronic axis and serve as reminders that historical experiences lie behind the texts, even if the texts themselves dispense with the notion of a simple chronological progression from during to after.

While a historical narrative of events is thus part of the material of Delbo's project, a reading of the three volumes demonstrates that the concept of "Auschwitz and after" is in fact not only a narrative but also, and more unusually, a double-edged chronotope: in Delbo's account, the problem of the "after" is already inscribed in the event, as much as the event persists in the aftermath. For Delbo, then, the opposite of diachrony is not synchrony or ahistoricism, but rather nonsynchronicity. Delbo filters the standard narrative form, before/during/after, through her particular construction of the concentrationary universe, not in order to flatten out time but to insist that history is always multiple and uneven. Defining the concentrationary universe as "Auschwitz and after" means looking at the Holocaust from the point of view of both the event and its aftermath and realizing that different times coexist both in the experiencing of events and in their reporting.

Traumatic realism brings together history, experience, and representation, but not in order to unite them. Rather, traumatic realism reveals their overlaps and their tensions. They come together *nonsynchronously*, in the heterogeneous spaces and times of the postgenocidal world. In the case of the concentrationary universe, traumatic realism must answer to a series of conflicting demands simultaneously. It must be there where death takes place, but it must also emerge from that place. It must bear witness to the specificity of the camp, but it must also account for its own survival and thus for the interpenetration of the extreme and the everyday or the during and the after. It must mark the radical difference between those who returned and those who did not, but it must radically put into question any homogenization or valuation of either category. And finally, it must insist on the "uselessness" of the knowledge it imparts, but it must recognize that uselessness is itself a teaching.[18] These problems are all fundamentally problems of representation. Their unavoidability for any account of the camps as a historical phenomenon or individual experience demonstrates that the question of a literature of the Holocaust is not an afterthought but an essential variable of the concentrationary universe. The traumatic realists' responses to these problems of representation build on Adorno's insights, but also make claims to new forms of historical documentation and linguistic reference. In demonstrating the significance of literature and in using literary space as a form of historical archive, Delbo, like Klüger, makes an intervention that is not only aesthetic but interdisciplinary. Attuned to the heterogeneity of genocide's events and effects, Delbo's literary practice dwells in the nonsynchronous tensions of "Auschwitz and after." It forswears the temptation of the grand narrative in order to foreground the scraps of the concentrationary universe and the disruptions of genocide: a stuffed bear left behind, a letter gone awry, a broken clock.

Part III

POSTMODERNISM, OR "THE YEAR OF THE HOLOCAUST"

Postmodernism, or "The Year of the Holocaust"

"Tonight, America remembers the Holocaust." With those words, ABC's late-night news show, *Nightline,* introduced a 28 December 1993 segment on the contemporary fascination with the events of the Nazi genocide. Drawing attention to "ethnic cleansing" in Bosnia, to the growth of the neo-Nazi movement in Germany, and to the crowds lining up for Steven Spielberg's hit film *Schindler's List* and the United States Holocaust Memorial Museum, *Nightline* declared 1993 "The Year of the Holocaust." Thinking about the logic of this odd declaration raises questions that help set the stage for a consideration of the Holocaust in the context of postmodernism: Why, fifty years after the murder of Jews in the camps of central and eastern Europe, does the Holocaust still prove worthy of network television coverage? What could the ongoing American and European obsession with the memory and history of those events possibly mean at a moment when diagnoses of collective amnesia by postmodern theorists also abound?[1] Finally, what do different texts and sites of mass-cultural memory, such as *Nightline, Schindler's List,* and the Holocaust museum, tell us about the contemporary status of Holocaust memory and representation and about representation in general?

The *Nightline* segment helps to clarify the transformation of the currency of the Holocaust presently taking place in mass culture, but it also draws our attention to a persistent demand in representations of extremity for an account of the medium and economics of representation — for an account, in short, of representation's status as public knowledge. On the most immediate level, the program creates a constellation by harnessing the past to the present. In almost direct opposition to the "after Auschwitz" chronotopes constructed by Adorno and Blanchot, however, which assume that the past maintains an unredeemed claim on the present and future,

"The Year of the Holocaust" collapses a historical event into the present. As the content of the show makes clear, this slogan does not refer to 1942, when Heydrich announced the Final Solution to fellow Nazi leaders at the Wannsee Conference; nor does it refer to the eleven-month period between March 1942 and February 1943 when, according to historians, over 50 percent of Jews who would die in the Holocaust were exterminated (Browning, *Ordinary Men*, xv). According to the logic of the show's introduction and contextualization (which is not necessarily wrong), the contemporaneity of the Holocaust lies both in its potential repetition in the genocidal war in Bosnia and in the active consumption of its images and history by the public. Living in "The Year of the Holocaust" means blindly repeating the past or consuming horror via simulation. It was the coexistence of ethnic violence and historical knowledge of the Nazi genocide with the actuality of video technology and an increasingly integrated global communications industry — the CNN-effect — that made 1993 the year the world / America remembered, or at least watched, a new Holocaust.

In order to grasp the specificity of the postmodern demand on representation, it is worth considering the structure of the medium most indicative of postmodernity: television.[2] The televisual medium of broadcasting coordinates *Nightline*'s temporal claims with an appropriate "space" and thus answers the questions: Where is it "The Year of the Holocaust," and how does America remember "tonight"? The work of Raymond Williams on television as a form of broadcasting helps to clarify the specificity of the medium. Unlike film, television (as well as radio) has developed as a form of communication not to a massed audience but rather to individual viewers (or small groups). This is not intrinsic to the technology, and, indeed, Williams points out, in Nazi Germany "the Party organised compulsory public listening groups and the [radio] receivers were in the streets" (*Television*, 24). Williams describes the "broadcasting model" of television that has developed in most capitalist countries as possessing a "deep contradiction" between "centralised transmission and privatised reception" (30). This contradiction underpins and legitimates *Nightline*'s otherwise preposterous claims about the relationship of one television program to national memory. The centralization of the broadcast, along with its dispersed reception, enables "America" to become, at some "virtual" level, the space that *Nightline* occupies; furthermore, the simultaneity of electronic broadcasting ensures that, if "memory" is declared the activity that the program promotes, then, yes, "tonight," America remembers.

But why does America remember *the Holocaust,* and what does memory mean when it is only authorized for one night before being replaced by some more pressing problem? In analyzing the content of television, Williams determined that "[i]n all developed broadcasting systems the characteristic organization [of programming], and therefore the characteristic experience, is one of sequence or flow." Since flow also characterizes the sequence of video imagery (as opposed to the frames-per-second of film), Williams was able to claim that "[t]his phenomenon, of planned flow, is then perhaps the defining characteristic of broadcasting, simultaneously as a technology and as a cultural form" (86). It is obvious upon recalling the synopsis of the show from 28 December 1993 that "planned flow" characterizes the programming of the Holocaust. The program creates a sequence in which contemporary and historical events are linked to advertised consumer products, other media representations (such as *Schindler's List*), and expert commentary. The associative position that the Holocaust occupies within this sequence is reinforced by the relationship between this show, all the other editions of *Nightline,* all the shows on ABC, and, indeed, on the other networks from which viewers may, with the push of a button, choose. "Tonight," in other words, refers to a particular moment that can only be singled out with difficulty from the overall flow of television. Television, as it has developed, fundamentally alters the kind of constellation through which an event can be grasped. As Williams writes,

> [i]n all communications systems before broadcasting the essential items were discrete. A book or a pamphlet was taken and read as a specific item. A meeting occurred at a particular date and place. A play was performed in a particular theatre at a set hour. The difference in broadcasting is not only that these events, or events resembling them, are available inside the home, by the operation of a switch. It is that the real programme that is offered is a *sequence* or set of alternative sequences of these and other similar events, which are then available in a single dimension and in a single operation. (87)

Television, in Williams's argument, significantly changes the way we think about events. Within the possibilities and constraints of the televisual medium (both its technology and its social organization) the "uniqueness" so much a part of most understandings of the Holocaust is radically undermined at the same time that knowledge of the event reaches a vast audience. To represent the Holocaust as one element in a "set of sequences" does not so much relativize the event as dissolve it in the flow of networks and channels. Even the dramatic declaration of "The Year of the Holocaust," which seems to establish a link of remembrance between the past and a substantial duration in the present, is only the citation of a fixed code ("The Year of the . . . ") whose meaning is not the durability of memory but its ephemeral quality in the public sphere. While network television can tolerate a variety of spatiotemporal configurations, the sequential model of fast-cutting and sound-bite analysis exemplified by the *Nightline* segment is certainly the dominant mode of news programming—a mode in which memory of the Holocaust does not stand much chance to emerge or persist in its specificity. Ironically, however, other "texts" that share aspects of *Nightline*'s logic may make a more lasting contribution to knowledge of the Nazi genocide. And, indeed, the way that *Nightline* condenses and reveals the salient material and political conditions of representation teaches us something that Adorno and Blanchot never address: that there are possibilities for knowledge even in the most commodified zones of culture.

In the final two chapters, I consider the significance of recent attempts to popularize and "Americanize" understanding of the Holocaust by situating them within the framework of "The Year of the Holocaust," a framework that implies the conjuncture of new communications technologies, conflictual contemporary politics, the mass-marketing of genocide, and the obsession with traumatic memories. Moving between genres, media, and discourses I chart the contours of the Holocaust's intensified presence in contemporary culture. At the same time, I suggest that it is not only *new* technologies and *contemporary* politics that affect understandings of the Holocaust. "The Year of the Holocaust" makes evident that media, technologies, and economics always frame acts of representation—that they are always lurking behind artists and their subjects, like the smiling Mickey Mouse face in Spiegelman's drawing. Likewise, if much ink has been spilled on the "Americanization" of the Holocaust, it becomes clear that there has been a parallel process of "Europeanization" by critics of modernity such as Adorno, Bauman, and Arendt, who lay the blame for the genocide at the feet not of the Germans (à la Goldhagen) but of western European modernity.

The recent fascination and obsession with the memory and aftereffects of events now more than fifty years old are not the same as the "new discourse" of Nazism provocatively explored and critiqued by Saul Friedlander in *Reflections of Nazism.* Writing at the beginning of the 1980s, Friedlander argued that although political and socioeconomic conditions had changed drastically from the interwar period, aspects of the psychological dimension of Nazism persisted after the war and started to reemerge in culture produced from the late 1960s on: "Nazism's attraction lay less in any explicit ideology than in the power of emotions, images, and phantasms" (14). Such a formulation was crucial to the emerging cultural studies of fascism and the Holocaust because it brought the question of representation to the fore. However, Friedlander's "criterion of uneasiness" (20), by which he grouped texts into the "new discourse," tended also to homogenize a variety of different approaches and to imply the existence of objective limits to representation that ought not to be transgressed but that were never substantiated. Friedlander, in short, simultaneously opened up the study of popular cultural representations of the Holocaust and Nazism and sought to police the production of such representations.

In any case, whether or not Friedlander was correct that films such as *Lili Marleen, The Damned,* and *Hitler: A Film from Germany* represent a troubling and dangerous flirtation with the attractions of Nazism, they certainly suggest a libidinal investment in the trappings and aesthetics of National Socialism, an investment that a decade or two later already seems dated. Such an ambivalent mode of "coming to terms" with history may not have fully disappeared, but from the vantage point of the present, it no longer constitutes the dominant engagement with the Nazi past (despite the growth of the various European neo-Nazi movements). This does not imply that the demons have been exorcised, but rather that the historical conditions of the imagination of the past are in the process of shifting. Many contemporary representations focus a simultaneous identification with the victims and "liberators" (usually, but not always, represented as American or embodying American ideals). The "styles or atmospheres" of Philip Roth's novels, Art Spiegelman's comic strips, Steven Spielberg's blockbuster film *Schindler's List,* or the permanent exhibit of the United States Holocaust Memorial Museum — the subjects of my final two chapters — share hardly at all in the "modes of fascination with kitsch and death" that Friedlander details in *Reflections of Nazism* (22). Rather, they shift the terrain of Holocaust discourse into an American imaginative space / time peopled by victims / survivors and heroes / liberators (however ironized these figures are in Roth and Spiegelman and regardless of where the stories actually take place). The producers of these representations tend to come from what Marianne Hirsch has called the generational space of "postmemory" — people haunted not by their own memories but by the memories they have inherited from their families, or (in my extension of the concept) from the culture at large. This new "new discourse" also indicates and corresponds to a shift in global cultural power from the European-dominated discourses of the critical theorists to the hegemony of American popular culture, all in an era in which the power of the United States is at once uncontested and on the decline.

One of the central paradoxes of postmodernism is the coexistence of an obsession with trauma — what Mark Seltzer calls "wound culture" and Hal Foster names "the return of the real" — with a sense that trauma has lost its disruptive edge. If the confrontation with extremity produced reformulations of the aesthetics and epistemologies of realism and modernism, it is not clear to me that a concept of "traumatic postmodernism" is needed or would make sense. On the one hand, postmodernism is precisely what remains after the wounding of the referential and metahistorical claims of the other moments. On the other hand, dominantly postmodern practices or sites — such as *Schindler's List* and the Holocaust museum — often salvage an Americanized modernity over against the ruins of Europe. Perhaps this is the best reason to continue to take the questions of realism and modernism seriously — their very anachronism points to what is missing from most discussions today: concern with the referential components of discourse and with the course of history.

Chapter 5

Reading Jewish

Philip Roth, Art Spiegelman, and Holocaust Postmemory

" '*He's dying, he's dying*. Look at him. *Tell them over there*. You saw it. Don't forget.' . . . '*Remember this, remember this*.' "

— Jan Karski in Lanzmann's *Shoah*

Holocaust Pornography

In the final comic set-piece of Philip Roth's novelistic memoir about his father, *Patrimony: A True Story*, Herman Roth attempts to cajole his author-son into helping one of his card-playing buddies from the Y get his memoirs of World War II published. Philip is understandably resistant — especially as his father has regularly asked him over the years to aid other aspiring authors of books about home mortgages or annuity funds. Of course, a book about the Holocaust is different, and Philip even admits that he has taught Holocaust memoirs and briefly knew Primo Levi.

The invocation of Levi and the description of his suicide hardly foreshadow a comic scene. Indeed, Philip wonders

> if Primo Levi and Walter Herrmann [his father's friend] could possibly have met at Auschwitz. They would have been about the same age and able to understand each other in German — thinking that it might improve his chances of surviving, Primo had worked hard at Auschwitz to learn the language of the Master Race. In what way did Walter account for *his* survival? What had *he* learned? However amateurish or simply written the book, I expected something like that to be its subject. (212)

But Walter's subject and the lesson he learned in Nazi Germany turn out to be quite different. In fact, they turn out to be comic and even obscene. According to Walter, he was "the only man left in Berlin," and his memoirs are the graphic depictions of his sexual exploits with the women who hid him—quite a twist on the usual anguish of Holocaust testimonies. "My book is not a book like Elie Wiesel writes," Walter honestly remarks. "I couldn't write such a tragic book. Until the camps, I had a very happy war" (212–13). What with Katrina and Helen and Barbara, Walter's war was more an orgy than the greatest tragedy of the century.

This odd episode at the end of *Patrimony* suggests that there might be something *pornographic* about making images and ultimately commodities out of the Holocaust. It is as if the fundamental obscenity of the events themselves cannot be represented without a pornographic contamination of the person doing the representing. Walter seems to grasp this truth unconsciously and displaces it into farce; this is perhaps the flip side of Levi's, and many other survivors', ultimately tragic inability to redeem their experience by representing to themselves the meaning of the camps. We gain insight into this irony and angst about the decorum of representing destruction by considering it as a particularly, although not uniquely, Jewish question. Well before what has come to be known as "the Holocaust," certain aspects of the debate surrounding the Nazi genocide and the question of representation were foregrounded in Jewish discourse. The examples of Roth and Spiegelman demonstrate how a biblically mandated suspicion of idolatry and image-making and a cultural claim to being the "people of the book" come to constitute specifically Jewish parameters, or at least "themes," of even secular Jewish writing. Although, as Daniel Boyarin has argued, there is a greater degree of complexity in attitudes toward the image in the Jewish tradition than popular interpretations of the "ban on graven images" imply, this very anxiety about the proper place of visual representation enriches the work of Roth and Spiegelman.[1]

The framework of "The Year of the Holocaust" reworks this preexisting relationship to representation by inserting it into a context in which both the Holocaust and its mass-cultural depiction are inescapable for Jewish-American writers and artists. The conflicting impulses for and against representation "after Auschwitz," as well as the risk that accompanies the circulation of images and texts in a capitalist economy, structure the responses to the Holocaust in Roth's writing and Spiegelman's comic-book memoir, *Maus*. However, instead of taking these conflicts as a cause for silence in the face of a distant catastrophe, both Roth and Spiegelman work from within the contradictions of their situation in the American-Jewish diaspora. Spiegelman's work partakes of what Marianne Hirsch, in an effort to define the specificity of the lives of survivors' children, has called "the aesthetic of post-memory" ("Family Pictures," 27). Postmemory occupies a position between the personal experience of memory proper and the impersonal "objectivity" of history (8). Although Roth does not belong to this generation, the manner in which his writing intersects with the Holocaust demonstrates the extent to which the postmemory predicament has come to be shared (albeit with crucial psychic and historical differences) by Jewish Americans more broadly. The cultural logic of postmemory thus provides the field in which both Roth and Spiegelman engage with the Holocaust.

Their situational self-consciousness as both linked to and distant from the Holocaust — which I would propose as a working definition for collective postmemory — allows them simultaneously to transgress and to uphold the ethical injunctions related to acts of representation "after Auschwitz." In this provocative practice, they follow different paths: in his fiction and memoir, Roth frequently returns to the uses and abuses of the Holocaust but does not attempt to represent the genocide as such; in relating the narrative of his parents' Holocaust experiences, Spiegelman creates comic-book images of Auschwitz but constantly and critically reflects on his process of creation. As my discussion of Spiegelman in the introduction already suggests, *Maus*, despite its pop-cultural format, also bears a resemblance to the work of the traumatic realists. His comic book combines the pedagogical and documentary impulses of Klüger and Delbo with their desire to inscribe traumatic wounds in the text through narrative innovation. Nevertheless, the terrain of Spiegelman, as a member of the postmemory generation, is much more the present than the past, and that present includes the issues of the commoditization and technologization of Holocaust memory that are not usually central to testimonial literature. The writings of Klüger and Delbo also raise questions about the relationship between the genocide and the "feminine" everyday. Similarly, the work of Roth and Spiegelman suggests the gendered dimensions of Jewish identity and Holocaust survival as they expose consciously or unconsciously the dynamics at work in elaborations of Jewish masculinity. Ultimately, in de-absolutizing Jewish identity and the experience of the Holocaust, Roth and Spiegelman displace, but do not negate, the place of the Nazi genocide in contemporary culture. Knowledge of the event is revealed as the product of ongoing acts of representation that inevitably juxtapose it with other historical and personal traumas and with seemingly irrelevant concerns, sometimes pressing, sometimes trivial. This tendency toward serialization of the Shoah is a mark of and response to "The Year of the Holocaust."

Operation Holocaust: Philip Roth and Jewish-American Identity

The coming together of Roth's self-consciousness about representation in general and his tragi-comic recognition of the inevitable contamination of representing the Holocaust can be glimpsed throughout much of his fiction. It culminates in the metafictional pyrotechnics of *Operation Shylock,* a text published in 1993 during "The Year of the Holocaust." In *Shylock,* Roth returns to material already present in *The Ghost Writer* (1979), *The Counterlife,* and *Patrimony* (1991) and recontextualizes it, situating American Holocaust representation (including his own) in a particular historical geography.

The Ghost Writer — published one year after the *Holocaust* miniseries had almost single-handedly set in motion the media deluge of interest in the Judeocide — marks Roth's first significant engagement with the representation of the Nazi genocide. Here, Roth engages with the Holocaust as "archetype" (in James Young's phrase from *Writing and Rewriting the Holocaust*) and reveals both this archetype's phantasmatic presence in Jewish-American life and its absurd distance from the banalities of that life. The paradoxical position of the Holocaust was already parodied in *Portnoy's Complaint* where Alex's mother pronounces the word "*Hamburgers*" with the same bitterness "as she might say *Hitler*" (33), as if to suggest the equal threat to Jewishness of *goyische* cuisine and Nazi genocide. While Alex Portnoy remains an unrepentant, if conflicted, self-hating representative of "the culture of the Diaspora" (265), his alter-ego from Roth's later work, Nathan Zuckerman, attempts to mobilize the fantasy of the Holocaust as a means of modulating that self-hatred.

In *The Ghost Writer,* Nathan Zuckerman's fantasy of marrying Anne Frank serves as a means of occupying a Jewish-American identity satisfactory both to his parents and to his sense of vocation as a writer. The premise of this short novel is that Nathan, a promising young writer, is suffering the wrath of his family for having written a short autobiographical story that is "bad for the Jews." Although the transgression involves the revelation of family secrets, the shame is a public one and involves the image of the Jew in the Christian imaginary. As Nathan's father complains, "your story, as far as Gentiles are concerned, is about one thing and one thing only. . . . It is about kikes. Kikes and their love of money. That is all our good Christian friends will see, I guarantee you" (*Zuckerman Bound,* 57). Since his son refuses to renounce his story, Nathan's father asks an esteemed, if self-righteous, judge to appeal to Nathan's sense of obligation and responsibility for his maligned people. The judge writes to Nathan and includes a questionnaire to spark his moral self-interrogation that poses questions such as, "Can you honestly say that there is anything in your short story that would not warm the heart of a Julius Streicher or a Joseph Goebbels?" (63). As an antidote to Nathan's self-hatred, Judge Wapter suggests a dose of mid-1950s Holocaust culture: "If you have not yet seen the Broadway production of *The Diary of Anne Frank,* I strongly advise you to do so. Mrs. Wapter and I were in the audience on opening night; we wish that Nathan Zuckerman could have been with us to benefit from that unforgettable experience" (62). It is this therapeutic and sentimental version of "Holocaust memory" that Roth works against in constructing Nathan's Anne Frank fantasy.

The moral authority that Nathan's parents and Judge Wapter evoke involves a confusion between the situation of the Jewish victims of Europe and the Jews situated, more or less comfortably, in the United States. In response to his mother's accusations of immodesty, Nathan points out the absurdity of the judge's position:

> "The Big Three, Mama! Streicher, Goebbels, and your son! What about the judge's humility? Where's his modesty?"
>
> "He only meant that what happened to the Jews — "
>
> "In Europe — not in Newark! We are not the wretched of Belsen! We were not the victims of that crime!" (64)

But, since the foundational paranoia of his parents' Jewish identity cannot be so easily exorcised, Nathan ends up caught in the same structure of delusion. He imaginatively brings Anne Frank, the icon of Jewish innocence, to America "in the flesh"—and not just in the theatrical version favored by the Wapters. In Nathan's late-night fantasy, the mysterious Amy, assistant and lover of Nathan's idol, the great writer E. I. Lonoff, becomes Anne Frank. Having survived against all odds, Anne makes her way to Lonoff and America, where she assumes the identity of Amy. When "her" diary and then play appear, she contemplates coming out of the closet, but moved by the powerful emotions her story produces in bourgeois theatergoers, Amy decides, "I knew I couldn't [reveal myself] when I heard that woman scream 'Oh, no.' I knew then what's been true all along: . . . I have to be dead to everyone" (75). The paradox of Anne / Amy's victimization / redemption provides another figure for Jewish Americans' relationship to the Holocaust and provides the fantasy space for Nathan's comic resolution to his identity crisis—he'll marry Anne Frank! " 'Married? But so fast? Nathan, is she Jewish?' 'Yes, she is.' 'But who is she?' 'Anne Frank' " (95). In revealing the Holocaust's "usefulness" to the establishment of politically correct Jewish identities, *The Ghost Writer* exposes one aspect of the "new new discourse" on Judeocide, the ambivalent focus on survival and death that corresponds to Jewish Americans' ambiguous position as a "well-off" minority with a deeply tragic and not-very-distant history.

The desacralizing of the Holocaust in an American context—implicit in *The Ghost Writer*'s parody of sentimental constructions of Jewishness—is both present and partially forgotten in *Patrimony*, a text that also alludes to another novel from the Zuckerman series. Although the Nazi genocide itself is peripheral to Roth's memoir, the Holocaust's legacies form the background of *Patrimony* against which Roth frames the story of his father's losing battle with cancer. Roth uses metaphors that call upon both timeless Jewish themes of memory and survivorship and historically specific evocations of the Nazis. Despite the father's obstinate "survivor" mentality, Herman's tumor, Roth writes, "would in the end be as merciless as a blind mass of anything on the march" (136). This Nazi-like image resonates uncannily with a passage from Roth's novel *The Anatomy Lesson*. Here, Roth describes not his father's actual death, but an imagined version of his mother's death (a death that in reality, we know from the chronology of *Patrimony,* must have prompted *The Anatomy Lesson*). But the categories of reality and imagination become here — as everywhere in Roth's writing — hopelessly confused, since the fictional version *anticipates* the memoir. Nathan Zuckerman's mother develops a brain tumor in this 1983 novel, as Herman Roth will a few years later. Admitted into the hospital for the second time, Zuckerman's mother

> was able to recognize her neurologist when he came by the room, but when he asked if she would write her name for him on a piece of paper, she took the pen from his hand and instead of "Selma" wrote the word "Holocaust," perfectly spelled. This was in Miami Beach in 1970, inscribed by a woman whose writings otherwise consisted of recipes on index cards, several thousand thank-you notes, and a voluminous file of knitting instructions. Zuckerman was pretty sure that before that morning she'd never even spoken the word aloud. (269)

The carefully situated Jewish mother's death serves here as a metaphor for the emergence in the Jewish community of a new understanding of "the Holocaust" in the late 1960s, an understanding that testifies to the spatially and temporally displaced effect on Jewish-American identity of the extermination of European Jewry (even, or especially, for Jews comfortably situated "in Miami Beach in 1970"). The association of Holocaust and tumor, forged by Roth in *The Anatomy Lesson,* reappears in *Patrimony,* a memoir that further measures the health of the collective and individual Jewish body.

Patrimony's last line, and most frequently repeated motif, is a slogan often applied to the Nazi genocide: "You must not forget anything" (238). This line, which so closely echoes my epigraph (some lines taken from Claude Lanzmann's film *Shoah*), also occurs in the passage where Philip gives his father a bath and pays special attention to the signifier of Jewish manhood (a passage that repeats similar reflections from *Portnoy's Complaint*):

> I looked at his penis. I don't believe I'd seen it since I was a small boy, and back then I used to think it was quite big. It turned out that I had been right. It was thick and substantial and the one bodily part that didn't look old. . . . I looked at it intently, as though for the first time, and waited on the thoughts. But

> there weren't any more, except my reminding myself to fix it in my memory for when he was dead.... *You must not forget anything.*

Here, the phallic law of the father takes on the particularly Jewish imperative to "remember everything accurately" (177), a commandment metonymically linked to the contemplation of the one "substantial" organ of his father's body that resists the deterioration of time. In *The Anatomy Lesson* Roth had already connected the deterioration caused by cancer with a maternal evisceration (of body and language). In *Patrimony*—despite the holocaust of cancer and the cancer of the Holocaust—the Jewish communal body survives in and through the memory of the solidity of the father: his "substantial" penis and his "vernacular" speech, with "all its durable force" (181).

The power and ultimately the sentimentality of Roth's portrait arise from his manner of combining traditional Jewish motifs of survival, memory, and the law with a subtle evocation of the Holocaust in order to depict a particular Jewish life in the diaspora. Roth's text simultaneously exposes the potential for pornographic kitsch in his account of Walter Herrmann and then risks drawing upon a kind of emotional kitsch in the depiction of his father. Such a paradoxical stance constitutes a particular, and in this case gendered, configuration of contemporary Jewish-American identity—one in which the abuses of the Holocaust have been made manifest by years of trivialization, but in which the Holocaust still serves as the dominant metaphor for collective and individual Jewish survival.

In his most recent Holocaust-related novel, *Operation Shylock,* Roth expands the scope of his critique beyond the more intimate accounts of Holocaust memory in *The Ghost Writer* and *Patrimony.* Although published in "The Year of the Holocaust," *Operation Shylock* disrupts the surface flux characteristic of *Nightline*'s presentation by constructing an alternative topography of Holocaust memory. If *Nightline* promises thirty minutes of late-night fame for every historical event, Roth subjects such modes of publicity to a biting satire that lays bare the always tendentious rhetorical sites in which Jewishness and genocide intersect. *Operation Shylock* is a metafictional "confession" that, from opening "Preface" to closing "Note to the Reader," acts out the old paradox whereby the final claim that "[t]his confession is false" (399) radically destabilizes the entire text, including that final claim. In interviews, Roth has even asserted the veracity of the most unbelievable element of *Shylock* — the secret and undisclosed mission the narrator undertakes for Israeli intelligence. Reviewers and reporters have been understandably suspicious of this claim, seeing it as Roth's own sly engagement with the "PR" machine. Esther Fein of the *New York Times* wrote of Roth's claim, "It is an ingenious performance, as if Mr. Roth means to extend the theme of 'Operation Shylock . . . ' from the pages of his book into a book-tour interview" (9 March 1993, C18). Instead of seeking an answer to this strange literary mystery — "Was He a Spy or Wasn't He?" as *Newsweek* wondered (22 March 1994, 71) — I will argue that the uncertainty has a determinate historical significance. The oscillation between fact and fiction, which the text and Roth's claims about it set into motion, bisects other unstable binary oppositions, many of which focus on questions of individual and collective identity. At the intersection of these paradoxes of genre and identity in *Shylock,* the Holocaust's uniqueness gives way to a *Nightline*-like sequence, but one that does not collapse history into a depthless present. Instead of turning the Holocaust into pornography or the ticket to authentic and "politically correct" American Jewishness, Roth, in *Shylock,* continues the exploration of how memory and identity coalesce and come undone in the wake of genocide.

Operation Shylock is the story of what happens when the writer Philip Roth discovers that someone posing as him in Israel is attending the trial of alleged Treblinka guard John Demjanjuk and espousing in the media a theory of diasporism, which encourages Ashkenazi Jews to re-emigrate from Israel back to their European homelands. Philip, still recovering from a psychotic bout with the drug Halcion, is already planning a trip to Israel to interview Holocaust survivor and novelist Aharon Appelfeld for the *New York Times.* Against his wife's reasonable recommendation that he simply contact his lawyer or the Israeli police, Philip decides to investigate the impostor himself, whom he names, in an attempt to reappropriate his stolen identity, Moishe Pipik (or "Moses Belly-button"). Philip's pursuit of Pipik turns out to be at once a form of self-conscious navel-gazing and a path into a tangled conspiracy involving, it would seem, PLO agents, Israeli intelligence operatives, recovering anti-Semites, and various other eccentrics of uncertain provenance. At the end, in the episode alluded to above, Philip agrees to go undercover in a Mossad operation code-named "Shylock," although the details of his actions are, for "security reasons," removed.

As this all-too-brief synopsis makes clear, *Operation Shylock* is not a representation of the Holocaust; yet the text probes Holocaust memory at different levels, mapping Jewish-American identity across these modes of remembrance. At the level of plot, *Shylock* turns on the importance of Philip's and Pipik's attendance at the Demjanjuk trial. This contemporary legal staging of the Holocaust calls upon its epoch-making ancestor, the Eichmann trial, an event that first brought the continued suffering of Holocaust survivors into a public space. Formally, the text incorporates, *en abîme,* Roth's *New York Times* conversations with Aharon Appelfeld about representing the Holocaust; it also includes allusions to various other Holocaust texts, including Roth's own *Ghost Writer* and Saul Bellow's *The Bellarosa Connection.* And, as a novel of ideas, *Operation Shylock* simultaneously espouses and ridicules a post-Holocaust philosophy of diasporism, which insists that a second Holocaust can only be averted through a reversal of Zionism and a reoccupation of Europe.

Most significantly for my purposes, Roth's interrogation of identity consists of what Nancy K. Miller (rewriting Adrienne Rich in *Getting Personal*) calls a "poetics of location," a process in which he places his Jewish-American narrator at a determinate distance from the Holocaust. Roth carefully sets his novel at various temporal and spatial crossroads. He makes a point of telling the reader that upon arriving in Jerusalem, Philip stayed not in his usual guest house but "at the American Colony, a hotel staffed by Arabs and situated at the other end of Jerusalem, virtually on the pre-1968 borderline between Jordanian Jerusalem and Israeli Jerusalem" (51). The historical resonance of this location is reinforced by the restricted time and place in which most of the novel takes place:

> It felt like a May afternoon, warm, breezy, lullingly serene, even though it was January of 1988 and we happened to be only a few hundred yards from where Israeli soldiers had teargassed a rock-throwing mob of young Arab boys just the day before.

> Demjanjuk was on trial for murdering close to a million Jews at Treblinka, Arabs were rising up against the Jewish authorities all over the Occupied Territories, and yet from where I was seated amid the shrubbery, between a lemon tree and an orange tree, the world could not have seemed any more enticing. (88–89)

By inscribing history into a hotel courtyard, Roth creates a site of memory in which a series of temporal turning points — the Holocaust, the occupation of the West Bank, the beginnings of the intifada — ambiguously and allegorically structures a geographical locale and an ethnic identity.[2] Philip's particular American Jewishness is determined, this setting implies, both by his implication in the aftermath of the Holocaust and in the crises of Zionism *and* by his comfortable, tourist's remove from them. At the same time, he is caught between Demjanjuk and Arafat and is sitting safely between two fruit trees. That is, between two fruit trees and opposite Jinx Possesski, a buxom Polish-American recovering anti-Semite, the "tantalizing layer cake of female excitement" who is in fact at this moment responsible for Philip's feeling of well-being. As enticing *shiksa,* Jinx excessively embodies a gendered vision of an Edenic non-Jewish America. Her tempting location amid the fruit trees demonstrates not only the archetypical masculinism of Roth's investigation of Jewishness (there are no significant Jewish female characters in the novel), but the extent to which space and time are always articulated with other kinds of categories, including gender and ethnicity.[3]

In *Shylock,* "space becomes charged and responsive to the movements of time, plot and history" (to re-cite Bakhtin's description of the chronotope), as Roth triangulates his novel's setting between the Holocaust and different historical moments in the State of Israel and the state of American Jewry. How does Roth's narrativization of this map complicate the novel's space/time configuration? The split subject who emerges from *Shylock*'s multidimensional map ought to be fractured along so many fault lines that identity no longer coheres, but in fact it is in incoherence that this American Holocaust Jew's identity has been formed. The forward movement of the narrative is driven by a series of encounters between Philip and his doubles, thus rendering identity either repetitive or sequential. Jinx, on the one hand, narrates her life as a "tale of lifelong servitude and serial transformations" (244), but, in fact, her life history serves the narrator's tale through the conventional titillation her sexual metamorphoses offer. Philip's encounters with Demjanjuk and Appelfeld, on the other hand, raise the question of identity specifically in relation to the Holocaust.

Demjanjuk's case turns around several types of identity crisis that link the slipperiness of identity to the facticity of fascism. Sitting opposite the accused mass murderer in a Jerusalem courtroom, where he has come to find the impostor "Philip Roth," known as "Pipik," Philip finds his own identity unsettled: "[W]hen, after sorting out the dozen or so figures on the raised platform at the front of the courtroom, I realized which one was the accused, not only did my double cease to exist, but, for the time being, so did I. There he was. *There he was*" (59–60). Initially overwhelmed by the singular presence of Demjanjuk, Philip soon begins to ponder the questions of identity and identification that constituted that strange trial. If Demjanjuk is Ivan the Terrible, then how to explain his overwhelmingly normal Americanness, the way in which he "lived sequentially . . . two seemingly antipodal, mutually excluding lives" (63)? If he is not Ivan the Terrible, then how to account for the series of eye-witness identifications by Treblinka survivors? In either case, everyday assumptions about the continuity and coherence of identity, memory, and testimony break down. But are the issues raised by the Demjanjuk trial simply a metaphor for Philip's identity crisis, or is that crisis in part produced by the issues of Holocaust memory and testimony indexed by the identification controversy? Given the triangulated rhetorical map of Jewish-American identity that Roth constructs, this question may be unresolvable.

The problem is complicated further by the presence of Aharon Appelfeld in the text. Demjanjuk is not so much a character in *Operation Shylock* as he is part of an event (his trial) that locates the story in space and time. But Appelfeld, the survivor and Israeli author of Holocaust novels such as *Badenheim 1939*, is one of Philip's key interlocutors. His presence links the question of identity and the status of the Holocaust to the metafictional paradoxes of the text. The discussions of Appelfeld's novels that Roth includes in occasional long indented paragraphs are taken from a published interview. They constitute "real" dialogue with a "real" Holocaust survivor. As such, they stand in marked contrast to Philip's conversations with other characters, which consist primarily of endless monologues and which self-consciously parody a multiperspectival Dostoyevskian novel. In the published discussion, Roth characterizes Appelfeld's novels as "depict[ing] the harshest reality and the most extreme form of suffering" (85)—about as far as you can get from *Goodbye, Columbus,* or *Portnoy's Complaint.*

These dialogues about the reality of fictions of extreme suffering are, in turn, embedded in a comic novel masquerading as reality; Appelfeld's "realness," in other words, lies at the center of what Philip (fictionally) calls "these fictions about the fictions of the self-divided" (115). This proliferation of generic levels evokes what Gérard Genette, writing about Proust, called a "whirligig": "an endless discussion between a reading of the novel as fiction and a reading of the same novel as autobiography" (cited in de Man, "Autobiography," 921). Paul de Man used Genette's insight to suggest that autobiography is "a figure of reading or of understanding that occurs, to some degree, in all texts" ("Autobiography," 921). In *Shylock,* Appelfeld's "presence" facilitates the text's "autobiographical moment." This is ironic, since, for de Man, the "specular moment" that constitutes the autobiographical reading "is not primarily a situation or an event that can be located in a history, but that is the manifestation, on the level of the referent, of a linguistic structure" (922). The suggestion that that moment—in this case, the citation of a published interview with a Holocaust survivor—might be primarily a linguistic event radically throws into question the attempt to historicize the Holocaust just as surely as it renders the Holocaust's uniqueness part of an omnipresent structure. Much of the discourse of the "uniqueness" of the Holocaust derives from the experience and autobiography of those who passed through the Nazi assault. Writing about Chaim Kaplan, who left a diary of the Warsaw Ghetto but did not survive it, George Steiner comments, "metaphysically an absolute uniqueness passes from the store of human resources" when such a person dies (*Reader,* 253–54). Within the whirligig of poststructuralist criticism, the "absolute uniqueness" of "experience" and "autobiography" has been destabilized, but must they be dehistoricized? Appelfeld himself comes close to de Man's formulation when, in conversation with Roth, he claims, "[T]he Jewish experience in the Second World War was not 'historical.'" But Roth shows how this lack of historical consciousness *is* historical: "[D]ehistoricizing the events and blurring the background, you[r novels] probably approximate the disorientation felt by people who were unaware that they were on the brink of a cataclysm" (*Shylock,* 84).

Appelfeld's "uniqueness" and "realness" as a survivor constitute an alternative Jewish identity that deserves further consideration. But, at least in *Shylock,* those qualities are not there primarily as signifiers of Holocaust authenticity. Rather, they anchor Philip's identity, which is what is truly at stake, but only through a mediating process of differentiation. Roth specifically contrasts Appelfeld's experience to Philip's: "Hiding as a child from his murderers in the Ukrainian woods while I was still on a Newark playground playing fly-catcher's-up had clearly made him less of a stranger than I to life in its more immoderate manifestations" (111). That there is a parasitic relationship between Appelfeld's authenticity and Philip's American exceptionalism emerges when the "real" (fictional) Philip Roth is confronted with the "fake" (fictional) Philip Roth. When the impostor asks, "Why should you converse with Aharon Appelfeld . . . and not with me!" Philip answers by meditating on their "drastically *bifurcated* legacy":

> Because . . . of Aharon's and my distinctly radical *twoness*. . . . [B]ecause we are anything *but* the duplicates that everyone is supposed to believe you and me to be; . . . because each recognizes in the other the Jewish man he is *not;* because of the all but incompatible orientations that shape our very different lives and very different books and that result from *antithetical* twentieth-century Jewish biographies. (200–201)

The "radical twoness" of these figures doubles the radical twoness of the text's generic instability, understood by de Man as a fundamental linguistic structure. Appelfeld's realness, which derives both from his status as a historical figure and his status as a survivor, contrasts to Philip's ambiguous and "antithetical" realness, as the narrator in a fictional text and as the possessor of an autobiography that resembles the author's in its "playground" safety.

The entire text follows from the presence of the impostor Pipik and the initial doubling of the proper name, Philip Roth. The narrative generated by this improper repetition is riddled with further historical doublings that act out Marx's insight from the *Eigh-*

teenth Brumaire: history occurs twice, "the first time as tragedy; the second as farce" (*Selected Writings,* 300). Besides the account of the Demjanjuk trial as a pale imitation of Eichmann in Jerusalem, there is the strange appearance in *Shylock* of a fictional version of the diary of Leon Klinghoffer — the Jewish-American man killed in the PLO's *Achille Lauro* hijacking. Used as a ploy to recruit Philip for the Mossad, Klinghoffer's diary is meant by Roth as a farcical repetition of Anne Frank's diary (and in this sense it is also a self-parody of *The Ghost Writer*). Filled with accounts of the weather, accommodations, and sight-seeing from his previous cruises, Klinghoffer's diary demonstrates the banality of American-Jewish normalization, but also its deadly connection to Middle Eastern politics. The contrast between Klinghoffer's middle-class American travelogue and Anne Frank's girl's-eye view of occupied Europe could not be more stark, except of course that both diarists meet a fate that has everything to do with their ethnic identity. History may be farce, but it is still history.

With the proliferation of references to texts and characters real and fantastic, we remain stranded between fiction and nonfiction. This ambiguity about the text's genre needs to be factored back into the map of Jewish-American identity, which I charted above, and reintroduced into the question about the rhetorical status of the Holocaust in *Operation Shylock*. Philip's twoness, his antithetical biography, is the narrative equivalent of his spatial location at a determinate distance from the events that surround him in Israel and that echo the genocidal history of the Holocaust. Do Israel's conflicts with the Palestinians have the same status for an American Jew as for an Israeli one? Is the Holocaust real for Philip as it is real for Appelfeld?

Since the 1967 Arab-Israeli war and the canonization of the Holocaust's uniqueness, Jewish Americans of all political stripes — Zionist, anti-Zionist, and critically Zionist — have recognized Israel and the Holocaust as the twin poles of their identity formation. In "The Year of the Holocaust," various media, including print, television, film, literature, and museums, have suggested that the Holocaust is as "real" to contemporary Americans as it ever has been. Steven Spielberg's film *Schindler's List* — to give another contemporary example — attempted to simulate the experience of the genocide by filming at the gates of Auschwitz and by miming the codes of newsreel footage (see the next chapter). *Operation*

Shylock tells a different story by interrogating the narratives that have anchored American Jews to the Holocaust and by judging their status ambiguously authentic and undecidably real. Roth's "confession" highlights the multiple mediations through which the Holocaust is known and parodies all attempts at direct knowledge; it thus *increases* our distance from the events of the genocide in order to block the kind of identification that Spielberg encourages. The spatial and temporal location in which *Operation Shylock* leaves readers is not Philip's illusory Edenic setting, but rather the anxious position of living in the shadow of an event known only from a remove, an event so constitutive of Jewish-American identity that its potential repetition and the disappearance of such a possibility are equally threatening.

The Holocaust is an irreducible metaphor in *Operation Shylock*. That is, it is both a part of the plot and figurative in its presence. Just as Philip Roth's name cannot remain unique in his own text, the Holocaust cannot remain unique for Americans. *Shylock* suggests that in the postintifada, post–Cold War world, ethnic struggle and potential genocide create too much pressure to maintain the rhetoric of uniqueness, although they do not override the memory that links the Holocaust to the bodies, living and dead, of all Jews, even those raised on the playgrounds of Newark, New Jersey.

"We Were Talking Jewish": Art Spiegelman's *Maus*

> *Sometimes it almost seems that "the Holocaust" is a corporation headed by Elie Wiesel, who defends his patents with articles in the Arts and Leisure section of the Sunday* Times.
>
> — Philip Lopate, "Resistance to the Holocaust"

> *I resist becoming the Elie Wiesel of the comic book.*
>
> — Art Spiegelman, "A Conversation with Art Spiegelman"

In moving from Philip Roth to Art Spiegelman — that is, from the comic to the comic book — the motifs of survival and suffering become radically reconfigured even as the subjects of that survival and suffering (the overbearing fathers, the rebellious sons) seem so similar. Within the context of the ban on graven images and the "mystique" of the text — from which Roth derives both his pornographic ironization and his narrative sentimentalization —

the two volumes of Art Spiegelman's "survivor's tale," *Maus,* come as a particular shock. Spiegelman transgresses the sacredness of Auschwitz by depicting in comic strip images his survivor father's suffering and by refusing to sentimentalize the survivor. A phrase from Roth's memoir actually suits Spiegelman's depiction of his father, Vladek, better than it does that of Herman: "[W]hat goes into survival isn't always pretty" (*Patrimony,* 126). While Spiegelman is no Walter Herrmann-esque comic pornographer of the Holocaust, his use of coded animal identities for the ethnic and national groups he depicts certainly strikes readers at first as somewhat "obscene." Spiegelman even admits that going into a comic-book store is "a little like going into a porno store" ("Conversation"). But the power and originality of Spiegelman's effort derive quite specifically from this shock of obscenity that demands that we confront "the Holocaust" *as* visual representation, as one more commodity in the American culture industry.

For Jewish readers, the challenge of *Maus* will likely be even harder to assimilate since the experience (and the memory) of the Holocaust, even for those of us who know it only at a distance, remains, fifty years later, one of the defining moments of Jewish-American identity. Although the situation is beginning to change, Jewish identity remains relatively undertheorized, if overrepresented, in contemporary culture and criticism.[4] Those of us who occupy Jewish subject-positions thus come to the task of what that most Talmudic of anti-Semites, Céline, has called "reading Jewish" with an impoverished set of tools that might help us to examine our being in America.[5] In this discussion of *Maus* I will pursue a double-edged strategy, demystifying Céline's assumption of an essential Jewishness while at the same time demonstrating how Spiegelman brings a secular Jewish interpretive specificity to his rendering of the Holocaust. *Maus* assists us in the intellectual and political task of theorizing Jewishness because, even if it rarely addresses Jewish identity directly, it does tell us at least as much about the contemporary situation of Jews in the North American diaspora as about "the Holocaust." Or rather, it meditates as much on the production of the concept of "the Holocaust" and of the concept of Jewishness as it does on Nazi inhumanity. In its acknowledgment of and entanglement in the marketplace, *Maus* contributes to and intervenes in what I have been calling "The Year of the Holocaust." As a comic book, *Maus* mobilizes the latter's sequential logic, but, like *Operation Shylock,* it draws a multidimensional historical map that cannot be reduced to the "presentism" of *Nightline*'s narrative.

Maus critiques popular productions of Jewishness and the Holocaust not from a safe distance, but from within, in an accessible vernacular form. In his "goodbye to *Maus*" comments published in *Tikkun,* Spiegelman worries that his books "may also have given people an easy way to deal with the Holocaust, to feel that they've 'wrapped it up' " ("Saying Goodbye," 44–45). While the texts' very commodity form participates in the marketing of the Holocaust (*Maus* and *Maus II* were first "wrapped up" together in boxed sets in the 1991 pre-Hanukkah / Christmas season), they also simultaneously resist this "wrapping up." As Robert Storr mentions in his program notes to the *Maus* exhibit at the Museum of Modern Art in New York City, Spiegelman creates a visual pun on the back cover of *Maus II* that connects the stripes of his father's prison uniform with the stripes of the jacket's bar code. The text's very "wrapping" asks the reader to consider its implication in a system of economic entrapment. The self-conscious irony of this parallel between imprisonment and commodity production marks one of the many places where Spiegelman rebels against the terms of his success; such cleverness, however, reminds us that this very rebellion constitutes a large part of the artist's appeal. This paradox, which is foregrounded everywhere in *Maus,* can be read as a comment not only on the status of memory and history in capitalist culture, but also on recent debates about the possibility and desirability of representing the Nazi genocide.

Among the last *Maus* images, which Spiegelman contributed to *Tikkun,* two in particular stand out as emblematic of the dangers that the artist recognizes in mass-marketing death. In the first, which I have discussed at length in the introduction, Spiegelman draws his characteristic "Maus" self-portrait standing in front of a smiling Mickey Mouse background and gazing mournfully at a "real" mouse that he cups in his hands. The uneasy coexistence of three levels of representation in the same pictorial space literalizes the artist's position: backed by the industry but everywhere confronted with the detritus of the real. In the second drawing, the artist sits in front of a static-filled TV screen and plays with his baby daughter, who is holding a Mickey Mouse doll; mouse corpses hang, silhouetted in the background, from nooses. This drawing transposes a frame from *Maus I* (84) in which Spiegelman depicts his family (Vladek, Anja, and the soon-to-be-dead Richieu) before a backdrop of Jews hung by the Germans in a Polish ghetto. This transposition, along with the drawing of the three mice, illustrates an aspect of repetition compulsion that the work as a whole enacts. The Nazi violence lives on, with the survivor son just as much the subject and object of the terror as his father.

Spiegelman's self-portrait on the jacket flap of *Maus II* also delineates this tension inherent in the relationships between the artist, his historical sources, his representational universe, and his public artworks.[6] Wearing a mouse mask, Spiegelman sits as his desk with *Raw* and *Maus* posters behind him and a Nazi prison guard outside the window. One morbid detail stands out: the picture reveals Art's ubiquitous cigarettes as "Cremo" brand. On page 70 of the second volume we find the key to this deadly pun when Vladek refers to the crematorium as a "cremo building." Such black humor implies that with every cigarette, with every image—and Spiegelman seems both to smoke and to draw relentlessly—he does not just represent the Holocaust, he literally brings it back to life (which is to say, death). Taken together, these disturbing portraits figure forth *Maus*'s strange relationship to the ashes of the real: simultaneously haunted by the inadequacy of representation in the face of the catastrophe of history and overconscious of the all-too-real materiality representations take on through the intervention of the culture industry.

The impossibility of satisfactorily specifying the genre of *Maus* expresses this representational paradox. After *Maus II* came out Spiegelman requested that his book be moved from the fiction to the nonfiction best-seller list; but, a few years earlier, in an introduction to a collection of "comix" from *Raw,* the magazine he edits with his wife, Françoise Mouly, Spiegelman remarks that he has been at work on his "comic-book novel, *Maus*" (Spiegelman and Mouly, 7). While perhaps merely an artist's whim, I read this seeming contradiction as grounded in the specificity of the problem of representing the Holocaust, an event taken at once as *paradigmatic* of human potential for evil and as a truly *singular* expression of that potential that frustrates and ought to forbid representation and all comparison with other events.

In the wake of this singular universal, fiction and fictionalization have seemed at times irrelevant, if not sacrilegious, and at other times the only modes for imagining the unimaginable. On the one hand, critics such as Theodor Adorno, Maurice Blanchot, Berel Lang, and Claude Lanzmann have questioned the place of poetry, fiction, and the image "after Auschwitz."[7] Although their positions are extremely complex and varied, these critics have frequently been understood as proscribing artistic representations in the face of the need for testimonial and witnessing. On the other hand, the historical trauma of the Nazi genocide also *de-realizes* human experience and thus creates a need for fiction. Accounts of the death camps in memoirs never fail to document the fictional, oneiric aura that confronts the newly arrived prisoner.[8] By situating a nonfictional story in a highly mediated, unreal, "comic" space, Spiegelman captures the hyperintensity of Auschwitz: at once, more real than real and more impossible than impossible.

Yet *Maus* also replies to the debates about representation in ways that go beyond formalist subversion of generic categories and that indeed shift the terrain of the debate onto the cultural conditions, possibilities, and constraints of Holocaust representation (thus displacing the frequently prescriptive epistemologies and ontologies of the debate set by Adorno, Blanchot, and Lang). Spiegelman frankly recognizes the inevitable commodification of culture, even the culture of trauma, in "The Year of the Holocaust." In *Maus*'s multimedia marketing (through magazines, exhibitions, the broadcast media, and now a CD-ROM version), as well as through its generic identity as a (non)fiction comic strip, Spiegelman's project refuses the modernist notion of autonomous culture that ultimately grounds Adorno's position. His handling of the Holocaust denies the existence of an autonomous realm in which aesthetic issues can be debated without reference to the material bases of their production. He heretically reinserts the Holocaust into the political realm by highlighting its necessary imbrication in the public sphere and in commodity production.

My parents survived hell and moved to the suburbs.

— Art Spiegelman, sketch for *Maus*

As a primarily visual artist, Spiegelman challenges dominant representations of the Holocaust by *drawing* attention to the pornographic effect of graven images within a Mickey Mouse industry dedicated to mechanical reproduction in the name of profit. But *Maus* also operates significantly on the level of text and, in doing so, takes part in the discursive production of contemporary Jewish identity. Spiegelman makes analogies between image and text "grammar" and claims that, unlike most of his projects, *Maus* is "a comic book driven by the word" ("Conversation"). This "word" can only refer to the words of the father that Spiegelman renders not as mystical text but as fractured speech — what Roth calls, in the case of his father, "the vernacular" (*Patrimony,* 181). As he makes clear in both volumes, Spiegelman created this comic book by taping Vladek's voice as he recounted his life and then transcribing the events with accompanying pictures into *Maus.* He makes a particular point of describing the pains he went to in order to ensure the "authenticity" of Vladek's transcribed voice. Many readers have testified that much of the power of *Maus* comes from the heavily accented cadences — the shtetl-effect — of Vladek's narrative.[9] Spiegelman's staging of an exhibit on the making of *Maus* at the Museum of Modern Art, complete with the actual tapes of Vladek from which he worked, has, for most people, tended to reinforce this aura of documentary realism.

However, in a perceptive discussion of *Maus* and the MOMA exhibit, Nancy Miller has pointed to the illusion that grounds this version of realism:

> What surprised me when I listened to the tape was an odd disjunction between the quality of the voice and the inflections rendered in the panels. For while Vladek *on tape* regularly misuses prepositions — "I have seen on my own eyes," "they were shooting to prisoners" [— and] mangles idioms . . . the total *aural* effect, unlike the typically tortured *visualized* prose of the dialogue in the comic balloons, is one of extraordinary fluency. ("Cartoons," 51)

A particularly good example of Spiegelman's unconscious tendency to *overdo* his father's accent comes in a passage, featured in the exhibit and broadcast on *Talk of the Nation,* in which Vladek recounts the shooting of a prisoner, a shooting that reminds him of having seen a neighbor shoot a rabid dog. In the book, Art has Vladek say, "How amazing it is that a human being reacts the same like this neighbor's dog" (*Maus II,* 82). But on tape, Vladek says simply and *grammatically,* "How amazing it is that a human being is like a dog." This passage also contradicts Spiegelman's assertion that the changes he made were dictated by the necessity of condensing Vladek's speech, since in this case he adds words. For related reasons of affect, Spiegelman occasionally alters Vladek's words to keep up with the changing language habits of contemporary English-speaking Jews, as when he renders his father's phrase "We were talking Jewish . . ." as "We spoke Yiddish . . ." (I, 150); this subtle semantic gentrification registers the uneasiness at the heart of Jewish identities, as well as their susceptibility to change over time.[10]

Spiegelman is right: the power of *Maus* does derive from his father's words and evocative accent. But a close analysis of these words demonstrates the artist's reconstruction of a marked dialect. In *Jewish Self-Hatred,* Sander Gilman discusses the perception of Jews as possessing a "hidden" and devalued language of ethnic difference called, appropriately enough for Spiegelman's work, Mauscheln. Gilman quotes "Hitler's racial mentor, Julius Streicher," for his description of this perceived "hidden language of the Jews": "Speech takes place with a racially determined intonation: *Mauscheln.* The Hebrews speak German in a unique, singing manner. One can recognize Jews and Jewesses immediately by their language, without having seen them" (312). Arguably, an element of self-hatred exists in Spiegelman's careful "Mauschelnizing" of *Maus,* displaced into aggression against the vernacular of the father. But another reading of the linguistic manipulations of the book, analogous to my reading of the images and the animal motif, would emphasize the irony, conscious or not, that uses caricature to unsettle assumptions about the "naturalness" of identities. Self-hatred and, more obviously, aggression against the father would then become not so much qualities of the work as two of its significant themes.

The source-tape of the passage from *Maus II* about the shooting of the prisoner / neighbor's dog carries another level of significance for an understanding of the verbal narration of the story. As John Hockenberry remarks to Spiegelman after playing the segment of tape on National Public Radio, during Vladek's telling of the story the barking of dogs can be easily heard in the background ("Conversation"). Nobody, including Vladek, I would guess, could definitively say whether the dogs simply triggered the memory of the association between the prisoner and the dog in Vladek's mind or, more radically, whether the association derived from the present circumstances of the narration. But, in either case, this example points to the importance of the moment of *enunciation* in the construction of a narrative.[11] This narratological insight is not simply a truism of literary analysis; *Maus* everywhere thematizes the constitutive relationship between the present and different moments of the past. The importance of this temporal structure emerges in various facets of the work: in the constant movement between the tense interviews between father and son and the unrolling of the Holocaust story; in the second volume's insistent self-reflexivity and thematization of writer's block; and in Spiegelman's practice — in exhibit and interview — of revealing the process of "making *Maus*." With the production of a CD-ROM version titled *The Complete Maus* — including sketches, source tapes, photographs, and other paraphernalia — Spiegelman's project has become fully conversant with the techniques of "The Year of the Holocaust." The *Maus* story now takes place in the nonlinear sequential space of contemporary computer technology and poses challenges to the singular place of narration that anchors the traditional act of witness. Not simply a work of memory or a testimony bound for some archive of Holocaust documentation, *Maus* actively intervenes in a changing present, questioning the status of "memory," "testimony," and "Holocaust," even as it makes use of them.

> *Pain is the most powerful aid to mnemonics.*
> — FRIEDRICH NIETZSCHE, *On the Genealogy of Morals*

Thus far I have not differentiated between the two volumes of *Maus,* but Spiegelman's style clearly changes during the course of the thirteen years of his work on this project. While both volumes focus on the interplay of the past in the present and the present in the past, as Spiegelman has remarked ("Conversation"), *Maus: A Survivor's Tale: My Father Bleeds History* concentrates more on the woundedness and wounding of the familial body, as its title suggests. Because Spiegelman wrote much of *Maus II: And Here My Troubles Began* in the wake of widespread popular acclaim, the second volume explicitly interrogates its own status in the public sphere, reflexively commenting on its production and interrogating the staging of "the Holocaust." But, given the serial nature of their publication in *Raw* over the course of many years, both volumes of *Maus* resist such easy binaries: the form and content of the comic strip's unfolding put into question the propriety of present / past and private / public distinctions.

Maus, among its many functions, serves to catalogue "the Jew's body," an important concept in emergent Jewish theorizing that has been elaborated most fully by Sander Gilman in his book of that name.[12] In focusing on multifarious "representations and the reflection of these representations in the world of those who stereotype as well as those who are stereotyped" (*Jew's Body* 1), Gilman draws attention to the constitutive character of "difference," a category that need not succumb to the kind of binary ossification *Maus* resists. Spiegelman, like Gilman, anatomizes various Jewish bodies, including his parents' bodies and his own; he draws attention to feet (20, 83), eyes (40), hands (51), the beard (65), and the voice (throughout). Subtly, but perhaps decisively, different are the Jewish / mouse noses, understood in contrast to the upturned snouts of the Polish pigs. When Vladek and Anja walk as fugitives through Sosnowiec, Spiegelman shows them hiding their noses by wearing pig masks (as he himself will later don a mouse mask). But while Vladek is able confidently to feign Polishness, Anja's body leaks Jewishness, her mouse tail drags behind her and signals the limits of her *goyische* drag: "Anja — her appearance — you could see more easy she was Jewish" (136).

The emphasis on the body and its difference, as all commentators have noted, reinscribes the same essential ethnic differences that drove the Nazi war machine. But this discourse on the body is fundamentally destabilized by the more pressing truth about the Jewish body under Nazism that haunts Spiegelman's story: its disappearance. Richieu's and Anja's absence and, by analogy, the absence of the millions of (Jewish and gay and Roma etc.) victims underlie Spiegelman's aesthetic choice of grappling with the Holocaust as an impossible visual text. Spiegelman's story does not seek, however, to flatten out analogous differences into a morality tale of universalist pluralism, but draws its power from negativity: an intimacy with death, pain, and loss motivates *Maus*'s memory-work.

In the first volume, the multiply disappeared story of Art's mother, Anja, constitutes the primary wound around which the story turns and points to an almost erased narrative of Jewish gender relations.[13] Anja's story is absent for three reasons, all significant: her original diaries from Poland were lost in the war (indicating the immediate destruction at the hands of the Nazis) (I, 84); Anja herself cannot tell her own story because she committed suicide twenty-three years after the war (indicating the unassimilable damage to the "survivors"); and Vladek later threw out her notebooks, in which she probably reconstructed her diaries (indicating the legacy of violence reproduced in some "survivors"). *Maus I* builds toward the revelation of Vladek's crime against Anja and memory, which Art names "murder" (159). Anja's suicide and Vladek's inability to mourn her death radically upset the notion of "survival" that ordinarily legitimates the Holocaust memoir; as Art puts it, "[I]n some ways [Vladek] *didn't* survive" (II, 90). I do not think it would be an exaggeration to read this first volume as an attempt to occupy, or speak from, the impossible position of the mother's suicide; in this, Spiegelman's project resembles Claude Lanzmann's *Shoah,* which attempts "less to narrate history than to *reverse the suicide*" of many of its potential sources (Felman and Laub, 216).

Spiegelman cannot actually reverse his mother's suicide, but he does question representations of Jewish women in his careful tracing of Anja's absent place of enunciation. Such a strategy takes on further significance given the relative lack of attention paid in dominant culture to the specific bodies and lives of Jewish women, a fact that emerges in the contrast between *Maus* and the respective academic and literary discourses of Sander Gilman and Philip Roth. In *The Jew's Body,* Gilman writes that "full-length studies of the actual roles of Jewish women in this world of representations [of the body] and their own complex responses are certainly needed and in fact such studies at present are in the planning or writing stages by a number of feminist critics." Gilman goes on to assert, however, that his own work "has generally focused on the nature of the male Jew and his representation in the culture of the West; it is *this* representation which I believe lies at the very heart of Western Jew-hatred" (5). Gilman points to the importance of the circumcised penis as an index of Jewishness, but, given the tendency of the last couple of generations of North Americans of all religions to circumcise their male children, perhaps this particular symbolic structure is waning. I don't find it unreasonable to assume, for example, that in a book dedicated to "the Jew's body," Orthodox women's shaved heads or the ubiquitous Jewish mother's body would merit chapters.[14]

Spiegelman, like Gilman, implicitly acknowledges the "need" for inquiry concerning the Jewish woman's body. But Spiegelman goes further in structuring his story around just such a lack and in repeatedly drawing attention to the gendered *violence* that has produced this empty space in his family history: Art's mother has had her voice forcibly removed by Vladek's stubborn annihilation of her diaries. The fictional and nonfictional writings of Philip Roth, which also mobilize family stories and historical motifs to reconfigure Jewish-American identity, similarly foreground the gender asymmetry of those very stories. But—unlike Spiegelman's portrait of Anja—Roth renders his fictional mother, Selma Zuckerman, as essentially and eternally without language: her writing, for example, is belittled as consisting only of recipes, thank-you notes, and knitting instructions. In *Patrimony,* he depicts his real mother not as a producer of language but as an archive; this "quietly efficient" woman was "the repository of our family past, the historian of our childhood and growing up" (36). There are, in the memoir, suggestions of a kind of patriarchal violence analogous to that enacted by Vladek — Bessie Roth's "once spirited, housewifely independence had been all but extinguished by [Herman's] anxious, overbearing bossiness"—but, unlike Anja, Bessie is never granted an autonomous voice that transcends the domestic sphere. Although she presided within what Roth calls "her single-handed establishment of a first-class domestic-management and mothering company" (37), the mother's restriction to this limited space by a patriarchal Jewish culture never becomes thematized since *Patrimony,* as its title suggests, is first and foremost the story of "the male line, unimpaired and happy, ascending from nascency to maturity" (230). The mother is notably absent from (although one wonders if she has taken) the family photograph that inspires this last formulation and that adorns *Patrimony*'s cover.

Both Roth and Spiegelman present narratives in which a certain version of history, the family, and the Holocaust implicitly disappears with the mother in the late 1960s and early 1970s. Selma Zuckerman dies after substituting "Holocaust" for her own name; Bessie Roth, the family "repository" and "historian," is "extinguished" upon Herman's retirement in the mid 1960s; and Anja takes her Holocaust testimony to the grave in 1968. In their wake, the history of the family and the "race" devolves into the hands of what Paul Breines, in a recent attempt to characterize post-1960s Jewish maleness, has called a "tough Jew." These three "tough" figures — Nathan, Herman Roth, Vladek — are all equally well described by what Roth calls "obsessive stubbornness" (*Patrimony,* 36). The quality is indeed ambiguous, seeming to provide at once the means for survival in difficult situations (whether historical or medical) and the resources for self- and other-directed violence in domestic and public spheres. While Roth's writing certainly produces ambivalent feelings about the "tough Jew," only Spiegelman foregrounds the ways in which this new Jewish subject has emerged through the repression (in two senses) of Jewish women's bodies and texts and the ways in which it can initiate new tales of violence.

The insertion in *Maus I* of the previously published "Prisoner on the Hell Planet" — the story of Anja's death — not only presents an expressionist stylistic rupture with the rest of the work, but reopens the wound of the mother's suicide by documenting the "raw" desperation of the twenty-year-old Art. We should not read "Prisoner," however, as a less mediated expression of angst, despite its "human" characters and the reality-effect of the inserted 1958 photograph of Anja and Art. Rather, the "presence" of the maternal body here vainly attempts to compensate for what, many years later, remain the unmournable losses of Anja's suicide and of the years of psychic and political suffering that her life represents for Art. "Prisoner" draws attention to itself as at once *in excess* of the rest of *Maus* — a "realistic" supplement framed in black — and *less than* the mother (and the history) it seeks to resuscitate. With artist's signature and date (1972) following the last frame, "Prisoner" also complicates *Maus*'s moment of enunciation — it simultaneously stands apart temporally and spatially from the rest of the work and is yet integrated into it. Like Art in this segment and throughout *Maus,* "Prisoner" cannot hide its difference from the totality of the family romance, but nor can it fully separate from the mother's story.

By highlighting, once again, the complexity of the time of enunciation in *Maus,* "Prisoner" points to the possibility of reading the work as part of a historical process that Spiegelman has focalized through the family, but that opens into questions of public culture and politics. The moment of Anja's suicide — May 1968 — serves as a touchstone for the countercultural rebellion that obviously informs Spiegelman's work. In the same year that "Prisoner" appeared in an underground comics magazine, for example, Spiegelman edited an (explicitly) pornographic and psychedelic book of quotations, *Whole Grains*. This book, dedicated to his mother, foreshadows some of the irreverence, eclecticism, and black humor of *Maus* (and even contains the quotation by Beckett that Art brings up in volume II, 45 — see below), but it serves more as a marker of the cultural material of Spiegelman's life/career than as a developmental stage on the road to his masterpiece. The 1960s cemented Spiegelman's identity as an artist, putting him in touch, through the underground comics scene, with other "damned intellectuals"; in *Maus* and in the pages of *Raw*, he continues this tradition of underground comics-with-a-message, even after "what had seemed like a revolution simply deflated into a lifestyle" (Spiegelman and Mouly, 6).[15]

Besides constituting a moment of general cultural upheaval, the late 1960s inaugurated a new era for Jews in North America, one that would provide the sociological setting in which and against which Spiegelman would create *Maus*. Around this time "the Holocaust" took on its central articulated importance in Jewish life — and it did so in a particular context. As Jewish liberation theologian Marc Ellis writes,

> it is in light of the 1967 war that Jews articulated for the first time both the extent of Jewish suffering during the Holocaust and the significance of Jewish empowerment in Israel. Before 1967, neither was central to Jewish consciousness; the Jewish community carried on with a haunting memory of the European experience and a charitable attitude toward the fledgling state. After the war, both Holocaust and Israel are seen as central points around which the boundaries of Jewish commitment are defined. (3)

For Ellis, it is imperative that Jewish people of conscience pass beyond the now-problematic dialectic of innocence and redemption that poses all Jews as innocent victims and sees the state of Israel as a messianic redemption. Theology, indeed all discourse, that partakes of the innocence / redemption dialectic ultimately serves as a legitimating apparatus for Jewish chauvinism and for the Jewish state, since, within its terms, we cannot acknowledge Jews as themselves victimizers, either as individuals or as a collective.

Spiegelman's *Maus* operates precisely in this troubled space "beyond innocence and redemption." The Jewish subjects he produces are certainly not innocent (they're barely likable), nor have they found redemption in Rego Park, the Catskills, Soho, or indeed anywhere. The depiction of Vladek — a survivor — as a purveyor of violence in his own home, especially against his second wife, Mala, raises the crucial question about how a people with such a long history of suffering (one that continues to the present) can in turn become agents of violence and torture. While neither volume of this comic strip addresses the question of Israel / Palestine (except for one ironic aside — II, 42), in an interview Spiegelman makes a rather interesting comment that I believe invites this contextualization. During the discussion of *Maus* on National Public Radio, Spiegelman alludes to the newscast that had opened the show. The top three stories, he notes, were on Pat Buchanan, South Africa, and an Israeli invasion of southern Lebanon in which Israeli tanks crushed UN peace-keeping vehicles. Spiegelman calls these three disturbing news stories evidence of the "constant reverb" of the past into the present that *Maus* seeks to illuminate, "if you dig my drift." The drift is that for post-1967 diasporic and Israeli Jewish communities any text that explicitly challenges sentimental renderings of the Holocaust also implicitly challenges that tragedy's dialectical double — the legitimacy of Israeli incursions into Arab land. Although it carefully and provocatively explores the specificity of different generations of Jewish-American identity, *Maus* does not *explicitly* raise the question of American Jews' relation to the policies of Israel. To do so would have been (in my opinion) to lose the mass audience so important to the book's effect among Jews and non-Jews. Revealing Jewish racism against African Americans, as Spiegelman does (II, 98–100), falls within the mainstream realm of possibility. The contrast between that scene's inclusion and the absence of a consideration of mainstream Jewish-American support for repressive Israeli policies indicates the presence of a politically mandated, if unconscious, limit to representation.[16]

In any case, the true strength of Spiegelman's critique comes from his presentation of a people situated "beyond innocence and redemption," in that implausible ethical space that Jews must occupy in relation to their troubled history. In this sense, I believe, Spiegelman avoids what Edward Said has justly called "a *trahison des clercs* of massive proportions," the "silence, indifference, or pleas of ignorance and non-involvement [on the part of Jewish intellectuals which] perpetuate the sufferings of [the Palestinian] people who have not deserved such a long agony" (xxi). To remember genocide without abusing its memory, to confront Jewish violence while acknowledging the ever-present filter of self-hatred — these are the difficult intellectual tasks that mark the minefield of identity explored in *Maus* through the "lowbrow" medium of comics.

Maus as a whole works through the desacralizing and secularization of Jewish experience, but the second volume, in particular, marks a further crisis in Jewish identity. Through a staging of his own anguish at the success of the first volume, Spiegelman interrogates the ambivalent concept of Jewish power, especially the cultural capital won through the re-presentation of the Holocaust. Spiegelman condenses in one frame (which has attracted the attention of nearly all commentators) the various forces that unsettlingly intersect in *Maus*.

At the bottom of the first page of the chapter "Auschwitz (Time Flies)" (II, 41), Spiegelman draws Art seated at his drawing board on top of a pile of mouse corpses. Outside his window stands the concentration camp guard tower that also figures in his "about the author" self-portrait; around the man in the mouse mask buzz the "time flies." Art's thought-bubbles read, "At least fifteen foreign editions [of *Maus*] are coming out. I've gotten 4 serious offers to turn my book into a T.V. special or movie. (I don't wanna.) In May 1968 my mother killed herself. (She left no note.) Lately I've been feeling depressed." Meanwhile, a voice-off — revealed in the next frame as a camera crew — calls ambiguously, "Alright, Mr. Spiegelman . . . We're ready to shoot!" Among other meanings hovering, like the flies, in this frame, the overlay of positions and temporalities communicates an important fact about anti-Semitism: its effects persist across time and situation; someone is always "ready to shoot," even when no Nazis are visible and the media are under your control.

But the successful, avant-gardist artist has another difficulty to confront: his own implication in the scene. Who, after all, is responsible for the corpses at Art's feet, this frame asks? Art's guilt and depression, as thematized here, arise from his inability to make his mother reappear or the corpses (past and present) disappear. Instead, he finds himself unwillingly positioned as a willing victim of the culture industry. This industry — against which Spiegelman constantly defines himself — underwent its own crisis in the years between the publication of the two volumes of *Maus*. Articles proliferated on the deterioration of American publishing, and Spiegelman's own publisher, Pantheon, underwent a change in direction that caused an uproar among intellectuals concerned about the disappearance of nonmainstream work. In *Maus II,* Art finds that he can only actively resist such commodification through the contradictory gesture of directly addressing his audience, and thus assuring that his success — based in the first place on such self-consciousness — will continue. Art's subsequent conversation with his shrink, Paul Pavel (who died in 1992), carries this double bind to its logical (in)conclusion. Pavel, a survivor, wonders whether, since "the victims who died can never tell THEIR side of the story, . . . maybe it's better not to have any more stories." Art agrees and cites the aforementioned Beckett quotation ("Uh-huh. Samuel Beckett once said: 'Every word is like an unnecessary stain on silence and nothingness' ") but then realizes the bind: "On the other hand, he SAID it" (II, 45).

The impossibility of staying silent, which Spiegelman's ceaseless work on *Maus* embodies, entails what Marianne Hirsch, following psychiatrist Dori Laub, has called "the aesthetic of the testimonial chain — an aesthetic that is indistinguishable from documentary" ("Family Pictures," 26; see also Felman and Laub) and that calls the reader into the story. The most striking example of this process, as Hirsch notes, comes at the end of the second volume when Spiegelman includes a photograph of his father taken just after his escape from the Nazis. This picture, sent to Anja as proof of his survival, was taken under strange circumstances: "I passed once a photo place what had a *camp* uniform — a new and clean one — to make *souvenir* photos" (II, 134). This photo, which could have been taken of anyone, survivor or not, "dangerously relativizes the identity of the survivor" (Hirsch, "Family Pictures," 25). Taken out of the context of Vladek's message to Anja, it also marks the becoming-kitsch of the Holocaust. Thanks to the miracle of mechanical reproduction anybody can be a survivor! Philip Roth draws on a similar iconography, but, at least in *Patrimony*, he leaves out Spiegelman's self-conscious ironization. Roth seeks to wrap his father simultaneously in the uniforms of sentimentality and "tough" Jewish survivorhood, a strategy that, we have seen, works through the abjection, or at least forgetting, of the mother's experience.

Spiegelman's relationship to the photograph is more complicated. He clearly recognizes the sentimental tradition it inaugurates, *but he also has to use it:* "I need that photo in my book," he exclaims (134). In a gesture worthy of Beckett, *Maus* "stains" the "clean" uniform of Jewish suffering in the Holocaust; it reveals the impure basis of all Auschwitz *souvenirs*. Spiegelman "needs" to offer us this uniform because it figures the act of reading: for those living "after Auschwitz" (even those who, like Vladek and Anja, lived *through* Auschwitz), the uniform provides a kind of access, albeit highly mediated, to the events themselves. As a "site of memory" the photograph — and by extension the book that contains it — creates the space of identification that Spiegelman relies on for affective and artistic success.

But identifications are always multiple, unforeseeable, and tinged with repudiation; readers are at least as likely to refuse to empathize with Vladek and instead to occupy Art's trademark vest — offered as a souvenir by an entrepreneuring "dog" (II, 42). The vest, as opposed to the uniform, represents the power and risk of writing (and drawing): the ability and the need of those raised in what Hirsch calls "postmemory" to reconfigure their parents' stories without escaping either their failure to revive the dead or their recuperation by a dominant non-Jewish culture. Between the vest and the uniform, *Maus* unravels as "a survivor's tale" of "crystalline ambiguity."[17] Spiegelman demonstrates how "the Holocaust" ultimately resists representation, but he uses this knowledge as authorization for *multiplying* the forms of portraiture. In this mongrelized, highbrow/lowbrow animal tale, ethnic and familial identities hover between a painful present and an even more painful past, between futile documentary and effective fiction. Simultaneously reproducing and recasting Holocaust history, *Maus* partakes of the melancholy pleasures of reading, writing, and talking "Jewish."

Unlike Roth, Spiegelman creates a documentary project that resonates with the practice of traumatic realism. By organizing the first volume of *Maus* around his mother's missing story, Spiegelman inscribes absence in narrative without sacrificing the need for the kind of historical knowledge made possible by art. While Spiegelman actually risks "Holocaust pornography" and creates images of Auschwitz, Roth interrogates the circulation of such images in different cultural locales (Jewish and non-Jewish, American and Israeli) without actually attempting to represent the Holocaust. But, despite their obvious differences of experience and style, Spiegelman and Roth both provide maps for locating the Holocaust in an age of postmemory. Employing the techniques and technologies of postmodern culture, they reframe the questions of imaging and representing the Holocaust posed first in a modernist mode by Adorno and Blanchot. In adopting ironic and popular idioms for their narratives, Spiegelman and Roth do not simply dispense with the injunctions of their philosophical forbears. Rather, they incorporate an interrogation of the limits of representation into the form and content of their work. "Postmodernism," as used by the postmemory generation, consequently refers not to a definitive break with modernist or realist aesthetics and ideologies, but to a reworking of their contradictions from a different cultural location. This cultural shift parallels the relationship between the "after Auschwitz" era and the histories that led up to it. In the "after after Auschwitz" moment, the Holocaust is not just the occasion for ethical and political evaluations of modernity or for realist documentation projects although it is the occasion for those things as well. In the work of the postmemory artists, the Holocaust is also part of a larger mediascape in which entertainment, pedagogy, and ethnic/national identity politics form an inseparable — but rapidly fluctuating and contested — sequence of images and ideas. At no point is this new era of cultural flux more visible than in "The Year of the Holocaust" proper, with the opening of *Schindler's List* and the United States Holocaust Memorial Museum.

Chapter 6

"Touch an Event to Begin"

Americanizing the Holocaust

Despite the potential for trivialization, "The Year of the Holocaust" provides a suggestive frame for beginning to understand the contemporary meanings of the Nazi genocide. Yet as the serious ironies of Roth and Spiegelman demonstrate, the particular configuration offered by *Nightline* in no way determines or even indicates what all of those meanings will look like. My subsequent discussions of *Schindler's List* and the United States Holocaust Memorial Museum will further elucidate the complexities and contradictions at the heart of current Holocaust discourses. The framework of "The Year of the Holocaust" suggests several parameters for the following discussion: the predominance of media and information technologies; the hegemonic position of American media in a global media environment; the "sequencing" of the Shoah in various spheres of the media with other genocides and histories of oppression, as well as with other images and commodities of a postmodern consumer culture; the simultaneous desires for immediacy and decorum in the field of Holocaust representation.

In producing meaning between some or all of these poles, artifacts of "The Year of the Holocaust" such as *Schindler's List* and the museum remain in tension with the modernist aesthetics and politics of Adorno and Blanchot; at the same time they signal the eclipse of certain distinctions between different realms of culture, economics, and politics that the latter writers maintain. The space/time coordinates of "after Auschwitz" in which Adorno and Blanchot perform their thought-experiments no longer constrain representation as they once did. But, at the same time, Adorno's reflections on literature after Auschwitz have been significantly absorbed into contemporary culture, as the tensions inherent in

Roth's and Spiegelman's critical uses of Holocaust "pornography" and "comix" make clear. This absorption signals both the "success" of Adorno's formulation and the dispersion of its power as his phrase becomes an academic and journalistic commonplace.

The mega-events of "The Year of the Holocaust" also reflect continued fascination with the place of the "real" and of "trauma" in the contemporary moment. Trying to evaluate the significance of those events entails thinking critically about the possibilities for documentation and historical knowledge in a technologically advanced age. Clearly, as I have demonstrated in my discussion of traumatic realism, new forms of documentation have arisen to grapple with the extremes of human existence in the twentieth century. The technological prowess of Spielberg's film and the museum in Washington suggests, on the one hand, that the contemporary media may be put to work for projects fostering collective memory and combating historical amnesia (and they remind us that questions of technology can never be separated from questions of history and memory). On the other hand, such technologies are not "neutral" in their implications for understanding the events of the Nazi genocide. The more the Holocaust becomes an archetype of the mass media, the more it finds itself invoked and circulated in sequences of unfamiliar images and ideologies. In "The Year of the Holocaust," understanding of the Nazi genocide becomes not only Americanized but ultimately globalized. As the "uniqueness" of the Holocaust becomes more difficult to maintain in a media-saturated culture, the Holocaust itself begins to function differently within the competing narratives of European and American history. No longer simply a challenge to European modernity, the Holocaust is now beginning to function as an anchor of American modernity, part and parcel of postmodern culture and economics, and central to the political landscape of global political power.

Schindler's List "after *Shoah*"

When Steven Spielberg's film *Schindler's List* was released in December 1993 the Holocaust memorial museum had already been open for several months, but as *Nightline* demonstrated, these two different genres of phenomena contributed to each other's renown by becoming linked as part of a greater public event: the Holocaust's resurgent currency. Like the Memorial Museum, the film was conceived and received simultaneously as a site of (moral and political) memory and as a lesson in history. As an incipient cultural monument, *Schindler's List* attracted responses of a quasi-ritual cast, with praise for, and citation of, the film coming to stand in for memorialization of the genocide itself. In his *New Yorker* review, for example, Terrence Rafferty suggested that Spielberg's symbolic act had a more than arbitrary relationship to Schindler's life-saving one: "The sheer unexpectedness of Spielberg's rigorous refusal to simplify his protagonist's motives seems to connect him, in a minor but distinct way, to Schindler himself" (129). Such a deliberate confusion of representation and historical event has become a ubiquitous part of the "postmodern condition" and provides a necessary framework for thinking about the place of the Holocaust in contemporary culture.

Meanwhile, politicians, educators, and activists were quick to seize upon the cinematically mediated heroism of Schindler in the face of Nazi anti-Semitism and annihilation as a history lesson for contemporary Americans. Thus, in New Jersey, Governor Christine Whitman proposed mandatory screenings of the film in order to promote "understanding" among students thought to be at the center of black-Jewish conflict. And in New York City, the Jewish Ad-Hoc Committee on Bosnia (JACOB) used the crowds lining up to see the film as an opportunity to pass out leaflets calling for action in the name of Holocaust memory to stop the Serbian genocide of Muslims in Bosnia.

These political, pedagogical, material, and semiotic practices to which Spielberg's film gave rise — and coverage of the film preceded its completion and extended well beyond its long and popular first run — demonstrate the degree to which the film was more of an event than a text. But while an understanding of the *Schindler's List* phenomenon necessitates the crossing of boundaries between media, genres, and disciplines, the film also deserves a more textual analysis. At the formal level, it is interesting to compare it to Claude Lanzmann's *Shoah*, a film that, according to intellectual publicity (not least by Lanzmann himself), set new standards for austerity in Holocaust representation and thus created a measure for previous and future representations. In responding to *Schindler's List*, Lanzmann took on the role of border guard and declared Spielberg's film inadequate to its subject matter. He thus protected the place of his own "sacred" film in the canon of Holocaust representation.[1] Such a critical move only reproduces what Miriam Hansen has called the "impasse" in theories of representation "after Auschwitz": the opposition of modernism to popular culture ("*Schindler's List* Is Not *Shoah*"). Contrary to Lanzmann's polemical attempt to differentiate himself from Spielberg's efforts, I find similar rhetorical claims to realism enunciated by both directors and their critics, as well as related attempts to create a mimetic correspondence between text and event, albeit with very different effects. The deconstruction of the opposition between these products of high and popular culture does not do away with their differences, but shifts the debate away from the representability of Auschwitz toward the uneven conditions of cultural production and reception.

Whatever the formal similarities and differences between the two films—and certainly the divergences outweigh the commonalities — they occupy structurally different positions within the interlocking state, civic, and financial spheres. *Schindler's List* not only embodies but also makes available a network of political, economic, and cultural meanings and practices that draw on, but extend well beyond, the film text and the novel on which it was based. As an "inspiring" entertainment commodity marketed within the global capitalist economy, *Schindler's List* has naturally circulated more extensively than Lanzmann's self-consciously difficult marathon and differently from the circumscribed public space of the Holocaust museum (although computer links take the museum into the evolving realm of cyberspace). The combination of *Schindler*'s moral and economic logics has produced effects and events that extend "The Year of the Holocaust" into profane realms not imaginable in relation to *Shoah*. Is this just another example of trivialization, as Lanzmann and other highbrow critics maintain? Or does the dissemination of *Schindler's List* help more people to "never forget"? The present cultural status of the Holocaust in the United States ensures that the answer to both questions is probably affirmative. The Holocaust has an unignorable "presence" in contemporary social life, but the relationship between that media-based appearance and the absent past toward which it gestures is subject to debate and negotiation.

This uncertainty in the relationship between appearance and historical reality in the context into which *Schindler's List* entered echoes a tension already at work in the source text for Spielberg's film, Thomas Keneally's novel, originally called *Schindler's Ark*. Keneally's work is a documentary, or nonfiction, novel, a genre that Barbara Foley has argued is particularly suited to depictions of the Nazi genocide ("Fact, Fiction, Fascism"). In a presumably unremarked irony, the copyright page of the recent edition of the novel includes the standard novelistic disclaimer: "This book is a work of fiction. Names, characters, places, and incidents are either products of the author's imagination or are used fictitiously. Any resemblance to actual events or locales or persons, living or dead, is entirely coincidental." While so ordinary as to almost escape notice, such a statement jars with the "author's note" that opens the novel. The note is attributed to "Tom Keneally," as if to assure us, by way of its informality, of its sincerity. Here, Keneally details his modus operandi, how he based his story on oral and written testimonies "enriched by a visit, in the company of Leopold Pfefferberg [one of the survivors], to locations that figure prominently in the book" (9). The overall historical truth of the Schindler story is not in question, although the discrepancy between the disclaimer and the note suggests the typically postmodern ploy whereby increasing testimony to authenticity only increases the story's aura of unverifiability and inauthenticity (as happens in *Operation Shylock*). Keneally solves this problem of ambiguity inherent in his project (regardless of the disclaimer) by appealing to precedent and by recasting the contradiction as a felicitous opportunity: "To use the texture and devices of a novel to tell a true story is a course that has frequently been followed in modern writing. It is the one I choose to follow here — both because the novelist's craft is the only one I can lay claim to, and because the novel's techniques seem suited for a character of such ambiguity and magnitude as Oskar." Recognizing that the notions of "craft" and "technique" immediately raise questions about factuality, Keneally goes on to assure us that he has "attempted, however, to avoid all fiction, since fiction would debase the record, and to distinguish between reality and the myths which are likely to attach themselves to a man of Oskar's stature" (10). Keneally displaces the inherent problems of the instability of genres onto the "ambiguity" of "Oskar" — once again using the informality of the first name to signify authenticity, but here the authenticity of someone who is already "novelistic" and "mythic." Perhaps the lesson of this prefatory material is to reveal the rhetorical strategies that *equally* underwrite both fictional and nonfictional texts. By their nature, these strategies (of which the novel includes examples of both) leave a margin of uncertainty that, given the history of Holocaust aesthetics, serves as a particularly troubling and fascinating pole of attraction.

While the author's note reveals the general rhetoricity of documentation, it ultimately leaves its own particular rhetoric unexamined. The problem here is not the blurring of the fiction/fact border, but an equally troubling and more subtle issue. Precisely in his reliance on factual testimonies Keneally misses the "truth" of the events he attempts to describe. Many reviewers of the film adaptation complained that Spielberg erased the individuality of the Jews in his movie, depicting them primarily as a group and bestowing upon them all of the stereotypes of anti-Semitic propaganda. Lawrence Langer was one of the few critics who defended this aesthetic choice as faithful to history, reminding us that Nazi policy worked at the level of the collective and discouraged the singling out of individual Jews (*Admitting,* 9). In any case, the same complaint cannot be made about the novel, which operates according to a somewhat different logic. In fact, Keneally balances his free indirect discourse between Schindler and a relatively well-differentiated Jewish "cast of characters." The disquieting quality of Keneally's depiction of Jews has other grounds. By basing his novel predominantly on a faulty interpretation of survivor testimony, Keneally imposes a false teleology on the events. Simply put: no Jewish character whose consciousness the narrative enters (even at the third-person distance) ever dies. Again and again the "Schindler Jews" are put into life-threatening circumstances only to be saved by "a special and startling deliverance" (152). The point is not that these all-but-unfathomable stories are not true—the least familiarity with the irrational rationality of the Holocaust confirms their likelihood—but that they couldn't not be true, based as they are on a certain reading of *survivor* testimony.

My point is not that survivor memoirs necessarily impose a false teleology of survival. Rather, the most powerful memoirs work against this omnipresent possibility by employing a variety of narrative means. Since the risk of teleology lies at the level of emplotment—the meaningful shape given to the events—not at the level of fact, many memoirists attempt to use narrative against itself. Refusing the potential comforts of narrative, such as the im-position of closure and meaningful wholeness, the writers I call traumatic realists undermine the conventions of storytelling without entirely forgoing narrative or its ability to document history. For instance, in Robert Antelme's *L'espèce humaine* and Primo Levi's *Survival in Auschwitz* the narratives culminate not in the expected joy of liberation but in an increasingly dark view of the "concentrationary universe." (This invented title of the recent English editions of Levi's book thus contradicts the narrative itself.) In Charlotte Delbo's *None of Us Will Return,* the possibility of such a celebratory conclusion is foreclosed entirely by the text's fragmentary micronarrative vignettes and expressionist images. Meanwhile, in the last volume of her trilogy, *The Measure of Our Days,* the traumatic effects of postcamp life are shown to far outweigh the "deliverance" of survival. And in Ruth Klüger, as in Delbo and so many other memoirists, the unavoidable fact that "she who writes, lives" always remains tied to the untold stories of the anonymous dead. Keneally's use of testimony in *Schindler's List* to affirm "survival" is thus not fictional, but it does not correspond to the majority of memoirs either.

At the limit, Keneally's depiction of these survivors borders on the grotesque. In a passage describing the liquidation of the Cracow ghetto, Keneally's original source, Leopold Pfefferberg, finds himself coming upon "a pile of victims. They lay, some of them, with their heads split open, their limbs twisted.... Somehow it did not occur to Pfefferberg to look for the bodies of his wife and the [family whom she was to hide with]. He sensed why he had been placed there. He believed unshakably in better years to come, years of just tribunals. He had that sense of being a witness which Schindler had experienced on the hill beyond Rekawka" (184). The narrative brutally objectifies the victims, rendering them as a "pile" of body parts; this is more an effect of the novel's strategy than of Nazi dehumanization since the author carefully avoids identifying any of these bodies and assures us that Pfefferberg's wife could not be included. As depicted by Keneally, the survivor's thoughts verge on the triumphalist, exalting his calling ("why he had been placed there") and his optimism in the face of an unredeemable mass murder. The passage also implies that justice *would* ultimately come, a piety contradicted by subsequent judicial history and by the magnitude of a crime for which proper atonement is all but unimaginable.[2] This is a perverse parody of the often expressed desire of the persecuted to survive *in order* to witness. Moshe the Beadle in Elie Wiesel's *Night* does not return from the killing fields to the village because he senses "better years to come," but rather worse ones (*Night Trilogy,* 13–17). In the logic of Keneally's novel, even the tattoo, the symbol of the permanent wound inflicted upon the survivors, takes on an inverted significance: "Henry Rosner arrived first. He too stood at the wire, his left arm bared and raised. 'The tattoo,' he called in triumph" (328).

The novel *Schindler's List* leaves out the most important aspects of the Jewish experience of the Holocaust and all but erases the genocide, replacing them with "deliverance" and heroism, concepts difficult to attribute to most examples of the survivor testimony on which it is based. If the first problem with Keneally's depiction of Jews is *which* Jews he portrays, the second is *how,* in the majority of cases, he portrays them. Here, the novel and film converge, as demonstrated by use in the 1993 edition of the novel of cover art taken from the film's publicity posters — the "List" superimposed over a strong hand and forearm lifting up a smaller, more childlike hand. Reminiscent of the Sistine Chapel creation scene, the poster for *E.T.*, or a Bennetton advertisement, this visualization captures both Keneally's and Spielberg's attitudes toward Schindler. The Jews are infantilized (almost bestialized in the novel's original "ark" logic) in the service of the German's heroization, if not deification. As the novel quotes a survivor, "He was our father, he was our mother, he was our only faith" (330). Only long after the war, when Schindler's life had become a series of marital and business failures, can "Oskar's children . . . become his parents" (397). Schindler's gender and generational crossing — from man to woman, from father to son — contributes to the sense of divinity Keneally creates around him: "If the man was wrong, if he lightly used his powers of passing on conviction, then there was no God and no humanity, no bread, no succor" (92). Or, more coyly but explicitly: "It is not too fantastic to say that he desired [the Jews] with some of the absolute passion that characterized the exposed and flaming heart of the Jesus which hung on Emilie's wall. Since this narrative has tried to avoid the canonization of the *Herr Direktor,* the idea of the sensual Oskar as the desirer of souls has to be proved" (350). The distance from *Herr Direktor* to *der Herr* [the Lord] is, it would seem, not so far. By canonizing the "good German," infantilizing the survivors, and then remembering them at the expense of the dead, Keneally's *Schindler's List* confirms the ironic insight that a temporarily infantilized Art gets from his analyst in *Maus:* "It's as if life equals winning so death equals losing" (II, 45).

The movie poster adds the slogan "The list is life" to the picture used on the book cover and thus establishes an equation crucial to the film's narrative. In this image the list names are superimposed, tattoo-like, on both the childlike "survivor's" arm and the strong "savior's" arm; once again, the mark of entry into the death-world of the extermination camp is inverted and recast as "life." In addition the tattoo marks both arms, linking them and annulling their difference, even as the vertical image hierarchizes the strong over the weak. The film's script assigns the famous lines, "The list is an absolute good. The list is life," to Stern instead of Keneally's anonymous narrator (see 290). In the book, Stern plays no visible role in the list's construction, and in fact, the list goes through various emendations as positions are bought, sold, and traded by Goldberg, a member of the Jewish police (and a figure amply represented by Spielberg, although not in this capacity). After the men are mistakenly sent to Gross-Rosen, the list is lost and then reconstituted somewhat differently by Goldberg. The women, as shown in the film, end up first at Auschwitz, where they in fact stayed for several weeks; although Keneally is vague on this point, it is virtually impossible that precisely the same three hundred women, without losses or exchanges, could have returned from Auschwitz to Schindler's factory in Brinnlitz. In other words, the film, even more than the novel, erases the randomness of the list and replaces it with *continuity.* A traditional film narrative demands recognizable and consistent characterization and a rational connection between characters' behavior and their fate. The events of the Nazi genocide, as represented even by the exceptional story of the "list," do not fulfill those narrative demands since they radically "deconstruct" any notion of continuous "character." The Holocaust also renders the notion of an "absolute good" nonsensical. Absolute good cannot exist in a context where survival is arbitrary and death the rule: the list always also conjures up the nonlist, uninterrupted genocide. The maintenance of continuity in Spielberg's version sutures the gap between "film character" and "Holocaust survivor," preserving the narrative logic of identification proper to classical Hollywood cinema.[3] The film has been rightly criticized for reducing the Jews to anti-Semitic stereotypes; this stereotyping also contributes to the maintenance of the type of character that the law of genre demands, and this has major implications for the kind of story that can be told.

The inclusion of Stern at the genesis of the list culminates a process, typical to film adaptations of novels, that constructs individual characters through composite portraits. Stern, who plays a much smaller role in the novel, takes on some of the attributes of other Jewish characters, such as Schindler's other "business associate," Bankier, and even of the dissident Nazi Titsch, who in fact composed the list with Schindler. In constructing Stern — the most individualized Jewish figure, along with the much-abused Helen Hirsch — as a collective subject, Spielberg might have activated the power of the testimonial, a genre that channels a collective experience through an individual voice. In the field of Holocaust literature, testimonial memoirs by writers such as Primo Levi, Elie Wiesel, David Rousset, and Charlotte Delbo have given expression to the systematic and collective specificities of the Nazi concentration and extermination camp universe. But, as the scene in which Stern is saved from deportation illustrates, Spielberg, like Keneally, has another project. When Schindler discovers that his accountant has "mistakenly" been put on a list of people to be deported from the ghetto, he rushes to the train station to extract him. While Spielberg demonstrates, through irony, that Schindler's motives at this point are primarily selfish, he nonetheless reproduces the idea that only a mistake could have sent Stern to the cattle cars. Set off against crowds of anonymous prisoners, the individuated Stern emerges as a grateful and relieved survivor, while the forgotten masses go, not mistakenly, but intentionally, to their (unrepresented, off-screen) deaths. In the narrative's logic, the survival of Stern is essential since he mirrors and upholds Schindler's accomplishments, giving them an interpersonal (i.e., "ethical") authenticity. What Keneally calls a "tender connection" between the two men is confirmed in the movie by Stern's presentation to Schindler, on behalf of the survivors, of a gold ring, fashioned from gold extracted from another character's tooth. While the extraction of a prisoner's tooth might, in a traumatic realist narrative, constitute an index of violence and loss, here it is rendered as comedy and sentimentality and as part of the film's act of closure. This homosocial ring ritual culminates the homeopathic "purification rites" for Schindler, who has been partially sullied by his (opportunistic) homosocial bonds with Amon Goeth and other Nazi leaders.

The scene of Stern's near-deportation indicates a more general ambivalence about the centrality of bureaucratic murder in the Nazi genocide. The film oscillates between the implicit acknowledgment of mass death and the disavowal or distancing of such death through the focus on the exceptional paths of the featured characters. The scenes of the women at Auschwitz focus the dilemmas of representing the Holocaust. As has been reported, Spielberg, in his quest for site-specific authenticity, wanted to film within Auschwitz, but was discouraged from doing so by the World Jewish Congress. A compromise was worked out in which Spielberg chose to film outside the camp, reconstructing the interior of the camp and using the front of the entryway as the back.[4] The arrival of the train carrying the women onto the (reconstructed) unloading ramp is an effective impressionistic evocation of the "night and fog" of Auschwitz, even if the *real* SS guardhouse in the background of the scene actually ends up looking like a stage set. Complete with dogs (albeit muzzled), dramatic lighting-effects, a haunting musical theme that contrasts sharply with the rest of the soundtrack, and impersonal camera angles emphasizing the camp's chaos, this sequence captures some facets of the "concentrationary universe" not because of the authenticity of the location or the testimony on which it is based, but because it employs to maximum effect the special effects of the cinematic medium. Spielberg's stylization of Nazi terror is equally present in the clearing of the Cracow ghetto, which also cites documentary conventions and incorporates them into the fictional world of the feature film. Significantly, these are the only two sequences in which the collective and impersonal (if not the bureaucratic) nature of that terror is represented.

It would be easy to condemn Spielberg's "aestheticization of politics" (*pace* Benjamin) by contrasting it to the starker aesthetic of Claude Lanzmann's *Shoah* (1985) — and this is indeed what Lanzmann himself does in an essay on *Schindler's List* that appeared in *Le Monde* upon the film's opening in France in March 1994. As its title suggests, Lanzmann's intervention, "Holocauste, la représentation impossible" [Holocaust, the impossible representation], concerns what Saul Friedlander has called "the limits of representation." The notion that representation of certain aspects of the Holocaust entails constraints particular to this event is not new and goes back to the dominant, if cursory, reading of Adorno on "poetry after Auschwitz." In the case of Lanzmann, the notion of representational limits proves contradictory, imprecise, authoritarian, and ill-suited to describing the heterogeneity of modes of Holocaust representation. Lanzmann begins by challenging the view dominant in the United States that Spielberg has captured "historical truth" (I). He defines the problem as one of a lack of correspondence between the film's symbolic act and the historical events represented: "It's the whole problem of the image and of representation. Nothing which happened resembles that, even if everything appears authentic" (VII).[5] While the failure of the correspondence theory of meaning is a commonplace in contemporary semiotics, Lanzmann's theory of representation is inconsistent. On the one hand, he demands historical authenticity; hence, he accuses Spielberg of overall distortion but praises him for including a scene in a Cracow pharmacy that he himself has seen and that therefore really exists (I)! On the other hand, historical authenticity is not what Lanzmann really demands, and his argument extends beyond the terms in which his critique of Spielberg seems at first to be couched.

Indeed, Lanzmann suggests in a provocative hypothetical example that there is something radically *antihistorical* about his position.[6] First, he establishes the uniqueness of the Holocaust as a function of its unrepresentability in a phrase that he reproduces word for word (without citation) from his 1979 article "De l'Holocauste à *Holocauste*" [From the Holocaust to *Holocaust*]: "The Holocaust is unique first of all in that it erects around itself, in a circle of flames, a limit which cannot be breached because a certain absolute is intransmissable: to claim to do so is to make oneself guilty of the most serious sort of transgression. Fiction is a transgression; I profoundly think that there is an interdiction of representation" (*Au sujet de Shoah*, 309).[7] Based on this understanding of interdiction, Lanzmann criticizes Spielberg's attempts to re-create Auschwitz (and almost film a gas chamber) and argues that such "reconstruction" is equivalent to a process of historical falsification [*reconstruire, c'est, d'une certaine façon, fabriquer des archives* (VII)]. He then shifts away from *Schindler's List* and into a tangential, disconcerting example: "[I]f I had found a film —

a secret film, because it was strictly forbidden — made by an SS man showing how 3,000 Jews — men, women, and children — died together, asphyxiated in the gas chamber of Crematorium 2 at Auschwitz; if I had found that, not only would I not have shown it, I would have destroyed it. I am not capable of saying why. It goes without saying" (VII).[8] The argument here goes well beyond "fictional" or mimetic representation and targets the image itself. In this part of his argument, Lanzmann allows no distinction between various degrees of mediation, so that even the hypothetical documentary footage has no priority over "reconstruction." But what history could proceed without documenting and reconstructing the events that it takes as its object? Why would the Holocaust represent a particularly unrepresentable event? And why should visual representation in particular be singled out as problematic?

Lanzmann does not provide answers for any of these questions, but rather confuses matters further by eliding the difference between the uniqueness of the Holocaust and the uniqueness of his own act of representation, *Shoah,* which he puts forward as a qualitatively different solution to the "impossible" problem of representation. The movement in Lanzmann's argument from the circle of fire to the fabrication of archives to their destruction remains unexamined. While his argument derives explicitly from a certain understanding of the ban on graven images, the rhetoric of destruction by fire cannot but create an uneasy echo of Nazi book burnings and crematoria and of the *Nazi's own* injunction against filming the genocide. Lanzmann's text activates the *Bilderverbot* [the ban on graven images] by providing a problematic paraphrase of Adorno's "poetry after Auschwitz" proposition (itself a secular version of the ban): "I truly thought, with humility and pride, that there was a before and an after *Shoah,* and that after *Shoah* a certain number of things could no longer be done. Now Spielberg has done them" (VII).[9] Lanzmann's paraphrase is unintentionally ironic (but also typical) in that the substitution of his film for the event itself (Auschwitz) reproduces exactly the logic that he detests in the reception of *Schindler's List* and that is typified by Rafferty's *New Yorker* review. Nevertheless, *Shoah* received the very same type of reception. In an "authorized" collection of essays and interviews pertaining to Lanzmann's film, *Au sujet de Shoah* [On the subject of *Shoah*], the film and the event often intermingle; frequently, the film title is not italicized, as in the very book title, creating confusion about whether genocide or cinema is at issue.

It is, in fact, this confusion between historical events and their representations (and between different meanings of representation)—a confusion promulgated by both Spielberg and Lanzmann and by many of their critics—that leads to absolutist positions on "representation." If representations have the power to displace historical events completely, then perhaps interdiction is a necessary stance. But if the event is radically cut off from representation and yet representation is an unavoidable fact of all modalities of communication, then interdiction amounts to a destruction of the historical archive. Despite the risks of distortion and displacement, representations of all sorts—including documentary footage, historical documentation, fictional and nonfictional narratives, and so on—remain the only access to historical events. No preconceived evaluation of which media are appropriate or inappropriate (i.e., the image) to a particular event can come to terms with either aesthetic representation, historical documentation, or the event they both seek to capture. While the discourses surrounding the films bear this point out, perhaps it is more interesting to show how *Schindler's List* and *Shoah* themselves almost converge—how, in fact, questions of representation cannot be expunged from the attempt to understand the Nazi genocide.

Lanzmann's nine-and-a-half-hour documentary consists of an extensive series of interviews (selected from hundreds of hours of film) with perpetrators, victims, and bystanders of the "Final Solution." Focusing exclusively on testimony and memory—with the exception of his conversations with political scientist Raul Hilberg and his readings of two written documents—Lanzmann forgoes the typical use of newsreel and archival footage (used to dramatic effect in documentaries such as Alain Resnais's *Night and Fog* and Marcel Ophuls's *The Sorrow and the Pity*). But in several fascinating sequences *Shoah* does perform a reenactment of the type he complains about in Spielberg. Lanzmann's documentary also stages an entry into Auschwitz, even if the terms of its representation are quite different from those in *Schindler's List.* While Filip Müller, one of the few survivors of the Auschwitz *Sonderkommando,* provides a voice-off narration of his arrival in the camp, Lanzmann's camera traces his path through the present-day memorial camp. This sequence differs dramatically from Lanzmann's usual technique of contrasting the horror stories of the survivors with repetitive, slow-tracking shots of the quiet and empty contemporary sites of memory (or oblivion). While the latter shots are impersonal, those accompanying Müller are presented as subjective through the use of a steadily moving hand-held camera and an itinerary that closely matches that of the narrative. The camera shows us the chimney as Müller mentions noticing it and then circles around the crematorium before entering it through a back doorway. Once inside, it continues to follow Müller's narration, turning quickly in reaction to twists in the story and mimicking his implied gaze. The camera surprisingly mimes the conventions of a thriller or horror film in which one character is being stalked and observed from the perspective of a pursuer. In fact, Lanzmann has been cited as describing *Shoah* as "at moments a crime film . . . [on the mode of] a criminal investigation" (Felman and Laub, 256n).

In an equally strange sequence, Müller describes the layout of the gas chamber / crematorium complex two times: the first description, narrated in a descriptive mode, is accompanied by footage that follows Müller's narration by using a plaster model of the crematorium, complete with bodies, on display at the Auschwitz Museum; Müller's second narrative describes the complex from the point of view of the doomed while the hand-held camera moves through the ruins of buildings at Auschwitz-Birkenau. As the camera reaches the gas chamber, the narrative changes and takes the perspective of the Nazis. We only hear Müller's evocation of what happened within the chambers after the camera has cut back to the witness and the distanced scene of the testimony's enunciation. The gas chamber scene represents both the telos of the narrative and that which cannot be represented or evoked visually, except from the outside. These sequences in no way make, or were meant to make, viewers think they were "there" — as the self-conscious use of the model and the ruins as "stage sets" demonstrates. Yet Lanzmann's camera-work is not simply a parody of any attempt to represent the universe of Auschwitz, since it enhances the power of sequences that concern some of the most unknown and extreme aspects of extermination. It is the contrast and the shifts between the "imitative" sequences and the non-"fictionalizing" context of the rest of the film that prevent viewers from reading the imitative shots as part of a "realist" mimetic universe, a fact that suggests the shifting contingency of generic categories and complicates the question of representation.

What is being stalked in such scenes is history, or perhaps more accurately, in Felman's words: "new possibilities of understanding history, . . . new pragmatic *acts* of historicizing history's erasures" (Felman and Laub, 253). But *how* historical understanding is being stalked is also crucial — the atypical camera-work indicates a visual-aesthetic dimension too often overlooked by critics, like Felman, whose emphasis falls on the word. The testimony of Müller, a *Sonderkommando* member with a much-too-intimate knowledge of the production of death, is particularly suited to an exploration of the possibilities for understanding and representing industrialized murder. In an interview with *Le Nouvel Observateur* at the time of the publication of Jean-Claude Pressac's *Les crématoires d'Auschwitz* — the book by the former denier that "proved" the existence of the gas chambers — Lanzmann cites Müller's testimony in *Shoah* as having described "in minute detail" virtually everything unearthed by Pressac. Referring to another survivor, Lanzmann states: "I prefer the tears of the barber of Treblinka in *Shoah* to the Pressac document on the gas detectors. His tears and his choked words are the very mark of truth: there is more truth in them than any material 'proof'" (Weill, "Auschwitz: Enquête," 49).[10] In his critique of Pressac, Lanzmann points to two aspects of his film that correspond to two poles of a decades-long debate about Holocaust representations (initiated perhaps by Adorno's comments on "poetry after Auschwitz"). As summarized by Gertrud Koch in an important essay on *Shoah*, these poles correspond to a "premodern aesthetic" committed to the communication of meaning and "a modernist aesthetic which aims at expression rather than communication" ("Aesthetic Transformation," 17). Müller's testimony *communicates* "in minute detail," claims Lanzmann, while the barber's *expresses* affect (tears) and the inability to communicate (his choked words).

In fact, as Koch argues, Lanzmann's aesthetic goes beyond this binary by providing a "montage of space and time" that "irritate[s] our realistic sense of spatiotemporal certainty: the presence of an absence in the imagination of the past is bound up with the concreteness of images of present-day locations" (21–22). In other words, in refusing to accompany narratives of annihilation with images of the past, but instead insisting on the anachronous image of the present, Lanzmann creates "the most extreme discrepancy between what there is to see and the imagination (*Vorstellung*) triggered by that seen" (23). For Koch, this syncretism of "indifference" and "horror" signals "an aesthetic transformation of the experience of the annihilation," a hybrid aesthetic form that eludes the problems of realism and modernism (23, 24). But the hand-held camera that explores the gas chambers and crematoria cuts across the realist/modernist debate in another, more disturbing way that is not fully acknowledged by Koch or most critics of the film. It seems to indicate a mute desire for a confirmation of horror beyond historical documentation, expressive affect, or the "presence of an absence" — a confirmation proper to artistic form. On the one hand, the hand-held camera becomes a ghostly presence haunting the camps — somewhat in the "spirit" of the traumatic realist details of Klüger and Delbo. On the other hand, this mimetic gesture suggests a desire to touch the real in a more direct way. That the gesture is accomplished through technological manipulation confirms the surprising hypothesis that the austere *Shoah* partially shares the terrain of "The Year of the Holocaust" with its unlikely sibling, *Schindler's List.*

In *Schindler's List,* Spielberg also approaches this aesthetic limit in the controversial sequence in Auschwitz where the women have their hair cut and are sent to the showers. Playing on the spectator's knowledge of the processes leading to gassing — which comes both from testimony, such as that alluded to above in *Shoah,* and from an earlier scene in which a character reported the rumors of this scenario — Spielberg painfully draws out the tension of the women's uncertain fate in a scene whose pornographic essence has the least to do with the masses of naked bodies. As in the entry into Auschwitz proper, the music changes dramatically when the women appear in what seems to be the antechamber of death — this time from the Auschwitz orchestral theme to a lone violin. As the women are herded into the showers, the camera takes the perspective of one of the prisoners, simultaneously creating identification and enhancing the chaos of the scene. Once in the shower room, however, the camera pulls back; as the door slams shut, the camera appears at a peep-hole, suggesting an entirely different identificatory position. The camera then returns to the shower room and moves between a bird's-eye view and more subjective angles, as the music swells and the women are ultimately given a reprieve from death. The camera's movement inside/outside and above/within the scene of death indicates contrary desires to "testify" from within an impossible space and to distance the film from what has been judged socially unrepresentable.

In this ambivalence, *Schindler's List* does not differ from *Shoah*'s occasional attempts to heighten the effect of the evocation of the gas chambers and crematoria with different imitative, but estranged, practices (using a model, using subjective camera shots). Where it does differ crucially is in the affect it produces in the spectator. By maintaining an unbridgeable gap between testimony and "being-there," Lanzmann marks the desire for the real without arousing the suspicion that he might attempt to simulate it. By using dramatic tension to arouse uncertainty, Spielberg displaces the horror from the actual (unrepresented) experience of the gas chambers to the fear that he might actually transgress the socially constructed line drawn around representations of mass murder. *Shoah*'s ambivalent, shifting modes of representation of the killing sites usually suggest that the transgression of taboo resides in the Nazis' social and historical actions and in the death-world of the gas chambers and crematoria that they created. *Schindler's List,* however, shifts the question of transgression to the field of representation, even as it ultimately retreats from crossing the line to a "tasteful" distance. Instead, Spielberg chooses to indicate the gas chambers through more traditional means, by following the gaze of the "Schindler" women as they watch others descend into the real gas chambers and "emerge" through the smokestack. The similar "aestheticization" and the dissimilar *effects* of that process that *Shoah* and *Schindler's List* bring to the representation of Auschwitz bear out Koch's useful clarification: "[T]he various patterns of meaning inscribed in the representations of the death camps cannot be distinguished according to literary forms or genres. Just as purely autobiographical, documentary literature is not free of the compulsion to search for meaning, aesthetically wrought works like Paul Celan's do not necessarily lapse into affirmative idealization because of their aesthetic stylization" (17).

There is one moment when *Schindler's List* might, arguably, be performing the same act of spatiotemporal disorientation as *Shoah* does in those scenes of "reenactment" in which the past comes to haunt the present. At the end of the narrative, when the war has ended and Schindler has fled, Spielberg breaks out of the diegetic frame of the narrative and momentarily disrupts spectator identification by presenting the "real" "Schindler Jews" alongside their fictional representatives. This uneasy coexistence of presentation and representation indicates an attempt to displace the realism / modernism opposition through a postmodern reflexivity. However, the sequence ultimately contributes to a process, found also in Keneally's novel, in which the appeal to a surplus of reality — actual testimony or actual bodies — unwittingly fictionalizes the real. The sequence begins with the liberation of the Brinnlitz factory by a lone Soviet soldier on a horse. When asked by Stern and the others which direction they should head in now that they are "free," the soldier warns: "Don't go east. That's for sure. They hate you there. I wouldn't go west either, if I were you." Faced with this seemingly impossible dilemma, the former prisoners ask where they can get food. The soldier gestures toward the horizon and asks, "Isn't that a town over there?" At this moment, the literal becomes metaphorical and a way out is proposed, as the scene changes and the Jews are pictured coming over a ridge in what the music suggests must be Israel. After shots that reveal the story's "dénouement" — Goeth's execution, Schindler's business failures — in classical Hollywood "nonfiction" style, an even more dramatic transformation takes place. The last captions describing Schindler's postwar canonization appear: "In 1958, he was declared a righteous person by the council of the Yad Vashem in Jerusalem, and invited to plant a tree in the Avenue of the Righteous. It grows there still." As the final sentence appears on the screen, the actors are seen coming over the hill and then suddenly the film shifts from black and white to color and the actors are replaced by "the Schindler Jews today." In the final precredit scene, the lead actors accompany the survivors they portrayed in the film, as together they place stones, according to Jewish ritual, on the Israeli gravesite of Oskar Schindler.

This sequence overlays a series of binary oppositions: black and white / color, past / present, diegesis / reality, actor / survivor, Europe / Israel. This ending offers both a surplus of reality meant to supplement and confirm the realism of the film's narrative and a syncretism of fiction and reality that destabilizes both the real and the fictional. In the former supplementary mode, *Schindler's List* repeats a gesture seen in other Holocaust films, most notably Agnieszka Holland's *Europa, Europa.* In Spielberg's film, as in

Holland's (where the living prototype of the protagonist appears at the end on his kibbutz), the site of the real is Israel, where both films locate the survivors. In associating Israel with the foundation of its narrative project, *Schindler's List* is again not far from *Shoah.* According to Felman, the "finding" of Chelmno survivor Simon Srebnik in Israel "is *the finding of the film* itself": "the discovery of Israel as the place where, on the one hand, the remnants of the extinguished European Jewery [*sic*] could gather (find each other), and where, on the other hand, Lanzmann, coming from outside, can for the first time look inside and discover the reality of the Jews" (255, 254). In her description of Lanzmann's discovery of a Jewish identity beyond the terms of the Sartrean existentialist analysis of the "Jewish question," Felman anticipates much of the discourse that accompanied *Schindler's List* about Spielberg's "born-again" Jewishness. For both directors, the cinematic project involves the construction of a diasporic Jewish identity in relation to the events of the Holocaust, but grounded in the "reality of the Jews," that is, Israel. Israel, as a presumed site of "realness" — an originary site of testimony in *Shoah* and the end point or telos for both films — provides the supplement which allows the directors, in their very different ways, to broach the problem of representing the Holocaust and, particularly in *Schindler's List,* to cross over the breach between aesthetics and reality, and between "inauthentic" American Jew and survivor.

At the same time that the mise-en-scène of the survivors at the end of a Hollywood film seeks to provide a historical grounding where it is perceived to be needed, the simultaneous inclusion of the actors produces an ambiguous mixing of representational worlds, which again has its correlate in Lanzmann's scenes of reenactment (i.e., the staged barbershop scene with the real survivor). This scene of actors hand in hand with survivors was probably meant to signify the intimate connection between the film and the history of the Holocaust—the film's fidelity to the real and to the individual survivors, and through them to the unnamed millions of victims to whom the film is dedicated. But the real cannot be produced, only its effect; the more vigorously representation tries to assert its unmediated nature, the more it piles effect upon effect. In this case, it is not the presence of the survivors as such that produces the vertiginous, if momentary, effect, since their presence has been announced by a variety of conventional means, from the shift into color to the text identifying them as "the Schindler Jews today." Rather, it is the return of the actors into the historical space of a contemporary Jerusalem cemetery that unsettles the relationship between the film and the real. The porousness of the boundaries between narrative and history *within* the film may be intended to enhance the confusion between the film as a whole and the history that is its referent, but instead it reduces the survivors to nonspeaking extras in their own lives.

The privileging of the exceptional survivors at the expense of the majority who had no means of escape ends by traducing the survivors themselves. The implied narrative trajectory from handsome actor to dignified survivor disallows the actual voices of the survivors — they in fact do not speak — because their stories might disrupt the seamlessness with which Spielberg has constructed his narrative of the Holocaust and its aftermath. No sense of the psychic or physical cost of survival — which is unavoidable in, for example, oral testimony — disrupts the pious graveyard finale. This ambivalence at the heart of the new discourse of survival opens the possibility for dubious interventions. Even Lanzmann, who generally makes no effort to spare any of his witnesses the opportunity to display their scars, may be unable to avoid rewriting certain survivor testimonies. In a note to *Holocaust Testimonies,* Lawrence Langer reports that Filip Müller, whose narratives chart the terrain of the gas chambers and crematoria of Auschwitz in *Shoah, stammers* and that Lanzmann edited out his speech impediment (210n). If true, this would add another layer of meaning to Lanzmann's act of coupling Müller's testimony with hand-held camera-work on location. In those sequences, breaks in the soundtrack of the narrative are "audible" (a kind of absent presence) and, if Langer were correct, would represent not just an attempt to synchronize the voice and setting (as in realist films) but an effort to eliminate the traumatic effect of the voice. In smoothing over narrative ruptures, Lanzmann rejoins Spielberg, who smooths out potential survivor testimonies and the complications they would add to his story of redemption. Both films would then display elements of what Eric Santner in "History beyond the Pleasure Principle" calls "narrative fetishism": the desire to cover over trauma and rupture with continuity.

Although *Schindler's List* and *Shoah* share certain representational techniques and, to some extent, each manipulates survivors and survivor testimony, they nevertheless do so to different effect. *Schindler's List,* on the one hand, reconstructs the sites of death not in order to re-present bureaucratic murder but as the pretext for a story that, exceptionally, eludes death: the reconstructed Auschwitz and "showers" are mere props, not because they are "simulations" but because they only serve as a backdrop for the survival story of the "Schindler Jews." Hence, Spielberg's sets can become palatable sites for "memory tourism." *Shoah,* on the other hand, revisits the extermination sites in order to find a metaphor for the persistence of death and the conditions for mass murder in a world that still, unbelievably, looks innocent. As Simon Srebnik says upon returning to Chelmno in a passage at the beginning of *Shoah* that determines how the contemporary images of the extermination sites should be read: "It was always this peaceful here. Always. When they burned two thousand people—Jews—every day, it was just as peaceful" (Lanzmann, *Shoah,* 6). Lanzmann's re-presentation of the extermination camps works because it demonstrates that the camps never were what we thought they were. Drawing on the disturbing juxtapositions characteristic of traumatic realism, he replaces the almost comforting otherworldliness of the "concentrationary universe" with a more "banal" proposal: genocide took place in ordinary villages under the watchful eyes of ordinary villagers. For that reason, it is eminently representable, especially in shots that seem to show nothing unusual. But for Lanzmann, unlike for the traumatic realists discussed earlier, the portrait of this everyday scenario relies on strangely antihistorical assumptions. In Lanzmann's own words, written after his first research trip to Poland: "[T]here is no need in Poland to reconstruct the Holocaust or to strain one's imagination; the Holocaust lets itself be seen immediately in the permanent and perennial sites."[11] The Poles and Poland in Lanzmann's film stand in for the nonsynchronous elements of the Holocaust, which Ernst Bloch, in "Nonsynchronism and the Obligation to Its Dialectics," connected with fascism several years before the genocide and which contrast to the technologically modern elements of the Holocaust (which Lanzmann also shows). In his belief that he can read Poland "immediately," without mediation, Lanzmann no doubt reproduces an anti-Polish discourse of primitivism and displaces blame away from the German center of the Holocaust's instigation. But, above all, the Polish scenes authorize Lanzmann's particular mode of representing the past *in and through* the present because "a voyage to Poland is first and foremost a voyage in time" (*Au sujet de Shoah,* 213). While Lanzmann's account of Poland is historically and politically simplistic, if not misleading, it is necessary to his project because it grounds his representational practices in a way analogous to Spielberg's reconstruction of Auschwitz and his "on location" filming.

In "The Year of the Holocaust," the relationships between the real, the fictional, and the historical are not only matters for theorists of representation and history, because those relationships are complicated by questions of technology and economics. Once the all-but-untenable absolutist position that Auschwitz cannot be represented has been given up, then the possibility of multiple points of view and multiple constructions must be entertained; as Berel Lang put it, "No single representation, in effect, without the possibility of another" ("Representation," 300). If both films (and many others) "represent the Holocaust," why should Lanzmann express such resentment over Spielberg's not altogether successful attempt? The fact remains that not all representations are equal. While *Shoah* was indeed warmly received by mainstream critics and had success in commercial runs in the United States, no possibility exists for a nine-and-a-half-hour documentary by a French intellectual to compete with a feature film by Hollywood's leading director, albeit a long one on an unpleasant subject. The struggle between *Schindler's List* and *Shoah* for control over the Holocaust's "image"—staged primarily, it should be noted, by Lanzmann himself and other middlebrow and highbrow critics—derives in part from the misguided totalizing ambitions of each film to tell the "definitive" story of the Nazi genocide, but it also reflects the current asymmetry of globalized communications. As the 1993 GATT controversy in France over the import of Hollywood films and American culture demonstrated, economics and culture are inextricable from each other and mutually determining under the conditions of late capitalism. Because of the cultural and economic power of the U.S. culture industry—which French cultural producers brought into renewed focus in the GATT battle—*Schindler's List* was able to sweep the globe, creating a situation in which all that many people around the world will know about the Holocaust is the marginal story of a minor element of its history. At the same time, however, the success of

Spielberg's film contributes to the possibility (and indeed the desire) for more knowledge about and more representations of the Shoah (and probably more screenings of *Shoah,* too, as Miriam Hansen has suggested). These tensions between the popularizing reach of American culture and the strictures of European cultural critique constitute important dimensions of the ongoing debates on Holocaust representation.

The effects of the asymmetry between Lanzmann's and Spielberg's films are foregrounded by considering the circulation and consumption of Holocaust-related images, services, and products that resulted from the publicity surrounding *Schindler's List.*[12] Unlike *Shoah, Schindler's List* also takes part directly in a larger dynamic of Holocaust commodification, both as a quintessential example of Hollywood "product" and as the source of some bizarre product "tie-ins." Interestingly, the film's music has been one of the most popular elements for appropriation, perhaps because it provides a way to evoke the film's dark subject without too literally re-presenting it — the "ban on graven (Holocaust) images" is obeyed, while the capital associated with its imaging is accrued. On 9 March 1995, Lincoln Center's Alice Tully Hall was the site for a concert called "Sound Tracks II: Great Music from the Movies," hosted by Jeffrey Lyons and Michael Medved of *Sneak Previews.* An advertising brochure promised that audiences could hear the Little Orchestra Society perform selections from *Sunset Boulevard, Citizen Kane, Now, Voyager,* and "John Williams' haunting music from *Schindler's List.*" It is precisely the possibility of fetishizing elements of *Schindler's List* (i.e., the soundtrack album, the stellar performance) that constitutes its continuity with the canon of classical Hollywood cinema and its discontinuity from the soundtrack-less *Shoah.*

A month before the Lincoln Center concert, at the World Professional Figure Skating Championships, no fewer than two skaters performed to that same "haunting" soundtrack — a soundtrack, it should be pointed out, that seemed to suit the aesthetics of figure skating quite nicely. American Paul Wylie donned a concentrationary gray outfit with Hebrew letters stitched into the back and performed a routine that included what the announcers described as a "controversial Nazi salute." The section of the soundtrack that Wylie chose for the beginning of his routine was from the scene in which the Schindler women are presumed to be about to enter the gas chambers, which turn out to be simply showers. In appropriating horror for the purposes of entertainment, Wylie was not far from the logic of the film itself, in which, in the "gas chamber" sequence, the horror turns out to be only a citation of horror for the purposes of suspense and narrative complexity. Sporting Holocaust drag earned Wylie the top score for artistic merit among the male competitors.

Yet more symbolically tangled was the German skater Katarina Witt's performance, which employed a different segment of the soundtrack. According to the alternating male and female accounts of NBC's announcers, Witt was "very much aware of the symbolism of a German skating to the *Schindler's List* music." "She plays the role of the little girl in the red coat in the movie.... Alive,... all grown up." Flashing her "trademark smile," Witt, according to the announcers, "delivered a message": "She told me that her generation is younger and different, but should never forget the Holocaust. She made that statement tonight." While obviously well-meaning (as was Witt's tribute to the people of Sarajevo at the 1994 Olympics), the symbolism and message of her performance were, at best, ambiguous. In a Holocaust film focused more on "life" than on the millions of innocent victims of Nazi bureaucratic murder, the little-girl-in-red sequence was a synecdoche for those victims — and might be seen as analogous to the traumatic detail of the teddy bear in Delbo's *Auschwitz and After.* By portraying that character as alive and all grown-up, Witt unwittingly negates the truth-content of the fiction, displacing history through a second-order re-presentation. Combined with her self-presentation as younger and different, Witt's statement uses fictional Holocaust signifiers (the music, the red outfit) to effect a double removal of the Holocaust from memory: contemporary Germans are far from the genocide, she implies, and, by virtue of this distance, are empowered to reverse its course. In this scenario (as mediated through its television coverage), the new German generation takes the place of the murdered Jewish one, donning its clothes, listening to its music, rewriting its history. "Younger" Germans identify *as* German by identifying *with* Jewish victims, thus implicitly claiming a victim identity vis-à-vis the shadow of the past, while hiding that victimization through the fantasy of (the little girl's) survival.[13]

In Witt's and Wylie's self-serving, if well-intended, philo-

Semitism, it is tempting, if somewhat cynical, to read a mirrored version of Horkheimer and Adorno's analysis of anti-Semitism: "The purpose of the Fascist formula, the ritual discipline, the uniforms, and the whole apparatus, which is at first sight irrational, is to allow mimetic behavior. The carefully thought out symbols (which are proper to every counterrevolutionary movement), the skulls and disguises, the barbaric drum beats, the monotonous repetition of words and gestures, are simply the organized imitation of magic practices, the mimesis of mimesis" (*Dialectic of Enlightenment,* 184–85). Except for Wylie's momentary miming of the Nazi salute, the performances are as far from fascist formulas and Nazi symbols as one could be. Yet in ritually re-presenting the symbols and uniforms of the victims, the skaters fall into a logic similar to the one the critical theorists associate with fascism, even as they evacuate its links with barbarism. We are, once again, both close to and far from Friedlander's "new discourse," Sontag's "fascinating fascism," or Rosenfeld's "return of the Führer" (*Imagining Hitler,* 1–12)—all analyses that convincingly point to a continued obsession with the seductions of power and sadism. The "return of the girl in red," however, indicates a parallel discourse of victimization and survival that is finding a willing audience in the United States and in parts of Europe.

While Spielberg's film has inspired some to imagine the return or the resurrection of Europe's murdered Jewish population (an act with distinctly Christian undertones that is parodied in Roth's *Operation Shylock*), it has inspired others to return to the sites of destruction themselves and thus to take part in what James Young calls "memory tourism." A *New York Times* Travel Section article titled "Remembering Poland's Jews" claims that " 'Schindler's List' and the 50th anniversary of the liberation of Auschwitz have reawakened interest in the country's Holocaust sites." Complete with a list of travel agencies and accommodations, but not (tastefully?) places to eat or drink, the article describes a tour that author Ruth Ellen Gruber took to some of these "Holocaust sites":

> In a shiny German-built minivan, on a sparkling clear day last summer, we drove down a road in Cracow, Poland, paved with Jewish gravestones. The stones were fake—and I knew it: just concrete casts of real tombstones, they led into a fenced enclosure of crumbling barracks and rusting barbed wire that were

> also, I knew, simply stage sets. My knowledge, however, did little to dispel my acute uneasiness. Three other tourists and I were on a guided tour of sites related to Steven Spielberg's movie "Schindler's List." . . . For nearly two hours we followed in the footsteps of both Oskar Schindler and Mr. Spielberg, sometimes tangled in a disconcerting mixture of celluloid and reality. (29 January 1995, 8)

When Holocaust sites come to include movie sets, we have definitely entered into the realm of what Gary Weissman, rewriting Barthes, calls "the *special effect* of the real" ("Fantasy of Witnessing," 300). Weissman's analysis of *Schindler's List*'s prepublicity remains valid for the postfilm tie-ins: "In representations of the Holocaust and Nazism, a fascination with the blurring of borders between fact and fiction, real and simulation, and the present and the past competes with an interest in the Holocaust itself" (296). Gruber's "acute uneasiness" can be read as that *frisson* that results not so much from driving over desecrated gravestones as from taking part in a memorial act that puts into question the distinctions between the opposing terms that Weissman enumerates and that constitute the poles that memory must maintain. In its destabilization of the boundaries between the real and the fictional, and not in the chronological accident of the date of its release, *Schindler's List* takes part in and helps to produce "The Year of the Holocaust": that strange combination of the Holocaust's omnipresence and its evacuation, both of which are made possible by technological reproduction and the economic forces of global capitalism.

The United States Holocaust Memorial Museum: Images, Identities, and the Feel of History

By combining artifacts, simulations and replications, and state-of-the-art technology, the United States Holocaust Memorial Museum in Washington, D.C., takes part in the same dynamic as *Schindler's List*. But it also creates solutions that do not simply reproduce the debates that set Spielberg against Lanzmann in an agonistic popular/modernist struggle. The USHMM consists of the most complex and, with all likelihood, the most lasting of the cultural phenomena collected under "The Year of the Holocaust" rubric. Although it opened in April 1993, the museum's particular engagement with the present struggle over the history and appearance of the past represents the outcome of a fifteen-year process involving political, intellectual, moral, and aesthetic negotiation. As a very specific kind of "text," the "memorial museum" calls for a methodology of reading that combines historical genealogy, phenomenological description, anthropological observation, political critique, and literary and art criticism. Because the museum collects so many elements into one unstable whole and thus demands an extremely heterogeneous critical practice to engage with it, we should not expect it to yield a singular meaning or significance, especially within a constantly changing cultural context. Like other sites of memory and knowledge production, the USHMM functions necessarily and (in part) intentionally as a place in which to observe what James Young calls the "activity of memory, by which artifacts of ages past are invigorated by the present moment, even as they condition our understanding of the world around us" (*Texture of Memory,* 14–15). In narrating and interpreting some aspects of the museum's activity of memory, we can distinguish the overlap of at least four interrelated levels: the museum's background (the commissioning and planning), its physical site (a combination of geography, architecture, and design), the exhibit contents (including questions of narrative, technology, and cultural identity), and the museum's reception (by popular, mass media, and intellectual publics). The USHMM is simultaneously a very particular and ambivalent Holocaust representation and a two-tiered pedagogical machine: it produces historical knowledge and emotional-subjective identifications at the same time that it embodies in its architecture and narrative a spatiotemporal map of the Nazi genocide.

Although a search for the museum's origins would have to consider a number of tangential phenomena extending all the way back to World War II, if not beyond (some of which I have already discussed), the usual place to start such a discussion would be with the founding by President Jimmy Carter in 1978 of the President's Commission on the Holocaust.[14] This presidential act took place in a highly politicized context involving concern on the part of Jewish Americans over Carter's sale of military equipment to Saudi Arabia, a sale perceived to threaten the security of Israel. This political context intersected with a cultural environment in which, with the televising of the *Holocaust* miniseries, interest in the Shoah was building among Jews and non-Jews alike. The fortuitous coming together of the historical-cultural and the contemporary political could only take place because of the links that had already been established in the wake of the 1967 Arab-Israeli war between the Holocaust and Israel. Within a year of the commission's founding, its chair, Elie Wiesel, had drafted a series of proposals that called for the establishment of a museum and a " 'living' monument." While those proposals have been implemented, another recommendation was rejected for political reasons: "[T]he group urged that a Committee on Conscience of prominent citizens be established to sound an alarm whenever and wherever human rights were violated," but the State Department and the "human rights" president rejected that proposal as potentially disruptive of, and embarrassing to, the U.S. government's security interests (J. Miller, 227).

As the president's commission gave way to the U.S. Holocaust Memorial Council, and the concrete planning and design of the museum got under way, political controversies both internal and external helped to shape the project. The external contests over memory and memorialization included Ronald Reagan's infamous Bitburg excursion (see Hartman, *Bitburg*)—at which time Wiesel asked the entire council to resign — and architect James Ingo Freed's struggles with the institutionalized aesthetics of Washington's Fine Arts Commission, which limited the degree to which the museum could provide "critiques of the monumental Washington front" (see Freed, 90). Various nation-states also attempted, with mixed results, to influence what the museum included and what it excluded. Thus, the German government's desire to see the success of the *Bundesrepublik* honored as a bulwark against fascism was not fulfilled, but Turkey succeeded in discouraging extensive consideration of the Armenian genocide, and the U.S. State Department successfully lobbied against provoking contemporary action through allusion to the ongoing Bosnian massacre.[15] Within the memorial council, disagreements ranged from global questions involving the overall shape of the exhibit's narrative to local decisions about which items to display. One controversy that has already received a great deal of attention concerned what to do with nine kilograms of human hair sent from the State Museum of Auschwitz (Linenthal, "Boundaries of Memory," 421–25; Ryback). The hair had been cut from the heads of victims just before or after they were gassed in order to be used in German industries. Although the council originally voted to include the hair as material evidence of the ghastly extremes that Nazi "rationality" took, opposition from many survivors and others resulted in a photograph replacing the actual hair in the museum's permanent exhibit. All of these matters are part of the museum's memory work and reveal the competing interests and perspectives involved in the production of Holocaust memory and representation. This history continues to echo in the ultimate form of the museum's exhibits and programs. Nevertheless, that final structure cannot be read only from a historical perspective, since it is continually reactivated in the present through the reception and modification of its finished form.

In considering the completed museum, one of its most salient and determining qualities is its location. In tune with its origins in a presidential decree, the museum is situated in a politically overdetermined site just off Washington's Mall. It is thus almost literally in the shadow of the Washington and Jefferson Monuments, and just a few hundred yards away from the various components of the Smithsonian's national museum complex. In such a situation, the USHMM has become an unlikely blockbuster tourist attraction, filled to capacity with visitors from school trips and tour buses. The crowds lining up to learn about the Nazi destruction of the European Jews thus represent not so much the expected ethnic identity politics of the contemporary United States, but rather the political economy of tourism in the nation's capital. Most, although certainly not all, are white and seem to come from middle-class Middle America. The result of the "official Washington" site and the government imprimatur seems to be the integration of the museum, if not the Holocaust itself, into the fabric of American historical memory.

This process of partial assimilation has been named "Americanization" by the former director of the museum's Research Institute, Michael Berenbaum. Embracing Americanization as the best means of importing historical knowledge of events in which Americans have been involved in a variety of ways, yet that remain primarily European, may be inevitable, but it is also risky. In an interview with journalist Philip Gourevitch, Berenbaum described what he intends by this term: "In America . . . we recast the story of the Holocaust to teach fundamental American values. . . . For example — when America is at its best — pluralism, democracy, restraint on government, the inalienable rights of individuals, the inability of government to enter into freedom of the press, freedom of assembly, freedom of religion, and so forth" (Gourevitch, "Behold Now Behemoth," 56). Gourevitch, in his thoroughgoing dismissal of the museum as just another "theme park," remains doubtful as to the relevance and efficacy of such a program, even as he subscribes to the very values enumerated by Berenbaum. Despite attempted Americanization, Gourevitch writes, "[t]he fact remains, however, that the Holocaust was a European event, and that even at its utter worst, America has been a place where the Holocaust — a program of genocidal extermination mandated and implemented by every organ of a nation-state — has never entered the realm of possibility. . . . To suggest that there are meaningful comparisons can only distort our already feeble understanding of European history and — worse — obscure our perception of current American reality" (56).[16] While Gourevitch is correct to question the efficacy of comparison, by suggesting that "denouncing evil is a far cry from doing good" (57), his own understanding of American history might surprise African Americans, Native Americans, and victims of the American war in Indochina (not to mention American refugees and survivors of Nazi Germany). In the light of the legacies of slavery, Native genocide, and other state-sponsored American crimes — regardless of whether they "equal" the Holocaust — Gourevitch's complaints about the museum seem close to those of the various governments who correctly sensed the political impact such a historical museum could have in the present. The history of the USHMM demonstrates, in other words, that Americanization need not satisfy all of the champions of American values, but remains a contested process.

In any case, the version of Americanization actualized by the museum does not necessarily bear out Gourevitch's fear that the museum will function as "a therapeutic mass-cultural experience" (57) or Berenbaum's hope that it will serve as a site of democratic pedagogy. Neither of those poles captures the complexity of the USHMM, which "Americanizes" the Holocaust in a way significantly different from that found in *Schindler's List* (although the film has also been described and used in terms of therapy and pedagogy). The film can be considered American by virtue both of its optimistic narrative and hero, whom *Le Monde* termed an "ambiguous champion of 'free enterprise' " (3 March 1994, 1; my translation), and of its status as entertainment (which facilitated the various product "tie-ins"). The USHMM Americanizes the Holocaust in more contradictory fashion: it simultaneously brings the Holocaust closer to the history of the United States and brings Americans closer to the history of the genocide (which could just as easily be described as "de-Americanization"). These two processes are themselves ambiguous, but never does the museum provide the kind of exceptional happy ending that the film does, and never does the museum's user-friendliness decay to the status of entertainment or become an object of perverse fascination (which does not discount that such reactions are still conceivable). The presence of a film of survivor testimony at the end of the permanent exhibit makes a sharp contrast to the end of *Schindler's List,* where the survivors are presented but not allowed to represent themselves.

This major event in European history is assimilated to the official version of American heritage primarily through a stress on the role of the United States Army in liberating some of the concentration camps and defeating Nazi Germany. School groups and tours who enter through the Fifteenth Street entrance pass through Dwight D. Eisenhower Plaza, dedicated in honor of the general and the allied forces. An engraved stone reads, "Victorious in battle, they brought the Third Reich to an end, encountered its concentration camps, liberated the survivors and bore witness to the Holocaust." On the exterior walls of the Hall of Remembrance that bounds the plaza are engraved quotations from Eisenhower and Presidents Bush and Reagan. The effect of this first introduction is to place the Holocaust squarely within U.S. military and political history. Such a placement is, of course, not without irony, given Reagan's Bitburg offense and the more relevant historical fact that Allied forces were by no means fighting to "liberate survivors" or "bear witness" to an event that had not yet been named and that the Allies' leaders had effectively ignored. Entering through the main Fourteenth Street entrance produces a comparable effect through the juxtaposition of a quotation from President Clinton with flags representing the American army units that liberated the camps.[17]

The permanent exhibit itself is framed by a similar rhetoric of American liberation. Upon entering the elevators that carry visitors to the fourth floor, where the exhibit begins, attention is focused through the use of a video monitor. When the doors close and the sound and images begin, everyday conversations tend to be silenced quickly and replaced by a hushed and serious demeanor that generally lasts throughout the exhibit visit. As the monitor displays footage of the first encounters of the American army with the camps, an American soldier recounts his experience of this discovery: "Sick, dying, starved people. . . . Such a sight as that, you . . . you can't imagine it. You, you just . . . things like that don't happen" (transcribed in Linenthal, "Boundaries of Memory," 407). The stuttering, incomplete sentences register and "translate" an unprecedented encounter that, it is subtly implied, the visitors are also about to have. As the GI's testimony ends, the elevator doors immediately spring open in front of a large photo of American soldiers standing over the charred remains of camp prisoners. In an adjacent video screen a soldier enters the frame and proceeds to observe and photograph victims who never made it out of the last cattle cars. These first minutes of the visit provide a powerful grid through which the remainder of the visit (which takes most visitors more than three hours) will be understood. They introduce the power of the video/film and photographic image, upon which much of the exhibit relies, and they focus this image through the gaze of American soldiers. Even if later components of the museum will significantly complicate this identification with the "liberators" by drawing attention to the government's less than consistently righteous response to the Shoah (e.g., the *St. Louis* refugee fiasco, the failure to bomb Auschwitz), the overall impression of the United States as a past and future bulwark against fascism and injustice persists, and, indeed, given the location of the museum, could do nothing else.

Nevertheless, the question of which notion of "Americanness" to incorporate into the Holocaust remains. In the final pages of his already classic study of Holocaust memorials, *The Texture of Memory,* James Young writes of the museum that "the visitors' experience will begin appropriately with America's first direct Holocaust experience — through the eyes of the American GIs who liberated Buchenwald and Dachau" (345). If Americanization is perhaps inevitable, it is by no means obvious that the only "appropriate" form it will take is through the equation of Americanness with the American army. Given the status of the United

States as a land of immigrants, a significant number of whom are either survivors of the Holocaust, as Young also remarks, or relatives of survivors and victims, not to mention perpetrators and bystanders, a significantly different point of view could have been established for the narrative that follows. Acknowledging from the beginning the Americanness of exile and suffering, and not just liberation — both outside of and within the United States — would have revealed a range of identifications well beyond that with the military. Such an alternative strategy might have powerfully fulfilled the dialectic of Jewish uniqueness and moral universality that characterizes the museum's overt mission. In short, whether Americanization is condemned or condoned, it needs to be recognized as an open-ended possibility, as subject to negotiation as democracy itself.

It is one of the peculiarities of the museum that this previous process of identification with the victors is experienced almost simultaneously with a countervailing force: identification with the victims. Even as visitors are held rapt by the video / voice-over of liberation in the elevator they are also being definitively removed from American "soil." The elevator, as the museum's architect and designer have emphasized, is the most dramatic of a series of design strategies meant to isolate visitors from present-day Washington. Besides being a celebration of contemporary democratic society, the museum is also a time machine that transports its visitors to another place in history. When visitors emerge from the elevator they have also been encouraged to assume — in a distanced way — a new identity. In one of the museum's controversial "experiential" ploys, one that has also undergone several emendations, visitors choose an identity card that bears the story of an individual Holocaust victim.[18] In the initial conception, the only information that the card originally contained concerned the "character's" prewar life; visitors were given identities that matched their gender and age. At various points, corresponding to turning points in the exhibit's historical narrative, a computer could be used to update the story. Because of technical difficulties, mechanization was replaced by other strategies. During an intermediate stage, visitors simply chose a card that revealed the life story of a victim. Currently, the cards have been redesigned as small booklets in order to preserve the narrative development of the original plan. Whether or not visitors actually use the cards as intended and form some kind of temporary identifications will vary — personally, I was not drawn in — but the cards certainly contribute to making what Young calls "a victim-imagined museum" (344). The doubled identifications that result from the layering of Americanness with victimization parallel those of *Schindler's List* in which the triumphal narrative of survival and rescue proposes two distinct characters for identification (Stern and Schindler), as well as a more distanced acknowledgment of the death of the "others."

As visitors are drawn into the museum's narrative, these two suggested points of view begin inevitably to come into conversation, if not conflict, with the cultural identities (ethnic, national, sexual . . .) visitors already carry with them. As the accounts of Miller and Linenthal indicate, the negotiation between competing claims of victimization vis-à-vis both the Nazi period (homosexuals, Poles, Roma . . .) and other histories of oppression (Armenians, African and Native Americans . . .) presented the exhibit's organizers with some of their most difficult challenges. The narrative they constructed in order to solve these tensions simultaneously places Jews at the center of a hierarchy of victims and renders them abstract by representing them only in the context of Nazi power. The combination of stratification and abstraction allows American identifications with the victims at the same time that it does not upset the American ideals of the liberators.

While the overarching narrative follows the persecution and extermination of Jews, twists and side-bars are added to account for the multiple "enemies of the state." A certain lack of resolution regarding the place of these enemies unsettles the linearity of the consideration of Jews in the Holocaust. Admirable efforts are made to personalize the Nazi's Jewish victims — both through the identity cards and through the most effective design feature, Yaffa Eliach's stunning tower of photos from the shtetl of Ejszyszki. Visitors receive mixed messages about the specificity of the other victims, however. While, for example, the Roma ("Gypsies") are first grouped generically with homosexuals, political prisoners, and Jehovah's Witnesses, we later read that "their fate closely paralleled that of the Jews," and indeed many text panels describe the effects of Nazi policy on "Jews and Roma." Visitors are left uncertain whether the hierarchy that places Jews "above" Roma is a function of a qualitative difference in Nazi policy and ideology or of the quantity of victims. In that first section on "enemies of the state," a video monitor personalizes the victims to a limited extent by identifying successive groups of others. Later, however, in the most visible display of non-Jewish "enemies," located just after visitors pass through an actual railroad car, a wall of mug shots is accompanied with a text that deprives such victims of their specificity: "These images of prisoners include political dissidents, Roma (Gypsies), homosexuals, Soviet prisoners of war, and criminals." It is impossible to match an identity with an image, just as it is impossible to know how to understand the relationships between such different categories. The ambivalence of the representation of non-Jewish victims — is their suffering also unique? — no doubt expresses the outcome of conflictual planning sessions as well as the complex realities of World War II history. The point is not that the museum's narrative is wrong or could have been done better, but that it structures response without determining it. The very lack of resolution in the treatment of the "mosaic of victims" leaves openings for other interventions, either within or beyond the walls of the museum. Thus, lesbian and gay activists could use the opening of the museum as the occasion for a vigil and rally meant to call attention to histories of homophobic violence, and African and Native Americans could point to the representation of Jewish history as evidence that it was time to represent their own particular American histories. While the very holes and contradictions in the museum's narrative and its relation to U.S. history in general sometimes generate such radically democratic initiatives, it is equally possible that they could generate *ressentiment*. Indeed, every time I left the museum I did not have to go far before I saw some anti-Semitic manifestation, usually in the form of swastika graffiti.

Besides the framing devices that establish point of view by interpellating visitors as American and victims, identification is also motivated or blocked by contradictions between and within the form and content of the museum's narrative. After the proleptic and ambiguous confrontation with liberation, visitors are taken through a condensed, primarily linear, chronology of the Third Reich, from the seizure of power to the end of the war. Within the main narrative of the museum, the histories on either side of the 1933–45 period are deliberately downplayed. On the one side, the centuries of Jewish history in Europe are reduced to a handful of uninformative sentences and a series of unexplained images (first on video screens, later in two powerful photography series); meanwhile, the histories of Christian anti-Semitism and German nationalism, two of the sources of Nazi ideology, are missing from the main narrative, although they are covered in two optional films. On the contemporary side, the final space of the exhibit provides images and texts dealing with the founding of Israel and emigration to the United States, but these postwar narratives are literally overshadowed by the presence in the same space of a large screen on which survivor testimony is continuously projected. Although the testimonies deal disproportionately with the themes of rescue and resistance, thus reprising elements of the final floor of the exhibit, they also inevitably return visitors to the narratives of the "Final Solution." When one woman survivor recounts her escape from Sobibor as having entailed "hopping on dead bodies," and another describes a death march in which "I saw girls breaking off their [frozen] toes like twigs," any happy resolution and triumphal overtones (pace *Schindler's List*) are undercut. The survivor testimonies provide a fitting culmination to the emotional component of the museum's project by confronting whatever identifications viewers have made with the victims and liberators with the terrible evidence of the persistence of trauma. They do not, however, make up for the lack of historical contextualization. The Nazi genocide is in no way mythified or mystified by the museum's narrative. Yet the foreshortened historical optic gives the mistaken impression that the event's uniqueness lies in its separation from the rest of history, not in its singular conjuncture of *"factors by themselves quite ordinary and common"* (Bauman, xiii).

The compactness of the narrative "story" is complicated by the "discourse" of the exhibit's design (to adopt the conventional distinction from narratology). The path of the visit consists of twists and turns, which provide occasional glimpses forward and backward in "time," while the visitors' space itself is constricted and narrow, causing frequent crowding throughout the three floors of the exhibit and constraining visitors to keep moving forward. The exhibit designers also effectively exploit Freed's deconstructivist architecture by foregrounding the asymmetries of the building and its bridges and glass panels, which prevent the enclosure of "proper" spaces. The exhibit thus spatializes time in a very particular way, rendering history visible as a complex layering of residual, dominant, and emergent traces that suggest but do not dictate connections between different moments. This layering inflects the understanding of historical time as aftereffect and retrospection found in Blanchot: on the one hand, the (re)visiting of spaces already glimpsed allows an "after the fact" reevaluation of the place of the past in the narrative that has led up to that present; on the other hand, the possibility of seeing ahead in time, which the twisting, porous design enables, suggests that things could have been different if emergent tendencies had been grasped in the past. The exhibit's layout also captures the geography of the Holocaust's terrible simultaneity in which bystanders and future victims stood by in apathy or ignorance as murder proceeded in neighboring towns or nations. In this dual insistence on necessity and contingency, the design synthesizes the two dominant schools of the last quarter-century's interpretation of the development of the "Final Solution": the meanderings of the functionalist "twisted road" to Auschwitz and the inevitable progression of the intentionalist "straight path" (see Marrus, *Holocaust,* 31–54). The intentionalists' belief that Hitler's career "reflect[s] a consistent murderous objective" (Marrus, *Holocaust,* 34–35) is communicated through the "flashback" from liberation to the origins of the Third Reich, which inscribes the memory of the narrative's conclusion back into its origins, and through the pressure exerted by the crowd to keep moving forward through the exhibit. At the same time, the functionalists' "picture of the Third Reich as a maze of competing power groups, rival bureaucracies, forceful personalities, and diametrically opposed interests" (Marrus, *Holocaust,* 40) is materialized in the nonlinear design of the exhibition space and the discontinuity of many of its images and artifacts. This dialectical understanding of history as a composite of agency and structure recalls the binary identifications with the liberators and the victims posited by the narrative's point of view.

The "Tower of Faces" section of the museum represents another significant source of identification and a tour de force of design that complicates further the museum's construction of meaning in history. The tower is a beautifully constructed, multiple-story structure containing hundreds of prewar family photographs from the shtetl of Ejszyszki in Lithuania. Visitors pass through the tower at two points in the exhibit narrative—once before and once after the killing. In Marianne Hirsch's eloquent formulation, "When we enter the Tower of Faces, we leave the historical account of the museum and enter a domestic space of a family album that shapes a different form of looking and knowing, a different style of recognition, one that is available to any viewer and that can connect viewers of different backgrounds to one another" (*Family Frames,* 254). Like the texts of traumatic realism, the tower shifts emphasis from the larger processes of history to a homeliness that necessarily haunts genocide but that is also accessible to ordinary visitors because of its familial form. The tower supplements the museum's synthesis of intentionalism and functionalism by puncturing both narratives with an extranarrative interlude. Although panels of text reveal the fate of the shtetl's inhabitants, the photographs remain unintegratable into narrative memory of the Holocaust because — like Klüger's socks or Delbo's teddy bear — their everydayness seems incommensurable with the extreme violence of genocide that they nevertheless index. Employed rhetorically, such traumatic indexes mobilize the familiar in the service of the radically unfamiliar.[19]

The narrative structure of the permanent exhibit reveals the museum's character as twofold: both a pedagogical tool for the dissemination of historical knowledge and a site of identifications meant to guide and evoke emotional responses based on personal interaction with the various "characters" in the story. Other nonnarrative elements — in particular the use of technology and the presence of artifacts and almost-authentic castings — also contribute to the pedagogical/experiential functioning of the museum. Cognizant of the Holocaust's challenge to celebration of the instrumental rationality of modernity, the museum's conceivers saw a possibility to intervene in "America's infatuation with technology, so predominant in other museums and memorials on the Mall. 'While the Air and Space Museum glorified the wondrous capabilities of technological know-how, the Holocaust museum will reveal the dark side of technology,' Michael Berenbaum said of his museum" (J. Miller, *One, by One,* 234). Despite this intention, video and computer technologies play important roles in the museum, even if their use is restrained compared to the high-tech Hollywood version of Holocaust history enshrined at Los Angeles's Museum of Tolerance. Indeed, Judith Miller reports, the computer system in the USHMM's Wexner Learning Center has been designed by someone who created a similar system for the Israeli Defense Forces (265). The computers, which are located both in the learning center and at strategic points in the permanent exhibit (usually involving American responses to the genocide), complement the "modernist" historical narrative with the nonlinear mode of knowledge particular to postmodern information technologies.

The learning center allows visitors to deepen their knowledge of particular aspects of the Nazi genocide by accessing encyclopedia articles, photographs, video and film clips, maps, and music, all available via computer. The computers' database (which is constantly being expanded and refined) is structured by the logic of hypermedia linkages. After choosing an initial topic, date, or keyword, users can follow up on other highlighted terms and pursue different themes through the use of different media: life in the ghetto might be illustrated by a Yiddish song, a personal anecdote, or a scholarly essay. Such a system provides an accessible means of producing different kinds of knowledge in the same technological "space"—that gained by the reading of "scientific" texts and that experienced through listening to survivor testimony. However, the multiplicity of paths that hypermedia allows through the computer database undermines certain aspects of historical understanding that the structure of the exhibit narrative creates. The connections between time and causality disappear as the pursuit of the highlighted terms in one article can lead to entirely different locations. Having selected the "Aftermath" menu option, for example, I was disconcerted to find that I was soon reading about conditions in the Warsaw Ghetto. As opposed to being dictated by some connection to historical conditions, there is a large degree of arbitrariness and whim in the movement between eras, events, and types of evidence. Perspective on spatiotemporal location breaks down as the hypermedia system promotes an illusory simultaneity of times and places. The predominance of sequencing and flow over constrained movement through time and space (as found in the exhibit narrative) produces a contradiction between the ease with which information is accessed and the difficulty with which such information can be assimilated and understood. This paradox grows out of the contradictory demands for historical documentation and public access to knowledge through information technologies that are condensed in "The Year of the Holocaust."

The computers located at particular points in the course of the permanent exhibit serve a somewhat different purpose since they are keyed to particular aspects of Holocaust history, usually American responses to the events in Europe. But, as with the use of technology in the learning center, they also ultimately and ironically facilitate an erroneous belief that knowledge can bypass mediation. Here, a menu is presented and a message provocatively reads, "Touch an Event to Begin." This suggestion of tactile links to knowledge connects technology to the museum's other experiential and sense-based strategies of pedagogy.

The idea that one can touch an event that happened fifty years ago on another continent is implicit in the museum's significant reliance on artifacts and castings. When visitors walk through a railroad car that transported Jews to their deaths, furtively touch part of the Birkenau barracks, or smell the rotting abandoned shoes of victims, a different kind of experience emerges from that produced by the reading of texts and the observation of videos and photographs (although these can also have bodily effects). While many of the artifacts displayed are extremely ordinary, their effect differs from that of the Tower of Faces and the other traumatic indexes since they are not only easily aestheticized, as Andrea Liss points out, but also easily *reachable*. The symbolic power of the socks in *weiter leben* derives from their inaccessibility, the way in which their everydayness is estranged by the barbed wire geography of the camps. In transporting artifacts from the camps to Washington, D.C., a risk accrues of simplifying the relationship between the extremity and everydayness of genocidal violence. If the conspicuous presence of "authentic" artifacts also often feels like a defensive move against highly visible Holocaust deniers (and one that to a degree stays within the logic of "proof" of those deniers), visitors I observed also demonstrate a desire for such tactile connection. In one temporary exhibit on the museum's lower level of painted tiles documenting the responses of school children who had visited the museum, other young visitors were drawn to run their fingers over the texture of the tiles (as I was also). In the special "walk-in" section designed for those too young for the main exhibit, "Remembering the Children: Daniel's Story," an emphasis is also put on touching the reconstructed house, ghetto, and concentration camp of the fictional Daniel. Children are invited to look under Daniel's bed, open windows to see "outside," and listen in as joyful, but ghostly, prewar voices echo in the house's kitchen. As a pedagogical tool for reaching children, such tactile and sense-based methods may be most effective, but, especially in the main exhibit, they are also potentially misleading in the ease with which they allow contemporary visitors to touch an event that in both its extremity and everydayness continues to elude us.

The affective, tactile connection to history promised by the museum clearly fills a need not fully satisfied by scholarly discourses on the Holocaust or even firsthand accounts of the camps, such as those I have discussed as examples of traumatic realism. There seems to be a direct correspondence between the heightened degree of mediation in recent Holocaust texts—such as Hollywood films and high-tech museums—and the belief that such texts can provide a direct access to history. The palpable desire for history in public responses to *Schindler's List* and the USHMM might be taken as a sign that postmodernism has not only meant the disappearance of a sense of history, as critic Fredric Jameson has suggested. Nor is contemporary fascination with the Holocaust easily aligned with the nostalgia mode typical of postmodern approaches to the past (see Jameson, *Postmodernism*). And yet there is no doubt that the museum, like other artifacts of "The Year of the Holocaust," embodies an ambivalence common in public history projects. In disseminating history and memory through a broad, collective address, the museum necessarily opens itself up to highly idiosyncratic appropriations.

In a short essay concerning visitor response to the Holocaust museum, one of the museum's most vocal critics, Philip Gourevitch, observed that visitors' "diverse reactions reflect the beliefs and attitudes they brought to the museum as much as anything they discovered within its walls." Diagnosing current interest in the Holocaust as one of many "fashions in popular history," Gourevitch argued pessimistically that "the Holocaust Museum provides a rhetorical exercise in bearing witness to dehumanization and mass murder from a seemingly safe distance" ("What They Saw," 45). The omnipresence of "subjective" (mis)readings of history by museum visitors is, of course, a sociological truism, and indeed, "The Year of the Holocaust" represents a fashion, even if one that has already lasted well beyond its fifteen minutes of fame. But while the museum never forces visitors beyond the "safe distance" of the spectator, rhetorical exercises in witnessing should not be underestimated.[20] This is true not simply because even the most authentic acts of witnessing are inevitably rhetorical, but because they derive their potential power precisely from that fact. Rhetorical dimensions of testimony and memorialization are essential to pedagogy and the expansion of historical knowledge in the same way that representations are. Gourevitch is content to accept only "one certain lesson" from the Holocaust: "that it happened" ("Behold Now Behemoth," 62). But testimony and certain acts of representation do more than give us "the facts"; they demand a change in our understanding of what is accepted history. Although its lessons are not comforting, the Holocaust did more than just "happen"; it emerged, it persisted, it persists.

The inevitability of rhetoric, representation, and mediation does not entail the erosion of judgment or the collapse of truth — even in "The Year of the Holocaust," when historical understanding seems to be undergoing a significant mutation. *Shoah* surpasses *Schindler's List* in its contribution to understanding the Holocaust not because it is less rhetorical but because it more rigorously searches for a form commensurate with the Holocaust's destruction of already existing forms and because it foregrounds the mediations inherent in its acts of representation; in that, it is supremely rhetorical. The Holocaust museum is not just a "theme park" or another of Washington's celebrations of Americanism because it literally twists the materials of its construction into a new shape, thus registering the real in a spatiotemporal choreography of unexpected subtlety. At the same time, the museum appeals to, creates, and sometimes satisfies desires for immediacy and identification that often conflict with its historical architectonics. Certainly no "text" — and no museum, feature film, or epic documentary — can embody the contradictory contents of history in a wholly coherent form. We need to articulate options that submit neither to the fallacy that representing the Holocaust could mean replacing a lived reality with a belated aesthetic nor to the defeatism that claims to rest content with knowing "that it happened." As caretakers of postmemory in a decidedly unredeemed landscape, no resource, be it fictional, rhetorical, or visual, can be spared.

Conclusion

After the "Final Solution"

From the "Jewish Question" to Jewish Questioning

We are not "the woman question" asked by somebody else; we are the women who ask the questions.

— Adrienne Rich, "Notes toward a Politics of Location"

Tu te tais, j'étais. Tu parles, je suis.

— Edmond Jabès, *Le livre des questions*

One of the most powerful moments during a visit to the United States Holocaust Memorial Museum in Washington came for me in a transitional section between exhibition floors. In this in-between space are collected artifacts and images of artifacts that in their dumb materiality speak loudly about the human lives that they indicate only obliquely. Here is found the wall-length photograph of hair from Auschwitz, human remains that aroused one of the most bitter disputes of the museum's planning. Also present is a poignant pile of shoes left by the Nazi's victims; the shoes emit a sour smell of passed time that adds another affective dimension to the sensory experience offered by the museum. There is a spare metal truck frame, which looks at first like the support for a missing exhibit, until you realize that this is the Majdanek "roast" on which the murdered were burned in lieu of a crematorium oven. The incompleteness of these artifacts is the point; they all gesture toward the absent and unrecoverable bodies of the dead.

Another exhibit in the same area points to the way that unrecoverable absence is inscribed on the bodies of survivors. A collection of photographs taken at a 1991 gathering of survivors in Los Angeles shows the tattooed arms that marked the Nazi's efforts to dehumanize their victims. On the one hand, the photographs, which show only arms, emphasize the success of that genocidal program by fragmenting the survivors' bodies and displaying the indelible sign of suffering. On the other hand, the collection of images represents an actually existing collective of survivors, an indication both of some survivors' defiant agency and of the persistence of Jewish community after the "Final Solution." In no way do the photographs propose a transcendence of the Holocaust: an adjacent group portrait shows four survivors from Salonika displaying their tattoos and staring at the camera with unredeemable expressions of anger and sorrow. Here, more than anywhere in the museum, including the final oral testimony section, the survivors return the gaze of Holocaust tourists and pilgrims. Their message is easy to read, yet unassimilable to "normal" everyday life: viewers are reminded that they were not *there,* but that the survivors live on, carrying their unredeemed experiences into the post-Holocaust era. The all-too-present tattoo marks another absence, another asymmetry between past and present: the gap between the survivors and the postmemory generation that is now drawn to their experience.

In her two-page short story "Three Days and a Question," Grace Paley interrogates the absences of victimized bodies and the gaps in communication between the victimized and the privileged that the museum's exhibits suggest. Drawing on the status of the Holocaust in the United States as both a metaphor for suffering and a specific historical experience, Paley succinctly raises many of the questions of representation that have occupied me throughout this book. The Holocaust-as-event is less present in this brief text than in most of the documents I have considered, but the vitality of its memory generates the sequence of three vignettes that constitute the story's associative narrative. Paley takes part in "The Year of the Holocaust" discourse by creating a sequence between qualitatively different historical experiences, but the effect is not a flattening or relativization of suffering; rather, her historical contextualizations make the question of genocide *more* real for her readers.

The passage of "Three Days and a Question" in which Holocaust memory is at stake is worth quoting at length. Paley's story begins here:

> On the first day I joined a demonstration opposing the arrest in Israel of members of Yesh Gvul, Israeli soldiers who had refused

to serve in the occupied territories. Yesh Gvul means: *There is a Limit.*

TV cameras and an anchorwoman arrived and *New York Times* stringers with their narrow journalism notebooks. What do you think? the anchorwoman asked. What do you think, she asked a woman passer by — a woman about my age.

Anti-Semites, the woman said quietly.

The anchorwoman said, But they're Jewish.

Anti-Semites, the woman said a little louder.

What? One of our demonstrators stepped up to her. Are you crazy? How can you . . . Listen what we're saying.

Rotten anti-Semites — all of you.

What? What What the man shouted. How you dare to say that — all of us Jews. Me, he said. He pulled up his shirtsleeves. Me? You call me? You look. He held out his arm. Look at this.

I'm not looking, she screamed.

You look at my number, what they did to me. My arm . . . you have no right.

Anti-Semite, she said between her teeth. Israel hater.

No, no he said, you fool. My arm — you're afraid to look . . . my arm . . . my arm. (*Long Walks,* n.p.)

Through the figure of the exposed arm Paley links this confrontation with two further encounters: one with a young homeless man whose arm is covered with Kaposi's sarcoma lesions, one with a Haitian cab driver who holds his arm up to the narrator and asks, à propos of U.S. refugee policy, "You tell me — this skin, this black skin — why? Why you hate this skin so much?" Having narrated these three encounters, Paley asks in the text's final lines: "Those gestures, those arms, the three consecutive days thrown like a formal net over the barest unchanged accidental facts. How? Why? In order to become — probably — in this city one story told."

In this story the tattooed arm of the Holocaust survivor holds a special place, not only as the initiating gesture of the series, but as the possessor of an already metaphorical charge. I don't mean simply the Holocaust's archetypical narrative of suffering, which has become, in its extremity, a source of analogy for other histories. Rather, the revelatory self-exposure of the survivor provides a first analogy between Jewish suffering and Jewish-inflicted suffering that grounds and authorizes the metonymical chain constructed with the segments on AIDS and racism. "There Is a Limit" is the name of the group for which the demonstrators rally, a name that in its Israeli context refers to a geographical and moral topography and that, in this story, comes to refer as well to the boundaries of ethnic identity and figuration. If, on the one hand, the notion of the limit signals a refusal to move beyond certain preestablished borders, on the other hand, the survivor's gesture implies the mutual implication of limits and their transgressions. In response to the passer-by's slur — "Rotten anti-Semites" — the man bears his arm, thus claiming the authority to speak from a Jewish subject-position about Jews and their responsibilities. The survivor reappropriates the essentializing inscription on the surface of his body, claiming the Jewishness that the Nazis once demonized, but he simultaneously transcends the limits of that identity as it has been institutionalized by an uncritically Zionist American-Jewish leadership. There is a moral limit to what humans ought do to each other, but it can only be established through the transgression of a limited ethnic identity always at risk of absolutization. Yet, the story proposes, the ethics of that transgression are not founded on a refusal of identity — that refusal is shown to be impossible in each of the three vignettes, in part because of the essentializing (but not essential) inscription on the body of otherwise very different racial, ethnic, and medical codes. The story's working out of an "anti-anti-essentialist" notion of ethnic identity is the place from which an ethics honoring difference emerges.[1]

Like Philip Roth in *Operation Shylock* or Art Spiegelman in *Maus*, Paley, in "Three Days and a Question," interrogates the narrator's identity as surely as she does various collective identities. Although the generic status of this story is never specified, Paley is easily recognized as a character since she carefully includes herself and her collaborator, artist Vera Williams, in each vignette. The sight of the homeless young man causes both the narrator and her friend Vera to see him from a certain perspective: "Separately, Vera and I think: A boy — only a boy. Mothers after all, our common trade for more than thirty years." Paley is not appealing to an essential notion of feminine and motherly compassion, as her contrast to the unsympathetic passer-by and her comment about parenting as a "trade" make clear. Nevertheless, she, like Roth and Spiegelman, genders her construction of Jewish-American identity. In *Operation Shylock*, for instance, Philip's determinate distance from the Holocaust and the oppression of Palestinians leaves him seated with a sexy shiksa in the Garden of Eden, eating, he tells us, from the "tree of fiction" (219). There is a powerful truth to Roth's comic portrait of Jewish-American masculinity, but Paley's narrator is elsewhere, inhabiting a blighted urban setting of conflict and disease. The references to mothering create a different sense of narrative time than can be found in Roth's metafiction, not the repetition of doubling, but the ethically implicated difference of generations, a difference exploited for other effects in *Maus*. The women's relationship to the boy complements the relationship between the survivor and the absent Jewish and Palestinian boys he is defending and between each segment of the story. This ethical, generational bond is explicitly not biological or familial, but rather, discursive, insofar as it involves the simultaneous recognition, in a rhetorical space, of difference and of the responsibilities that hold *across* differences.

In foregrounding the temporal difference of generations, as well as ethnic and racial differences, Paley rejoins Walter Benjamin, who in his critique of the concept of history took it as an ethical imperative to attempt to "wrest tradition away from a conformism that is about to overpower it.... Only that historian will have the gift of fanning the spark of hope in the past who is firmly convinced that even the dead will not be safe from the enemy if he wins. And this enemy has not ceased to be victorious" ("Theses," in *Illuminations*, 255). Multiple generations are at stake in Paley's story: in attempting to act justly in an unjust world, the survivor claims his identity not only in the name of the future, but also in memory of the dead. Performing an *après coup* intervention worthy of Blanchot, the survivor declares in his recognition of differences among Jews that, from now on, the "purity" of identity and narrative is situated before Auschwitz. The assumedly Jewish passer-by, on the other hand, can only maintain her "traditional" sense of Jewishness by not acknowledging the tattoo on the survivor's arm and thus repressing the challenge of the Holocaust to all conventional identities. Through this contrast, Paley suggests (like Adorno and Blanchot before her) that after Auschwitz an ethical demand ought to link the present to the past, the self to the other, and different histories of oppression to each other in such a way that coming to terms with the past necessitates coming to terms with the present in a public setting.

The rhetorical analogizing of identities and locations suggested by "Three Days" works in the interests of both solidarity and singularity, or, in the terms of Holocaust discourse, universality and uniqueness. Nowhere does Paley suggest an equation between the Holocaust, the struggle for Palestinian self-determination, AIDS, and the Haitian refugee situation. In this sense, she provides a recasting of Adorno's injunction concerning Holocaust representation: to equate histories of suffering after Auschwitz would be barbaric. But it is in the very marking of differences that literature can play a role. Instead of drawing on the interdictions of the second commandment to ground her approach to the Holocaust, as Adorno does, Paley draws on another, equally demanding but more affirmative, Jewish tradition: the ethics of questioning. Her story can be read as belonging to the tradition of the Passover Haggadah that asks, Why is this night different from all other nights? As all writers and artists who approach the Holocaust are forced to ask at some point, Why and how is this suffering different from all others? Why and how is it similar?

Paley does not provide direct answers of course, but she suggests the importance of the place of enunciation of narratives in constituting their differences. Just as the museum exhibit on tattoos depicted survivors gathered in the multiply diasporic setting of Los Angeles, where they simultaneously mourned and made the best of their displaced condition, Paley situates her survivor in an American setting, but one that might also be international—in front of the Israeli embassy or the United Nations. Portraying a survivor who is also a kind of liberator or rescuer in his role as activist, Paley joins the recent American Holocaust texts, such as *Schindler's List* and the museum, that have combined those roles as well. But Paley's rescuer is neither a businessman nor a soldier, and thus her portrait brushes conventional notions of Americanness against the grain. At the same time, he refuses to take a position with the helpless mass of survivors; in stepping forward to confront injustice he assumes the agency that contemporary obsessions with victimization and infantilizing representations like *Schindler's List* would deny him. "Three Days and a Question" demonstrates, as do many elements of the Holocaust museum, that the Holocaust is already part of U.S. history and that considering the genocide in an American framework is not necessarily a matter of trivialization.

Like the other contemporary American work with which I framed this book—Art Spiegelman's drawing—Paley's story provides a version of traumatic realism. The successive acts of pointing that Paley's three characters perform exploit the referential function of language, but the object indicated — the human arm — is revealed as already coded; it is in fact the very violent act of coding at which they point. The tattoo is a material trace of suffering that the survivor carries into the postwar world of the everyday, but it is not suffering itself. The bearing of the tattoo, even as artifact of the Holocaust, is an example of the kind of indirect reference, also found in Klüger and Delbo, whereby material objects stand in for the forceful absence of physical violence. Paley's story, like the works of the other "traumatic realists," stages questions about the ethical relationship to history. But also, because of its setting in the public space of the polis, "Three Days" demonstrates how questions of representation are tied to questions of political agency: the survivor's referential gesture is also an activist's gesture.

Nevertheless, Paley is cognizant of what constitutes the dominant space of late-twentieth-century America, and so she stages her ethnic ethics in front of the media — remember the reporter with her "narrow" notebook whose question prompts the confrontation. Television cameras and newspaper reporters, present also in *Operation Shylock,* in Art's confrontation with his success in *Maus,* and in the uses and abuses of *Schindler's List,* bring us back to *Nightline* and the year America remembered the Holocaust. The presence of the mass and broadcast media in those various texts demands an acknowledgment of the modes of publicity that are simultaneously essential to ethics in a postmodern world and disruptive of the face-to-face encounter that has traditionally grounded the ethical. The texts of Americanization follow *Nightline* in linking the issues raised by the Holocaust with a variety of contemporary political dilemmas. They do not, for the most part, yield to the format of flux that dissolves the event into the smooth surface of entertainment. Rather, they bring unlike elements together as a means of disrupting commonplace notions about what constitutes events and identities. In so doing, they show themselves to be heirs to the project of public enlightenment that Adorno outlined in "What Does Coming to Terms with the Past Mean?" While a comic-book version of the Holocaust or a national memorial museum would not have been assimilable to Adorno's vision, such projects nevertheless contribute to a working through of a collectively disastrous past and thus suggest new orientations toward the future.

Grappling with the cultural implications of the Holocaust necessitates, in part, rethinking the continuities and discontinuities of history. In its elegant brevity Paley's story links the three parts of my project: the realist demand for reference — here indexed by the simultaneous representational and material quality of the survivor's tattoo — the modernist ethical imperative to reconceptualize culture "after Auschwitz," and the postmodern acknowledgment that culture, like barbarism, is continuously being transformed by the techniques and technologies that contributed to "The Year of the Holocaust." It would be as wrong to establish a radical break between those three modes of coming to terms with the past as it would be to equate them.

The recent omnipresence of the history and memory of the destruction of the European Jews in the social text of First World postmodernism registers the survival of incomplete theoretical and practical tasks into the post–Cold War new world order. Holocaust postmodernism maintains realist claims of reference and the ideals of the incomplete project of modernity, while simultaneously exposing the impossibility of direct reference and modernity's necessary failures — all while looking to the stylistic novelty of postmodernism for clues as to how to fulfill and transfigure the past. The postmodern arts of memory practiced by Roth, Spiegelman, the Holocaust museum, and sometimes *Schindler's List,* take their place among other new forms of remembrance, from video testimony to computer memory banks and Internet resources. Yet as long as they maintain a critical edge toward this "progress" in the technologies of memory, they also keep alive the modernist project of ethical critique and the sense of loss registered by traumatic realism.

The deadly persistence of religious, racial, and ethnic hatred continues to haunt the present, as do the specters of genocide and economic decline. Demonstrating in intimate detail what it means to live in the wake of catastrophes, "Three Days and a Question" brings the overarching problems of periodization and cultural practice back to the level of everyday life. In working out from the Holocaust in the direction of other histories of oppression, such as that of Haitians, Paley contributes to an ongoing dialogue among diasporic groups and what Paul Gilroy in *The*

Black Atlantic calls "other consciousnesses of affliction" (215). There are no guarantees that the analogies pursued by Paley will satisfy all who participate in the dialogue, a dialogue that always takes place under unequal conditions. But given the global warming of the nationalist climate, the risk of anti-anti-essentialism may have to be taken. In these years of the Holocaust, the genocide lives on in the bodies of survivors and the minds of the comfortable, even as its reality reappears on city streets everywhere.

Notes

Introduction

1. This book focuses primarily on the significance of the Nazi genocide of European Jews, a genocide whose singular challenge to understanding lies in its successful erasure of eastern European Jewish culture through a deployment of primarily modern means. But Jews were by no means the only victims of National Socialism, and nor are they the only subjects of this book. In various sections of this study I will address the difficult question of how simultaneously to preserve the particularity of the suffering of different groups and to acknowledge the common fate and more general implications of all of the victims. Much work remains to be done in this area. In particular, I am convinced that most Holocaust scholars have not fully come to terms with Henry Friedlander's powerful argument in *The Origins of Nazi Genocide* that not only Jews but also Roma (Gypsies) and the handicapped were singled out for genocidal elimination. Even scholars who would reserve the concept of genocide for the destruction of European Jewry are beginning to pay more attention to the multiple forms of racism embodied in what Michael Burleigh and Wolfgang Wippermann call "the racial state." Future projects will need to continue to think about how changes in the historical understanding of the Holocaust intersect with theoretical and cultural considerations of its impact. Although problematic in many ways, including its unfortunate title, Michael Berenbaum's edited volume *A Mosaic of Victims* contributes to this project.

2. These contradictions are illustrated by some of the major popular and academic controversies surrounding understanding of the Holocaust in the last decades: the German historians' debate [the *Historikerstreit*], the exchange between historians Saul Friedlander and Martin Broszat over the question of the Holocaust's "historicization," and the often acrimonious conflict over Steven Katz's *The Holocaust in Historical Perspective*, whose vigorous assertion of the uniqueness of the Nazi genocide prompted outraged responses by scholars of Native American and Roma (Gypsy) history, among others. The debates surrounding Daniel Goldhagen's *Hitler's Willing Executioners* also turn on similar questions of the ordinary and particular.

3. This book is not a work of historiography and makes no claims to enlarging or emending the historical record of the Nazi genocide. It is, nevertheless, an attempt to think through some of the difficulties of representing the Holocaust that I believe are fully as relevant to historians as to artists, writers, critics, and the general public. While references to historiographical debates are generally made in passing through footnotes, I do believe that the arguments made here are in keeping with some of the recent developments in Holocaust histori-

ography and may provide a conceptual framework for them. In particular, my emphasis on the intertwining of the everyday and the extreme is shared by Saul Friedlander, as his comments in *Nazi Germany and the Jews* illustrate: "It is the relationship between the uncommon and the ordinary, the fusion of the widely shared murderous potentialities of the world that is also ours and the peculiar frenzy of the Nazi apocalyptic drive against the mortal enemy, the Jew, that give both universal significance and historical distinctiveness to the 'Final Solution of the Jewish Question' " (6). See also my comments in note 1.

4. Arendt, *Eichmann in Jerusalem* and *Jew as Pariah,* 251. This quotation comes from Arendt's exchange of letters with Gershom Scholem concerning her Eichmann book. Arendt's view seems to have changed over time, as she admits to Scholem. An earlier essay from 1950 argues for an understanding of the Nazi concentration camps as a radical break with Western notions of logic and reason that renders it opaque to "normal" social science. See Arendt, "Social Science Techniques," 365–78. Arendt's itinerary thus moves in a direction opposite from the dominant, popular understandings of the Nazi genocide.

5. See Browning, *Ordinary Men;* Goldhagen, *Hitler's Willing Executioners;* Marrus, *Holocaust in History,* 1–7. Marrus points out that histories of the Holocaust have not always been "detached" and "professional" but have tendentially become so (5).

6. See Wiesel, *Against Silence,* 158; Lanzmann, "Obscenity of Understanding"; Cohen, 83, 1; Lyotard, *Differend* and *Heidegger.*

7. It is obvious that this schema represents a simplification. There are important exceptions to this division of labor, such as Tzvetan Todorov (a literary scholar who falls in with the historians' realist view), and there are significant figures in between, such as Saul Friedlander and Dominick LaCapra. Another fascinating aspect of this division is that it also often breaks down around the question of subject-position: literary scholars, for example, are concerned primarily with the testimonies of *victims,* while the major historical controversies have tended to focus on the *perpetrators.* Psychologists are notable for working in both areas. Although I seek to complicate the realist/antirealist divide, I do tend to fall into the disciplinary division of labor around the question of subject-positions, since I do not focus in this book on perpetrators, but rather on victims, bystanders, and latecomers (members of generations born after the Holocaust). For some of my thoughts on representing perpetrators, see my article "Documenting Barbarism."

8. I am not the only one to attempt to move beyond this deadlock. I am in great sympathy with the project of Saul Friedlander to develop a new mode of writing Holocaust history, first outlined in *Memory, History, and the Extermination of the Jews of Europe* and put into practice in *Nazi Germany and the Jews.* Similarly, Dominick LaCapra's stress on "working through" as a way out of the opposition between "repetition-compulsion" and "total mastery" bears a certain resemblance to the position I put forward here. See *History and Memory,* 46n.

9. In *The Return of the Real,* Hal Foster introduces a concept of traumatic realism that is close to my own (130–36). Foster uses this concept to supplement readings of contemporary neo-avant-garde art, especially those of the work of Andy Warhol, as either purely referential or purely simulacral (130). In Fos-

ter's fine reading, Warhol's repetitive images of accidents both "*screen* the real understood as traumatic" and *point* to the real that "*ruptures* the screen of repetition" (132). In chapter 3, I develop a notion of traumatic realism that has a similarly double relationship to the real. However, while Foster follows Lacan closely in equating the real with trauma, I seek to install a rift between the two categories in order to specify the differentiated relationship between the extreme, the real, and the traumatic. My differences with Foster are partly a product of subject matter — a concern with neo-avant-garde art as opposed to Holocaust testimonies — but more significantly they arise from my more critical attitude toward poststructuralist psychoanalytic approaches to trauma.

10. Andreas Huyssen, whose work has influenced my own, also discusses postmodernism and modernism as relational terms, but doesn't address the question of realism in that context (see "Mapping"). Fredric Jameson comes closest to my formulation in his essay "The Existence of Italy," in which he theorizes a dialectical relationship between realism, modernism, and postmodernism in film history (see *Signatures*). But his account is ultimately tied to the teleology of an account of the stages of capitalist development — a project that is important but not necessarily helpful in the context of the Holocaust. Two important works that have thought the Holocaust in terms of the relationship between modernism and postmodernism are LaCapra, *Representing,* and Bartkowski. Both LaCapra and Bartkowski consider the Holocaust as establishing a break between the modern and the postmodern. While there is much convincing about this argument, I have found that returning to the question of realism complicates such a periodization.

11. Among many important works that engage with Benjamin, Jonathan Boyarin's original use of his work in *Storm from Paradise* continues to inspire my own.

12. The construction of constellations seems a particularly suitable methodology for thinking through the Nazi genocide since, as Fredric Jameson reminds us, the concepts that join together in the constellation are not meant by Benjamin to capture the "representative, characteristic, typical or average" aspects of reality, but rather "must register its extremes; only in its ultimate convulsive manifestations can the real be grasped, not in its least common denominators" (*Late Marxism,* 56).

13. Working through as the goal of historical understanding is a motif found most explicitly in the work of Dominick LaCapra. See *Representing* and *History and Memory.* A very different, rather provocative perspective is advanced by van Alphen in *Caught by History.* Van Alphen values precisely the way that certain works of art and literature act out, or in his vocabulary "reenact," the traumas of the Holocaust, thus producing a "Holocaust effect." He writes, "When I call something a Holocaust effect, I mean to say that we are not confronted with a representation of the Holocaust, but that we, as viewers or readers, experience directly a certain aspect of the Holocaust or of Nazism, of that which led to the Holocaust" (10). While there is much of value in van Alphen's work and interesting points of contact with my own book (such as the emphasis on the importance of the index), it is also filled with vague and indefensible assertions about the relationship of art to historical events. While acting out may in fact be an important element of working through catastrophic histories, as LaCapra

argues, the notion that "we" can reexperience the Holocaust is absurd and dangerous. My notion of traumatic realism is meant to mediate between positions, like van Alphen's, that seek to bypass the problem of representation and those poststructuralist positions that seek to reduce all approaches to the Holocaust to representation.

14. While my focus is primarily on the relationship of the Nazi genocide to its aftermath, there is also important work being done on the "prehistory" of the Holocaust. See Omer Bartov's convincing argument in *Murder in Our Midst* proposing what I would call a constellation between genocide and the industrial killing inaugurated by World War I. Some of my own thoughts on the pre-Holocaust can be found in chapter 2 on Blanchot.

15. For an initiation into trauma studies with a literary and cultural emphasis, see Cathy Caruth's book, *Unclaimed Experience,* and her edited collection, *Trauma.* See also Geoffrey Hartman's important review essay, "On Traumatic Knowledge," and his book *The Longest Shadow,* as well as Felman and Laub's *Testimony.* On trauma and history, see Dominick LaCapra's work cited above and Friedlander's *Memory, History.* For clinical approaches, see Laub and Auerhahn. In *Worlds of Hurt,* Kali Tal provides a provocative nonpsychoanalytic framework for thinking about trauma. James Berger's review essay, "Trauma and Literary Theory," provides a helpful, critical account of trauma-related work by Caruth, LaCapra, and Tal. Elizabeth J. Bellamy's *Affective Genealogies* provides a sophisticated reading of French philosophy and psychoanalysis "after Auschwitz."

16. See *Holocaust Testimonies,* but also Langer's collected essays, *Admitting the Holocaust.* In *Travelers, Immigrants, Inmates,* Bartkowski has done similarly important work that reads Holocaust memoirs alongside other narratives of displacement and estrangement.

17. See Young's *Texture of Memory* and Segev's *Seventh Million.* Young's earlier study of "narrative and the consequences of interpretation," *Writing and Rewriting the Holocaust,* has also been a crucial resource for this study, as have the works of Eric Santner, in particular his book *Stranded Objects* and his essay "History beyond the Pleasure Principle." Also important to the study of literary representations of the Shoah are Sara Horowitz's *Voicing the Void,* Sidra Ezrahi's *By Words Alone,* and Alvin Rosenfeld's *A Double Dying.* My chapters on memoir have been indelibly marked by the work of Nancy K. Miller. See *Getting Personal* and *Bequest and Betrayal.*

18. See Marianne Hirsch's moving and insightful *Family Frames* for the coining of postmemory as a category for thinking about the space of the generations born after the Holocaust.

19. The concepts, representations, and cultural practices that I group under the sign of these constellations are not meant to be crudely equated; nor do I mean to imply that every representation or practice must belong only to one constellation or that the constellations are themselves necessarily unified. The constellations are rather abstractions — albeit ones with material effects — meant to bring structure (and sometimes contradictory structure) to the multiplicity of instances through which the Holocaust has been made present in and to the postwar world.

Part I. Modernism "After Auschwitz"

1. For an illuminating discussion of the temporality of one particularly troublesome tendency in narrations of the Holocaust, which he calls "backshadowing," see Bernstein.

2. It is not only the Holocaust, however, that shakes the self-understanding of the modern; the crisis of the modern has been exacerbated as well by decolonization, feminism, and the political and economic changes that have wrought the postmodern world. For other critiques of modernity "from below," see Gilroy (*Black Atlantic*), Bhabha, and Jardine (*Gynesis*).

3. The work of Dominick LaCapra is fascinating in this context. LaCapra dissents on the question of the Holocaust's modernity and argues that it contains both modern elements and the return of a repressed sacrificial logic. Although he argues for the Holocaust as a rupture between the modern and the postmodern, his notion of the return of the repressed implies the kind of complicated temporality I am invoking here. See *Representing the Holocaust* and *History and Memory*.

4. The work of Sigrid Weigel has been crucial in helping me to reach these conclusions. See her *Body- and Image-Space*.

5. Dominick LaCapra also repeatedly stresses the related importance of acting out in processes of working through. See *Representing the Holocaust*.

1. After Adorno

1. For misquotations, see note 2. Among the many citations, see, for example: in philosophy, Lyotard, *Differend;* Claussen, "Nach Auschwitz"; in theology, Rubenstein, *After Auschwitz;* Metz, "Suffering unto God"; Fackenheim, *To Mend the World;* in aesthetics, Zuidervaart, *Adorno's Aesthetic Theory;* Eagleton, *Ideology of the Aesthetic;* in literary and cultural criticism, Langer, *Holocaust and the Literary Imagination;* Howe, "Writing and the Holocaust"; Steiner, *Language;* Santner, *Stranded Objects*. See also Maurice Blanchot's reflections in *Apres coup,* the subject of my next chapter. As I discuss below, Charlotte Delbo's memoirs were titled *Auschwitz et après,* recently translated by Rosette Lamont as *Auschwitz and After*.

As testimony to the continued interest in Adorno and Auschwitz in the German context, two volumes have recently appeared. Manuel Köppen's edited volume *Kunst und Literatur nach Auschwitz* is an interdisciplinary set of interventions growing out of a recent conference. Reclam has also issued an important source book titled *Lyrik nach Auschwitz?* that collects excerpts from Adorno's work in which the status of Auschwitz is in question and responses by poets and critics to his dictum. The editor's introduction by Petra Kiedaisch is the only essay that I know other than the present one and the one by Claussen cited above that draws attention to the variety of Adorno's articulations and to the frequent partial or mis-citations of Adorno's critics. However, while Kiedaisch and Claussen are at pains to emphasize the continuity of Adorno's thought, I argue here for discontinuities in his articulations of Auschwitz. In this sense I am closer to Sigrid Weigel, who, while not providing a systematic reading of Adorno's oeuvre, does emphasize the differences between the writings of the 1940s and those of the 1960s. See Weigel, "'Kein philosophisches Staunen.'"

2. The first phrase (or paraphrase) is from Steiner, *Language,* 53. See discussion below. The second case, from Shoshana Felman's contribution to the volume, coauthored with Dori Laub, *Testimony: Crises of Witnessing in Literature, Psychoanalysis, and History* (33), is slightly stranger. Felman subtly, but significantly, misquotes Adorno's *Negative Dialectics* (362)—"it may have been wrong to say that after Auschwitz you could no longer write poems"—thus detracting from the tentativeness of Adorno's sentence and adding the question of "possibility," which, as we will see, is a complex one. Nevertheless, on the back cover of *Testimony,* the quotation is the standard, correct one from Adorno's original statement, nowhere cited by Felman or Steiner. There, however, Adorno is referred to as an "Austrian musicologist"!

3. It is worth noting that in German "nach Auschwitz" means not only "after Auschwitz" but "to Auschwitz." I was reminded of this by the monument to the deportation of Berlin Jews in which a metal memorial panel notes that transport after transport was deported "nach Auschwitz." The tension between living after Auschwitz and being repeatedly transported back toward it lies at the basis of both the monument and Adorno's reflections on culture in the wake of catastrophe.

4. Gary Weissman pointed out to me the possible poetic seductiveness of the near assonance in "after Auschwitz."

5. While we in the United States have, since the 1960s, conventionally called that totality of events the Holocaust, it is unlikely that Adorno, at least in his earliest writings, had the same object in mind when he referred to Auschwitz. More likely, he was referring to the totality of Nazi barbarism, and not necessarily its specifically Jewish component. It is important to keep in mind that the general significance of Auschwitz changed along with Adorno's conceptualization of it—although Adorno's prophetic reference to what would become the best known of the camps also makes clear how influential his thought was in this very history.

6. For an extended discussion of Adorno's interventions in democratic pedagogical practice and theory, see Hohendahl, "Education after the Holocaust," in *Prismatic Thought,* 45–72.

7. On Nazism and language, see also Victor Klemperer's important early study, *LTI.*

8. With *In Bluebeard's Castle,* Steiner appears to be making a somewhat different, perhaps more Adornian, argument. Here he wants to read the inhuman events of the twentieth century, now referred to as the "Thirty Year's War" of 1915–45, as anticipated by the ennui of nineteenth-century culture. However, even in negating the pastoral view of the last century and the more general nostalgia for past "golden ages," his writing still preserves the sentiment of decline. Implicit in such phrases as "undermining European stability," "the dissolution of civilized norms," and "the breakdown of the European order" (22, 25, 29) is the same investment found in *Language* in the greatness of European culture, even at the same time that that culture's impotence before barbarism is exposed. To get out of this bind, Steiner constructs a "religious" theory of culture, which is particularly un-Adornian in its anachronistic idealism.

9. Cited in Santner, *Stranded Objects,* 165n. See Jardine, "Copyright 2000," 6.

10. The spatiotemporal articulation of modernity as consisting of a constant break between the "space of experience" and the "horizon of expectation" can be found in Koselleck.

11. In "Cultural Criticism and Society," Adorno writes: "The cultural critic is barred from the insight that the reification of life results not from too much enlightenment but from too little" (*Prisms,* 24). Considering Adorno's ideas in the light of debates over modernity and postmodernity, Albrecht Wellmer, in *The Persistence of Modernity,* argues for a notion of postmodernity as a "second" or "postmetaphysical modernity": "a modernity without the dream of ultimate reconciliations, but [which] would still preserve the rational, subversive and experimental spirit of modern democracy, modern art, modern science and modern individualism" (viii).

12. The key sentence in German reads, "Kulturkritik findet sich der letzten Stufe der Dialektik von Kultur and Barbarei gegenüber: nach Auschwitz ein Gedicht zu schreiben, ist barbarisch, und das frißt auch die Erkenntnis an, die ausspricht, warum es unmöglich ward, heute Gedichte zu schreiben" (Adorno, *Gesammelte Schriften,* 10.1:30).

13. For some of Adorno's reflections on his U.S. exile, see "On the Question: What Is German?" and "Scientific Experiences of a European Scholar in America." The latter account, in particular, represents a more positive take on his experiences in America than the wartime and immediate postwar writings do. In *Prismatic Thought,* Hohendahl argues convincingly that this "pro-American reorientation" was "motivated by the confrontation with postwar Germany" (43).

14. Adorno, "Commitment," 312. In German, this passage begins, "Den Satz, nach Auschwitz noch Lyrik zu schreiben, sei Barberei, möchte ich nicht mildern" (Adorno, *Gesammelte Schriften,* 11:422). *Satz* is more neutral than "saying," meaning "sentence" or "phrase," but the sense of self-citation is still present.

15. See also the important consideration of the "Jewish question" in postwar Germany in Rabinbach, "The Jewish Question." For the Israeli perspective on the politics of *Wiedergutmachung,* see Segev, *Seventh Million.*

16. For consideration of Benjamin's influence on Adorno's *Negative Dialectics,* see Buck-Morss, *Origins of Negative Dialectics,* and Jameson, *Late Marxism,* 49–58.

17. See the essays collected in Saul Friedlander, *Memory, History,* for insights into the growth of Holocaust memory in different national contexts. For the U.S. context in particular, see Novick, "Holocaust Memory."

18. For an example of this error, see Rosenfeld, *Double Dying* 13.

19. Adorno, *Negative Dialectics,* 362–63. The German makes it clear that the "could" and the "can" of these sentences refer not to an ability but to an ethical principle: " . . . darum mag falsch gewesen sein, nach Auschwitz ließe kein Gedicht mehr sich schreiben . . . ob nach Auschwitz noch sich leben lasse, ob vollends es dürfe . . . " (Adorno, *Gesammelte Schriften,* 6:355). The verbs *lassen* and *dürfen* used here denote "allowance" and "permission."

20. Miriam Hansen has made a similar point about Adorno's notion of ex-

perience in the context of her brilliant forward to Oskar Negt and Alexander Kluge's *Public Sphere and Experience:* "[T]he 'structure' of Adorno's experience was not merely a generalized perception of 'horror'; it was the insistence on a fundamental *Zusammenhang* (relation, connection, context), the persistence of the past in the present that maintained the imperative to engage the legacy of mass annihilation across generational boundaries" (xix).

21. For a critique of the version of the *Bilderverbot* implicit in Adorno's approach to Auschwitz, see Klaus Laermann, " 'Nach Auschwitz,' " 11–15.

22. In a famous passage from one of his *Historikerstreit* interventions, Habermas wrote: "There [in Auschwitz] something happened, that up to now nobody considered as even possible. There one touched on something which represents the deep layer of solidarity among all that wears a human face; notwithstanding all the usual acts of beastliness of human history, the integrity of this common layer had been taken for granted.... Auschwitz has changed the basis for the continuity of the conditions of life within history" (cited in Friedlander, introduction to *Probing the Limits,* 3). Given recent events in Bosnia and Rwanda, the most frightening fact about the "touching" of this layer is that it seems to open up genocidal possibilities at least as much as it serves as a warning against reoccurrences.

23. See, especially, Lyotard, *Postmodern Condition.*

24. See Huyssen's discussion in "Mapping" (266).

25. Jameson's wording here is ironic given that he popularized Althusser's critique of "expressive causality" and championing of "structural causality" in *The Political Unconscious,* 23–58. For Althusser's development of these ideas see "Contradiction and Overdetermination," in *For Marx* (87–128), and Althusser and Balibar, *Reading Capital.*

26. This account of the Holocaust as a possibility within modernity that forever modifies our notion of the latter is close to Zygmunt Bauman's in *Modernity and the Holocaust:* "From the fact that the Holocaust is modern, it does not follow that modernity is a Holocaust" (93). Bauman's ideas on the causality of the Holocaust, however, tend to be closer to the combinatorial logic put forward by Jameson in a very different context.

27. Adorno in conversation with Ernst Bloch in Bloch, *Utopian Function,* 12.

28. See Jameson, "Reflections in Conclusion." See also Zuidervaart's extensive critique of Adorno's aesthetics for a useful discussion of its strengths and weaknesses. Zuidervaart is also quite critical of Jameson's theory of postmodernism, although this section of his book is less convincing to me.

29. For a defense of the possibilities of mass-cultural representation of the Nazi genocide that pays particular attention to one important mass-cultural text, the television miniseries *Holocaust,* see Huyssen, "Politics of Identification."

30. For the articulation of a "popular modernist" position on the representability of the Holocaust that seeks to elude the outmoded antinomies of modernist art, see Hansen, "*Schindler's List* Is Not *Shoah.*" I discuss *Schindler's List* and *Shoah* in chapter 6.

31. See, for example, Adorno, "What Does Coming to Terms with the Past Mean?" 124–29.

2. Before Auschwitz

1. The most recent, and perhaps strangest, moment in Blanchot's ongoing engagement with the past is his 1994 *récit L'insant de ma mort,* which seems to recount an incident during the occupation when Blanchot was almost assassinated by the Nazis for taking part in resistance activities. This unexpected text has already received detailed commentary from Derrida in *Demeure* and brief discussion in Mesnard (329–31) and Mole (163–67).

2. For a critique of Blanchot's melancholy, see in particular Rose, *Mourning.*

3. Leslie Hill provides an exemplary treatment of Blanchot's complete works, even if he comes to very different conclusions from mine with respect to Blanchot's early anti-Semitism. Both Gary Mole's and Gerald Bruns's books provide a more full integration of Blanchot's political, critical, and literary writings than was previously available. Neither, however, dedicates as much space to the journalism as Ungar does in *Scandal and Aftereffect.* I am sympathetic in particular to Mole's insight that "[t]he Shoah . . . can be posited as the unnarrated experience that fragments Blanchot's text from within" (143), although we read different texts for that evidence and come to somewhat different conclusions about the efficacy of the Holocaust's indirect impact. Much integrating work remains to be done that does not segregate Blanchot's different texts from each other—that is one of the projects to which this chapter contributes. My larger aim, however, is to think about what such an integrated picture of Blanchot's work might tell us about the larger problems of the responsibility of bystanders and the limits of representation in the face of extreme events.

4. The example I have in mind here is Gregg's *Maurice Blanchot,* but this text is typical of the mainstream of Blanchot studies.

5. For two different examples of this kind of political erasure in critical works of unquestionable importance, see Londyn (13) and Shaviro (828).

6. Sternhell and Loubet del Bayle do not paint the same picture of the era, by any means, but their accounts complement each other. Loubet del Bayle evenhandedly accounts for the tenuous ideological unity that characterized the diverse nonconformist movements. Sternhell is more tendentious in unhesitatingly characterizing the groups as fascist, but he provides a crucial account of the role anti-Semitism played in forging their coherence. Loubet del Bayle downplays this aspect of nonconformism, one important for this study and one that radically alters the sense of the movements as soon as it enters into the mix. See, for example, Loubet del Bayle's "Une Tentative de Renouvellement," in which he chronicles the nonconformists' view of the crisis in civilization without once mentioning the pivotal mobilizing role of anti-Semitic rhetoric in their theories. The interlocking discourses of crisis and Jewishness will reappear in my discussion of Blanchot's political writings.

7. Allan Stoekl provides a somewhat different reading of Blanchot's text on Montherlant, commenting that "Blanchot holds Montherlant to a more rigorous silencing than the one Montherlant would perform on himself in his politically naive and garrulous self-portrait" *(Politics, Writing, Mutilation,* 32). Stoekl does suggest, however, that certain key political questions (and questions about politics) are "beyond the reach of Blanchot's novelistic or critical practice" and that

"the specificities of political defiances and dilemmas" should not and could not under any circumstances be "stripped away" (36, 35). Despite this imperative, Stoekl's own text suffers from a certain stripping of specificity; after raising the question of the relationship between Blanchot's "rightist articles" and his "hermetic works of fiction and Heideggerian criticism" (22), he provides no account or analysis of the early writings, thus leaving the mistaken impression that they are transparent and missing an opportunity to explore the specificity of the later works in light of the early ones.

8. In the most significant account of Blanchot's early writings since Ungar—and indeed one of the most complete and convincing texts on Blanchot—Leslie Hill makes a similar point in assessing Blanchot's "diffidence regarding autobiographical narrative": "[T]he question raised by Blanchot's own particular political evolution is not a question requiring autobiographical disclosure, but, more abruptly and more trenchantly, a question that is inseparable from the issue of ethical and political responsibility" (20).

9. This work has been translated as *Vicious Circles.* While I use this translation, with occasional modifications, I refer to the text throughout as *Après coup* since that French phrase proves crucial to my analysis.

10. "[E]n le prenant pour maître, je l'enchaînai à sa souveraineté. Et nous fûmes liés de telle sorte qu'il se vit obligé, pour redevenir lui-même, de me dire: 'je te berne, car je ne suis qu'une bête,' mais, sur cet aveu, je redoublai d'adoration et, à la fin, il n'y eut plus l'un auprès de l'autre qu'un triste animal gardé par un serviteur qui en écartait les mouches. Un rayon de soleil, dressé comme une pierre, les enfermait tous deux dans une illusion d'éternité. Ils jouissaient béatement du repos" (*Après coup,* 80).

11. Translations from *L'amitié* are my own.

12. Leslie Hill, in his otherwise excellent analysis, derides the claim of Blanchot's anti-Semitism and argues that "to date, no evidence of any real substance has ever been produced to support it" (36). Although Hill objects to Todorov's "unnecessarily coy" assertion of Blanchot's anti-Semitism, his own refutation of the charge could be seen as itself coy: "Anti-semitism, then, as Blanchot was well aware, was always present in some form or another in *Combat* and *L'Insurgé,* if not over his signature, then at least sometimes alongside it; and this is the reason...that it is of course possible to read as indirectly anti-semitic both the two references to the Jews in his pieces for *Combat* and the ambiguous language used in one or two further articles for *L'Insurgé*" (38). The rhetoric of ambiguity and the minimization of seriousness (e.g., using the phrase "dangerously ambiguous" [47] instead of simply "dangerous") does not do justice to the issues at stake or the actual rhetoric of Blanchot's texts, as I suggest in this section.

13. The original lines read: "[O]n sent qu'il s'égare dans un domaine qui n'est pas le sien," and "il faut séparer nettement ses aspects politiques et ses aspects artistiques ou culturels" (*Le Soir,* 12 August 1941: 2).

14. "D'un point de vue purement artistique, cette attitude s'avère féconde et productive, puisqu'elle cantonne la littérature dans un domaine nettement limité dans lequel elle jouit d'une entière liberté. Elle n'entraine donc pas de changement dans les problèmes du style dont elle n'entrave pas les évolutions normales. En fait, il n'y a donc pas de rupture de continuité entre la littérature française d'avant

et d'après la campagne de 1940, et le lecteur ne sera à aucun moment désorienté par une manière d'écrire qui ne lui est pas habituelle."

15. I am referring here to Santner's notion of "narrative fetishism," which seeks to diagnose narratives that erase and deny the trauma that called them into being in the first place. I return to this concept when I develop the notion of traumatic realism in the following chapter. See Santner, "History beyond the Pleasure Principle."

16. It also resonates with other, unsatisfactory accounts of Blanchot's career. Typical of these problematic attempts at forgetting are those found in the capsule biography given by Blanchot's publishers at the beginning of *Thomas l'Obscur.* There, we find no mention of his political writings, although we learn that "his first literary contributions are for reviews: *Journal des Débats, L'Insurgé* et *Aux Écoutes*" (my translation; n.p.). The biography goes on to note that "in 1940, despite being without resources and speaking German perfectly, he categorically refuses to collaborate with the occupier." As this sentence indicates but cannot say, this refusal only takes on significance in light of Blanchot's previous writings. Such an omission is not unique in the French context, as any reader of similar air-brushed biographies in the novels of Céline will note.

17. A bibliography of Blanchot's writings for *L'Insurgé* can be found in *Gramma* 5 (1976). This issue and the previous one (3, no. 4 [1976]) are both dedicated to Blanchot and contain extensive bibliographies of his writings from before and after the war, as well as the excellent account of his political thinking by Holland and Rousseau. There are also reprints of various political texts, again both from before and after, and many important critical studies, including Derrida's "Pas" (reprinted in *Parages*). Unfortunately, these issues are rare and hard to come by, especially in the United States. This may be one of the reasons these early texts remain underdiscussed. Now an even more complete bibliography is available in Hill.

Both *L'Insurgé* and *Combat* are available on microfilm at the Bibliothèque Nationale, the former in the Salle des Périodiques, the latter in the main reading room. *L'Insurgé* was cofounded by Thierry Maulnier, the editor of *Combat,* who also wrote a weekly column for the paper. It was published every week from 13 January 1937 until 27 October 1937. At the time it stopped publishing, the journal claimed to have twenty thousand readers, including two thousand subscribers. The stoppage was for "political reasons," the editors asserted in a front-page editorial of that last issue, in order to enlarge the field of their political action and continue their wholesale opposition to the "political degeneracy of the French nation."

18. "La critique qui échappe par principe aux infiltrations indélicates de l'esprit de parti parce qu'il est le contraire de l'esprit critique ne peut pas échapper à une question qui lui est essentielle et qui la conduit à se demander si, dans un temps où la révolution est souhaitable, il n'y a pas quelques affinités à reconnaître entre la notion de révolution et les valleurs littéraires."

19. "Ce qui importe davantage, c'est la force d'opposition qui s'est exprimée dans l'oeuvre même et qui est mesurée par le pouvoir qu'elle a de supprimer d'autres oeuvres ou d'abolir une part du réel ordinaire, ainsi que par le pouvoir d'appeler à l'existence de nouvelles oeuvres, aussi fortes, plus fortes qu'elle ou de

déterminer une réalité supérieure. Ce qui compte aussi, c'est la force de résistance que l'auteur a opposée à son oeuvre par les facilités et les licenses qu'il lui a refusées, les instincts qu'il a maîtrisés, la rigueur par laquelle il se l'est soumise."

20. On the relationship between France and the state/nation opposition in Blanchot and 1930s discourse, see Holland and Rousseau, 29–34. For another context in which fascist discourse mobilizes this binary, see Theweleit, *Male Fantasies.*

21. "Il est l'interlocuteur qu'on ne craint pas parce qu'il ne parle jamais de la force, mais du désarmement; ... l'adversaire qu'on ne respecte pas parce qu'il n'est même pas l'héritier de la civilisation qu'il devrait défendre."

In "De la révolution," Blanchot had already suggested that "some of the great classical works are today accomplishing their design in preparing for us a universe where great works are newly conceivable and in transmitting to us, not a fully formed inheritance, but the reasons, the hope, and force to assemble our personal inheritance, to become our own inheritors" [quelques-uns des grands ouvrages classiques accomplissent aujourd'hui leur dessein en nous préparant un univers où les grandes oeuvres soient à nouveau concevables et en nous apportant non pas un héritage tout fait, mais les raisons, l'espoir et la force de rassembler notre héritage personnel, de devenir notre propres héritiers].

22. "[L]e seul moyen présentement de sauver notre pays est de l'abattre dans ce qui représente le mieux son abjection."

23. "[S]e révèle impossible à tenir face à un nationalisme hitlérien insoutenable et à un état national impuissant à s'instaurer."

24. Blanchot is reported to have served for a few months as the literary director of Jeune France, part of the Vichy government's cultural apparatus. That was his last known right-wing commitment. Other reports have him already changing sides as early as 1938. Hill provides an informative and concise version of these years.

25. "L'indigne gouvernement Sarraut, qui semble avoir reçu la mission d'humilier la France, comme elle ne l'a pas été depuis vingt-cinq ans, a porté ce désordre à son comble.... Il a commencé par entendre l'appel des révolutionaires et des Juifs déchaînés dont fureur théologique exigeait contre Hitler toutes les sactions tout de suite.... On n'a rien vu d'aussi perfide que cette propogande d'honneur national faite par des étrangers suspects dans les bureaux du quai d'Orsay pour précipiter les jeunes Français, au nom de Moscou ou au nom d'Israël, dans un conflit immédiat" ("Après le coup de force germanique," *Combat* 4 [April 1936]).

26. "Il est nécessaire que cette révolution soit violente, parce qu'on ne tire pas d'un peuple aussi aveuli que le nôtre les forces et les passions propres à une rénovation par des mesures décentes, mais par des secousses sanglantes, par un orage qui le bouleversera afin de l'éveiller" ("Le terrorisme, méthode de salut public," *Combat* 7 [July 1936]).

27. It might be interesting to compare Blanchot's words to Heidegger's "decisionism" in his lectures between 1936 and 1940 on Nietzsche, the lectures that Heidegger claims staged "a confrontation with National Socialism." See David Farrell Krell's introduction to the paperback edition of Heidegger, *Nietzsche.* Heidegger writes, for example, that "thinking in the grand style is genuine ac-

tion, indeed, action in its most powerful—though most silent—form," and that "that which is to come is precisely a matter for decision" (cited in Krell, xv). This is clearly not the place for a discussion of the relationship between Heidegger's political commitments and his thinking, but such a discussion is part of the framework of any discussion of Blanchot's and poststructuralism's relationship to politics.

28. I am grateful to Sylvère Lotringer for reminding me of this possibility.

29. On "sur-vival," see Derrida's essay "on" Blanchot, "Living On." Derrida writes there of "the story, the narrative, of 'Living On' as differance, with an a, between archeology and eschatology, as differance in apocalypse" (94). This essay and three others touching on Blanchot were collected by Derrida in French in his book *Parages.* See "Pas" in that collection, for a reading of the doubleness of the *pas.*

30. It is thus significant that Blanchot's 1994 *récit* dealing with the Occupation, *L'instant de ma mort,* should end also with an invocation of the "from now on": "Seule demeure le sentiment de légèreté qui est la mort même ou, pour le dire plus précisément, l'instant de ma mort désormais toujours en instance." Derrida makes this phrase, and particularly the word *désormais,* the subject of his concluding remarks in *Demeure* (138–39).

31. "Il est vraiment honteux de voir tant de Français perdre tout sang-froid quand on leur parle d'Hitler et craindre, en ne s'exprimant pas assez sévèrement sur l'Allemagne, de paraître moins patriotes que les communistes."

32. See Hirsch and Spitzer, "Gendered Transactions," for a critique of "Orphic creation" in Claude Lanzmann's *Shoah.* Drawing on the model provided by Klaus Theweleit, Hirsch and Spitzer understand the Orphic paradigm as one in which masculine culture attempts to "bypass the generativity of women," using them as intermediaries on the way to a form of reproduction between men (15). I do not deny this less savory aspect of the Orpheus model; indeed, I find it at many places in Blanchot's work. However, in this instance, and in light of the other aspects of Blanchot's historical and biographical context, *Death Sentence*'s revision seems to be working through the myth in order to demonstrate its impossibility and its danger.

33. "[D]éfense d'un juif innocent": "ce qui les justifiait d'écrire, de savoir et de penser. L'étrangeté de leur intervention est que celle-ci fut collective, alors que leur exigence exaltait la singularité."

34. See Stoekl, "Blanchot, Violence, and the Disaster," for a less sympathetic reading of the essay "Etre juif." Stoekl is rightly troubled to find there certain inverted evaluations of the anti-Semitic portrait of Jews. But, placed within the larger project of Blanchot's "coming to terms with the past," and read alongside the Antelme essay, the considerations on Jewishness appear as part of an ethico-political stance that radically puts anti-Semitism and fascism into question.

35. Other than Blanchot's reference to this important resistance figure, many of his references to the collectivity of the political turn on the experience of May 1968 (which I have suggested is not separable from the question of the Shoah for Blanchot). For this rethinking of communism and community, see *The Infinite Conversation* (especially the prefatory note) and *La communauté inavouable,* as

well as the postwar political essays collected in the *Gramma* issues dedicated to Blanchot.

Part II: Realism in "The Concentrationary Universe"

1. I should make clear that this is not an "antipoststructuralist" position. Just as I draw on exponents of realism such as Lukács and Auerbach in my formulation of traumatic realism, I also recognize that poststructuralism contains essential resources for this project. The Kristevan notion of the "abject" and Barthes's "punctum" clearly contribute to a theorization of traumatic realism. Nevertheless, the dominant reading of poststructuralism, at least in the United States, has until recently downplayed such themes in favor of a thoroughgoing suspicion of representation.

2. In *Writing and Rewriting the Holocaust,* James Young makes a powerful and convincing argument about the significance of such a concept of representation for the understanding of victims of the Holocaust at the time of the events. See especially the introduction, "Narrative and the Consequences of Interpretation" (1–11). Jameson's notion of realism as a form of cognitive mapping is also related to what Bruce Robbins has recognized as a more general contemporary critical "tendency to translate the realism debate out of the epistemological language in which it is usually formulated and into social terms" (225). While I find this short response-essay by Robbins extremely suggestive, I would rather assert that in notions of realism such as Jameson's and the one under development here the epistemological and social coexist and are inseparable.

3. For an extended discussion of the possibilities of indirect reference, see Caruth, *Unclaimed Experience.*

4. It is ironic, if fitting, that in Barthes's late incarnation as a willfully vulgar realist in *Camera Lucida,* it is precisely the indexical quality of the photograph—the trace it communicates of its subject's presence—that constitutes the stakes of his argument. While this autobiographical-critical text is complex and fascinating, it seems to contain a very simple reversal of the earlier antirealist Barthes: from a critic who held out no possibility of reference to one who claims a direct and quasi-mystical experience of reference. See Marianne Hirsch's suggestive discussion of Barthes, with special attention to the index and its relation to trauma, in the introduction to *Family Frames* (1–15).

5. Saul Friedlander writes that "commentary should disrupt the facile linear progression of the narration, introduce alternative interpretations, question any partial conclusion, withstand the need for closure" (*Memory, History,* 132). Friedlander himself has now written such a narrative history in *Nazi Germany and the Jews.*

3. "The Barbed Wire of the Postwar World"

1. This view has been expressed prominently by historian Deborah Lipstadt in her book on Holocaust denial: "[B]ecause deconstructionism argued that experience was relative and nothing was fixed, it created an atmosphere of permissiveness toward questioning the meaning of historical events and made it hard for its proponents to assert that there was anything 'off limits' for this skepti-

cal approach" (18). While Lipstadt realizes that "proponents" of deconstruction are not themselves deniers, her account of the role of poststructuralism in fostering Holocaust denial remains unconvincing. The insistence that knowledge of the Holocaust depends on the establishment of facts conveyed by realist forms of representation is given its most uncompromising philosophical articulation in the works of Berel Lang. See, for example, *Act and Idea in the Nazi Genocide* and "The Representation of Limits."

2. Despite his long-standing and articulate, if contested, role as spokesperson for Holocaust survivors, Elie Wiesel is also strongly associated with the calls for silence. This paradox extends all the way back to the mystical invocation of silence in *Night,* a memoir whose Yiddish pretext, *Un di Velt Hot Geshvign,* offered a more aggressive political indictment of the world's silence. On the ambiguous question of silence in Wiesel, see Naomi Seidman's brilliant essay. Jean-François Lyotard is the most prominent critic of realism. His critique of realist modes of art and understanding is not limited to the case of the Holocaust, but it finds a muted, if still impassioned, expression there. See, for example, his comments on realism in *Postmodern Condition,* 73–79; in *Differend,* 33, and elsewhere; and in *Heidegger,* 9.

3. This quotation is cited and discussed in White, "Historical Emplotment," 50.

4. Rousset's representation of that world was already recognized and canonized in Hannah Arendt's 1951 account titled *The Origins of Totalitarianism* (441).

5. Arendt proposes the concept of "banality" in *Eichmann in Jerusalem.* See also her exchange of letters with Gershom Scholem in *The Jew as Pariah,* where she denies the autonomous existence of radical evil and asserts that extremity derives from an intensification of banal evil.

6. I am grateful to Gary Weissman for demonstrating to me the importance of the category of experience in Langer's work. See his "Lawrence Langer."

7. My critique of Langer's unmediated notion of experience in this paragraph is inspired by Joan Scott's important essay "Experience."

8. Langer, *Holocaust Testimonies,* and Todorov, *Face à l'extrème,* were both published in 1991, although Langer had already developed his general framework in a series of previous books and essays.

9. In his *New York Times* review of Todorov's book, Neil Gordon makes some of these same points (29). While I agree with Gordon that "[b]y so sedulously omitting from his moral vision those who experienced something beyond 'a threshold of suffering,' Mr. Todorov severely limits the moral reach of his book," I do not agree that the problem is with "the intellectual limitations of 'interpretation.' " It lies rather with Todorov's particular mode of interpretation.

10. See Langer's concluding discussion of Charles Taylor's *Sources of the Self: The Making of the Modern Identity,* which he counterposes to his own subject, articulated in the title of his essay "Sources of the Diminished Self: The Unmaking of Modern Identity" (*Holocaust Testimonies,* 198–205). Langer leaves open the question of how precisely to conceive of this unmaking. Did it lead to the postmodern? back to the premodern? or to some kind of hiatus in the modern,

along the lines of a Habermassian "unfinished project"? This is one of the larger questions that concerns me in this study.

11. I am in no way suggesting a parallel, or even comparison, between the Nazi-constructed camp world and life along the United States/Mexico border, which serves as Anzaldúa's subject matter and prime example of the borderland. What interests me in Anzaldúa's work (in this context) is precisely the manner in which she transforms a geopolitical marker into a powerful conceptual constellation that allows her in turn to rethink geography and history.

12. On *weiter leben*'s duality of genre, see Lezzi. Lezzi refers to Saul Friedlander's call for the self-conscious inclusion of commentary in the writing of Holocaust history. See "Trauma and Transference" in Friedlander, *Memory, History.*

13. Although developed in the very different context of an exploration of concepts of " 'new' German identity after unification," Leslie Adelson's discussion of Klüger's "positionality" is similar to my reading of "displacement" and "differentiation." See her insightful discussion of *weiter leben* in "Ränderberichtigung." The quotation is from p. 85; my translation back into English.

14. Also significant in this context is the question of gender in theories of realism and traumatic realism. Commenting on this passage from *Mimesis,* Barbara Johnson points out that "[w]hat Auerbach calls 'minor, unimpressive, random events' . . . can all be identified as conventional *women's* activities." Johnson goes on to criticize Auerbach for seeking to subsume these everyday details in a universalist framework "which has always been unavowedly male" (165–66). Through its emphasis on the persistence of the socks and the intersection of the everyday and the extreme, *weiter leben* could be seen as resisting the universalist subsumption that Johnson terms male. Indeed, the two major examples of traumatic realism in this book are by women writers, Klüger and Delbo. Nevertheless, I am reluctant to generalize based on such a small sample because the question of gender and genocide is an extremely complex one. While I think it is possible that the kinds of attention to the everyday demonstrated in these traumatic realist texts derive in part from the authors' gendered positions both inside and outside the camps, I would not reduce the traumatic realist project to a question of gender, nor would I necessarily exclude male writers from this category (Primo Levi is one who comes immediately to mind).

15. Mark Seltzer also defines trauma as the breakdown in such distinctions. See Seltzer, "Wound Culture," and *Serial Killers.*

16. The notion of a "shared/divided place" is borrowed from Yasemin Yildiz's reading of Klüger and Jean Améry. Her concept of *geteilte Zeiten* puns on the German verb *teilen,* which can mean both to share and to divide. See Yildiz, "Sharing Divided Times."

17. I am thus sympathetic to Judith Butler's critique of Zizek and his deployment of the concept of the real. Butler's convincing critique turns, in part, on the question of Zizek's analysis (or nonanalysis) of concentration camps as instantiations of the real. See Butler, "Arguing with the Real," in *Bodies That Matter,* esp. 201–3.

18. I have found Dominick LaCapra's important distinction between "structural" and "historical" trauma quite helpful here: "One may argue that structural

or existential trauma appears in different ways in all societies. It may be evoked or addressed in various fashions: in terms of the passage from nature to culture, the eruption of the pre-Oedipal or presymbolic in the symbolic, the entry into language, the encounter with the Real, the inevitable generation of aporia, and so forth.... [H]istorical trauma is related to specific events, such as the Shoah or the dropping of the atom bomb on Japanese cities." LaCapra argues against conflating the two forms of trauma, even as he suggests the necessity of pursuing "the problem of relations between the two." See LaCapra, *History and Memory,* 47. Similarly, I am trying to distinguish between the real and the traumatic in a nonfetishistic way that takes into account what Klüger would call their "differentiation."

19. On the importance of accidents for trauma theory, see Caruth, *Unclaimed Experience,* 6–7.

20. On the importance of lack of community, communication, and empathy in the constitution of trauma, see Laub and Auerhahn.

21. For more on Klüger and trauma, see Lezzi.

22. On Klüger's modes of address to the postwar world, see Yildiz, "Sharing Divided Times."

4. Unbearable Witness

1. This biographical sketch is based on information found in the testimony/memorial book, *Le convoi du 24 janvier.* See especially the introduction ("Le départ et le retour," 9–22), the entry under Charlotte Dudach, née Delbo (100–102), and that under Madeleine Doiret (88–90).

2. Delbo thus expresses here a very different understanding of the French language, and of language in general, from that expressed by Shoshana Felman in her interpretation of Lanzmann's film *Shoah.* Commenting on the fact that French, the native language of the filmmaker, is not the language of any of the witnesses interviewed in the film, Felman writes: "It is a metaphor of the film that its language is a language of translation, and, as such, is doubly foreign: that the occurrence, on the one hand, happens in a language foreign to the language of the film, but also, that the significance of the occurrence can only be articulated in a language foreign to the language(s) of the occurrence" (Felman and Laub, 212). Delbo's book (as well as a grasp of history) makes clear both that the occurrence did take place in French (both for some victims and some perpetrators, such as the French police or Vichy bureaucrats who enthusiastically persecuted Jews and the resistance) and that no language is foreign to such catastrophic occurrences, because all languages can be turned into the language of torture.

3. All translations from *Le convoi* are my own.

4. On the question of ordinary and extraordinary problems of communication, see also Primo Levi's essay "Communicating," in *Drowned and Saved,* 88–104.

5. See also the equally well-known passage from Levi's essay "Shame," in the same collection: "[W]e, the survivors, are not the true witnesses.... We survivors are not only an exiguous but also an anomalous minority: we are those who by their prevarications or abilities or good luck did not touch bottom" (83).

6. A similar passage is found in the opening chapter of *None of Us Will Return,* called precisely "Arrivals, Departures": "They would like to know where they are. They have no idea that this is the center of Europe. They look for the station's name. This is a station that has no name" (5). The use of third-person narration gives the passage a more universal significance, but because of that does not as concretely attach the metaphor of the *in-nommé* to the particular experiences of the prisoners.

7. My reading of these scenes complicates Langer's comment, which is nonetheless true, that "atrocity creates a breach in the chain of events, in what we normally call the history of an individual" (*Age of Atrocity,* 232). The breach in the history of an individual is clear, but I would suggest that the continuation of the chain — the fact that *history goes on nonetheless* — weighs equally heavily on the witness.

8. One of the ironies of Delbo's *Auschwitz and After* project is that, while obviously aware of Adorno's "after Auschwitz" dictum, Delbo's writing is filled precisely with lyric. For an account of the belated reception of Adorno in France, see Richard. He makes the point that in France, writing of all sorts was intimately connected to resistance and not perpetration (as in Germany) and therefore less likely to be submitted to a radical "ban on representation." Richard's argument fits partially for Delbo, but it passes lightly over French collaboration and anti-Semitism and does not account for Delbo's early appreciation of the problem of "writing the disaster."

9. See also the facsimile letter from one of the women in the "Documents" appendix of *Le convoi.* The letters were often delivered by railroad workers who found them on the tracks.

10. See Langer's literary contextualization of this splitting: "A new kind of 'double' emerges, a split personality not tormented by inner psychological contradictions like so many of Dostoevsky's characters, but by the incompatibility of the former crisis of facing life and death with the superficial choices which comprise existence in normal society" (*Age of Atrocity,* 233).

11. Dori Laub, seminar visit, City University of New York Graduate Center, March 1995.

12. Ida is not the only woman in Delbo's accounts for whom childbearing has been rendered traumatic. For Mado, from Delbo's own convoy, and thus not Jewish, the *revenants* that haunt her after the birth of her son are ghosts not of her own family but of her comrades: "When my son was born, I was suffused with joy.... At the very same moment as this sweet, enveloping water of joy was rising around me, my room was invaded by the ghosts of our [*nos*] companions.... I saw again this woman — you remember this peasant woman, lying in the snow, dead, with her dead newborn frozen between her thighs. My son was also that newborn" (261–62; translation modified). The different specters that haunt Ida and Mado are another testimony to the simultaneous commonality and particularity of Jewish and non-Jewish deaths in Auschwitz.

13. All translations from *La mémoire et les jours* (*Days and Memory*) are my own.

14. See Cathy Caruth's comments on one quality that "seems oddly to inhabit all traumatic experience: the inability fully to witness the event as it occurs,

or the ability to witness the event fully only at the cost of witnessing oneself" ("Trauma," 7). The second possibility seems to apply particularly to Loulou.

15. An important complement to Jacques's testimony is that of his wife, Denise, rendered lyrically by Delbo: "I had such a hard time bringing Jacques back ashore / I did all I could to bring him back, back to life. / Not a moment left to think of myself" (326). Denise's words testify to the gendered structures of mourning and the inequity of everyday caregiving (a significant theme in *Measure*), as well as to the nascent feminist consciousness of the late 1960s. Because the feminist movement helped precisely to put the importance of the everyday into relief, I believe that both Delbo's and Klüger's insights into the traumatic interrelationship of the everyday and the extreme are also feminist insights.

16. See Sigrid Weigel's related comments on Benjamin's critique of "einer fundamentalen Vorstellung von 'Geschichte' überhaupt als eines der Zeit sinnvoll sich vollziehenden Verlaufs, eine Konzeption, die jeglicher Geschichtsphilophie zugrundeliegt, welche die Erkennbarkeit einer Vernunft in der Geschichte zur Voraussetzung philosophischer Sinndeutung der Geschichte machen muß" (" 'Kein philosophisches Staunen,' " 123). Although written briefly "before Auschwitz," Weigel convincingly argues that Benjamin's "Uber den Begriff der Geschichte" was, perhaps because of its proximity to the disaster, already attuned to the epistemological challenge of the Holocaust.

17. The epistemological reference here is to Donna Haraway's "Situated Knowledges," in *Simians,* 183–201.

18. Compare Shoshana Felman's discussion, in her chapter on Lanzmann's *Shoah,* of "the philosophical challenges and the concrete impossibilities/ necessities that such a testimony from inside the death camp would entail" (Felman and Laub, 228). Felman's account is similar to mine, except in that she considers the camps as a site of "Otherness," where the capitalization implies the kind of "closed" account of the concentrationary universe that I am countering with an open account.

Part III: Postmodernism, or "The Year of the Holocaust"

1. Andreas Huyssen takes up this question in a compelling fashion in *Twilight Memories.*

2. For an excellent cultural history of the Holocaust on American television, see Shandler.

5. Reading Jewish

1. In a subtle consideration of the complexities of Jewish relations to the image, Daniel Boyarin demystifies the "commonplace of critical discourse that Judaism is the religion in which God is heard but not seen" (532). His essay has implications that go beyond this religious context and are important to secular Jewish representations as well.

2. The importance of the intifada is reinforced since the events have been set at the uprising's origins, a year earlier than Roth has claimed the events "really" happened.

3. Much of Roth's writing—at least from *Portnoy's Complaint* through *Operation Shylock*—can be seen as confirming for Jewish "ethnicity" Paul Gilroy's insight (which draws on Stuart Hall) that "gender is the modality in which race is lived" (*Black Atlantic,* 85). Thus, Roth's different configurations of gender will necessarily correspond to different (aspects of) Jewish identities, most of which are coded masculine.

4. Apart from work cited elsewhere in this chapter, a few critics stand out for their theoretical sophistication in attempting to understand the Holocaust and Jewishness in an American context. On the Holocaust, see Young, *Writing and Rewriting the Holocaust* and *Texture of Memory.* On Jewish identity, see the work of Sander Gilman and of Daniel Boyarin and Jonathan Boyarin. See also my review essay of Boyarin, "Sites of Memory, Sites of Forgetting." The Boyarins' collection *Jews and Other Differences* provides an excellent introduction to the "new Jewish cultural studies."

5. In a 1937 anti-Semitic pamphlet, Céline wrote, "J'espère qu'à présent vous savez lire 'juif.'" This sentence is cited in Kaplan, *Relevé,* 25.

6. See also Marianne Hirsch's discussion of this self-portrait in "Family Pictures."

7. On Adorno and Blanchot, see chapters 1 and 2, respectively. See also Lang, *Act and Idea,* 144–45. On Lang, see White, "Historical Emplotment," 44–48. On Lanzmann, see the next chapter.

8. See, for example, Levi, *Survival in Auschwitz,* and Antelme.

9. Alice Y. Kaplan wrote, for example: "Spiegelman gets the voice right, he gets the order of words right, he manages to capture the intonations of Eastern Europe spoken by Queens" ("Theweleit," 155).

10. The evidence for this alteration comes from the exhibit *Art Spiegelman: The Road to "Maus,"* at the Galerie St. Etienne, 17 November 1992–9 January 1993. The phrase "talking Jewish" was one I heard my grandmother use, but one that makes me (and, I would guess, Spiegelman) uncomfortable to hear. I suspect that the Jewish / Yiddish difference figures a generational divide.

11. Maurice Anthony Samuels, in a very fine unpublished essay, makes a similar point about the interplay between past and present in *Maus* and reads Art as "a parody of the traditional historian in what amounts to a parody of realist historiographic methods" (49–50).

12. Despite anatomizing a wide range of texts on Jewish themes, Gilman surprisingly makes no mention in *The Jew's Body* of Spiegelman or *Maus.*

13. See Nancy Miller's and Marianne Hirsch's articles for readings of Anja's absence that have influenced my own.

14. In her 1992 performance piece about the struggles in Crown Heights between Hasidic Jews and Caribbean and African Americans, *Fires in the Mirror,* Anna Deveare Smith included a perceptive monologue on Hasidic women's wigs, which she immediately contrasted with the Rev. Al Sharpton discussing his "James Brown" coiffure.

I do not mean to imply that circumcision and the wearing of wigs are parallel phenomena, since only the former derives from a biblical injunction and since it holds more fully for different types of Jews (although Gilman does point out that assimilated German Jews in the nineteenth century questioned the need for circumcision [*Jew's Body,* 91]). Rather, I think more emphasis needs to be placed on the *heterogeneity* of Jewish bodies across various lines of socio-sexual demarcation: not "the Jew's body," then, but Jewish bodies. A full treatment of this question of Jewish women's bodies in *Maus* would need to consider the role of Art's wife, Françoise, and Mala, Vladek's second wife, both of whose marginalization is not always treated as self-consciously as the question of Anja (see Hirsch on this topic).

A broader account of gender politics in Spiegelman's work would also take into account his controversial Valentine's Day cover for the *New Yorker* (15 February 1993), which featured a painting of a Hasidic man kissing a black woman. A fairly direct reference to the same tensions explored by Smith in her performance, this "Valentine card" succeeded only in enraging black and Jewish communities. Spiegelman's avowedly utopian wish that "West Indians and Hasidic Jews... could somehow just 'kiss and make up'" ("Editors' Note," 6) was directed at racial tensions but did not take account of the intersection of race with gender and sexuality. On the one hand, the image of a white man with a black woman connotes a whole history of sexual exploitation grounded in racial domination, while, on the other hand, a Hasidic man (as Spiegelman does acknowledge) is forbidden from touching a non-Jewish woman. With respect to the present context, I would also note the (not) accidental erasure of the Jewish woman (as well as the presumably threatening black man) from this vision of reconciliation. The scenario effectively points to an ambiguity of Jewish "ethnicity": Jews will, depending on the context, appear as white, as other than white, or as both simultaneously (as here).

15. For an essay that situates *Maus* within a tradition of Jewish comics, see Buhle. For a consideration of *Maus* as part of the emergent genre of the comic-novel, see Orvell. Other recent and important essays on *Maus* include Rosen, Staub, and Landsberg. See also the chapters on Spiegelman in Liss, *Trespassing,* and LaCapra, *History and Memory.*

16. In recent years, the Jewish-American community has begun to express an increasingly diverse range of opinions about the State of Israel and the politics of peace in the Middle East. This is partly due to the Oslo accords between Israel and the PLO, partly due to the assassination of Prime Minister Rabin, and partly due to discord between the various branches of Judaism over the vexed question of "who is a Jew."

17. Spiegelman claims that the phrase "crystalline ambiguity" was his favorite description by a critic of *Maus* ("Conversation"). The only other place I have seen the phrase is in Spiegelman's own comments in *Tikkun,* where it appears unattributed. Talk about taking self-reflexivity seriously!

6. "Touch an Event to Begin"

1. For a disturbing description of *Shoah* as "a sacred film," see Elisabeth Huppert, "Voir (*Shoah*)," in *Au sujet de Shoah,* 152. Lanzmann's own descriptions of his film often come close to this theological hyperbole, as when he describes it as an "incarnation" of knowledge of the Holocaust (see, e.g., *Au sujet*

de Shoah, 282). LaCapra's "Lanzmann's *Shoah*" has many valuable reflections that signal a similar unease with such sacralizing logic.

2. See Jean Améry's essay "Resentments," in *At the Mind's Limits,* for a blistering attack on the possibility of justice for the Holocaust survivor.

3. In this light, it is surprising that Lawrence Langer, one of the most stringent critics of Holocaust representations, should argue that "[w]ith few exceptions, director Steven Spielberg resists the temptation to let old values invade new terror" (*Admitting,* 9).

4. See Weissman, "A Fantasy of Witnessing," for an analysis of the filming process and its media coverage.

5. "C'est tout le problème de l'image, et tout le problème de représentation. Rien de ce . . . qui s'est passé se ressemblait à ça, même si tout paraît authentique."

6. I am in sympathy with LaCapra's reading of the discourse surrounding this film in "Lanzmann's *Shoah.*" His argument parallels my own in a number of places. See also Hansen's important "*Schindler's List* Is Not *Shoah,*" which also looks at the two films together.

7. "L'Holocauste est d'abord unique en ceci qu'il édifie autour de lui, en un cercle de flamme, la limite à ne pas franchir parce qu'un certain absolu est intransmissible: prétendre le faire, c'est se rendre coupable de la transgression la plus grave. La fiction est une transgression, je pense profondément qu'il y a un interdit de la représentation."

8. "[S]i j'avais trouvé un film existant — un film secret parce que c'était strictement interdit — tourné par un SS et montrant comment 3,000 juifs, hommes, femmes, enfants, mouraient ensemble, asphyxiés dans une chambre à gaz du crématoire 2 d'Auschwitz, si j'avais trouvé cela, non seulement je ne l'aurais pas montré, mais je l'aurais détruit. Je ne suis pas capable de dire pourquoi. Ça va de soi."

9. "Je pensais vraiment avec humilité et orgeuil qu'il y avait un avant et un après *Shoah,* et je pensais qu'après *Shoah* un certain nombre de choses ne pouvaient plus être faites. Or Spielberg l'a fait."

10. "Je préfère les larmes du coiffeur de Treblinka dans 'Shoah' au document Pressac sur les détecteurs de gaz. Ses larmes and sa parole étranglée sont le sceau même du vrai: il y a là plus de vérité que dans n'importe quelle 'preuve' matérielle."

11. "[N]ul besoin en Pologne de reconstruire l'Holocauste ou de s'efforcer à l'imagination, l'Holocauste se donne immédiatement à voir à travers la permanence et la pérennité des lieux."

12. See the essays collected in Loshitzky for the extent of the intellectual response to Spielberg's film and for essays on its reception in different national contexts.

13. A similar dynamic is probably at work in the cult status surrounding Anne Frank (which obviously extends beyond Germany). Identifying with Frank facilitates the emergence of a certain kind of adolescent identity that simultaneously normalizes the Holocaust victim and adds pathos to ordinary teenage angst. In a recent tribute to Frank in a Presbyterian church in New York City, publicizing the new "definitive" edition of her diary, the diary's publisher, Doubleday, gave out blank diaries inscribed with Anne Frank's name to all in attendance.

The blank pages of "My Diary" seek to elicit identification with the victim, but create a strong ambivalence, not least because of this "gift's" links to the implied (necrophiliac) consumption of her posthumous book.

14. A fascinating discussion of the museum's development in the context of Jewish-American memory and identity politics can be found in Judith Miller's *One, by One* (220–75). Edward Linenthal's excellent book-length history of the museum titled *Preserving Memory: The Struggle to Create America's Holocaust Museum* comprises the most complete account of the museum's emergence. My discussion of this history is based primarily on Miller's book and on Linenthal's book and his review essay "The Boundaries of Memory."

15. The German example is discussed in Linenthal, "Boundaries of Memory" (427). Linenthal discussed the other examples in a presentation at the third Lessons and Legacies conference on 24 October 1994 at Dartmouth. At that time, Linenthal described these incidents as examples of "burdensome" or "hypocritical public memory." That discussion can also be found in *Preserving Memory.*

16. I would be curious to know whether Gourevitch has changed his opinion about the relevance of the Holocaust to "current American reality" in light of his more recent writings on the genocide in Rwanda. In his brilliant account of that event, *We Wish to Inform You That Tomorrow We Will Be Killed with Our Families,* Gourevitch includes a searing indictment of the West's mishandling of and complicity in the genocidal situation in Africa. While the Rwandan genocide was in no way "American," it nevertheless illustrates the extent to which the world is still very much in need of a post-Holocaust pedagogy — which is not necessarily to say that the museum in Washington alone can provide such a lesson.

17. Only more knowledgeable visitors would probably recall that the Soviet army liberated the most famous extermination camps, such as Auschwitz — a historical detail which Spielberg, to his credit, does not distort.

18. See the extensive critical discussion in Liss, 13–26.

19. See Liss's excellent discussion of the tower, 26–37.

20. See Landsberg for an optimistic account of the museum's pedagogical possibilities. Her concept of "prosthetic memory" is provocative and important, if sometimes, to my mind, too celebratory.

Conclusion

1. "Anti-anti-essentialism" is theorized by Paul Gilroy in *Black Atlantic* and demonstrated throughout his readings of black cultures in *Small Acts* and *"There Ain't No Black in the Union Jack."* Gilroy writes that anti-anti-essentialism "sees racialized subjectivity as the product of the social practices that supposedly derive from them" (*Black Atlantic,* 102). Although this applies equally well to ethnic identities — and indeed may throw into question the opposition between "race" and ethnicity — the medicalization of identity clearly poses other problems for theory. Paley is close in her formulation of ethics to Lévinas's linkage of ethical imperatives and the human face and to R. Radhakrishnan's insight into the intertwining of ethics and ethnics.

Bibliography

Adelson, Leslie. "Ränderberichtigung: Ruth Klüger and Botho Strauß." In *Zwischen Traum und Trauma — Die Nation: Transatlantische Perspektiven zur Geschichte eines Problems,* ed. Claudia Mayer-Iswandy, 85–97. Tübingen: Stauffenburg-Verlag, 1994.

Adorno, Theodor. *Aesthetic Theory.* Trans. C. Lenhardt. New York: Routledge and Keegan Paul, 1984.

———. "Commitment." In *The Essential Frankfurt School Reader,* ed. Andrew Arato and Eike Gebhardt, 300–318. New York: Continuum, 1982.

———. "Erziehung nach Auschwitz." In *Erziehung zur Mündigkeit.* Frankfurt: Suhrkamp, 1970.

———. *Gesammelte Schriften.* 20 volumes. Frankfurt: Suhrkamp, 1970–86.

———. *Minima Moralia.* Trans. E. F. N. Jephcott. New York: Verso, 1974.

———. *Negative Dialectics.* Trans. E. B. Ashton. New York: Continuum, 1973.

———. *Notes to Literature.* Vol. 1. Trans. Shierry Weber Nicholsen. New York: Columbia University Press, 1991.

———. "On the Question: What Is German?" Trans. Thomas Y. Levin. *New German Critique* 36 (fall 1985): 121–31.

———. *Prisms.* Trans. Samuel and Shierry Weber. Cambridge, Mass.: MIT Press, 1981.

———. "Scientific Experiences of a European Scholar in America." In *The Intellectual Migration: Europe and America, 1930–1960,* ed. Donald Fleming and Bernard Bailyn. Cambridge, Mass.: Harvard University Press, 1969.

———. "What Does Coming to Terms with the Past Mean?" In Hartman, ed., *Bitburg,* 114–29.

Althusser, Louis. *For Marx.* Trans. Ben Brewster. New York: Pantheon, 1969.

———. *Lenin and Philosophy.* Trans. Ben Brewster. New York: Monthly Review Press, 1971.

Althusser, Louis, and Etienne Balibar. *Reading Capital.* Trans. Ben Brewster. London: Verso, 1979.

Améry, Jean. *At the Mind's Limits.* Trans. Sidney Rosenfeld and Stella P. Rosenfeld. New York: Schocken Books, 1986.

Antelme, Robert. *L'espèce humaine.* Paris: Gallimard, 1957.

Anzaldúa, Gloria. *Borderlands / La Frontera: The New Mestiza.* San Francisco: Spinsters / Aunt Lute, 1987.

Arendt, Hannah. *Eichmann in Jerusalem: A Report on the Banality of Evil.* Rev. ed. New York: Penguin, 1965.

———. *The Jew as Pariah: Jewish Identity and Politics in the Modern Age.* Ed. Ron Feldman. New York: Grove Press, 1978.

———. *The Origins of Totalitarianism*. New York: Harcourt Brace Jovanovich, 1973.
———. "Social Science Techniques and the Study of the Concentration Camps." In Rosenberg and Myers, eds., 365–78.
Aschheim, Steven E. *Culture and Catastrophe: German and Jewish Confrontations with National Socialism and Other Crises*. New York: New York University Press, 1996.
Astro, Alan, ed. *Discourses of Jewish Identity in Twentieth-Century France*. Special Issue of *Yale French Studies* 85 (1994).
Auerbach, Erich. *Mimesis: The Representation of Reality in Western Literature*. Trans. Willard Trask. Princeton, N.J.: Princeton University Press, 1953.
Austin, J. L. *How to Do Things with Words*. Cambridge, Mass.: Harvard University Press, 1962.
Au sujet de Shoah: Le film de Claude Lanzmann. Paris: Belin, 1990.
Bakhtin, M. M. *The Dialogic Imagination*. Trans. C. Emerson and M. Holquist. Austin: University of Texas Press, 1981.
Barthes, Roland. *Camera Lucida: Reflections on Photography*. Trans. Richard Howard. New York: Hill and Wang, 1981.
———. "The Reality Effect." In *French Literary Theory Today*, ed. Tzvetan Todorov, 11–17. New York: Cambridge University Press, 1982.
Bartkowski, Frances. *Travelers, Immigrants, Inmates: Essays in Estrangement*. Minneapolis: University of Minnesota Press, 1995.
Bartov, Omer. *Murder in Our Midst: The Holocaust, Industrial Killing, and Representation*. New York: Oxford University Press, 1996.
Bauman, Zygmunt. *Modernity and the Holocaust*. Ithaca, N.Y.: Cornell University Press, 1991.
Bellamy, Elizabeth J. *Affective Genealogies: Psychoanalysis, Postmodernism, and the "Jewish Question" after Auschwitz*. Lincoln: University of Nebraska Press, 1997.
Benjamin, Walter. *Gesammelte Schriften*. Vol. 1.2. Frankfurt: Suhrkamp, 1974.
———. *Illuminations*. Trans. Harry Zohn. New York: Schocken Books, 1969.
Berenbaum, Michael. *The World Must Know: The History of the Holocaust as Told in the United States Holocaust Memorial Museum*. Boston: Little, Brown and Company, 1993.
———, ed. *A Mosaic of Victims: Non-Jews Persecuted and Murdered by the Nazis*. New York: New York University Press, 1990.
Berger, Alan L. *Crisis and Covenant: The Holocaust in American Jewish Fiction*. Albany: State University of New York Press, 1985.
Berger, James. "Trauma and Literary Theory." *Contemporary Literature* 38, no. 3 (1997): 569–82.
Bernstein, Michael Andre. *Foregone Conclusions: Against Apocalyptic History*. Berkeley: University of California Press, 1994.
Bhabha, Homi. *The Location of Culture*. New York: Routledge, 1994.
Blanchot, Maurice. *L'amitié*. Paris: Gallimard, 1971.
———. *Après coup*. Paris: Editions de Minuit, 1983.
———. *L'arrêt de mort*. Paris: Gallimard, "L'imaginaire," 1948.
———. Articles and reviews in *Combat* (1936–37) and *L'Insurgé* (1937).

———. *La communauté inavouable.* Paris: Minuit, 1983.

———. *Death Sentence.* Trans. Lydia Davis. Barrytown, N.Y.: Station Hill Press, 1978.

———. *L'écriture du désastre.* Paris: Gallimard, 1980.

———. *L'entretien infini.* Paris: Gallimard, 1969.

———. *The Infinite Conversation.* Trans. Susan Hanson. Minneapolis: University of Minnesota Press, 1993.

———. *L'instant de ma mort.* N.p.: Fata Morgana, 1994.

———. "Les intellectuels en question." *Le Débat* 29 (1984): 3–28.

———. *La part du feu.* Paris: Gallimard, 1949.

———. *Le pas au-delà.* Paris: Gallimard, 1973.

———. *The Space of Literature.* Trans. Ann Smock. Lincoln: University of Nebraska Press, 1982.

———. *The Step Not Beyond.* Trans. Lycette Nelson. Albany: State University of New York Press, 1992.

———. *Thomas l'Obscur.* Paris: Gallimard, 1950.

———. *Thomas the Obscure.* Trans. Robert Lamberton. Barrytown, N.Y.: Station Hill Press, 1988.

———. *Vicious Circles.* Trans. Paul Auster. Barrytown, N.Y.: Station Hill Press, 1985.

———. *The Writing of the Disaster.* Trans. Ann Smock. Lincoln: University of Nebraska Press, 1986.

Bloch, Ernst. "Discussing Expressionism." In Bloch et al., 16–27.

———. "Nonsychronism and the Obligation to Its Dialectics." *New German Critique* 11 (1977): 22–38.

———. *The Utopian Function of Art and Literature: Selected Essays.* Trans. Jack Zipes and Frank Mecklenburg. Cambridge, Mass.: MIT Press, 1988.

Bloch, Ernst, et al. *Aesthetics and Politics.* London: New Left Books, 1977.

Boyarin, Daniel. "The Eye in the Torah: Occular Desire in Midrashic Hermeneutic." *Critical Inquiry* 16 (spring 1990): 532–50.

Boyarin, Daniel, and Jonathan Boyarin. "Diaspora: Generation and the Ground of Jewish Identity." *Critical Inquiry* 19, no. 4 (summer 1993): 693–725.

———, eds. *Jews and Other Differences: The New Jewish Cultural Studies.* Minneapolis: University of Minnesota Press, 1997.

Boyarin, Jonathan. *Storm from Paradise: The Politics of Jewish Memory.* Minneapolis: University of Minnesota Press, 1992.

Brecht, Bertolt. "Against Georg Lukács." In Bloch et al., 68–85.

Breines, Paul. *Tough Jews: Political Fantasies and the Moral Dilemma of American Jewry.* New York: Basic Books, 1990.

Broszat, Martin, and Saul Friedlander. "A Controversy about the Historicization of National Socialism." *New German Critique* 44 (1988): 85–126.

Browning, Christopher R. *Ordinary Men: Reserve Battalion 101 and the Final Solution in Poland.* New York: HarperCollins, 1992.

Bruns, Gerald L. *Maurice Blanchot: The Refusal of Philosophy.* Baltimore: Johns Hopkins University Press, 1997.

B'Tselem. "The Wrong Arm of the Law: Torture Disclosed and Deflected in Israeli Politics." *Tikkun* (September/October 1991): 13–14, 86–88.

Buck-Morss, Susan. *The Origins of Negative Dialectics.* Hassocks, U.K.: Harvester Press, 1977.
Buhle, Paul. "Israel and Jewish Self-Identity." *New Politics* 6, no. 2 (winter 1993): 40–49.
———. "Of Mice and Menschen: Jewish Comics Come of Age." *Tikkun* (March/April 1992): 9–16.
Burleigh, Michael, and Wolfgang Wippermann. *The Racial State: Germany, 1933–1945.* New York: Cambridge University Press, 1991.
Butler, Judith. *Bodies That Matter: On the Discursive Limits of "Sex."* New York: Routledge, 1993.
———. *Gender Trouble: Feminism and the Subversion of Identity.* New York: Routledge, 1990.
Butler, Judith, and Joan W. Scott, eds. *Feminists Theorize the Political.* New York: Routledge, 1992.
Caruth, Cathy. "Recapturing the Past: Introduction." In Caruth, ed., 151–57.
———. "Trauma and Experience: Introduction." In Caruth, ed., 3–12.
———. *Unclaimed Experience.* Baltimore: Johns Hopkins University Press, 1996.
———, ed. *Trauma: Explorations in Memory.* Baltimore: Johns Hopkins University Press, 1995.
Celan, Paul. *Poems.* Trans. Michael Hamburger. New York: Persea Books, 1989.
Céline, Louis-Ferdinand. *D'un château l'autre.* Paris: Gallimard, 1957.
Certeau, Michel de. *L'écriture de l'histoire.* Paris: Gallimard, 1975.
Claussen, Detlev. "Nach Auschwitz." Diner, ed., 54–68.
Cohen, Arthur A. *The Tremendum: A Theological Interpretation of the Holocaust.* New York: Continuum, 1993.
Conan, Eric, and Henry Rousso. *Vichy, un passé qui ne passe pas.* Paris: Fayard, 1994.
Cooke, Miriam, and Angela Woollacott, eds. *Gendering War Talk.* Princeton, N.J.: Princeton University Press, 1993.
Darnton, John. "Does the World Still Recognize a Holocaust?" *New York Times,* 25 April 1993, 4.1.
Davis, Natalie Zemon, and Randolph Starn. Introduction to *Representations* 26 (spring 1989): 1–6.
Delbo, Charlotte. *Aucun de nous ne reviendra.* Paris: Minuit, 1970.
———. *Auschwitz and After.* Trans. Rosette Lamont. New Haven: Yale University Press, 1995.
———. *Une connaissance inutile.* Paris: Minuit, 1970.
———. *Le convoi du 24 janvier.* Paris: Minuit, 1965.
———. *Days and Memory.* Trans. Rosette Lamont. Marlboro, Vt.: Marlboro Press, 1990.
———. *La mémoire et les jours.* Paris: Berg International, 1995.
———. *Mesure de nos jours.* Paris: Minuit, 1971.
———. *Who Will Carry the Word?* In Skloot, ed., 268–325.
Deleuze, Gilles, and Félix Guattari. *Anti-Oedipus: Capitalism and Schizophrenia.* Trans. Robert Hurley, Mark Seem, and Helen Lane. Minneapolis: University of Minnesota Press, 1983.

———. *Qu'est-ce que la philosophie?* Paris: Minuit, 1991.

———. *A Thousand Plateaus.* Trans. Brian Massumi. Minneapolis: University of Minnesota Press, 1987.

de Man, Paul. "Autobiography as De-facement." *Modern Language Notes* 94 (1979): 919–30.

———. *Blindness and Insight: Essays in the Rhetoric of Contemporary Criticism.* 2d ed. Minneapolis: University of Minnesota Press, 1983.

———. *Wartime Journalism, 1939–1943,* ed. Werner Hamacher et al. Lincoln: University of Nebraska Press, 1988.

Derrida, Jacques. *Demeure: Maurice Blanchot.* Paris: Galilée, 1998.

———. "Living On: Border Lines." In Harold Bloom et al., *Deconstruction and Criticism,* 75–176. New York: Seabury, 1979.

———. *Margins of Philosophy.* Trans. Alan Bass. Chicago: University of Chicago Press, 1982.

———. *Memoires: For Paul de Man.* Rev. ed. Trans. Cecile Lindsay et al. New York: Columbia University Press, 1989.

———. *Parages.* Paris: Galilée, 1986.

———. *Specters of Marx: The State of the Debt, the Work of Mourning, and the New International.* Trans. Peggy Kamuf. New York: Routledge, 1994.

Diner, Dan, ed. *Zivilisationsbruch: Denken nach Auschwitz.* Frankfurt: Fischer, 1988.

Eagleton, Terry. *The Ideology of the Aesthetic.* Cambridge: Blackwell, 1990.

Ellis, Marc. *Beyond Innocence and Redemption: Confronting the Holocaust and Israeli Power.* San Francisco: Harper and Row, 1990.

Ezrahi, Sidra DeKoven. *By Words Alone: The Holocaust in Literature.* Chicago: University of Chicago Press, 1980.

Fackenheim, Emil. *To Mend the World: Foundations of Post-Holocaust Jewish Thought.* New York: Schocken Books, 1982.

Felman, Shoshana, and Dori Laub. *Testimony: Crises of Witnessing in Literature, Psychoanalysis, and History.* New York: Routledge, 1992.

Foley, Barbara. "Fact, Fiction, Fascism: Testimony and Mimesis in Holocaust Narratives." *Comparative Literature* 34 no. 4 (1982): 330–60.

Foster, Hal. *The Return of the Real: The Avant-Garde at the End of the Century.* Cambridge, Mass.: MIT Press, 1996.

Foucault, Michel. *The Archaeology of Knowledge.* Trans. A. M. Sheridan Smith. New York: Pantheon, 1972.

Freed, James Ingo. "The United States Holocaust Museum." In Young, ed., 89–101.

Freud, Sigmund. *Standard Edition of the Complete Psychological Works of Sigmund Freud.* Trans. James Strachey. London: Hogarth, 1955.

Friedlander, Henry. *The Origins of Nazi Genocide: From Euthanasia to the Final Solution.* Chapel Hill: University of North Carolina Press, 1995.

Friedlander, Saul. Introduction to Friedlander, ed., 1–21.

———. *Memory, History, and the Extermination of the Jews of Europe.* Bloomington: Indiana University Press, 1993.

———. *Nazi Germany and the Jews, Vol. 1: The Years of Persecution, 1933–1939.* New York: HarperCollins, 1997.

———. *Reflections of Nazism: An Essay on Kitsch and Death*. Trans. Thomas Weyr. Bloomington and Indianapolis: Indiana University Press, 1993.

———, ed. *Probing the Limits of Representation: Nazism and the "Final Solution."* Cambridge, Mass.: Harvard University Press, 1992.

Furst, Lillian. *All Is True: The Claims and Strategies of Realist Fiction*. Durham, N.C.: Duke University Press, 1995.

Garver, Zev, and Bruce Zuckerman. "Why Do We Call the Holocaust 'The Holocaust?' An Inquiry into the Psychology of Labels." *Modern Judaism* 9, no. 2 (1989): 197–211.

Gilman, Sander. *Jewish Self-Hatred: Anti-Semitism and the Hidden Language of the Jews*. Baltimore: Johns Hopkins University Press, 1986.

———. *The Jew's Body*. New York: Routledge, 1991.

Gilroy, Paul. *The Black Atlantic: Modernity and Double Consciousness*. Cambridge, Mass.: Harvard University Press, 1993.

———. *Small Acts: Thoughts on the Politics of Black Cultures*. New York: Serpent's Tail, 1993.

———. *"There Ain't No Black in the Union Jack": The Cultural Politics of Race and Nation*. Chicago: University of Chicago Press, 1991.

Goldhagen, Daniel Jonah. *Hitler's Willing Executioners: Ordinary Germans and the Holocaust*. New York: Knopf, 1996.

Gordon, Neil. "The Threshold of Suffering." *New York Times Book Review*, 11 February 1996, 29.

Gourevitch, Philip. "Behold Now Behemoth: The Holocaust Memorial Museum: One More American Theme Park." *Harper's Magazine* (July 1993): 55–62.

———. *We Wish to Inform You That Tomorrow We Will Be Killed with Our Families: Stories from Rwanda*. New York: Farrar, Straus, and Giroux, 1998.

———. "What They Saw at the Holocaust Museum." *New York Times Magazine*, 12 February 1995, 44–45.

Gregg, John. *Maurice Blanchot and the Literature of Transgression*. Princeton, N.J.: Princeton University Press, 1994.

Gutman, Yisrael, and Michael Berenbaum, eds. *Anatomy of the Auschwitz Death Camp*. Bloomington: Indiana University Press, 1994.

Habermas, Jürgen. *The Philosophical Discourse of Modernity*. Trans. Frederick Lawrence. Cambridge, Mass.: MIT Press, 1987.

Hamacher, Werner, Neil Hertz, and Thomas Keenan, eds. *Responses: On Paul de Man's Wartime Journalism*. Lincoln: University of Nebraska Press, 1989.

Hansen, Miriam Bratu. Foreword to Oskar Negt and Alexander Kluge, *Public Sphere and Experience*. Trans. P. Labanyi, J. Daniel, and A. Oksiloff, ix–xli. Minneapolis: University of Minnesota Press, 1993.

———. "*Schindler's List* Is Not *Shoah*: Second Commandment, Popular Modernism, and Public Memory." *Critical Inquiry* 22 (winter 1996): 292–312.

Haraway, Donna. *Simians, Cyborgs, and Women*. New York: Routledge, 1991.

Hartman, Geoffrey. *Beyond Formalism: Literary Essays, 1958–1970*. New Haven, Conn.: Yale University Press, 1970.

———. "Introduction: Darkness Visible." In Hartman, ed., *Holocaust Remembrance*, 1–22.

———. *The Longest Shadow: In the Aftermath of the Holocaust.* Bloomington: Indiana University Press, 1996.

———. "On Traumatic Knowledge and Literary Studies." *New Literary History* 26 (1995): 537–63.

———, ed. *Bitburg in Moral and Political Perspective.* Bloomington: Indiana University Press, 1986.

———, ed. *Holocaust Remembrance: The Shapes of Remembrance.* Cambridge: Blackwell, 1994.

Hayes, Peter, ed. *Lessons and Legacies: The Meaning of the Holocaust in a Changing World.* Evanston, Ill.: Northwestern University Press, 1991.

Hill, Leslie. *Blanchot: Extreme Contemporary.* London: Routledge, 1997.

Hirsch, Marianne. *Family Frames: Photography, Narrative, and Postmemory.* Cambridge, Mass.: Harvard University Press, 1997.

———. "Family Pictures: *Maus* and Post-Memory." *Discourse* 15, no. 2 (1992–93): 3–29.

Hirsch, Marianne, and Leo Spitzer. "Gendered Translations: Claude Lanzmann's *Shoah.*" In Cooke and Woollacott, eds., 3–19.

Hobsbawm, Eric. *The Age of Extremes: A History of the World, 1914–1991.* New York: Pantheon, 1994.

Hohendahl, Peter Uwe. *Prismatic Thought: Theodor W. Adorno.* Lincoln: University of Nebraska Press, 1995.

Holland, Mike, and Patrick Rousseau. "Topographie-parcours d'une (contre-) révolution." *Gramma* 5 (1976): 8–41.

Horkheimer, Max, and Theodor Adorno. *Dialectic of Enlightenment.* Trans. John Cumming. New York: Continuum, 1972.

Horowitz, Sara. *Voicing the Void: Muteness and Memory in Holocaust Fiction.* Albany: State University of New York Press, 1997.

Howe, Irving. "Writing and the Holocaust." In Lang, ed., 175–99.

Huyssen, Andreas. "Mapping the Postmodern." In *Feminism/Postmodernism,* ed. Linda Nicholson, 234–77. New York: Routledge, 1990.

———. "Monument and Memory in a Postmodern Age." *Yale Journal of Criticism* 6 no. 2 (1993): 249–61.

———. "The Politics of Identification." *New German Critique* 19 (1981): 117–36.

———. *Twilight Memories: Marking Time in a Culture of Amnesia.* New York: Routledge, 1995.

Jabès, Edmond. *Le livre des questions.* Paris: Gallimard, "L'imaginaire," 1963–65.

Jameson, Fredric. Foreword to Lyotard, *Postmodern Condition,* vii–xxi.

———. *Late Marxism: Adorno, or, the Persistence of the Dialectic.* New York: Verso, 1990.

———. *The Political Unconscious: Narrative as a Socially Symbolic Act.* Ithaca, N.Y.: Cornell University Press, 1981.

———. *Postmodernism, or, the Cultural Logic of Late Capitalism.* Durham, N.C.: Duke University Press, 1991.

———. "Reflections in Conclusion." In Bloch et al., 196–213.

———. *Signatures of the Visible.* New York: Routledge, 1992.

Jardine, Alice. "Copyright 2000." *Copyright* 1 (fall 1987): 6.

———. *Gynesis: Configurations of Woman and Modernity.* Ithaca, N.Y.: Cornell University Press, 1985.

Johnson, Barbara. *A World of Difference.* Baltimore: Johns Hopkins University Press, 1987.

Kaplan, Alice Y. "Paul de Man, *Le Soir,* and the Francophone Collaboration (1940–1942)." In Hamacher, Hertz, and Keenan, eds., 266–84.

———. *Relevé des sources et citations dans "Bagatelles pour un massacre."* Tusson: Editions du Lerot, 1987.

———. "Theweleit and Spiegelman: Of Men and Mice." In *Remaking History,* ed. Barbara Kruger and Phil Mariani, 151–72. Seattle: Bay Press, 1989.

Katz, Steven T. *The Holocaust in Historical Context.* Vol. 1. New York: Oxford University Press, 1994.

Keneally, Thomas. *Schindler's List.* New York: Touchstone, 1982.

Kiedaisch, Petra, ed. *Lyrik nach Auschwitz?* Stuttgart: Reclam, 1995.

Klemperer, Victor. *I Will Bear Witness: A Diary of the Nazi Years, 1933–1941.* Trans. Martin Chalmers. New York: Random House, 1998.

———. *LTI: Notizbuch eines Philologen.* Leipzig: Reclam, 1990.

Klüger, Ruth. *weiter leben: Eine Jugend.* Munich: Deutscher Taschenbuch Verlag, 1994.

Knowlton, James, and Truett Cates, trans. *Forever in the Shadow of Hitler?* Atlantic Highlands, N.J.: Humanities Press, 1993.

Koch, Gertrud. "The Aesthetic Transformation of the Image of the Unimaginable: Notes on Claude Lanzmann's *Shoah.*" *October* 48 (1989): 15–24.

Köppen, Manuel, ed. *Kunst und Literatur nach Auschwitz.* Berlin: Erich Schmidt Verlag, 1993.

Koselleck, Reinhart. *Futures Past: On the Semantics of Historical Time.* Trans. Keith Tribe. Cambridge, Mass.: MIT Press, 1985.

Krell, David Farrell. Introduction to the paperback edition of *Nietzsche,* by Martin Heidegger. Trans. D. F. Krell. Vols. 1 and 2. San Francisco: HarperSanFrancisco, 1991.

Kristeva, Julia. *Pouvoirs de l'horreur.* Paris: Seuil, 1980.

Kritzman, Lawrence D., ed. *Auschwitz and After: Race, Culture, and "the Jewish Question" in France.* New York: Routledge, 1995.

Lacan, Jacques. *Ecrits: A Selection.* Trans. Alan Sheridan. New York: Norton, 1977.

———. *Ecrits I.* Paris: Seuil, "Points," 1966.

———. *The Four Fundamental Concepts of Psycho-analysis.* Trans. Alan Sheridan. New York: Norton, 1981.

LaCapra, Dominick. *History and Memory after Auschwitz.* Ithaca, N.Y.: Cornell University Press, 1998.

———. "Lanzmann's *Shoah:* 'Here There Is No Why.'" *Critical Inquiry* 23 (winter 1997): 231–69.

———. *Representing the Holocaust: History, Theory, Trauma.* Ithaca, N.Y.: Cornell University Press, 1994.

Laermann, Klaus. "'Nach Auschwitz ein Gedicht zu schreiben, ist barbarisch': Überlegungen zu einem Darstellungsverbot." In Köppen, ed., 11–15.

Landsberg, Alison. "America, the Holocaust, and the Mass Culture of Memory: Toward a Radical Politics of Empathy." *New German Critique* 71 (spring-summer 1997): 63–86.

Lang, Berel. *Act and Idea in the Nazi Genocide.* Chicago: University of Chicago Press, 1990.

———. "The Representation of Limits." In Saul Friedlander, ed., 300–317.

———, ed. *Writing and the Holocaust.* New York: Holmes and Meier, 1988.

Langer, Lawrence L. *Admitting the Holocaust.* New York: Oxford University Press, 1995.

———. *The Age of Atrocity: Death in Modern Literature.* Boston: Beacon, 1978.

———. *The Holocaust and the Literary Imagination.* New Haven: Yale University Press, 1975.

———. *Holocaust Testimonies: The Ruins of Memory.* New Haven: Yale University Press, 1991.

———. *Versions of Survival: The Holocaust and the Human Spirit.* Albany: State University of New York Press, 1982.

Lanzmann, Claude. "Holocauste, la représentation impossible." *Le Monde,* 3 March 1994, "Arts et Spectacles," I, VII.

———. "The Obscenity of Understanding: An Evening with Claude Lanzmann." In Caruth, ed., 200–220.

———. *Shoah: An Oral History of the Holocaust.* New York: Pantheon Books, 1985.

Laub, Dori, and Nanette C. Auerhahn. "Failed Empathy — a Central Theme in the Survivor's Holocaust Experience." *Psychoanalytic Psychology* 6, no. 4 (1989): 377–400.

Leupin, Alexandre. "La fiction et Auschwitz (Hermann Broch et Maurice Blanchot)." *L'Esprit Créateur* 24, no. 3 (1984): 57–67.

Levi, Primo. *The Drowned and the Saved.* Trans. Raymond Rosenthal. New York: Vintage, 1989.

———. *Survival in Auschwitz.* Trans. Stuart Woolf. New York: Collier, 1961.

Lévinas, Emmanuel. *Totalité et infini.* Amsterdam: Martinus Nijhoff, 1971.

Levine, George, ed. *Realism and Representation: Essays on the Problem of Realism in Relation to Science, Literature, and Culture.* Madison: University of Wisconsin Press, 1993.

Lezzi, Eva. " 'weiter leben': Ein deutsches Buch einer Jüdin?" *Rundbrief Frauen in der Literaturwissenschaft* 49 (December 1996): 14–20.

Linenthal, Edward T. "The Boundaries of Memory: The United States Holocaust Memorial Museum." *American Quarterly* 46, no. 3 (1994): 406–33.

———. *Preserving Memory: The Struggle to Create America's Holocaust Museum.* New York: Penguin, 1995.

Lipstadt, Deborah. *Denying the Holocaust.* New York: Free Press, 1993.

Liss, Andrea. *Trespassing through Shadows: Memory, Photography, and the Holocaust.* Minneapolis: University of Minnesota Press, 1998.

Londyn, Evelyne. *Maurice Blanchot: Romancier.* Paris: Editions A.-G. Nizet, 1976.

Lopate, Philip. "Resistance to the Holocaust." *Tikkun* (May/June 1989): 55–65.

Loshitzky, Yosefa, ed. *Spielberg's Holocaust: Critical Perspectives on "Schindler's List."* Bloomington: Indiana University Press, 1997.

Loubet del Bayle, Jean-Louis. *Les non-conformistes des années 30.* Paris: Seuil, 1969.

———. "Une tentative de renouvellement de la pensée politique française." *MLN* 95 (1980): 789–807.

Lukács, Georg. *The Historical Novel.* Trans. H. Mitchell and S. Mitchell. Lincoln: University of Nebraska Press, 1983.

———. "Realism in the Balance." In Bloch et al., 28–59.

Lyotard, Jean-François. *The Differend.* Trans. George Van Den Abbeele. Minneapolis: University of Minnesota Press, 1988.

———. "Discussions, or Phrasing 'after Auschwitz.'" Trans. Georges Van Den Abbeele. In Kritzman, ed., 149–79.

———. *Heidegger and "the jews."* Trans. Andreas Michel and Mark Roberts. Minneapolis: University of Minnesota Press, 1990.

———. *The Postmodern Condition: A Report on Knowledge.* Trans. Geoff Bennington and Brian Massumi. Minneapolis: University of Minnesota Press, 1984.

Makdisi, Jean Said. *Beirut Fragments: A War Memoir.* New York: Persea, 1990.

Marrus, Michael R. *The Holocaust in History.* New York: Penguin, 1987.

———. "The Use and Misuse of the Holocaust." In Hayes, ed., 106–19.

Marrus, Michael R., and Robert O. Paxton. *Vichy France and the Jews.* New York: Basic Books, 1981.

Marx, Karl. *Selected Writings.* Ed. David McLellan. Oxford: Oxford University Press, 1977.

Mehlman, Jeffrey. *Legacies of Anti-Semitism in France.* Minneapolis: University of Minnesota Press, 1983.

Mesnard, Philippe. *Maurice Blanchot: Le sujet de l'engagement.* Paris: L'Harmattan, 1996.

Metz, Johann Baptist. "Suffering unto God." *Critical Inquiry* 20, no. 4 (1994): 611–22.

Milchman, Alan, and Alan Rosenberg. "Two Kinds of Uniqueness: The Universal Aspects of the Holocaust." In Millen, ed., 6–18.

Millen, Rochelle L., ed. *New Perspectives on the Holocaust: A Guide for Teachers and Scholars.* New York: New York University Press, 1996.

Miller, Judith. *One, by One, by One: Facing the Holocaust.* London: Weidenfeld and Nicolson, 1990.

Miller, Nancy K. *Bequest and Betrayal.* New York: Oxford University Press, 1996.

———. "Cartoons of the Self: Portrait of the Artist as a Young Murderer." *M/E/A/N/I/N/G* 12 (1992): 43–54.

———. *Getting Personal.* New York: Routledge, 1990.

———. "Hadassah Arms." In *Reconfiguring Jewish-American Identity,* ed. Jeffrey Rubin-Dorsky, 153–68. Madison: University of Wisconsin Press, 1996.

Mitchell, W. J. T., ed. *On Narrative.* Chicago: University of Chicago Press, 1981.

Mole, Gary. *Lévinas, Blanchot, Jabès: Figures of Estrangement.* Gainesville: University Press of Florida, 1997.

Neusner, Jacob. *Stranger at Home: The Holocaust, Zionism, and American Judaism.* Chicago: University of Chicago Press, 1981.

Nietzsche, Friedrich. *On the Genealogy of Morals.* Ed. Walter Kaufmann. New York: Vintage, 1969.

Nora, Pierre. "Between Memory and History: *Les Lieux de Mémoire.*" *Representations* 26 (spring 1989): 7–25.

Novick, Peter. "Holocaust Memory in America." In Young, ed., 159–65.

Orvell, Miles. "Writing Posthistorically: *Krazy Kat, Maus,* and the Contemporary Fiction Cartoon." *American Literary History* 4 no. 1 (spring 1992): 110–28.

Paley, Grace. *Long Walks and Intimate Talks.* With Paintings by Vera B. Williams. New York: Feminist Press, 1991.

Patraka, Vivian. "Situating History and Difference: The Performance of the Term *Holocaust* in Public Discourse." In Boyarin and Boyarin, eds., 54–78.

Paxton, Robert O. *Vichy France: Old Guard and New Order, 1940–1944.* New York: Columbia University Press, 1972.

Prendergast, Christopher. *The Order of Mimesis.* Cambridge: Cambridge University Press, 1986.

Rabinbach, Anson. "The Jewish Question in the German Question." In Rabinbach, ed., 159–92.

———, ed. Special Issue on the "Historikerstreit." *New German Critique* 44 (1988).

Radhakrishnan, R. "Ethnicity in an Age of Diaspora." *Transition* 54 (1991): 104–15.

Rafferty, Terrence. "A Man of Transactions." *New Yorker,* 20 December 1993, 129–32.

Rich, Adrienne. "Notes toward a Politics of Location." In *Blood, Bread, and Poetry: Selected Prose, 1979–1985,* 210–31. New York: Norton, 1986.

Richard, Lionel. "Auschwitz und kein Ende." In Köppen, ed., 23–30.

Robbins, Bruce. "Modernism and Literary Realism: Response." In Levine, ed., 225–31.

Rose, Gillian. *Mourning Becomes the Law: Philosophy and Representation.* New York: Cambridge University Press, 1996.

Rosen, Alan. "The Language of Survival: English as Metaphor in Spiegelman's *Maus.*" *Prooftexts* 15 (1995): 249–62.

Rosenberg, Alan, and Gerald E. Myers, eds. *Echoes from the Holocaust: Philosophical Reflections on a Dark Time.* Philadelphia: Temple University Press, 1988.

Rosenfeld, Alvin H. "Another Revisionism: Popular Culture and the Changing Image of the Holocaust." In Hartman, ed., *Bitburg.* 90–102.

———. *A Double Dying: Reflections on Holocaust Literature.* Bloomington: Indiana University Press, 1980.

———. *Imagining Hitler.* Bloomington: Indiana University Press, 1985.

Ross, Kristin. "Two Versions of the Everyday." *L'Esprit Créateur* 24, no. 3 (1984): 29–37.

Roth, Philip. *Operation Shylock.* New York: Vintage, 1994.

———. *Patrimony: A True Story.* New York: Simon and Schuster, 1991.
———. *Portnoy's Complaint.* New York: Random House, 1969.
———. *Zuckerman Bound: A Trilogy and Epilogue.* New York: Fawcett Crest, 1986.
Rothberg, Michael. "Documenting Barbarism: Yourcenar's Male Fantasies, Theweleit's Coup." *Cultural Critique* 29 (winter 1994–95): 77–105.
———. "Sites of Memory, Sites of Forgetting: Jewishness and Cultural Studies." *Found Object* 2 (1993): 111–18.
Rousset, David. *Les jours de nôtre mort.* Paris: Pavois, 1947.
———. *The Other Kingdom.* Trans. Ramon Guthrie. New York: Reynal and Hitchcock, 1947.
———. *L'univers concentrationnaire.* Paris: Pavois, 1946.
Rubenstein, Richard. *After Auschwitz: Radical Theology and Contemporary Judaism.* New York: Bobbs-Merrill, 1966.
———. *The Cunning of History: The Holocaust and the American Future.* New York: Harper Torchbooks, 1987 (1975).
Russo, Henry. *Le syndrome de Vichy de 1944 à nos jours.* 2d ed. Paris: Seuil, "Points," 1990.
Ryback, Timothy. "Evidence of Evil." *New Yorker,* 15 November 1993, 68–81.
Said, Edward. *The Question of Palestine.* New York: Vintage, 1992.
Samuels, Maurice Anthony. "Representing the Holocaust: Art Spiegelman's *Maus* and the Postmodern Challenge." Manuscript, 1990.
Santner, Eric. "History beyond the Pleasure Principle: Some Thoughts on the Representation of Trauma." In Saul Friedlander, ed., 143–54.
———. *Stranded Objects: Mourning, Memory, and Film in Postwar Germany.* Ithaca, N.Y.: Cornell University Press, 1990.
Scott, Joan W. "Experience." In Butler and Scott, eds., 22–40.
Segev, Tom. *The Seventh Million.* Trans. Haim Watzman. New York: Hill and Wang, 1993.
Seidman, Naomi. "Elie Wiesel and the Scandal of Jewish Rage." *Jewish Social Studies,* n.s., 3 (fall 1996): 1–19.
Seltzer, Mark. *Serial Killers: Death and Life in America's Wound Culture.* New York: Routledge.
———. "Wound Culture: Trauma in the Pathological Public Sphere." *October* 80 (spring 1997): 3–26.
Shandler, Jeffrey. *While America Watches: Televising the Holocaust.* New York: Oxford University Press, 1999.
Shapiro, Susan. "*Ecriture Judaïque:* Where Are the Jews in Western Discourse?" In *Displacements: Cultural Identities in Question,* ed. Angelika Bammer, 182–201. Bloomington: Indiana University Press, 1994.
Shaviro, Steven. "Complicity and Forgetting." *MLN* 105 (1990): 819–32.
Shohat, Ella. *Israeli Cinema: East/West and the Politics of Representation.* Austin: University of Texas Press, 1989.
Skloot, Robert, ed. *The Theatre of the Holocaust: Four Plays.* Madison: University of Wisconsin Press, 1982.
Smock, Ann. "Disastrous Responsibility." *L'Esprit Créateur* 24, no. 3 (1984): 5–20.

Spiegelman, Art. "A Conversation with Art Spiegelman." Interview by John Hockenberry. *Talk of the Nation*. National Public Radio, 20 February 1992.

———. *Maus: A Survivor's Tale: My Father Bleeds History*. New York: Pantheon, 1986.

———. *Maus II: A Survivor's Tale: And Here My Troubles Began*. New York: Pantheon, 1991.

———. "Saying Goodbye to *Maus*." *Tikkun* (September/October 1992): 44–45.

Spiegelman, Art, and Françoise Mouly, eds. *Read Yourself Raw*. New York: Pantheon, 1987.

Starobinski, Jean. "*Thomas l'Obscur*: Chapitre premier." *Critique* 229 (1966): 498–513.

Staub, Michael. "The Shoah Goes On and On: Remembrance and Representation in Art Spiegelman's *Maus*." *MELUS* 20, no. 3 (fall 1995): 33–46.

Steiner, George. *In Bluebeard's Castle*. New York: Atheneum, 1971.

———. *Language and Silence: Essays on Language, Literature, and the Inhuman*. New York: Atheneum, 1967.

———. "The Long Life of Metaphor: An Approach to the 'Shoah.' " In Lang, ed., 154–71.

———. *A Reader*. New York: Oxford University Press, 1984.

Sternhell, Zeev. *Neither Right Nor Left: Fascist Ideology in France*. Berkeley: University of California Press, 1986.

———. *Ni droite ni gauche: L'idéologie fasciste en France*. Paris: Editions Complexe, 1987.

Stoekl, Allan. "Blanchot, Violence, and the Disaster." In Kritzman, ed., 133–48.

———. *Politics, Writing, Mutilation: The Cases of Bataille, Blanchot, Roussel, Leiris, and Ponge*. Minneapolis: University of Minnesota Press, 1985.

Tal, Kali. *Worlds of Hurt: Reading the Literatures of Trauma*. New York: Cambridge University Press, 1996.

Theweleit, Klaus. *Male Fantasies*. Vol. 1, *Women, Floods, Bodies, History*. Trans. Stephen Conway. Minneapolis: University of Minnesota Press, 1987.

Todorov, Tzvetan. *Face à l'extrême*. Paris: Seuil, 1991.

———. *Facing the Extreme: Moral Life in the Concentration Camps*. New York: Henry Holt, 1996.

———. "Reflections on Literature in Contemporary France." *New Literary History* 10, no. 3 (1979): 511–31.

Tomiche, Anne. "Rephrasing the Freudian Unconscious: Lyotard's Affect-Phrase." *Diacritics* 24, no. 1 (1994): 43–62.

Ungar, Steven. "Night Moves: Spatial Perception and the Place of Blanchot's Early Fiction." *Yale French Studies* 57 (1979): 124–35.

———. "Paulhan before Blanchot: From Terror to Letters between the Wars." *Studies in Twentieth-Century Literature* 10, no. 1 (1985): 69–80.

———. *Scandal and Aftereffect: Blanchot and France since 1930*. Minneapolis: University of Minnesota Press, 1995.

Van Alphen, Ernst. *Caught by History: Holocaust Effects in Contemporary Art, Literature, and Theory*. Stanford, Calif.: Stanford University Press, 1997.

Van Pelt, Robert-Jan. "A Site in Search of a Mission." In Gutman and Berenbaum, eds., 93–156.

Von Moltke, Johannes. "Exhibiting Jewish Lifeworlds." *Found Object* 3 (spring 1994): 11–31.

Weigel, Sigrid. *Body- and Image-Space: Re-reading Walter Benjamin.* Trans. Georgina Paul with Rachel McNicholl and Jeremy Gaines. New York: Routledge, 1996.

———. " 'Kein philosophisches Staunen' — 'Schreiben im Staunen': Zum Verhältnis von Philosophie und Literatur nace 1945: Benjamin, Adorno, Bachmann." *Deutsche Vierteljahresschrift* 70, no. 1 (1996): 120–37.

Weill, Claude. "Auschwitz: Enquête sur la mécanique de l'horreur." *Le Nouvel Observateur* 1508 (30 September–6 October 1993): 42–49.

Weissman, Gary. "A Fantasy of Witnessing." *Media, Culture, and Society* 17 (1995): 293–307.

———. "Lawrence Langer and the Holocaust Imagination." Paper given at the Annual Scholars' Conference on the Holocaust and the Churches, 1996.

Wellmer, Albrecht. *The Persistence of Modernity: Essays on Aesthetics, Ethics, and Postmodernism.* Cambridge, Mass.: MIT Press, 1991.

White, Hayden. "Historical Emplotment and the Problem of Truth." In Saul Friedlander, ed., 37–53.

———. "The Value of Narrativity in the Representation of Reality." In Mitchell, ed., 1–23.

Wiesel, Elie. *Against Silence: The Voice and Vision of Elie Wiesel.* Ed. Irving Abrahamson. New York: Holocaust Library, 1985.

———. *From the Kingdom of Memory: Reminiscences.* New York: Summit, 1990.

———. *The Night Trilogy.* Trans. Stella Rodway. New York: Farrar, Straus, and Giroux, 1987.

Wieviorka, Annette. "Jewish Identity in the First Accounts by Extermination Camp Survivors from France." In Astro, ed., 135–51.

———. "On Testimony." In Hartman, ed., *Holocaust Remembrance,* 23–32.

Wilkomirsi, Binjamin. *Bruchstücke: Aus einer Kindheit, 1939–1948.* Frankfurt: Jüdischer Verlag, 1995.

Williams, Raymond. *Television: Technology and Cultural Form.* New York: Schocken Books, 1975.

Wyschogrod, Edith. "Concentration Camps and the End of the Life-World." In Rosenberg and Myers, eds., 327–40.

Yahil, Leni. *The Holocaust: The Fate of European Jewry, 1932–1945.* New York: Oxford University Press, 1990.

Yildiz, Yasemin. "Geteilte Zeiten: 'Dialoge' und Adressierung in den Holocaustzeugnisse von Ruth Klüger und Jean Améry." M.A. thesis, University of Hamburg, 1997.

———. "Sharing Divided Times: Responses to the Uses of the Holocaust in the Works of Ruth Klüger and Jean Améry." In *Hearing the Voices: Teaching the Holocaust to Future Generations,* ed. Michael Hayse et al., 173–80. Merion Station, Pa.: Merion Westfield Press International, 1999.

Young, James E. *The Texture of Memory: Holocaust Memorials and Meaning.* New Haven: Yale University Press, 1993.

———. *Writing and Rewriting the Holocaust: Narrative and the Consequences of Interpretation.* Bloomington: Indiana University Press, 1988.

———, ed. *The Art of Memory: Holocaust Memorials in History.* New York: Prestel, 1994.

Zizek, Slavoj. *The Sublime Object of Ideology.* New York: Verso, 1989.

Zuidervaart, Lambert. *Adorno's Aesthetic Theory: The Redemption of Illusion.* Cambridge, Mass.: MIT Press, 1991.

Index

MICHAEL ROTHBERG is assistant professor of English at the University of Miami. He has published articles on literature and theory in such journals as *a/b: Auto/Biography Studies, Contemporary Literature, Cultural Critique, English Literary Renaissance, Found Object, New German Critique,* and *Romanic Review.*